The Crisis of the Italian State: From the Origins of the Cold War to the Fall of Berlusconi and Beyond

Patrick McCarthy

St. Martin's Press
New York

Design by Acme Art, Inc.

Library of Congress Cataloging-in-Publication Data

McCarthy, Patrick, 1941-
    The crisis of the Italian state: from the origins of the Cold War
to the fall of Berlusconi / Patick McCarthy.
        p.   cm.
    Includes bibliographical references and index.
    ISBN 0-312-16359 (paperback)
    1. Italy—Politics and government—1945. I. Title.
JN5451.M38   1995
320.945'09'045—dc20   95-11890
                                                              CIP

First St. Martin's Griffin edition: February, 1997
10 9 8 7 6 5 4 3 2 1

*To the memory of my parents
Anne and William McCarthy*

CONTENTS

FREQUENTLY USED ABBREVIATIONS

AD   Alleanza democratica; Democratic Alliance

AN   Alleanza nazionale; National Alliance

CCD   Centro cristiano democratico; Center of Christian Democracy

CGIL   Confederazione generale italiana del lavoro; Italian General Confederation of Labor

CSIL   Confederazione italiana sindacati lavoratori; Italian Confederation of Labor Unions

CNL   Comitato di liberazione nazionale; Committee of National Liberation

Comit   Banca commerciale italiana; Italian Bank of Commerce

CSM   Consiglio superiore della magistratura; Supreme Council of Magistrates

DC   Democrazia cristiana; Christian Democratic Party

ENI   Ente nazionale idrocarburi; National Petroleum Company

FI   Forza Italia; Let's Go Italy

IRI   Istituto per la ricostruzione industriale; Institute for industrial reconstruction

Lega   Lega Nord; Northern League

MSI   Movimento sociale italiano; Italian Social Movement

PCI   Partito comunista italiano; Italian Communist Party

PDS   Partito democratico della sinistra; Democratic Party of the Left

PPI   Partito popolare italiano; Italian People's Party

PSI   Partito socialista italiano; Italian Socialist Party

RC   Rifondazione comunista; Communist Refoundation

BIOGRAPHICAL SKETCHES

These brief biographical notes are designed to help the reader situate the characters of my story. Often the sketches depict only the aspects of a life that are discussed in the book. Thus Italo Calvino is presented as a left-wing intellectual; space does not permit an account of his work as a whole. People whose lives are described within the text are not included here: Enrico Berlinguer, Silvio Berlusconi, Enrico Cuccia, Antonio Di Pietro, Leonardo Sciascia, and others fall under this category.

AGNELLI, GIANNI Born Turin, 1921. Grandson of Giovanni Agnelli. Took over the running of Fiat 1966. Chairman of Employers Association, 1974-76 where he helped negotiate wage indexation. Resigned as CEO of Fiat 1996.

AGNELLI, GIOVANNI Born 1866. Founded Fiat in 1899 and ran the company almost until his death in 1945.

AGNELLI, SUSANNA Born 1922. Sister of Gianni. Minister of Foreign Affairs in the Dini government.

D'ALEMA, MASSIMO Born 1949 into a Communist family. Has spent his entire active life in the PCI-PDS. Former Secretary of the Young Communists and former editor of *L'Unità*. Replaced Occhetto as Secretary of the PDS in 1994. An architect of the Center-Left's victory.

ALFIERI, CARMINE Camorra leader, rival of Raffaele Cutolo. Arrested in the post-1992 war against organized crime. Has turned state's evidence.

AMATO, GIULIANO Born 1938, University Professor. Elected member of parliament for the PSI in 1983. Held many government posts including Treasury Minister 1988-89. Influential in reform of banking system. Close collaborator of Bettino Craxi. Prime Minister 1992-93.

D'AMBROSIO, GERARDO Member of Milan pool of magistrates who launched the Clean Hands investigation. Believed to be favorable to the PDS.

AMBROSOLI, GIORGIO Appointed by government to sort out Michele Sindona's financial misdealings. Refused cover-ups. Murdered by U.S. Mafia at Sindona's behest in 1979. Film of his life, *A Middle-class Hero,* 1995.

ANDREATTA, BENIAMINO Born 1928. University Professor of Economics. DC Senator 1976-present. Minister of Treasury, 1981-82. Minister of Foreign Affairs in Ciampi government 1993-94. Minister of Defense in the Center-Left government.

ANDREOTTI, GIULIO Born 1919. Has spent entire adult life in DC. Protégé of De Gasperi. Considered close to Vatican. Perennial Minister. Prime Minister during the Historic Compromise years 1976-79 and again 1989-92. Had his own faction, the Andreottiani. Influential in Sicily via Salvo Lima. 1995 sent to trial for alleged ties with Mafia.

ARLACCHI, PINO Sociologist, expert on organized crime. Elected to parliament on PDS list, 1994. Member of anti-Mafia Commission.

BADALAMENTI, GAETANO Leading member of Mafia family defeated by the Corleonesi in the early 1980s. Now in prison in the United States.

BARESI, FRANCO Captain of AC Milan and of Italy. One of the world's great defensive soccer players.

BASSOLINO, ANTONIO Born 1947. Active in the PCI. Elected to Central Committee 1972. Elected Mayor of Naples 1993.

DE BENEDETTI, CARLO Born 1934. Industrialist and financier. 1978 CEO and main shareholder of Olivetti. Chief owner of *La Repubblica* and *L'Espresso.* Has admitted paying bribes to obtain government contracts.

BERLUSCONI, PAOLO Born 1949. Business associate of his elder brother Silvio. Under investigation in the Clean Hands operation.

BIONDI, ALFREDO Born 1928. Lawyer. 1968 elected member of parliament for the PLI. Minister of Justice in 1994 Berlusconi government.

BORSELLINO, PAOLO Born Palermo, 1940. Magistrate who played leading role in the campaign against Mafia. Murdered July 1992.

BOTTAI, GIUSEPPE 1895-1959. One of founders of Fascism. Minister of Education 1936-43. Fostered intellectual dissent but kept it within strict limits.

CAGLIERI, GABRIELE 1926-93. Engineer and executive in chemical industry. Had links with PSI. Vice-chairman of Enichem. 1989 named head of ENI. 1993 committed suicide after the Enimont scandal broke.

CALVI, ROBERTO Financier, owner of Banco Ambrosiano. Backed by Vatican. Ties to Michele Sindona and Licio Gelli. 1981-82 fraud was uncovered and Calvi was jailed; the press reported stories of huge bribes to politicians; Calvi was found dead, hanging beneath a bridge in London. It is unclear whether he committed suicide or was murdered.

CALVINO, ITALO Born 1923. Communist intellectual who broke with the PCI in 1956, author of *La giornata di uno scrutatore* (1963), which offers a critical but sympathetic view of the party.

CARLI, GUIDO 1914-92. Governor of the Bank of Italy 1960-75, President of Confindustria 1976-80. Minister of the Treasury in 1989-92 Andreotti government.

CARNEVALE, CORRADO Born 1931 in province of Agrigento. President of a section of Supreme Court which reviews decisions made by lower courts. Accused of using this power to overturn sentences passed on Mafiosi. Investigated in September 1992 and suspended from the magistrature in April 1993.

CASELLI, GIANCARLO Born Piedmont, 1940. Sent to Palermo as head of anti-Mafia pool of magistrates in December 1992.

CAVOUR, CAMILLE 1810-61. Piedmont statesman, whose diplomatic skills helped unite Italy. Favored separation of church and state.

CEFIS, EUGENIO Born 1921. Collaborator of Mattei. 1967 President of ENI. 1970-77 President of Montedison.

DALLA CHIESA, CARLO ALBERTO 1920-82. General of the Carabinieri. 1978 led successful anti-terrorist campaign. Appointed Prefect of Palermo in 1982 and quickly murdered by Mafia.

CIAMPI, CARLO AZEGLIO Born 1920. Governor of the Bank of Italy 1979-93. Prime Minister 1993-94. Minister of the Treasury in the Center-Left government.

COLLODI, CARLO Tuscan author, published *Pinocchio* in 1880.

COLOMBO, EMILIO Born 1920. Elected to parliament in 1948. DC chieftain in the Basilicata. Perennial Minister including Prime Minister and Minister of Foreign Affairs.

CONSO, GIOVANNI Born 1922. Magistrate and University Professor. Minister of Justice in Amato government. Drafted March 1993 decree which aroused popular fury.

CORBINO, EPICARMO Liberal Party politician. Minister of Treasury in early postwar governments. Supporter of austerity and opponent of currency exchange.

COSSIGA, FRANCESCO Born 1928. Cousin of Enrico Berlinguer. Elected DC member of parliament 1958. Minister of Interior during Moro kidnapping. President of the Republic 1985-92.

CRAXI, BETTINO Born 1934. Secretary of the PSI 1976-93. Prime Minister 1983-87. Ally of Silvio Berlusconi. Massive accusations of corruption 1992-present. Currently resident in Tunisia. Bombards Italy with faxes proclaiming his innocence and everyone else's guilt.

CRISPI, FRANCESCO 1818-1901. In united Italy a left-wing leader with authoritarian inclinations. 1894 harsh repression of Sicilian protest. Supported colonization but had to resign as Prime Minister after the Italian army was defeated by the Abyssians at the battle of Adua 1896.

CRISTOFORI, NINO Born Ferrara, 1930. Andreotti's emissary to Emilia-Romagna. Under-secretary in the 1989 Andreotti government.

CROCE, BENEDETTO 1866-1952. Philosopher, historian, literary critic. Neo-Hegelian, he was the leading thinker of Liberal Italy. Slow to oppose Mussolini, he became a focus of cultural resistance to Fascism. Influenced Antonio Gramsci as well as the post-World War II generation.

CURTÒ, DIEGO Born Messina, 1925. Acting President of Milan court. Sequestered the extra shares which Raul Gardini bought to gain outright control of Enimont. Curtò was accused of accepting a bribe in return for this action. Imprisoned September 1992.

CUTOLO, RAFFAELE Leader of one branch of Camorra. 1981 he negotiated with the Red Brigades terrorists the release of Antonio Gava's henchman, Ciro Cirillo. He is currently in prison.

DINI, LAMBERTO Born 1931. Banker. 1976-80 official of the IMF. 1979-94 Director General of the Bank of Italy. Minister of Treasury in 1994 Berlusconi government. Prime Minister from December 1994 to March 1996. Formed his own, small, centrist party. Minister of Foreign Affairs in Center-Left government.

DONAT-CATTIN, CARLO Born 1919. DC chieftain in Piedmont. Perennial Minister. Leader of faction, Forze Nuove.

DOSSETTI, GIUSEPPE Born 1913. Organized Catholic anti-Fascist groups. Joined the DC in 1945 and became leader of the left-wing faction. Resigned from parliament in 1952. Abandoned political life in 1956 and was ordained a priest 1959.

DRAGO, NINO Born 1924. DC leader in Catania. Mayor of city 1964-66. First elected to parliament 1968.

FAINA, CARLO Born 1894. Worked at Montecatini 1926. Named President of company 1956. Was President when Montecatini fused with Edison.

FANFANI, AMINTORE Born 1908. University Professor. Joined the DC in 1945, elected to Parliament in 1946. Held numerous ministerial posts, including Prime Minister. Appointed Senator for life in 1972.

FALCONE, GIOVANNI 1939-92. Magistrate at Palermo who led the anti-Mafia campaign. His investigation helped lead to 1986 trial. 1991 moved to Rome where he worked for Ministry of Justice. In 1992 (outside of Palermo) the Mafia murdered Falcone, his wife, and his three bodyguards.

FELLINI, FEDERICO 1920-93. Film director. Films include *Le notte di Cabiria* (1957), *La dolce vita* (1959), which includes an attack on the corruption of prosperous Italy, and *La voce della Luna* (1989), a diatribe against modernity.

FERRUZZI, SERAFINO 1908-79. Founded the family firm, Ferruzzi of Ravenna. Began with transportation of grain, built up a food-products conglomerate and then diversified. Remained unpretentious and was nicknamed "the Peasant." He was one of richest men in Italy.

FINI, GIANFRANCO Born 1952. Joined the MSI at an early age. Replaced Almirante as Party Chairman 1987. 1993-present led the party's revival and its 1995 transformation into AN.

FORLANI, ARNALDO Born 1925. Lawyer and DC chieftain in the Marche. Frequently Minister. 1989-92 Party Secretary in CAF period. Investigated in Clean Hands operation.

GARDINI, RAUL Born 1933. Son-in-law of Serafino Ferruzzi whom he succeeded as head of company. 1987 took over Montedison. Launched the Enimont venture. Later broke with rest of Ferruzzi family. When the Enimont scandal broke in 1993 Gardini committed suicide.

GASPARI, REMO Born 1921. DC chieftain in the Abruzzo. Perennial Minister.

DE GASPERI, ALCIDE 1881-1954. Born in Trento that then belonged to Austria. Member of the Austro-Hungarian parliament 1911-18. Helped found PPI. Imprisoned 1927-28 and then found refuge in Vatican library. Leading role in organizing DC from 1942 on. Prime Minister in December 1945. Won landmark elections 1948. Led party and government until 1953.

GAVA, ANTONIO Born 1930. DC boss in Naples, a position he inherited from his father Silvio. President of the provincial Council of Naples 1963. Member and then President of the Regional Council of Campania 1970. Elected to parliament 1972. Held several ministerial posts including Interior. 1993-present accused of ties with Camorra.

GELLI, LICIO Born 1919. In his youth he was a Fascist. Created masonic lodge, Propaganda 2 (P2), which reached its peak in 1970s. Its members, politicians, businessmen, and policemen, plotted against democracy while enriching themselves by drugs and arms trade, financial fraud, and blackmail. List of members discovered 1981. Gelli fled, was jailed in Switzerland, escaped, and was recaptured. Despite numerous charges filed against him, he lives a normal life in Italy.

GENTILE, GIOVANNI 1875-1944. Philosopher and politician. Neo-Hegelian and friend of Croce. Belief in thought as action led him to Fascism. Initiated reform of secondary education 1922-24. Killed by partisans.

GIULIANO, SALVATORE 1922-50. Bandit, of peasant origin, officially on the run after 1943. Linked with Sicilian independence movement. Committed murders and robberies on behalf of large landowners. In 1947 organized May Day massacre at Portelle delle Ginestre. Captured and died of poison in prison. His role taken over by Mafia.

GRONCHI, GIOVANNI 1887-1978. A founder of PPI. Active in DC from 1943. President of the Republic 1955-62. On the Left of party with authoritarian tendencies.

LAMA, LUCIANO 1921-1996. Partisan in Romagna. Trade unionist and PCI member. 1970-86 General Secretary of CGIL. Associated with wage restraint during Historic Compromise. Elected to senate 1987. On the Right of party, considered a reformer. Died shortly after Center-Left's victory. Massive funeral in Rome.

LA MALFA, UGO 1903-79. An anti-Fascist who became the leading figure in the PRI. Expert in economics, believer in the free market but also in informed state intervention. Considered close to Northern industrial circles.

LA PIRA, GIORGIO 1904-77. Joined DC 1945, member of Dossetti's faction. Mayor of Florence 1951-57 and 1961-66. Active opponent of the Vietnam war.

LAURO, ACHILLE 1982-87. Arms dealer and politician. Founded the largest private Italian shipping line. Mayor of Naples 1951-58. Practiced a crude form of clientelism. Monarchist who went over to MSI in 1972.

LEONE, GIOVANNI Born Naples, 1908. Elected to parliament for DC 1946. President of Republic from 1971-78. Forced to resign after accusations of corruption.

LEVI, CARLO 1902-75. Artist, writer, and anti-Fascist. His most famous book, *Christ stopped at Eboli* (1945), describes his confinement in Lucania. *L'Orologio*, a novel about the early postwar, has been much discussed recently.

LIGRESTI, SALVATORE Born Catania, 1932. Entrepreneur based in Milan. Prominent in construction and owner of the insurance company SAI. Further interests in motorways, hotel chains, and clinics. Associate of Craxi. Frequently investigated during Clean Hands operation. His holding group fell into difficulties and has been tended by Enrico Cuccia.

LIMA, SALVO Born Palermo, 1928. Spent his entire active life in DC. City councilor and then mayor of Palermo. 1968 elected to parliament. 1979 withdrew to European Parliament. Close ties with Andreotti. Widely regarded as the DC's ambassador to Mafia. Murdered by Mafia 1992 probably because he could no longer fulfil his promises.

DE LORENZO, FRANCESCO Born Naples, 1938. Member of parliament for PLI. Minister of the Environment 1986, Minister of Health 1989-92. Multiple accusations against him in Clean Hands investigation.

LUZZATTI, LUIGI 1841-1927. Economist and politician. Favored state invention in industry and also the creation of cooperatives.

MANCINO, NICOLA Born 1931. Lawyer and politician. DC provincial secretary for Avellino, and regional secretary for Campania. Elected senator in 1976. Minister of Interior in Ciampi government. Now member of PPI.

MARTELLI, CLAUDIO Born 1943. Joined the PSI in 1967, became secretary of the Milan branch in 1975. Craxi's number two. In 1989 became Deputy Prime Minister. Implicated in Clean Hands investigation suddenly abandoned politics in 1993.

MARTINAZZOLI, MINO Born 1931. Elected Senator for the DC in 1972, and member of parliament in 1983. Considered honest. Became Party Secretary during the Clean Hands investigation but could not avert electoral defeat in 1994. Withdrew from politics but has returned as Mayor of Brescia.

MATTEI, ENRICO 1906-62. Businessman, partisan commander, member of DC. At AGIP he headed the successful search for hydrocarbons in the Po Valley. Founded ENI and challenged the international oil companies. Associated with Neo-Atlanticism. Died in an air crash which many Italians believe to have been orchestrated by his enemies, although there is scant proof.

MATTIOLI, RAFFAELE 1895-1973. Economist, civil servant, and banker. Played a leading part in rebuilding Comit after the interwar crisis. Retained his role in the postwar years. Helped create Mediobanca.

MAZZOTTA, ROBERTO Born 1940. Elected member of parliament for the DC in 1972, national deputy-secretary of the DC 1979. In 1987, with no previous experience of banking, named Chairman of Italy's largest savings bank, Cariplo (Cassa di Risparmio delle Province Lombarde). Forced to resign during Clean Hands investigation.

MENICHELLA, DONATO 1896-1984. Director General of IRI 1933-43. Governor of the Bank of Italy 1948-60. One of Italy's great civil servants.

MERZAGORA, CESARE Born 1898. 1920-27 with Comit. 1938 General Manager of Pirelli. 1948 elected to senate as DC independent. Appointed President of the senate in 1958 and Senator for life in 1963. 1968-78 President of Italy's largest insurance company, Assicurazioni Generali. In 1972 moved away from DC.

DE MITA, CIRIACO Born Avellino, 1928. 1963-present DC parliamentarian. Became leader of the Left faction. 1982-89 Party Secretary. Clashed with Craxi. 1988-89 Prime Minister. Lost both posts at start of CAF period. Despite accusations that he misused government funds, sent after the Irpinia earthquake, De Mita has survived the Clean Hands investigation.

MORANDI, RODOLFO 1902-55. Socialist politician. Minister for Industry 1946-47. Helped set up SVIMEZ, an organization to develop the South.

MORO, ALDO 1916-78. Elected to parliament for the DC in 1948. Considered the supreme mediator. Key role as Party Secretary and Prime Minister in the Center-Left years. 1976 President of the DC and, along with Berlinguer, architect of the Historic Compromise. Kidnapped, held hostage, and murdered by the Red Brigades in 1978. His letters from prison are a last attempt to mediate.

NAPOLITANO, GIORGIO Born 1928. Joined the PCI in 1945. Became leader of the party's Right, seeking to transform the PCI into a Western European Socialist party. Worked on economic issues during the Historic Compromise and on foreign policy for much of the 1980s. Supported the transformation of the PCI into the PDS 1989-91. Minister of the Interior in Center-Left government.

OCCHETTO, ACHILLE Born 1936. 1963-66 Secretary of the Young Communists. Elected to parliament in 1976. 1979 member of the Central Committee. 1988 appointed secretary of PCI and next year undertook the slow but successful transformation into the PDS. Secretary of PDS until defeat in European elections of 1994.

ORLANDO, LEOLUCA Born 1947. DC politician and Mayor of Palermo. Rebelled against DC collaboration with Mafia and formed La Rete, a left-wing, Catholic protest party, which performed poorly in the national elections of 1992 and 1994. Orlando was reelected Mayor of Palermo in 1993.

PAJETTA, GIANCARLO Born Piedmont, 1911. Member of clandestine PCI. Arrested and sentenced to 21 years in prison in 1933, released in 1943. Vice commander of the

Garibaldi brigade during the Resistance. Held many leadership posts in postwar PCI. Famous for the independence of his thought. Died during the transition to PDS, troubled by splits in party.

PANNELLA, MARCO Born 1930. In 1956 supported the Partito Radicale when it split from the PLI. Used civil disobedience and referenda to obtain social reforms. In the 1970s the Radicals led struggle for divorce and abortion. However since 1992 Pannella has resisted the transformation of the system that allowed him to be a leader of dissent.

PARENTI, TIZIANA Member of Milan pool. Anti-PDS, she quarrelled with other members of pool. She resigned and was elected to parliament on the FI list. However she has also been critical of FI. At present head of parliamentary anti-Mafia Commission.

PARRI, FERRUCCIO 1890-1981. Anti-Fascist journalist. In 1943 helped found the Action Party and the Justice and Liberty partisans. Prime Minister in 1945, his overthrow marks the end of the Resistance's attempt to shape the postwar government.

PASOLINI, PIER PAOLO 1922-1975. Writer and film director. Active in Friulan PCI but was expelled from the party in 1949 because of his homosexuality. Remained close to the PCI and also admired peasant Catholicism. In his last years he denounced modernity, condemning technology and consumerism as new forms of Fascism in books such as *The Lutheran Letters*. Murdered in a homosexual incident that has never been fully explained.

PELLA, GIUSEPPE 1902-81. DC politician. Prime Minister in 1953-54 when EDC was a great issue.

PERTINI, ALESSANDRO 1896-1990. Militant Socialist from 1918 and ardent opponent of Fascism. Socialist parliamentarian, unloved by Craxi. Named President of the Republic in 1978, he became very popular by speaking out on issues such as the government's incompetent response to the Irpinia earthquake.

PICCOLI, FLAMINIO Born 1915. DC chieftain in Trento. Generally belonged to the Doroteo or Centrist faction. Has held many posts in party and government.

POPE PIUS XII (EUGENIO PACELLI) 1876-1958. Elected Pope in 1939. Reluctant to speak out against Nazism but strongly anti-Communist. Provided leadership in Italy after the collapse of Fascism. Authoritarian, he was also devoted to Mary and defined the dogma of the Assumption. In his last years feared the ravages of lay, modern society.

PRANDINI, GIANNI Born 1940, active in DC youth groups, became President of the Brescia DC in 1969. Rival to Martinazzoli. Elected to parliament in 1972. His period as Minister of Public Works provided him with limitless opportunities for "taxing" construction companies and he has been a target of the Clean Hands investigation.

PREVITI, CESARE Born 1934. Lawyer among whose clients was Silvio Berlusconi. Minister of Defence in Berlusconi government. 1994 appointed coordinator of FI. Considered close to AN.

PRODI, ROMANO Born 1939. Economist, University Professor. Linked with DC Left. 1982-89 chairman of IRI. Returned to post in 1993-94 and was active in privatization. 1995 formed the Olive Tree coalition with the PDS and other, smaller groups. Won 1996 elections and is at present Prime Minister.

RIINA, TOTÒ Considered head of Sicilian Mafia. His family, the Corleonesi, defeated other families in the wars of early 1980s. Arrested in 1993. Supposedly on the run, he had for many years been living a normal life in Palermo. In prison has conducted a campaign to discredit the Mafiosi who have turned state's evidence. Even by Mafia standards Riina is considered a violent man. He is currently on trial (Spring 1995) for the murder of Falcone.

RIZZOLI, ANGELO 1889-1970. Publisher and industrialist. His publishing empire expanded after the World War II to include the periodicals *Europeo* and *Oggi*. He also produced films by Fellini, De Sica, and Rossellini. His son Andrea and his grandson Angelo followed in his footsteps. In 1974 the firm took over the great newspaper of the Milan bourgeoisie, *Il Corriere della sera*. However the Rizzolis encountered financial difficulties and became entangled with Gelli and the P2. In 1985 the publishing house was taken over by Gemina, where the Agnellis are major shareholders.

ROMITI, CESARE Born 1923. Industrial executive. Joined Fiat as Central Manager of finance, planning and control in 1974, in 1976 became Managing Director of Fiat S.p.A. Masterminded the restructuring of Fiat in early 1980s and handled the bitter dispute with the unions in autumn 1980. Has been accused since 1992 of knowing Fiat paid bribes to obtain contracts. Played leading role in restructuring Fiat 1994. Succeded Gianni Agnelli as CEO 1996.

ROVELLI, NINO Born 1917. 1966 Chairman of Società Italiana Resine (SIR). Considered close to Andreotti.

RUFFOLO, GIORGIO Born 1926. Economist. 1956-62 head of research and public relations of ENI. 1983 elected to parliament as a Socialist. Unloved by Craxi. 1987 named Minister of the Environment. Elected in 1994 on the AD list.

RUINI, CARDINAL CAMILLO Born 1931. Ordained 1954, became bishop in 1983. Head of Italian Council of Bishops. Considered very anti-PDS.

RUMOR, MARIANO 1915-90. A DC chieftain in Veneto. Ally of Antonio Bisaglia. Doroteo. Numerous party and ministerial posts. Prime Minister 1968-70 and 1973-74.

DE SANCTIS, FRANCESCO 1817-83. Critic and literary historian. Imprisoned for activities against the Bourbons 1850-53 and exiled first to Turin 1854-55 and then to Zurich 1856-60. Returned to Naples after Unification and became Minister of Education 1861-62. 1872 awarded chair of literature at Naples University. His *Storia della letteratura italiana* is a hegelian analysis of Italian society and culture from its beginnings to the nineteenth century. De Sanctis was admired by both Croce and Gramsci.

SARACENO, PASQUALE Born 1903. Economist and planner. Worked at Comit and then in 1933 at the reorganized IRI. 1946 helped found SVIMEZ. One of Italy's most able technocrats.

SARCINELLI, MARIO Born 1934. Worked at Bank of Italy. 1979 briefly jailed because he refused to bail out Sindona and other DC proteges with taxpayers' money. Recently appointed head of Banca nazionale del lavoro.

SATTA, SALVATORE 1902-75. Born at Nuoro in Sardinia. Professor of law and writer. Author of *De Profundis* (1948) and one of the best postwar Italian novels, *Il giorno del giudizio*.

SCALFARO, OSCAR LUIGI Born 1918. Magistrate, devout Catholic and DC politician with a reputation for honesty. 1983-87 Minister of Interior. Elected President of Republic 1992.

SCELBA, MARIO 1901-91. DC politician. Minister of Interior from 1947 to 1953. Did not hesitate to use force to keep order in a tense period.

SECCHIA, PIETRO 1903-73. Founder member of the PCI at Livorno Congress of 1921. 1931 jailed by Fascist government. Released in 1943 he became a Resistance leader. After the Liberation he frequently opposed Togliatti, calling for a tougher line.

SCHIMBERNI, MARIO Born 1923 in a modest Roman family. Held several posts in chemical industry. Went to Montedison 1977. Appointed chairman 1980. Forced out by Gardini 1987.

SEGNI, MARIO Born 1939. Elected to parliament for the DC in 1976. Took up cause of electoral reform and the method of the referendum. Leading role in organizing the 1991 and 1993 referenda. Left DC in 1993 and formed his own movement but did not join forces with the Left. In 1994 elections he returned to the Catholic fold but his Patto won only 4.6 percent of the vote. Dropped out of Center-Left coalition before 1996 elections.

SFORZA, CARLO 1872-1952. Foreign Minister in the Giolitti government 1920-21. In opposition throughout the Fascist years. In 1943 he returned to Italy and gravitated towards the lay parties. As Foreign Minister, 1947-51, he supervised the peace treaties and Italy's entry into the Atlantic alliance.

SIGNORILE, CLAUDIO Born 1937. Joined PSI in 1956. On the Left of the party. Formed an alliance with Craxi in 1976 but saw his power gradually whittled down. Various government posts.

SINDONA, MICHELE Born 1920 in Sicily. Tax expert and financier. Ties with Andreotti and Vatican. Acquired Banca Privata and Franklin Bank (New York) which was declared insolvent in 1974. Sindona's Italian empire collapsed too and he was eventually imprisoned. Member of P2. He died of poison while he was in prison.

SINIGAGLIA, OSCAR 1877-1953. A far-sighted dirigist. Went to IRI in 1930. After the war he headed the public steel company, Finsider, and helped Italy develop a modern steel industry.

SPADOLINI, GIOVANNI 1925-94. Was the director of *Il Resto del Carlino* (1955-68) and of *Il Corriere della sera* (1968-72). In 1972 he was elected Senator for the PRI. Held several ministerial posts and was the first non-DC Prime Minister 1981-82. 1987-94 Speaker of the Senate.

STURZO, LUIGI 1871-1959. Politician and priest. Founded the Partito Popolare in 1919. As Party Secretary opposed Fascism but lost the support of the Vatican. In 1924 he went into exile.

TAMBRONI, FERNANDO 1901-63. DC parliamentarian. In 1960 he formed a government which ruled with the support of the neo-Fascists. The big anti-Fascist demonstrations, which were put down by the police with many deaths, showed that the MSI was not a legitimate coalition partner for the DC.

TAVIANI, PAOLO-EMILIO Born 1912. Leader of the Resistance in Liguria. Elected member of parliament for the DC in 1945. Helped negotiate the Coal and Steel Pool. Perennial minister. Member of Doroteo faction.

TOGLIATTI, PALMIRO 1893-1964. Friend of Gramsci. Co-founder of *L'Ordine nuovo* (1919) and of PCI (1921). Led the party after the arrest of Gramsci. Leading role in Third International. Collaborated in Stalin's crimes but saved the PCI ruling group. In 1944 launched the new party at Salerno. Established the strategy of parliamentary methods and cooperation with the Catholics. Moved, albeit slowly, away from Moscow between 1956 and his death in 1964.

TRENTIN, BRUNO Born France 1926. Trade Unionist. 1941-45 fought in the Resistance in France and Italy. 1949 began work at CGIL and in 1950 joined the PCI. On the Left of party, he was an advocate of worker control. Active in Hot Autumn of 1969.

Trentin grew more moderate and, as Secretary of CGIl, he supported Occhetto's transformation of the PCI into the PDS. In 1993 he helped negotiate the new framework of Italian labor relations. Now retired.

VALERIO, GIORGIO Born 1904. Engineer. Career in electrical industry. Managing director of Edison at moment of nationalization.

VALLETTA, VITTORIO Born 1883. President of Fiat from 1946 to 1966. Considered responsible for Fiat's postwar success and for its tough labor relations.

VANONI, EZIO 1903-56. DC politician, economist and planner. Elected Senator in 1948. As Minister of Finance (1948-54), he began a reform of the tax system, introducing annual individual tax returns. As Minister of the Budget (1954-56), he put forward, along with Saraceno, a development plan that stressed public intervention in the economy.

VIGANÒ, RENATA 1900-76. Active in the Resistance alongside her husband Antonio Meluschi. Her novel *L'Agnese va a morire* (1949) and the film based on it have been much discussed in the recent debates about the Liberation.

VIOLANTE, LUCIANO Born 1941. Worked for 11 years as judge in Turin. Elected to parliament for the PCI in 1979. As member and then Chairman of the anti-Mafia Commission he exposed the links between the political class and organized crime. Resigned as Chairman in 1994. The Mafia has threatened to kill him. At present he is Speaker of the House.

VISCONTI, LUCHINO 1906-76. Film director, close to PCI. Made *Rocco e i suoi fratelli* in 1960. Other films include *L'Ossessione* (1942), which launched neo-realism, and *Il Gattopardo* (1963).

PREFACE TO THE PAPERBACK EDITION

Since the hardback edition of this book was finished, Italy has lived through eighteen months of sporadic, disorderly change accompanied by the dogged persistence of old habits. The Center-Left's victory in the elections of April 1996 seems like a decisive step towards political stability, but in fact nothing could be less certain.

All the material contained in the hardback edition has been included in this one, but the last two pages of Chapter 9 have been incorporated into Chapter 10 and some of the biographical sketches have been updated. Two chapters, 10 and 11, have been added. Chapter 10 reviews the events of 1995 and takes into account developments at the local level. Chapter 11 deals with the 1996 elections and the new Center-Left government. These chapters discuss contemporary Italy within both the context of the process of change that began in 1992 and of the debate about the Italian state.

I wish to renew my thanks to Veronica and Kate for continuing to put up with a husband/father who spends so much time thinking about the Camorra, the Italian Council of Bishops, and A.C. Milan.

—Patrick McCarthy
Bologna, June 1996

PREFACE

This book grew out of the last chapter of a book that I coedited on the Italian elections of 1992. In "Inching Towards a New Regime" I tried to trace the consequences of that election on the period that ended with the April 18, 1993, referendum on institutional reform. It was a simple narrative account written as events were taking place. In fact, many public figures who played important roles in my first draft were under arrest in the final version.

The Crisis of the Italian State represents an attempt to grasp the causes of the Italian upheaval. It, too, has been written in close proximity to the events. Silvio Berlusconi's government fell in December 1994 just when I was attempting my analysis of it, and I could merely note Lamberto Dini's appointment as Prime Minister before dispatching my manuscript to the publisher. So the tale I am telling is unfinished and it ends, as any book on contemporary Italy should, with three dots . . .

Essentially this work is a historical essay. Chapters 2 through 7 each begin with a significant issue of the last three years and then uncover its origins. Not that I have the pretention of writing a history of postwar Italy: there are already many excellent histories and I have drawn liberally on them. Similarly chapter 5, which deals with economics, is in no sense an analysis of the entire Italian economy. It picks out certain strands in the economy that help explain current issues like the Enimont venture or the privatization program. So I have used history to explain the turbulent years from 1992 to 1995.

My starting point emerges in chapter 1 from a review of the events that separate the 1992 elections from Berlusconi's coming to power. Italians have quite simply been living through a fourth attempt to (re-)found the state. This obliges me to undertake the daunting task of defining what the "problem" of the state is and how it emerged from the Unification period.

Chapter 2 argues that the third (re-)founding at the Liberation had run its course with the demise of the Christian Democrats. It then goes back to look at how that regime emerged and where its weaknesses lay. Chapter 3 sets the postwar state in its international context because, unlike many observers, I argue that Italy had considerable room to maneuver and that more decisions were made in Rome (which includes the Vatican) than in Moscow, Washington, or Brussels.

Chapters 4 and 5 draw on the Clean Hands investigation to examine the structure of systemic clientelism that underlay the postwar order. Although that order was in no sense a complete failure, clientelism undermined the Liberation attempt to construct a state that could pass the tests of representation and efficiency, and it led to the events of 1992 to 1995. Chapter 6 analyzes the historic compromise as the most serious bid to remedy the weaknesses of the postwar order, while chapter 7 looks at the last actors to take the stage: Bettino Craxi's Socialists and the regime's grave digger, the Northern League.

Chapter 8 deals with two years, February 1992 to March 1994, in their historical context. It depicts this period as a regime crisis and modernization crisis; it examines the attempts to set up a new political and economic order. Chapter 9 analyzes the Berlusconi government as the product both of those attempts and of the resistance to them. The conclusion does not definitely end the tale, but offers some reflections on its main protagonist, the Italian state.

Two principles have guided me throughout the work. The first is that in limiting the importance ascribed to the international setting, or rather in trying to show how it meshed with "Italian Time," one has to deal with a host of Italian issues. These include not merely the political actors but the Church, the Mafia, the magistrates, the big companies, and many others. To deal with all of them is an enormous and probably foolhardy undertaking, but it is necessary if one believes that the present upheaval has multiple causes, of which changes in the behavior of social groups—the magistrates or the small industrialists of northern Italy—are the most important.

The second principle is my conviction that Italian society and government can indeed change, that many Italian commentators exaggerate their country's weakness and that the present attempt to refound the state will not inevitably turn into a restoration. On the last point Silvio Berlusconi has—at least until now—done his utmost to prove me wrong. But in general the skeptical, lucid pessimism that informs much good Italian commentary seems to me a trait of Italian political culture rather than the correct conclusion to draw from Italian history.

I have enjoyed the advantage of writing this book at the Bologna Center of the Paul H. Nitze School of Advanced International Studies, where I am surrounded by colleagues whose knowledge and experience of Italy are greater than mine. For their kindness in reading several chapters and suggesting improvements, I wish to thank Vera Zamagni, John Harper, Gianfranco Pasquino, and Thomas Row. Others who have been generous with their knowledge of Italy include Fernanda Minuz, David Ellwood, and Adrian Lyttelton. Several friends from the Facoltà di Bologna have provided me with insights and information: Marco Cammelli, Filippo Cavazzuti, Carlo

Guarnieri, and Piero Ignazi. I also wish to thank Gianfranco Brunelli, Valentino Di Leva, Geoffrey Dyer, and Eric Jones.

Under these circumstances the conventional phrase that all errors are the author's responsibility takes on fresh meaning. I am also responsible for all opinions and judgments. All translations from Italian to English are my own.

Several Bologna Center students have helped me dig out information: Barbara Matusik, Zach Messitte, and David Riggs.

I wish to thank the Nitze School and the Bologna Center for granting me a sabbatical semester in 1994 during which much of this book was written. Robert Evans, the Director of the Center, has been unfailing in his encouragement, as has David Calleo, the Director of European Studies at the Nitze School. The Center's library staff has been helpful and efficient and I would also like to express my gratitude to the staff of the Istituto Gramsci of Bologna. Meera Shankar's skills were invaluable in producing the final version of the manuscript.

Zaki Laïdi not merely enabled me to publish this study in French, but also stimulated me to write it.

Finally I wish to thank my wife, Veronica, and my daughter, Kate, for putting up with me.

— Patrick McCarthy
Bologna, January 1995

1

Corruption and the Overworked State

By the end of 1994 Italy had lived through three years filled with many kinds of turmoil. Hundreds of her politicians had been charged with taking bribes. The man who incarnated the postwar political order, Giulio Andreotti, stood accused of working with the Mafia, while the party that dominated that order, the Democrazia cristiana (DC) had all but vanished. Italy's most famous companies, Fiat and Olivetti, admitted offering bribes to obtain public contracts. A leading exponent of family capitalism, the Ferruzzi of Ravenna, saw its empire disintegrate, while another company, Fininvest, had tried to take over the government. A country that had always flaunted its Europeanism had seen its currency forced out of the European Monetary System (EMS). If many of these developments were unwelcome, there were also successes: a serious attempt was made to deal with the huge public debt; a privatization program, which included Italy's leading bank, the Banca Commerciale Italiana (Comit), was underway; the head of the Mafia, Totò Riina, had been arrested. Moreover a new electoral system was installed, which worked fairly well in March 1994, creating two broad coalitions of Left and Right in place of the many small parties, and gave to the Right coalition a majority, albeit an unstable one.

No one thread can guide us through this labyrinth of change. One could argue that behind the sound and fury of magistrates closing prison doors behind politicians lay a process of economic modernization, which began earlier but had been blocked by the old political system. This offers a plausible interpretation of the governments led by Giuliano Amato (from 1992 to 1993) and Carlo Azeglio Ciampi (from 1993 to 1994). One could also argue that behind the sound and fury there lay nothing at all and that Silvio Berlusconi's government (from May to December 1994) represented a restoration of the postwar regime.

The simplest way to begin is to consider the most famous of these events, the public contracts auctioned off by the political class. As the Clean Hands investigation launched by the Milan magistrates revealed, this was no ordinary corruption case for at least two reasons. First, the number of incidents was so great as to indicate that bribery was the norm rather than the exception. Second, the auctions formed part of a system without which the political order, as it existed from the 1950s to the 1990s, could not survive.

This special brand of corruption was widely known before the Milan magistrates began to expose it. It had a name—clientelism; journalists and political scientists had demonstrated that it was an integral part of the postwar settlement, while historians had explained that it flourished a century ago. Italy has just "celebrated" the hundredth anniversary of the Banca Romana scandal, which involved leading politicians such as Giovanni Giolitti and Francesco Crispi in the near-demise of the bank.[1]

Immediately three questions arise: Why has clientelism suddenly become a subject of scandal? How did it assume such importance in the postwar period? Why do its roots go so deep? One answer to the first question looks outward: "The end of the Cold War has enabled Italy to get rid of a political class that seemed to be eternal."[2] This is certainly true in that the collapse of the Soviet empire prompted the Partito comunista italiano (PCI) to change its name and perhaps also its identity between 1989 and 1991. That removed the DC's role as a bulwark against Communism and hastened its decline.

However, world time and national time do not move in harmony. The PCI had been seeking a new identity since the end of the historic compromise in 1979, while the DC's share of the vote dropped more in the 1983 elections, when East-West relations were tense, than it did in the 1992 elections. It would be more correct to say that the interplay of national history and the East-West confrontation created a political settlement in 1948 that grew into a stable order. After going through various phases, in the 1980s this order began slowly to crumble under both international and domestic pressures (such as the increasing independence of northern Italian society). These pressures erupted in the volcano of events in 1992 through 1994.

Systemic clientelism was a vital element in this order. Simply defined, *clientelism* means the plunder of the state by one or several political parties and the simultaneous use of the state to plunder the private sector. Clientelism depended on and spawned other traits of the postwar order. The most important was the domination by one party, the DC, and the lack of alternation of parties in government. Other traits were the fragmentation of parties and interest groups and a strong Communist Party. The postwar order was coherent and it evolved both in response to international pressures, which constituted one of the several reasons for the exclusion of the PCI, and partly according to its own logic. The Partito socialista italiano (PSI) learned from the DC and then outdid its mentor in plundering. The occupation of public and private space by the parties of government led them to strike bargains with most groups in society. Segments of the DC came to terms with the Mafia and traded a degree of impunity for votes.

Yet it would be wrong to imagine that this order was wholly bad. It was democratic, if imperfectly so. The quarter or third of the electorate that voted Communist saw its representatives barred from government, but they held power at the local and regional levels and from the 1960s on they were consulted on many national issues. The PCI itself was a heretical Communist Party, although less heretical than some kind observers pretend. The political order fostered enormous if unbalanced economic growth and the DC softened some of the tensions it brought with it. There is a thin line between certain kinds of clientelism—especially the southern Italian version—and mediation.

The basic foreign policy choices, which were as much made by Italy as forced upon her, were correct. Membership in NATO brought security cheaply, while the decision to break with Fascist autarky and to move toward European unity and the open world economy can hardly be faulted. The manner in which this long march was organized may be criticized and certainly the price was high. In the 1950s rapid industrial growth, export-led and concentrated in the North, maintained the historic gulf between North and South, strained big cities like Milan and Turin, and alienated the workers. They presented their bill in the 1970s when social tension ran higher in Italy than in Britain or France.

Repeatedly Italian society devised ways to adapt to European Community (EC) requirements. When the government entered the EMS in 1979, it won the concession of a wider band. In the early 1980s industry—especially small industry—was flexible enough to switch exports from Germany, where the enforced stability of the lira against the mark made them more expensive, and toward the United States, where the high Volcker dollar made sales easier.

In 1992 adaptation was more difficult. At Maastricht, Italy had committed herself to bring government debt, which was running at more than 100 percent of GDP, down to 60 percent. High German interest rates forced Italian rates up, worsening the debt and causing a run on the lira, which then had to be protected by even higher rates. In September 1992 the parties of government, which had derived prestige from Italian participation in the EC, suffered the humiliation of watching the lira drop out of the EMS. Meanwhile EC measures to reduce surplus steel forced closures and cut backs at Taranto in the vulnerable South. Symbolically the Bagnoli plant, opened in 1908 as part of the attempt to industrialize the South, was closed under EC pressure some 80 years later.

Italy responded with another burst of modernization: the privatizations, the Fiat restructuring, and the expansion of the stock market are examples. The Employers Association, small businessmen, and the expanding urban middle class of Lombardy and much of the North had begun in the late 1980s to wonder whether Italy could continue to afford such an expensive political class. Their protest took various forms: support for electoral reform to shift power from the party secretaries to the voter, demands for administrative decentralization, and, most important, the rise of the Northern League.

So the Clean Hands investigation is best understood as the eruption of a regime crisis.[3] It is not really a moral issue, certainly not the moral revulsion of a "good" people against "evil" leaders. Daily life in Italy is marked by a diffuse micro-illegality, of which tax evasion is the most obvious manifestation. One estimate is that more than $300 billion in revenue goes undeclared each year. Salary earners succeed in hiding only 6.5 percent of their earnings, but the self-employed conceal 59 percent of theirs. Conversely people have to buy goods to which they are entitled as citizens from bureaucrats and politicians. A driver's license, a hospital bed, or a residence permit may frequently be obtained without unreasonable delay only by offering cash. In a characteristic confusion of state and market, state representatives have set up a false market.[4]

Similarly incipient clientelism is present in the way Italians use personal contacts to avoid going through the usual administrative procedures. Bureaucratic delays are circumvented by mutual favors. Such behavior is inseparable from the good personal relations that are such an attractive feature of everyday Italian life. Moreover I do not wish to suggest that Italians disregard morality or are all equally dishonest. The political class is the most to blame because it exercises the greatest power, and the moral sensibility of many Italians was apparent in their furious reaction to the Amato decree of March 1993 and the Berlusconi decree of July 1994, which undid the work of the Milan magistrates. Other elites, such as the business community, bear their share of responsibility. My aim is to demonstrate that the real issue in the Clean Hands investigation is the systemic clientelism associated with the postwar order.

Clientelism became systemic in the mid-1950s, when the DC could no longer rely on anti-Communism to win elections and also wanted a measure of independence from the Church. Its solution was to buy support by taking over state resources and channeling them to its voters. This process worked, and the next step, taken in the late 1950s, was to expand the nationalized sector to provide fresh resources. Since clientelism consumes legitimacy by reducing the state's ability to arbitrate and since there was no alternative government to place a check on the DC, the process continued and grew. The next phase, associated with the nationalization of the electrical industry in 1964, was to place a tax on the private sector whenever it did business with the state sector or used the state's services. By the 1980s, the PSI had grown strong enough to impose its own taxes and there came a period of competitive clientelism. At this point Enrico Berlinguer could declare that the moral question had become the dominant political question. Clientelism was the core of the regime so the Clean Hands campaign marks Italian society's attempt to break with the degeneration of the postwar settlement. It is unlike the Watergate investigation that purged the aberrations of the U.S. political order, leaving the order intact.

Two examples will suffice to demonstrate this. Although the Milan magistrates began their inquiries before the 1992 elections, there can be little doubt that, had the ruling DC-PSI coalition won a decisive victory, the investigation would have been blocked, as previous investigations had been. The second example is the behavior of the magistrates themselves. Previously they had splintered and formed alliances with the factions of the political class. Indeed many of them have been accused of contributing to corruption: Corrado Carnevale has supposedly protected the Mafia, and Diego Curtò played a role in the Enimont intrigue where Raul Gardini paid huge bribes to politicians in order to sell his share of a chemical venture back to the state. The magistrates took action in 1992 because they saw that the political class was weak and that they could act with impunity. That Milan should take the lead was logical. The PSI city government, dominated by Bettino Craxi's friends and relations, had flaunted its dishonesty. This provoked the dual response of a Lega surge, which resulted in the 1993 election of Marco Formentini as mayor, and a legal onslaught led by Antonio Di Pietro, who has been depicted, in the best traditions of Italian populism, as a Molisan peasant, but behind whom stood a corporation that understood that its allies were about to collapse and that it must seek a new role.

If clientelism was characterized by a desperate need to grow because it was simultaneously self-destructive, then the distinguishing trait of the old regime was its penetration into every nook and cranny of Italian life, where it encouraged illegal activity. The magistrates have mown down elites, some of whom have incurred greater public censure than others. The political class was the primary target: Craxi, who had killed the goose that laid the golden eggs, was too naively arrogant to last long; Andreotti, "Alcide De Gasperi's heir," resisted better but was accused of more serious crimes. The civil service could not escape, not even the Ministry of Foreign Affairs where diplomats and administrators have been accused of making profits out of Italian aid to the Third World. Next came the representatives of the state sector, such as Gabriele Cagliari, who committed suicide; then the great private economic dynasties and Raul Gardini, who also committed suicide. Enimont posed the difficult question of the "publicized" economy, while the Ferruzzi collapse raised the separate if complementary issue of family capitalism. Cesare Romiti and Carlo De Benedetti made their acts of confession and have—so far—been forgiven.

The private sector has been allowed to plead that it was a mere victim of the old regime. This is dubious, for Gardini considered that bribes were normal and he paid them "in order to establish regular, reliable dialogue with the political system." When Fiat's construction subsidiary, Cogefar, was found to have paid bribes to obtain public contracts, Romiti waited and then condemned the political parties, while offering to cooperate with the magistrates and furnish them with documentation. In February 1994 the documentation turned out to be incomplete and a top Fiat manager was fired for suggesting that Romiti knew more than he was revealing. The notion that bribes were exacted from helpless companies hardly fits the conflictual but symbiotic relationship between the private sector and the state. Nor can one help remembering that Fiat's founder, Giovanni Agnelli, offered to finance the Turin Fascist Party and that Vittorio Valletta, who ran Fiat for decades, was known to distribute largesse.[5]

However, the employers' pleas, the economic shortcomings of the DC-PSI coalitions, and the hardship created by the world recession enhanced the prestige of the entrepreneurs and helped Berlusconi win the 1994 elections. The charges against the Minister of Health, Francesco De Lorenzo, left the medical profession untouched but brought into fresh disrepute the public health service, whose inefficiency had already provoked a flood of protest. So Clean Hands worked against the state, which was fair but had far-reaching consequences. De Lorenzo's cohort Duilio Poggiolini, a fairy-tale villain with a shrewish wife and a chest full of gold, was a doctor, academic, and bureaucrat. Only the last category was discredited by him.

One of the most intriguing cases is soccer, where the stadiums built for the 1990 World Cup involved much bribery and where the owners of the Rome, Lazio, Turin, and Naples clubs have all been investigated. Yet enthusiasm for soccer has, if that can be possible, increased. Not only did Italians follow the 1994 World Cup with passion and anguish, but Berlusconi turned his ownership of AC Milan into a key theme of his electoral campaign. That he stands accused of having paid part of star player Gigi Lentini's transfer fee in Switzerland to avoid taxes was forgotten as his team won the European Champions Cup shortly after he won the election. As the Italian elites were mown down, soccer emerged as a form of populist patriotism. Franco Baresi, the great defensive player, was more of a hero than ever because Craxi had become a pariah.

One of the rare elites to emerge unscathed was the upper echelon of the Bank of Italy, which explains why its president, Carlo Azeglio Ciampi, became Prime Minister in 1993. For the rest there seems no reason why the Clean Hands investigation should not go on forever. In June 1994 a new continent of corruption was discovered: some of the taxation police had systematically taken bribes from companies, which they then allowed to make false tax returns. This also involved allowing companies to conceal the names of their real owners. Since the firms were receiving illegal goods for their bribes, it became harder than ever to believe they were mere victims. Many of the bribes had been distributed after the Milan magistrates began their investigation, which indicates how tenacious the practice had become.

In an especially dark cranny of Italian society lived the Secret Services. The army chief of staff, General Canino, resigned amid rumors of plots against the government, and revelations that high Secret Service officials had lavished funds, supposedly designated for clandestine missions, on themselves and their lovers. Although comic, this had a sinister side because the Secret Services were a pillar of the postwar order. They were the government's weapon against subversion but also against the legal activities of the PCI. Elements in the Secret Services had ties both with right-wing terrorism and with the Mafia, as the trial of the government official Bruno Contrada revealed.

A thorough investigation of the Secret Service archives might throw light on the many mysteries of the old order such as the bombs placed at Piazza Fontana in 1969 or at Bologna station in 1980; right-wing conspiracies like the Rose of the Winds, which flourished in the 1970s; the police's puzzling inability to rescue Aldo Moro in 1978; and the nature of CIA involvement in Italian affairs. Some Secret Service members understood that Clean Hands was no ordinary investigation of corruption but the instrument of regime crisis. Having much to lose, they counterattacked by making charges against a string of Interior ministers—a post occupied by the DC for the past 47 years—including the incumbent, Nicola Mancino, and the President of the Republic, Oscar Luigi Scalfaro.

The logical explanation is that, while unable to execute a coup, this element of the Secret Service wanted to block the transition to a new regime. Scalfaro had pledged there would be early elections, but if he were indicted and forced to resign, the elections would be postponed. The Secret Servicemen who made the accusation that Scalfaro had taken money, Riccardo Malpica and Maurizio Broccoletti, were not men of great substance—it is intriguing that no more serious attempt was made to save the old order—but their action serves as a further proof of what was at stake.

After Unification, Benito Mussolini's seizure of power in 1922, and the Republic created after his fall, a new regime was struggling to be born. By sweeping away the political and administrative elite and demonstrating how most other elites had collaborated, the Milan magistrates were unwittingly preparing the ground for the fourth attempt to (re-)found the Italian state. The end of the Cold War, the need to modernize the economy, the emergence of social groups that considered the postwar order too expensive and too inefficient, and perhaps most of all its own excesses were bringing the old order down. There was a demand for citizenship, which found expression in the pressure for an electoral system that gave more power to the voter, and that helped inspire the anti-Mafia campaign.

All this does not mean that the bid to create a new regime will succeed or that it will mark an improvement. On the contrary it has been argued that it will fail, as did the three others. Italy has always, so the tale runs, been governed by blocs that either exclude or else embrace and stifle opposition. Eventually they collapse beneath their internal contradictions, but the forces that compose them re-emerge and govern under new names.[6] Another commentator sums up: "behind all the innovations of two years of crisis the old principle of change without change re-emerges, massively victoriously."[7]

This view, which is associated with Giuseppe Tomasi Di Lampedusa's novel, *The Leopard,*[8] underestimates the changes in previous shifts of regime, such as Mussolini's suppression of democracy or the postwar shift to Catholic rule. Such a fatalistic interpretation, which tends to become a self-fulfilling prophecy, blinds observers to Italy's dynamism. The postwar economic transformation was, despite its distortions, a great adventure.

Certainly there was continuity throughout the earlier regime shifts. For example, the Liberation the bureaucracy and the entrepreneurial class survived unscathed. So this time the democracy and relative prosperity of the Republic will—one hopes!—remain intact. Less desirable elements of continuity are likely: it is hard to imagine that the Mafia, the Camorra, which runs crime in Naples, and the 'ndrangheta, which operates in Calabria, can be obliterated. Moreover some actions by the Berlusconi government, such as the onslaught on state television, the reluctance to embrace austerity, and above all the attempt to block the Clean Hands investigation, provide compelling arguments for the believers in change without change.

Yet Berlusconi's government lasted only seven months and segments of Forza Italia (FI) resisted Fininvest, which never quite managed to take over the government. Admittedly it may yet succeed. A key issue is the long-sought electoral reform: the switch from full proportional representation (in which the number of seats a party obtains is directly determined by the number of votes it receives nationally) to the British, winner-take-all, constituency-based system for 75 percent of the seats, with proportional representation limited to the remaining 25 percent. Critics who argue it has produced the old squabbling, weak coalition government might remember that the French Fifth Republic's voting system, introduced in 1958, did not produce coherent Right and Left blocs until the parliamentary elections of 1967, that it took five years to complete the new constitutional arrangements, and that 23 years were needed before there was alternation of parties in power! The trend away from a plethora of small parties has begun in Italy, further electoral reform is much discussed, and Massimo D'Alema, the new secretary of the ex-PCI, the Partito democratico della sinistra (PDS), has given priority to the formation of a broad Center-Left coalition.

Moreover Berlusconi's attempt to take over state television, the Bank of Italy, and the magistrates encountered strong opposition from public opinion. The "fax people" remembered that government by clientelism meant the occupation of the state by parties and lobbies, which then expanded the state's power over the economy and throughout civil society. Many right-wing voters had hoped that Forza Italia's neoliberalism and the Lega's federalism were instruments to push back the invasion of the overbearing state.

The programs of FI and of the PDS demonstrate that Right and Left alike sought a state that was strong because, to borrow Michel Crozier's term, it was modest. Shorn of its huge public sector and bureaucracy, it would delegate financial power to the regions and organize a genuine market economy. Governments with secure majorities based on fewer and less faction-ridden parties would be better able to bargain in fora like the European Union at a time when the state's role as negotiator has grown more important. Such at least are the aspirations.

Whatever the outcome, it remains true that the fundamental problem during the last three years has been the state. Since its formation it has fallen short in its two duties of representation and efficiency. It has been "besieged": deprived of broad support and facing strong enemies, such as the Catholics in the post-Unification period.[9] Unable to project its national project outward on a population, many of whom did not feel themselves to be its citizens, it protected itself from them with a large but defensive bureaucracy.

Such a state had various options, none of them satisfactory. It could resort to authoritarianism, as Mussolini did; it could win tainted support by clientelism; it could simply remain absent, as the Liberal state did in most of southern Italy. To these various faces of the state—authoritarian, overbearing, and absent—the governed responded with fitful rebellion (Southern banditry in the post-Unification years), with absence of their own (a reliance on the black economy), or with offering tainted support by forming clientelistic networks. These were confrontations between non-citizens and a non-state. The government had to compete with other foci of loyalty like Moscow or the Vatican, while the individual found other communities like the family.

Unity is all the more sought after because it is rare. There is no English equivalent of the *tessitore,* the politician who knows how to weave together a political alliance, because British and American parties dissolve less easily into factions. It is equally hard to translate *stare insieme,* which is a more intense experience than "being together." The individual, perhaps because he is not a full citizen, needs a community.

Such generalities are of limited value, and it is more important to stress, against the Lampedusian pessimists, that the problem of the Italian state is not crippling. Each country has its anomaly. Italian commentators tend to admire the strong French state, which French observers often consider remote, over-centralized, and hence weak. A country's defects are the reverse side of its merits. The absent Italian state has spawned a race of small entrepreneurs, whom Britain, whose citizens demonstrate astonishing loyalty to their state, might envy. In any case the Italian state was not absent when confronted in the 1970s with left-wing terrorists; it dispatched them fairly efficiently. Similarly a strong sense of citizenship was present among the Resistants of World War II. Nor has postwar Italy been without "state's men": Alcide De Gasperi, Enrico Berlinguer, and Ugo La Malfa are merely three examples.

Yet the problem of the state remains and is illustrated by a historical coincidence. In the spring of 1979 the historic compromise, the postwar order's last attempt to correct itself by including people in the government who represented the excluded one-third of the population not ridden with clientelism, collapsed. At that precise moment the general public had the opportunity to read Salvatore Satta's novel, *The Day of Judgement.* Its hero, Don Sebastiano, is a notary and hence the representative of the Liberal state in Nuoro. However, he perceives the state as a magical realm, where the king and his ministers are beyond all criticism and where the notary's stamp is a sacred object that he wields with awe. As the book advances Nuoro changes, but no more modern sense of the state emerges. Instead society disintegrates like Don Sebastiano's family, and his only genuine contact is the feudal bond that ties him to his farmer, Zio Poddanzu.

Satta's novel illustrates the difficulty that his fellow Sardinian, Berlinguer, had failed to overcome. To examine it in a historical perspective we must glance at the period after Unification.

THE STATE—OVERBEARING OR OVERWORKED?

The Italian state was condemned to interventionism. Italy's industrial weakness left her with no option but to supplement private initiative with public money, government contracts, and protectionism. Steel is one of many examples. In 1911 after a series of difficulties, a private consortium was formed to take over the Bagnoli, Piombino, and Savona steel plants and it was guaranteed subsidies and increased tariffs. State intervention often brought about improvement and post-Unity Italy's economic record is respectable. The Banca Romana scandal was possible because banks had the right to issue money; afterward issuing money was entrusted, with certain exceptions, to the newly established Bank of Italy and proceeded in a more orderly manner.

Although the dearth of entrepreneurial skills has been much exaggerated,[10] Italian businessmen did turn too readily to the government and a vicious circle was set up. Unable to survive on its own, private industry formed powerful lobbies to demand public help. Even when the results were less disastrous than the tariffs that provoked the commercial war with France between 1886 and 1890, the effect was to weaken the state's ability to act as an independent arbiter. Its intervention was excessive and incoherent. Meanwhile the private sector failed to develop into a strong capitalist class capable of running a large number of big industries on its own. It had successful companies like Ansaldo and banks like Comit, and perhaps more should not have been expected. But private industrialists continued to rely on a state that could not respond satisfactorily. In turn this damaged their confidence in the Rome governments. So the political class had too little autonomy from the entrepreneurial class and yet succeeded in weakening it.[11] That the new industries, such as chemicals and electricity, required complex organization, made public-private cooperation even more difficult. World economic time was not kind to the new nation.

State resources were limited by the national debt, which stemmed from the wars of Unification. In 1866 revenue covered only 40 percent of public expenditure and government paper had to be floated at the exorbitant interest rate of 8 percent. The problem was exacerbated by tax evasion. Although a kind of progressive income tax was introduced as early as 1864, indirect taxes on food fell most heavily on the poor and a tax on grinding wheat and corn provoked one of many rebellions in 1869. Despite this the Right, which governed the fledgling state for the first 15 years, performed well.

The state's narrow social base and its inability to win the allegiance of the masses were identified by Antonio Gramsci as its greatest weakness. It was an inherited problem: from the eighteenth century on, the southern peasants watched the enclosure of common land; in the Napoleonic years they were promised that it would be given back but, since this never happened, they felt for all governments, including their new Italian masters, a profound mistrust. Tomasi Di Lampedusa depicts their skepticism in *The Leopard* but overstates their passivity. For example, Giuseppe Garibaldi's landing in Sicily was accompanied by peasant uprisings, which he put down.

Camille Cavour, the first Prime Minister of the new state, never visited the South, which correctly saw in Unification yet another foreign conquest. The big landowners formed an alliance with the northern industrialists and obtained tariff barriers to protect their grain. Southern industrialists suffered from northern competition and the masses were ignored by the government except when taxes and military service fell due. The Mafia existed long before Unification but it assumed a more organized form at this point.

After 1860, or more correctly after 1876 when the Left that was already dominant in Sicily came to power in Rome, the state imposed an authoritative rule even as it talked of democracy and citizenship. The ruling class, made up of the old landowners but also of the new middle class that had bought up Church land, bought protection from the Mafia. While acting as a mediator between the rich and the poor, the Mafia was already an autonomous force with a variegated social structure, active in Palermo as well as in the countryside. Its presence was made possible by the absence of the state, its "opponent, model and accomplice."[12]

The state was absent in the South because it was overworked in the North. Even here and in the Center it had to struggle to create citizens. In 1860 the masses did not speak Italian, but dialects, while in Turin the traditional language of the court was French. Local traditions, in part the legacy of the city states, were powerful. Yet Unification fostered in the northern bourgeoisie the sense of building a new Italian nation. This fueled the industrial ambition of Giovanni Agnelli and Vittorio Valletta: the *I* in FIAT stands for Italy and the *T* for Turin.

The state found its philosophy in the neo-Hegelianism of Francesco De Sanctis and Benedetto Croce. Although he was criticized as undemocratic and reluctant to oppose Mussolini's seizure of power, Croce's view of the Italian state as a moral and intellectual force influenced two generations of educated youth. It led many of them to Marxism, which did not please him, and fostered anti-Fascism, which did. Neo-Hegelianism jostled with the disenchanted fatalism that was another legacy of the past but was reinforced by the state's fragility and has thrived since. That fragility also left a space to be filled by the many brands of populism, of which Gramsci's was merely the most sophisticated.

More influential than Croce in shaping the state's economic role was Luigi Luzzatti, who believed that intervention was necessary in ordinary as well as in exceptional periods. Since he also championed cooperatives and mutual aid societies, Luzzatti's thought penetrated Catholic circles. The Church remained by far the strongest cultural influence. Even in an ex-Papal state like Romagna the people distinguished between the Vatican, which they hated, and the local clergy, whom they considered close to them. At the other extreme the Church was dominant in the Veneto, where it helped the peasantry to weather the 1880's Depression.

The weakness of post-Unification Italy is revealed by the most famous literary work it produced: *Pinocchio* (1880). The orthodox reading is that it is a parable of the state where the puppet becomes a citizen through acquiring a moral conscience. But the Marxist and Catholic readings are equally convincing: that Pinocchio's urge for freedom marks his alienation from the new capitalist Italy and that Pinocchio cannot save himself but needs the help of the Fairy who represents Mary. In my opinion Carlo Collodi's book is an image of the state besieged by the Socialists and the Catholics.

After 1876 the pitfalls of the state's narrow social base became apparent. The lack of parties with broad, active membership and clear programs meant that parliament broke down into clans clustered around a chieftain. Holding power became more important than using power and clientelism was rampant. The ambivalent need for and distrust of authority meant that liberal Italy oscillated between two kinds of leadership: compromising tacticians and self-proclaimed strongmen, such as Giolitti and Crispi.

A comparison with the Third Republic is illuminating. In France as well politics turned into a game where, behind the labels of Right and Left, centrist coalitions were formed, overthrown, and rebuilt. Corruption scandals, such as the Panama affair, were frequent. However, a glance at the respective education systems reveals the difference. Whereas the Italian state schools made little impact because of inadequate funding and scant sense of mission, the French elementary schoolmaster exerted enormous influence. The French middle class may have chosen a limited state but it was, as Gramsci felt, a strong class. It beat back Boulanger and the anti-Dreyfus movement, whereas the Italian middle class could not do without Mussolini. The Third Republic pushed through a divorce law, whereas in Italy divorce was not definitively legalized until 1974.

The role of the Catholic Church was very different in the two countries. Emile Combes's anti-clericalism was narrow-minded, but the break with the Church and the legacy of the (nowadays unjustly decried) Revolution gave the Third Republic a firm identity. In Italy the Vatican resisted the birth of the new state and contributed to its demise. In 1864 the encyclical *Quanta cura* denounced modernity and liberalism. Although Cavour's disestablishment legislation made a distinction between upper and lower clergy—parish revenues were left intact while diocesan were not—the Church began to support peasant revolts in the South. After 1870, Pius IX, supposedly a prisoner in the Vatican, obtained a favorable interpretation of the laws that regulated the Church's financial situation. He still forbade Catholics to vote in national, but not local, elections.

The result was that the Church competed with the state as a focus of people's loyalty. It exercised much influence within the state while refusing to recognize it. Anti-clericalism was not strong enough to become the cement of the new Italy but it prevented Catholics from identifying with the regime. In 1905 Catholics were allowed to vote. But although Giolitti tried to draw them into the political game with the 1913 Gentiloni pact, they entered when the game was being destroyed by universal suffrage and the post-1918 economic turmoil. The Partito popolare italiano (PPI), which maintained a certain distance from a Vatican that considered it an experiment, did not define its role as defending a Republic led by lay politicians like Giolitti and blessed with a strong Socialist party. It was outmaneuvered by Mussolini and abandoned by the Vatican. In 1922 the new Pope Pius XI opted for the Fascists over the PPI, which lamented the lack of Church support in the 1924 elections. The Vatican allowed Mussolini to break up the PPI and then struck an excellent bargain with him in 1929.[13]

As one reviews the historic problem of the Italian state one is struck by the disparity between its exiguous resources and the demands made upon it. It was created by an efficient but small kingdom, which employed conquest, craft, aid from dangerously strong foreign powers, and an alliance with a scattered, brave but vague nationalist movement. The new state could rely on no national culture, whether defined by language or worldview. The organization that came closest to embodying such a culture, the Church, was its enemy. Soon after it was founded the new state was challenged by a Socialist movement, which, because the masses were divided and pre-political, took messianic forms (such forms were unthinkable in a state like Britain, where a strong, homogeneous working class operated within a long parliamentary tradition). Onto this state was placed the burden, imposed by world time, of turning Italy into a modern nation endowed with an industrial economy and a more than subsistence agriculture. To continue the work of Unification, colonies had to be acquired and a seat at the European councils had to be won.

Unsurprisingly the Italian state was frenetically active as it sought to catch up. Because it pillaged one group to help another, it satisfied none. The strong plundered it and the weak fled it. It was absent and overbearing because it was overworked. It bequeathed to Fascism its dilemma to which Giovanni Gentile's answer was simple: "The State is the great will of the nation and hence its great intelligence. There is nothing it does not know and never does it remain aloof from what concerns the citizen, whether economically or morally."[14] By professing to offer such a solution Mussolini's regime aggravated the problem. Masked behind rhetoric for 20 years it again became the key issue in 1943.

Of the state's two rivals in the years from Unification to Fascism, the Catholics were stronger than the Socialists. In the third phase of the state's history they would not stand aside and criticize.

2

The Postwar Settlement: Catholic Hegemony?

One indication that the years from 1992 to 1994 mark the end of the postwar order is the collapse of the Democrazia cristiana (DC). In the 1992 elections the DC vote dropped by 4.6 percent from the 1987 figure to 29.7 percent, which was around 20 percent below its landmark result of 1948. A target of protest even before the Clean Hands investigation, the DC was swept away by the magistrates' revelations. A splinter group had already formed: in 1991 the ex-DC mayor of Palermo, Leoluca Orlando, began the Rete (Network) with Sicilian Catholics disgusted by their party's ties to the Mafia. In the 1992 elections the Rete, which had become a left-wing movement with a strong moral conscience, gained 1.7 percent.[1]

In 1993 the DC split into three groups: the largest rallied around the party's new secretary, Mino Martinazzoli, who tried to clean house and who went back to the name Partito popolare italiano (PPI); a second band left with Mario Segni, the leader of the campaign for institutional reform, and eventually formed an electoral alliance with the PPI under the name Patto Segni; the third group abandoned Martinazzoli and, when Silvio Berlusconi entered politics, ran under the Forza Italia banner as the Centro cristiano democratico (CCD). A fifth band took the name Cristiano sociali and ran as part of the left-wing coalition, the Progressisti.

The 1994 elections mark a Catholic diaspora. The group that went to the Right fared better than the two that went Left, for the CCD won 32 seats, whereas the Rete won 9 and the Cristiano sociali 6. The PPI-Patto Segni remained at the Center and was hurt by the new electoral system. The two allies gained 11.1 percent and 4.6 percent respectively but were limited to 46 seats. In a situation as fluid as the Italian it is impossible to say even now that the Catholics are finished as an organized political force, but there is scant chance of their recovering their former dominance.

The Church, so self-confident in the postwar years, stuck by "its" party but appeared not to grasp what was happening, much less what to do about it. Before the 1948 elections Cardinal Ildefonso Schuster of Milan had stated that "votes may be given only to candidates or lists of candidates who offer the surest guarantees that they will exercise their mandate according to the spirit of and following the guidelines of Catholic morality."[2] The coded message to vote for the DC was repeated before every election up to and including that of 1992. Before the 1994 elections the hierarchy was ambiguous.

Cardinal Camillo Ruini, the president of the Council of Bishops, harked back to the language of the postwar period when he asserted that "the soul of the Italian people, the cement of their unity and their greatest moral strength lie in their Christian faith."[3] He added logically that "the Church can in no sense give up propagating its moral and social teachings, even where they overlap with politics." But in the days that followed conflicting statements came from the Council, which defined the Church's role now as furnishing the faithful with general moral guidelines, or alternatively exhorting them to vote for Martinazzoli's party.[4]

Certainly the bishops backed the attempt to reform the DC without splitting it. They punished Segni for leaving the party and helped guide him back toward it. In January 1994 Pope John Paul II declared that Catholics should be "united and coherent,"[5] which was powerful language because "Catholic unity" had been another coded exhortation to vote DC. But again conflicting interpretations were given to the Pope's statement. As the elections drew closer Cardinal Ruini made a specific statement about the need for "a movement inspired by Christian beliefs,"[6] while many diocesan newsletters endorsed the PPI and, albeit less warmly, Mario Segni's movement, the Pact.

The Church was facing three problems. The most obvious was the decline of religion: in the postwar years around 70 percent of Italians attended Sunday mass; by the mid-1980s the figure was 25 percent.[7] Then, too, fewer Catholics heed the Church's instructions on how to vote: one poll cited the lowly figure of 15 percent.[8] Many former DC voters deserted to the Lega in the 1992 elections. Finally, Catholic activists who still link politics with religion are infuriated by DC corruption. In 1991 they supported Segni's referendum on electoral reform when the hierarchy hesitated. The Rete had the backing of a group of Palermo Jesuits.

After the elections Cardinal Ruini had kind words for Forza Italia, which had offered increased funding for Catholic schools in the name of choice. However Ruini was at once criticized by other bishops,[9] and the Church, while it could discreetly press for an alliance between the PPI-Patto and the Right, could hardly abandon the PPI after calling on the faithful to support it. Pope John Paul seemed to suggest another option: the Church would speak out in its own right on political matters.[10]

The bishops had raised the question of whether the Church bore any responsibility for political corruption and concluded rather hastily that it did not. In fact the Vatican has not emerged unscathed from the Clean Hands operation. Dubious money from the drug companies financed its conferences, while its bank, Istituto per le opere di religione (IOR), was used to move funds around in the Enimont deal. These may appear to be minor issues but they force one to consider the Church's role in systemic clientelism.

In general the hierarchy is likely to maintain considerable cultural influence in Italy, but it will not play the linchpin role it played from 1943 to 1948. What of the Catholics' old antagonists and allies, the Communists? The PCI was transformed with partial success into the PDS between 1989 and 1991. In the 1992 elections the PDS won a disappointing 16.1 percent of the vote, while the breakaway group that wanted to remain Communist, Rifondazione comunista (RC), was pleased with its 5.6 percent. The PCI-PDS's exclusion from government and the spoils thereof enabled the PDS to survive the Clean Hands investigation and in 1993 it was Italy's strongest party. However the Progressisti, the left-wing coalition gathered around the PDS, were defeated clearly in the 1994 elections as the PDS won 20.4 percent of the vote and RC 6 percent, while the Progressisti gained 215 seats to the Right's 366.

So the PDS has taken up the role of opposition in the new parliament. Unlike the PCI it is not an illegitimate candidate to govern and the international constraint of the U.S. veto has vanished. However in an age where ideology is supposedly in decline, anti-Communism played a major role in the 1994 elections. Explaining why he could not form an alliance with Occhetto, Segni cited the "Westernness" of his values.[11] If this harked back to the 1948 elections, Berlusconi was far more explicit. He promised "show trials and prison" if the Left won and described the 1994 contest as a choice between "freedom and slavery."[12] Contemporary anti-Communism is very different—it appears to show that if the Communist does not exist, the anti-Communist will invent him—from the postwar brand. Its existence does not contradict my thesis that the years 1943 to 1992 form a historical period that has ended.

We must now turn to the beginning of that period to examine its major protagonists and the kind of state they created.[13] Orthodoxy holds that events in Italy were shaped by their international context, namely, the nascent East-West conflict.[14] I would like to suggest that Italians had more control over their destinies than is usually thought, that the most important "international" actor was the Vatican and that the U.S. role was decisive in maintaining the postwar settlement, but secondary in shaping it.

AN ANGELIC BUT VERY DETERMINED PASTOR

The last assertion must be considered first. A glance at the chronology of events reveals that four long years separate the overthrow of Mussolini in July 1943 from the announcement of the Marshall Plan in June 1947. Even if we situate in mid-1946 the American decision to consider the USSR a major threat that must at all costs be checked, we must still conclude that De Gasperi became Prime Minister in December 1945 and that the DC emerged as the largest party in the elections of June 1946 without massive U.S. backing. In fact the United States was slow to select the DC as its champion: De Gasperi's trip to Washington in January 1947 brought little financial aid to Italy, although more was promised at the moment when he dismissed the PCI and PSI from the government in May 1947.

By the next year the United States was pouring in resources and simultaneously threatening not to include Italy in the forthcoming Marshall Plan if the Left won the April elections. Since the Italian economy looked in sorry shape in 1947 this threat certainly widened the DC's margin of victory. The United States did not rule out direct military intervention in the event of a Communist uprising, although it rather saw itself supporting an Italian effort.[15]

From this moment until William Casey's intervention in the local elections of 1985, U.S. governments deployed firm statements, economic aid, Hollywood's dream machine, illegal financing of friendly parties, and bagloads of dirty tricks to keep the PCI out of power. It is hard, however, to demonstrate that the Italians could not have achieved this on their own.

Between 1943 and 1946 the United States had many policies and policy-makers but it did not envisage Catholic hegemony. In the April 1948 crusade the Vatican provided more battalions than the Americans. One feels that the DC exploited American anti-Communism. Catholic unionists wanted to split off from the Communist-led Confederazione generale dei lavoratori italiani (CGIL) so the AFL-CIO put up the money. The United States lavished subsidies on Giuseppe Saragat's Social Democrats, who broke away from the Socialist Party, in the hope of getting working-class support for the government, but the Social Democrats were never more than a useful, minor ally for the DC.

The period from 1943 to 1946 was when the foundations of Catholic power were laid. In 1943 the existing order disappeared.[16] The coup of July 25 dispatched Mussolini, while the armistice of September 8 led to the disintegration of the army, the flight of the king, and the collapse of the Fascist state. All that remained was the war.

Space permits only a few snapshots of the chaos, the details of which are well known. In Sicily, bandits, separatism, and the Mafia all grew stronger. During the Allied rule of Naples 60 percent of the goods that arrived at the port ended up on the black market.[17] Sardinia was cut off from the mainland during the winter of 1943-44. No coal was distributed, bread was rationed at 150 grams a day, and people ate grasses that they gathered in the fields. The division between South and North was reasserted, while Milan and Turin were abandoned to the Wehrmacht and Allied bombing.

Where there had been an order of sorts suddenly there was none. Gentile's statement ceases to be rhetorical and becomes ironic. It has been noted that the damage done by the war to Italian industry was relatively slight: no more than 8 percent of the 1938 productive capacity.[18] But this fails to include the damage to roads, bridges, and railways, which made a direct impact on the population. Moreover the cultural disarray caused by the collapse of the 20-year-old regime was painful. On September 8, many people simply gave up and went home. The case of the young Pier Paolo Pasolini was typical. Rounded up by the Germans while he was serving with his unit near Livorno, Pasolini escaped, hid in a ditch, and then made his way across Italy to Friuli and his mother.

The shock was all the greater because Fascism had been so pervasive. It is erroneous to assume that Mussolini's ineptitude, demonstrated by his decision to fight a war for which he had not prepared, had left space for other foci of loyalty. One proof is the lack of opposition. Until the war Mussolini had little to fear and opinion turned against him only as military defeats mounted. Even the Turin strikes of March 1943 began as an economic protest and then took on a political dimension.[19]

Fascism compensated for its inefficiency by being many-sided.[20] It had forged alliances with industry and with the Church. Although it repressed the working class it offered at least some young workers in Turin their first taste of such modern pleasures as the cinema and soccer. When potential rebels arose among the educated youth, Giuseppe Bottai was dispatched to explain to them that their sentiments were a return to the original sources of Fascism. Indeed the example of culture reveals how difficult it was to oppose. Pasolini's early writing is a discourse of cultural opposition that is striving unsuccessfully to become political.

Only after July 1943 does he realize there had been in him a "political man whom Fascism had wrongfully suffocated without my knowing it."[21]

The best commentary on the 1943-45 years is Satta's *De Profondis*. His pessimistic vision blinds him to the conflict between Fascists and anti-Fascists, but enables him to seize the disintegration. Freedom "cannot be reduced to a political or even a legal issue . . . each of us must conquer and preserve . . . that Christian liberty, which is based on self-denial." All human institutions, including the state, are built on individual effort, which has collapsed in Italy. Looting and trading on the black market are the marks of an "individualism which serves only itself" and there are now "ten or twenty Italys or as many as there are citizens . . . in the disintegration of the state each person becomes a state unto himself."[22]

Vacuums are quickly filled. The mood of helplessness indicated one obvious solution to the question of who should run the country: foreigners. The arrival of U.S. troops, many of Italian origin, inspired the dream of America. Among the working class of northern Italy the myth of the USSR preceded PCI proselytizing, while socialism was associated less with Palmiro Togliatti's new party than with the arrival of the Red Army. Groups that were not helpless dealt directly with the foreigners. In March 1947 Vittorio Valletta, whom the Allies had helped back to power, drew up Fiat's shopping list and headed for Washington. The habit of appealing to foreigners to quash one's domestic enemies grew rapidly. In February 1945 Vittorio Emanuele Orlando, the veteran right-wing leader, sent a memorandum to American officials saying that the PCI "was in complete control" of the political situation.[23] Influential Italians pleaded helplessness in order to exploit the foreigner, not in order to be governed by him.

The vacuum left by Fascism was filled by the Vatican rather than by the Allies. As Mussolini's ally, the Papacy could appeal to the segments of the population that had supported him. While he could lay no claim to anti-Fascism, Pius XII had taken care to separate himself from the regime, and he had his own shock troops, the Catholic Action. He had earned respect by remaining in Rome when the king fled. The Church devoted itself to sheltering the population from the war. It tried to persuade the Allies not to bomb and the Nazis not to deport.

It was inevitable that in the disintegration of their country Italians should turn to the Church.[24] It was still the greatest cultural influence. "How can you not be a Catholic if you are born in Italy?" asked Federico Fellini. Bombing encourages prayer and Pius XII offered an emotional brand of religion replete with pilgrimages, processions, and miracles, which Fellini would chronicle with ironic sympathy in films like *The Nights of Cabiria*. Pius stressed devotion to Mary, whose Assumption into heaven would be proclaimed as doctrine in 1950.

However if Mary was forgiving and if the processions provided a respite from fear, the main trait in Pius's strategy was authority. In the film *Pastor Angelicus* (1942) the Pope is presented as the supreme leader, a more authentic version of Mussolini.

The Vatican had prepared for the demise of Fascism. In 1929, the year of the Lateran Pacts, Alcide De Gasperi was given a poorly paid post in the Vatican library. He was being held in reserve. The Church began to distance itself from Fascism after the 1938 Hitler-Mussolini agreement because of the Nazis' anti-Catholic policies. In 1940, Italy's entry to the war seemed to the Vatican a blunder and, as opinion turned against Mussolini, so did the Church. In his Christmas Day message of 1942 the Pope condemned racism. By now the ex-Popolari were regrouping.

Not that the Vatican displayed any great liking for democracy. It toyed with authoritarian solutions: in July 1943 Catholic Action wanted to take over the Fascist organizations, which implies that some Vatican leaders were considering a post-Fascist government based on king-army-church. September 8 put an end to such dreams and in December Monsignor Domenico Tardini, a close advisor to the Pope, could write that "without doubt it will be necessary to return to democracy," although he added that "the Italians are not ready for a republic."[25]

The Vatican's willingness to oppose the restoration of democracy has probably been exaggerated, as have its doubts about the nascent DC and De Gasperi.[26] In December 1945 Tardini complained that the party had drifted too far to the Left, but as early as 1942 the Vatican began presenting De Gasperi to the Americans as a postwar leader, while in December 1945 Tardini urged them to help make De Gasperi a successful Prime Minister. The more difficult questions are what sort of democracy and what sort of state the Vatican wanted for Italy. One must consider the Pope's priorities and the Church's view of the state.

On the first question, country time and world time ran together: the Pope's priority was the defeat of Communism. Reluctant to speak out against Hitler, Pius was ever willing to repeat that Communism was evil. The Vatican turned a deaf ear to Franklin D. Roosevelt's claim that he could integrate the USSR into a world order or persuade it to stop persecuting religion. As early as 1942 Tardini was worried that postwar chaos would provide Communism with its chance. The Pope watched with growing alarm the spread of the Communist-led Resistance in northern Italy and warned that trouble could result because the masses were "emotionally unstable and unpredictable."[27]

The Vatican feared the worst in Eastern Europe, but it was determined to prevent the spread of Communism into Western Europe and to limit Communist influence in Italy. To achieve these goals it wanted the United

States to remain in Europe, so in 1943 Tardini generously offered Italy to the Americans as "a magnificent base in the heart of Europe and of the Mediterranean from which to undertake both a civilizing mission and a vast economic operation." One may suspect that Tardini's faith in the U.S.'s ability to spread civilization was less strong than he pretended. The Vatican shared the Italian flair for exploiting helpful foreigners.

In Italy the Vatican wanted the DC in power with the PCI confined to opposition. It would have preferred a monarchy, for it distrusted the concept of anti-Fascism and it disliked the Comitato di liberazione nazionale (CLN). The Vatican was tempted by alliances between the DC and the Right, including the Movimento sociale italiano (MSI) after it was founded in December 1946, but it was willing to admit that there were practical reasons for not making them. The Vatican was determined to retain the power it had gained in 1929 and to have the Lateran Pacts (which gave the Church much power over education and marriage as well as much freedom from paying taxes), written into what, after June 1946, it recognized would be a Republican constitution.

The prime problem with this plan was not that it was too right-wing. Historians of the postwar period dwell too much on the supposed lost opportunity of creating a Social Democratic Italy.[28] From the way that the 1943 vacuum was filled, the opportunity to create such an Italy was small, as I shall argue in discussing the Resistance, the PCI, and the postwar economic decisions. Our focus, however, is different: from the viewpoint of the 1992-94 crisis the key question is why the third attempt to (re-)found the Italian state proved unsatisfactory. Neither Right nor Left has any monopoly on creating a state that is representative and efficient. The Vatican's vision was clear-sighted and doubtless it considered that it was helping create a strong Italy, endowed with religious and moral authority and capable of resisting international Communism. In fact though it was creating a state that, while different from earlier versions, did not resolve their shortcomings. To explain why this was so, we must consider the Church's various views of the Italian question.

During each incarnation of the state the Vatican's role was different. At Unification, it stood aloof and acted as an alternative focus of loyalty. During Fascism, it formed a wary alliance as it helped to legitimize the state, while gaining power through the Lateran Pacts.

In the third phase, the Church was participating more and gaining more power. Whereas the Fascist Party had been a rival, the DC was virtually the Church's creation. Between the two lay a tiny space that De Gasperi would try to expand. But the dominant party of government in the new Republic was dependent on the Church's organization to get itself elected. Moreover, political legitimacy was subordinate to religious legitimacy, which resided in the Vatican.

This situation was in harmony with the Church's teaching. The suppos-edly progressive Pope Leo XIII accepted democracy, but he considered it one form of social arrangement among many. It could not claim to represent right or justice, which were concepts enunciated by the Church. Following Aquinas's thought, the Church defined the common good and it demanded that govern-ments measure themselves against it.[29] In and of itself, this established the Vatican as the source of legitimacy, but two other factors strengthened its position. In the interwar period, an age of dictatorships, the Church became more dictatorial. Where Benedict XV had been modest, Pius XI was authori-tarian. The struggle against Communism took its toll.

Although Pius XII accepted democracy, his Catholicism was a total worldview. When he saw a new social trend he sought to assimilate it: the cinema erupted into Italian life after the war and by 1950 one third of all cinemas were run by parish priests. It is easy to smile at Pius's obsession with the length of women's skirts but control of people's bodies is vital. The Church understood that, if it could set the rules of sexual behavior, it could easily set the rules of politics.

The second factor was that the chaos of depression and wars reinforced the Augustinian notion of history as a battle against unflagging evil. Bringing to this struggle his personal pessimism, Pius XII considered most human institutions harmful and states among the most harmful.[30] There existed an incompatibility between the things of Caesar and the things of God. To Pius the new republic was undesirable but necessary: a barrier between himself and his faithful but a base from which to launch his international crusade against Communism. One is tempted to revise Cavour's statement and speak of a hegemonic church in a non-state.

The affirmations made by DC politicians in favor of incorporating the Lateran Pacts into the Constitution show that they understood and accepted their subordinate position. Guido Gonella, who was Minister of Education in 1946, calls for freedom of religion for the individual and then moves without transition to assert that Catholicism must be the state religion: "The fundamen-tal institutions of the state must be based on Christian ethics." Another spokesman refuses to restrict Catholicism to the private sphere or to admit that public institutions might be neutral. Either the schools teach religion or else they will be "areligious, which for practical purposes means anti-Christian." Giorgio La Pira, Giuseppe Dossetti's supporter, denied that there could be a lay state: Man had a religious nature and social institutions must reflect it.[31]

The supremacy of the Vatican over the DC was the prime cause of the new state's weakness. Instead of acquiring legitimacy through representation and efficiency, it received legitimacy from the papacy. Ultimately, this could only be the shadow of the legitimacy accorded to Pius. If to non-Catholics, of whom there was, despite Fellini's comment, a good number, such a state could only be a foreign body from which they were excluded, to Catholics it was a secondhand garment. The source of the DC's later systemic clientelism lies in this lack of sovereignty. If the state was legitimized only, but completely, by the Vatican, then the DC need demonstrate no sense of the state. From the 1950s on it would treat the public domain as its private property. The bishops were too hasty in refusing responsibility for political corruption. The looting of the Cassa per il Mezzogiorno was counterpoint to the cult of Mary. Such behavior by the party it endorsed troubled the Vatican only when it threatened the DC's ability to win elections. For the rest of the time, clientelism emphasized human frailty and the need for the angelic pastor.

In practice the Vatican was more directly besmirched by corruption through the property speculation in Rome, which took place in the 1950s under the so-called Vatican's mayor, Salvatore Rebecchini, or through IOR's collaboration with Roberto Calvi. But the papacy's greatest responsibility in the current crisis is that it removed from the DC the need to acquire legitimacy by running the state institutions fairly and objectively. The novelist Leonardo Sciascia offered a theological explanation in *Todo Modo*: the priest, Don Gaetano, who finds God in the contemplation of human stupidity, argues that, since Christ has come, all things are permitted to men. Sciascia's particular target in the DC was Giulio Andreotti, whose choice of friends—Pope Paul VI and Salvo Lima—indicated an affinity with Don Gaetano's sublime cynicism. The investigation of Andreotti's alleged Mafia ties is the most important single event in the present regime crisis.

To place the prime responsibility for the troubles of the postwar settlement on the Vatican is not to condemn it. No other force could have filled the 1943 vacuum. From its perspective—and from Italy's—it may have been right in according priority to the struggle against international Communism. Certainly history, in the shape of Joseph Stalin, did little to help the new Italian state. We must next look at the DC and the domestic political context.

A PARTY IN SEARCH OF AN IDENTITY

In the 1946 elections the DC had no control over the hierarchy or over its electorate. The Vatican delivered the vote with its doctrine of Catholic unity. Seventy-five percent of DC parliamentarians belonged to Catholic Action, which claimed 2.5 million members to the DC's 1 million. The party joined eagerly in the growing anti-Communist crusade. As early as 1942 De Gasperi had outlined to U.S. officials the plan for a postwar government that did not include the Communists.[32] During the 1946 elections the Pope invited Italians to choose between "over a thousand years of Christian civilization" and "a materialist state devoid of spiritual ideals, of religion and of God."[33]

By now it was becoming clear that the Resistance, while politicians of many hues would invoke it as the Republic's moral base and while it was certainly the Republic's ideal, was not going to determine the Republic's reality. The strength of the MSI in the 1994 elections casts retrospective doubt not on the moral value of anti-Fascism but on its strength in the country. The notion of a renovating "Wind from the North" that somehow failed—because of Allied opposition, southern inertia, or Togliatti's skepticism?—to sweep away the failings of Italy's past, is only partly correct. All three opposing forces were present, but so were others, and the Resistance was too weak to overcome them.

The Resistance was too small and it came too late. At the end of 1943 there were a mere 9,000 partisans and not until 1945 did the number rise to 100,000. By then the compromise with Italy's past was already taking shape. Like the French Resistance, the Italian movement possessed internal fissures that emerged once, or even before, the invader was defeated. Osoppo, where Pasolini's brother was killed, was only one case where the PCI and Partito d'Azione partisans came to blows. Although it acquired a mass following, the Resistance was not the expression of the entire working class, much less the entire nation.

Since this was a civil war and a class war as well as a national struggle against the Nazis,[34] it provoked hostility from many in the business community. It dethroned Vittorio Valletta whom it later allowed back; it is hard to see how both actions could have been correct. The DC had been present in the Resistance—Enrico Mattei is one example among many—but most of its supporters stood aside from it. This helps explain why Mario Scelba, once he became Minister of the Interior in February 1947, removed Resistants from the public administration as fast as he could.

The partisans personified the vision of a genuine national community: they were what the new state ought to have been. But their ethic of solidarity—citizenship at its best—was a projection of themselves rather than a national reality. This discrepancy lies at the heart of *L'Agnese va a morire,* Renata Viganò's novel about the Romagna Resistance, which reads quite differently in 1995 than it did when Einaudi first published it in 1949. Agnese is driven to rebellion when her husband dies in deportation and she becomes a mother to the young partisans. So a link is made between the family and the Resistance network, which is to be the nucleus of the postwar social order. Yet Viganò notes that many working-class families and villages chose to ignore the Resistance and to collaborate with the Germans. Indeed she hints that the partisans are outsiders: one of them, La Disperata, is an orphan who loses his fiancée when her family discovers he has become a partisan. Moreover Agnese, who has lived in solitude—"for more than fifty years, her whole life, she had fended for herself and she expected little from others"—also dies alone.[35] The novel thus foreshadows the postwar failure to link the individual and the collective in the citizen-state dialogue.

The Resistance's defeat came as early as November 1945. Its victories had increased the CLN's power until, after Germany's surrender, Ferruccio Parri became Prime Minister of a government that included the six Resistance parties. Parri, however, achieved little. In Carlo Levi's novel he is depicted as a saint who belongs to an imaginary Italy that is eternal, suffering and full of miracles. Both the Communist and Christian Democrat politicians are depicted as quietly pleased when Parri falls in November, the Christian Democrat with more reason—he knows that "he has the winning cards in his hand and his mind is at ease."[36] In December De Gasperi became Prime Minister.

The Vatican had enlisted Allied support for De Gasperi and it was now that northern Italy was returned to Italian control. De Gasperi's was a generically conservative government,[37] as was dictated by the two economic choices that were slowly and painfully being made: to internationalize the Italian economy and to do so by allowing the private sector to take the lead. Thus De Gasperi, who had talked of worker participation in industry, abandoned the works councils that the Resistance had created. A month after he took office the ban on laying off workers was partially lifted and in February 240,000 lost their jobs. However the exact nature of DC conservatism remained to be defined. Moreover, while it is correct to see an emerging alliance between the Catholic party and the lay northern industrialists, the two groups were very different.

The DC's strength was demonstrated in the June 1946 elections. It won 207 seats, while the PCI claimed 104, and the Socialists 115. By straddling the issue of republic or monarchy, De Gasperi preserved a large chunk of the 64 percent southern vote for the monarchy. The emergence of the Fronte dell'uomo qualunque (FUQ), which won 30 seats, demonstrated a reaction against anti-Fascism and reminded the DC that there were votes to be won among the lower middle class that disliked—and exaggerated—the strength of the Northern Wind.

The founding of the MSI and its relative success in the Rome local elections of October 1947—4 percent and three councilors—reinforced the lesson. Despite its left-wing Fascist leadership, the MSI's voters were the conservative southern lower middle classes—it grew as the FUQ flagged—and its overlap with the DC was demonstrated when the MSI Rome councilors backed Salvatore Rebecchini for mayor. The MSI was tenacious enough to survive 50 years of DC domination and to constitute a tenuous link between the Berlusconi government and Mussolini's regime. However, in 1947 it was yet another sign that Italian society was far less left-wing than northern and central Italy had seemed to be in 1945.

Although this trend was working mostly for the DC, its success was threatened in the autumn of 1946. Inflation soared, but with the Communists and Socialists in his government De Gasperi could not deflate the economy, and in September the Liberal Treasury Minister, Epicarmo Corbino, resigned. Yet De Gasperi needed the Left for the signing of the unpopular Peace Treaty and for the parliamentary vote on the Lateran Pacts. Once these obstacles were overcome in February and March 1947 respectively, he could oust the Left from the government in May with the enthusiastic support of his party, the industrialists, and above all the Vatican. By now world time had caught up with national time and the U.S. authorities had finally learned the truth about the Soviet regime that the Vatican had been expounding to them since 1940. Marshall aid was announced and Americans took the responsibility for decisions largely made by Italians.

What sort of party was it that, one year of excitement later, dominated the postwar settlement? There was no contradiction between its popular base and its conservatism: both the Gaullists and the British Conservatives enjoy strong support outside the middle and upper classes. Exponents of change without change who stress the continuity with Fascism are right that the lower middle classes, who had found in Mussolini a bulwark against working-class demands, now turned to the DC. But the political order was different: there were now elections and freedom of speech.

The DC's alliance with the Northern lay capitalists did not make it the party of capitalism. It did not pass antitrust laws or modernize the stock market. The traditional pattern of a private sector that relied too heavily on governments it distrusted was continued.[38] But this time the government had fewer ties with industry than in Giolitti's age and was more willing to intervene. The "publicized" economy was 25 years away, but the DC of 1948 felt no admiration for the market.

On the positive side the DC's definition of itself as Catholic gave it flexibility with policy as well as in dealing with most of the many different sectors of Italian society. The old alliance between northern industrialists and southern landlords could not suffice in an age of mass democracy. In the early 1950s the DC pushed through a moderate land reform in the South: it broke up some of the big estates, whose owners received generous compensation, and it distributed the usually uncultivated land to small farmers. They received state aid via the Cassa per il mezzogiorno (a fund set up in 1950 by the government to promote development in the South). Social tensions in the South, where the battle for the land had broken out as soon as Fascism collapsed, were alleviated and a new version of the old alliance was formed.

The DC's willingness to use the state was demonstrated by its decision to maintain and expand the nationalized sector. In the 1940s and 1950s it worked well: ENI is the best-known example, but it is also probable that Italy would never have developed a modern steel industry without the public sector, guided by Oscar Sinigaglia.

The DC's virtues were pragmatism and mediation. In the tumultuous process of socioeconomic change that marked the 1950s and 1960s these were important virtues. The parallel with the post-Unification period is obvious and once more the Italian state was overworked. Good motorways were built but the rail network lagged. Social services were expanded but they were often chaotic.

The defects of DC government in the period before the Naples congress of 1954 were the reverse side of its merits, because both may be traced back to the umbilical cord that tied the party to the Vatican. The DC excluded the groups in northern and central Italy from mediation who were not Catholic and who bore the brunt of the economic reconstruction. Toward them the state was overbearing, not to say authoritarian. Secondly DC governments mediated socioeconomic change but they did not direct it in either of the classical conservative ways: by *dirigisme* or by acting as arbiter of a liberal economy.

The group that suffered most at DC hands was the northern and central Italian working class. Mario Scelba's use of the police during strikes and demonstrations went far beyond minimum force. In 1950 the shots fired into a Modena crowd, which had assembled to protest against factory layoffs, were no exception. Between 1947 and 1950 some 60 workers were killed by the police, while more than 3,000 were wounded in 1950 alone.[39]

Along with this went a certain cultural repression. The Church and its party left the press alone because there was a parallel Catholic press, but they extended their control over radio and television. Film censorship took place and Andreotti felt justified in denouncing Vittorio De Sica's *Umberto D*. The DC, which kept the Ministry of the Interior for itself, also tried to monopolize the Ministry of Education to ensure that the Catholic religion was taught in state schools and that state money flowed to Catholic schools.[40]

Groups that had government support joined in the repression. At Fiat, Vittorio Valletta got rid of PCI and CGIL militants, isolated them in special workshops, and gave bonuses to workers who supported in-house or Catholic unions. His methods were mild when compared with Sicilian tactics. On May 1, 1947 the bandit Salvatore Giuliano fired into a crowd of demonstrators. The Sicilian landowners were using the bandits in the struggle to keep their land. Later Giuliano was killed by the Mafia with police connivance.[41] The Mafia had resumed its pre-Fascist role of protecting the landowners, while itself profiting from land reform. Initially separatist, it became Monarchist or Liberal and then—demonstrating its ability to adapt to new developments—it began the alliance with the DC that was sealed in the mid-1950s and lasted until the 1990s.

Not all these actions were equally grave, and opposition groups bear their share of responsibility. The PCI did nothing to improve labor relations in Fiat. That, too, has been a feature of Italian history: opposition groups seek not a change of government but a different political order. The PCI was a revolutionary party, or pretended it was. This compelled—or allowed—the DC-led governments to use force. But repression damaged their capacity for representation and hence the legitimacy of the new republic.

The DC's second weakness was that, while hyperactive, it lacked a project. The Gaullists were historically identified with the state and the British Conservatives with their empire. Other Christian Democrat parties devised projects, which gave them direction and around which they rallied support. The Germans created the social market based on a mixture of free enterprise and codetermination, while the Dutch and Belgian Christian Democrats developed their Catholic sense of an organic society into an efficient corporatism. By contrast the DC did not use its excellent *dirigistes* like Pasquale Saraceno and its culture of interventionism to plan the Italian economy. The Vatican had a clear project of which the DC was a part; the DC had none.

Indeed the concept of the "besieged" state may be applied to the DC of the 1948-54 years. Despite its landslide triumph (which was in reality the Church's victory), it faced an exacting master in Pius XII, a grumbling rival in the northern industrialists, and an implacable opponent, albeit less mighty than it pretended, in the PCI. This led it to surround itself with a bureaucracy that defended the government from the country rather than allowing the government to shape the country. The public administration, which would fuel opposition to the regime in the late 1980s, played for the DC and its allies the role it had played for previous governments.

It passed, unscathed, from the second to the third incarnation of the state. However it was not a Fascist bureaucracy for it had made the same tranquil transition in 1922. Mussolini had circumvented the state apparatus when it suited him, but he had left it largely intact. In 1943 Badoglio got rid of the few

Fascists whose loyalty was in doubt, but neither he, nor—more surprisingly—the left-wing ministers in the postwar governments, nor the DC undertook a reform, much less a purge, of the civil service.

The bureaucracy of post-Unification Italy was drawn from Piedmont and Sardinia and was modeled on the French civil service. From 1900 on, Southerners flooded into it because they had few options in the private sector and because their juridical, formalistic culture gave them an advantage. The bureaucracy was conservative and rigid and the fragmentation of Italian society produced a plethora of regulation, difficult to explain and slow to apply. The conservative mind-set of this civil service facilitated its transition to Fascism.

It also appealed to Pietro Badoglio, whose government from 1943 to 1944 was made up of military and civilian bureaucrats. For the same reason the Resistance purged the northern civil service, which had continued to obey the Salò Republic and the German occupiers. The Resistance appointed its own prefects, but the upper echelons of the career service fought back. They found support from the Liberal Party, and one of the reasons for Ferruccio Parri's fall was the issue of the political prefects.

The Left either failed to understand the importance of the state apparatus or was too timid to challenge it, so the bureaucracy won out. At first it distrusted the upstart Christian Democrats, but since the middle and lower echelons of the civil service were drawn from the lower middle class that was rallying to the DC, agreements were soon reached. "We'll be better off with the priests," is how Carlo Levi sums up the reaction in the Roman offices. So it proved. Before the 1948 elections the DC granted salary increases to most levels of the bureaucracy and after the election the civil service embraced the new masters of the state.[42]

Forty-five years later the fruits of this symbiotic relationship were apparent in the Clean Hands investigation, when many groups, including the taxation police, were accused of accepting bribes. In the late 1980s, reform of the civil service had become a demand in the growing protest against the regime while the habit of buying votes through promised salary increases in the public sector had contributed both to the public deficit and to spiraling wage costs in the private sector.

Democracy and efficiency have become lesser priorities than self-preservation and preservation of the political order. Thus "citizens" confront a remote bureaucracy protected by its intricate regulations. Despite outstanding exceptions, such as the elite that had run IRI and the nationalized banks under Mussolini and that served the Republic equally well, the postwar civil service has been ill-equipped to manage a modern economy and, unfortunately, it has played its defensive role all too well.

The DC's need for identity was apparent in the years 1948-54 and two major attempts were made to provide one. The first was initiated by De Gasperi and the second by Giuseppe Dossetti. De Gasperi had read the liberal French Catholic thinkers like Montalambert and his Austrian experience had allowed him to study a Catholic state that was not dominated by the Vatican. From his years in the PPI he drew contrasting conclusions, one of which was that Luigi Sturzo had been correct in separating Papacy and party.

De Gasperi sought to emulate him in a different way: by seeking alliances with non-Catholic parties, some of them on his left. His aim was to allow the DC to mediate between Church and society, which would create the space for an autonomous Italian state that was Catholic, but not solely Catholic. The precise character of this autonomy and whether De Gasperi's concept of it varied from period to period are subjects of controversy.[43] At the very least De Gasperi understood the need for the government to avoid being driven to the right and to make its own decisions.

The development of the anti-Fascist movement in the last year of the war suited him well, because it created an alternative pole to the Vatican and widened his room for maneuver. It was an obstacle to the Vatican's recurrent temptation, exhibited as late as the Rome local elections of 1952, to push the DC into forming alliances with the Far Right. In the 1946 referendum De Gasperi resisted Papal pressure to call on DC supporters to vote for the retention of the monarchy.

By late 1946 De Gasperi could see that both economic and foreign policy considerations were rendering impossible his coalitions with the Left. As a Catholic and a conservative he had no reason to seek permanent cohabitation with the PCI, although he was less crudely anti-Communist than someone like Luigi Gedda. De Gasperi continued to consider the PCI a legitimate part of the Republic, although the Cold War had removed its legitimacy as a party of government. His service to the Republic was his intuition that it needed the PCI, if it were not to collapse into civil war.

After his outright victory in the 1948 elections De Gasperi continued to seek coalition partners. The Liberals and the Republicans provided a link with the lay business community of northern Italy; the Social Democrats offered a symbolic bond with the working class. By forging such ties De Gasperi hoped to strengthen the fragile sense of national unity. The lay parties would lighten the weight of Catholic rule.

De Gasperi's openness should not be exaggerated. The second lesson he had learned from his PPI years was that the tie with the Vatican was essential: without it the PPI had been easy prey for Mussolini. Moreover he did not have the power to move far from Pius XII who controlled the DC electorate. De

Gasperi had no interest in building up the party's organization; the DC's role was to back his government. But such a non-party could not support him against Pius and Catholic Action. Anyway De Gasperi was not above using the Vatican to quell the attacks made on him by the Dossettiani. His vision was different from Pius's, if only because he thought in terms of citizens and states. But he believed in Catholic unity and in negotiating with non-Catholics from a position of strength.

This explains why he altered the election rules in 1953 so that the DC-led coalition might, with a reduced share of the vote, maintain its outright majority. Only then could the DC extend tolerance to coalition partners who would have no other options. Moreover aside from his one great intuition, De Gasperi did not articulate a vision of society. He did not rein in Scelba and he neither endorsed the free market nor defined a coherent pattern of public intervention. He left the DC neither capitalist nor anti-capitalist but perhaps both. It remains true that De Gasperi saw the Italians not merely as the faithful but as the sum of various cultural groups.

All these criticisms and more were made by Dossetti, who battled De Gasperi from 1946 until 1951, when he gave up politics. Where De Gasperi read Montalambert, the Dossettiani's bible was Jacques Maritain's *L'Humanisme intégral* (1936), of which they offered their own interpretation. Dossetti believed—against the Augustinian view—that Christianity could transform the human condition. There should be no separation of Church and party, which meant no subordination of party to Church. There should be no concessions to lay values, although the Catholic party would work with all social groups. The DC should assert itself and take up the difficult but glorious task of building a truly Christian society. This would require a long political struggle during which the Catholic party would be apostolic but never sectarian, while lay values would of themselves become Christian.

Since the ideal Christian society was based on the brotherhood of man Dossetti looked toward the PCI. He rejected historical materialism but he relished the future classless society. The Dossettiani attacked Luigi Einaudi's liberalism and affirmed that the market could not create full employment; state intervention was necessary. La Pira invoked Maynard Keynes and William Beveridge as well as the New Deal and he wrapped them in quotations from St. Matthew's gospel. The Keynes of the *Cronache sociali* (Social Chronicles) was not a reformer but a Franciscan. While it looked kindly on the Labor Party, Dossetti's magazine criticized the nationalization program (because it gave too much power to the centralized state) and preferred co-ops. The vision present in La Pira's widely read "L'attesa della povera gente" is a utopian Catholic populism.[44]

As such it could not fill the void in DC culture. Although unwelcome to the Vatican, which distrusted its view of the Church-party relationship as well as its kindness to the PCI, it was as integrally Catholic as De Gasperi's more prosaic strategy of an outright majority. If Dossetti could not govern with the PCI, then he wanted to govern alone. Nor did he offer a solution to the problem of the state, which was supposed to dissolve into the reborn Christian community.

However as long as they were active both De Gasperi and Dossetti demonstrated an awareness of the DC's predicament. After they left it became "pragmatic, empirical and directionless."[45] The judgment is harsh but it sums up the situation: the Catholic party had failed to re-found the state, but its power was assured.

DILEMMAS OF A REVOLUTIONARY PARTY

The opportunity to take control of the new republic was conceded to the DC by its ally-antagonist, the PCI: "In reality the Communists never challenged the DC's leadership."[46] The struggle between the two seemed equal but, even before the United States entered the fray in late 1946, it was not. Anti-Communist tirades about Cossacks watering their horses in Roman fountains masked the imbalance of a conflict between the Vatican, the industrialists, the state apparatus, and most of the middle class on one side, and the northern and central Italian working class on the other. The Soviet threat was, arguably, great, but the internal threat of Communism was not, although the fear of Communism was real. This made the PCI seem stronger than it was, while it increased the real strength of the DC. Moreover the PCI had no better solution than its rival to the problem of the Italian state.

Togliatti's speech at Salerno reflects a moment when the interests of the international Communist movement, as defined by Stalin, overlapped with the interests of the Italian Communist Party, as defined by its secretary. Entry into the Badoglio government, the formation of as broad an alliance as possible and the subordination of Socialism to the national struggle against the Nazis suited the war goals of the USSR. They also constituted Togliatti's plan to re-establish in Italy a Communist Party that could work legally to block any return of Fascism, while gradually expanding its own influence.

In April 1944, not anticipating the breakup of the anti-Nazi front, Togliatti envisaged the creation of a new mass party to replace the Third International model of a revolutionary elite. He foresaw a prolonged period in government during which the PCI would penetrate civil society and then, in indeterminate form, the establishment of hegemony. Here again, the failure of this strategy stemmed from domestic Italian considerations, although the East-West split worsened the defeat.

First, the social bloc, which was supposed to gather around the project, was internally contradictory. Progressive democracy was to become the rallying-point for a coalition of the industrial workers, the peasantry, and broad segments of the middle class. The reactionary, monopolistic bourgeoisie would be isolated and the workers would spearhead the vast, national-popular alliance. The rather obvious drawbacks were that the lower middle classes were the group most imbued with Fascism and that the entrepreneurs wielded much of the economic power.

Nor were the Gramscian underpinnings of the project any more convincing. The dominant view of Gramsci's prison writings is that they are an "open" work, subject to diverse interpretations.[47] In the way he chose to present them, Togliatti, who understandably neglected the earlier, more radical articles of *Ordine nuovo* (New Order), emphasized the themes of a long march through the existing institutions, the weakness of an Italian capitalism dismissed as parasitic and Malthusian, and hence the inevitability of hegemony. The results were positive in that they strengthened the new party's commitment to parliamentary democracy and to its own growth in membership, but negative in that they discouraged the PCI from acting rapidly to shape the emerging postwar structures, especially the economic structures. That task could be postponed until the social bloc was in place and the parliamentary alliances were working. Hegemony was relegated to a remote future and yet it served to justify present prudence.[48]

This seems to contradict Gramsci's view that the precise nature of capitalist development was unpredictable and could be altered by the strategy of the working-class movement. Nor is it clear that, when he writes of penetrating civil society, Gramsci means the existing organizations. However Togliatti's conservative reading justified his extreme caution during his period as Minister of Justice, when he left the Rocco code—the criminal law procedures introduced under Mussolini—intact; offered an amnesty that the magistrates were able to use to let serious Fascist crimes, including torture, go unpunished; and defended the corps of magistrates, although it had a conservative bias and had been subservient to the dictatorship.

Such minimalism was paralleled in the economic sphere, where the PCI failed to press for Mauro Scoccimarro's currency reform, which would have combated inflation and allowed the taxation of war profits. Even the agricultural reform of the Communist Minister, Fausto Gullo, which did promote peasant ownership of land, was watered down with Togliatti's acquiescence. When inflation soared in 1946 the Communist ministers in the government made no serious attempt to fight it with selective credit controls.

For the PCI's failure to use, much less change, the state, there are two main reasons. The first is the priority that Togliatti gave to working with the DC. This led him to weep no tears for the Parri government and to support De Gasperi's premiership. Parri was the incarnation of the Resistance, which was a source of PCI strength but that Togliatti distrusted. In part this reflected an aristocratic skepticism, typical of the Third International, about popular uprisings. In part it was the Roman perspective that stressed political action rather than the guerrilla war waged in the North. But mostly it was fear that the new party would be guided down dangerous paths that led away from the goal of cooperation with the Catholics.[49]

Togliatti's upbringing was marked by Catholicism: his uncle had been a priest, his parents attended Sunday mass, and he had contacts with the Salesians whose faith had social ramifications. But this was not the reason for the tenacity with which he pursued the alliance with the DC. The ostensible reason was the DC's role as representative of the Catholic masses, who could be won over to left-wing positions. If one doubts Togliatti's inexhaustible variations on this theme, it is because one respects his realism. His true motive was the need to legitimize the PCI. His pessimism was revealed in a conversation with some young Communists who were waxing lyrical about the changes the PCI would make. It will be enough, Togliatti replied, if in a year's time we are not all in jail.[50]

The sense of illegitimacy would haunt the PCI and one cannot dismiss Togliatti's fear as groundless. One can, however, ask whether the PCI would not have done better to fight for structural changes—whether currency reform or renewal of the state apparatus—that would have enabled it to bargain better with the DC. Repeated acts of conciliation merely invited De Gasperi to use and then discard his ally. Moreover minimalist practice could not atone for maximalist doctrine: the identification with Stalin's USSR. Nor could a PCI, which had to support the daily demands of its working-class constituency for wage increases, restrictions on layoffs, and controls on the price of food, hope to appease the Liberals and private-sector industrialists, to whom De Gasperi had entrusted the economy.

How can one explain Togliatti's persistence? Certainly he relied too much on his personal relationship with De Gasperi. When he exulted that the PCI's vote in favor of the Lateran Pacts would earn it 20 years in the government,[51] he was underestimating the Vatican's toughness. The Church felt no gratitude for Communist support. The explanation that best suits Togliatti's realistic, pessimistic worldview is that he believed that the Catholic

Church was uncontrollable.[52] The PCI had no choice but to strike a deal with it, even if the deal was bad.

If the Communists allowed the DC to monopolize and undermine the state, a second reason lay in their own culture. Their maximalist doctrine taught them that the Italian state was nothing more than the sum of the capitalist forces within it. Intervention to remedy the shortcomings of the economy was nonsense because the state "was no different from the machine it was supposedly repairing."[53]

This view, which drew on Lenin's theory of imperialism, had survived Communist participation in the Popular Fronts. While it was certainly used by Togliatti to justify his minimalism, it was not a mere tactic. Rather it overlapped with the admiration for the USSR as a "different" society and with the rejection of Social Democratic experiments such as the Atlee government. As such it was an essential trait of PCI identity. It appealed to the militants of northern and central Italy who had fought in the Resistance for a new, Socialist society.

Such revolutionary purity did not mesh perfectly with Togliatti's choice of parliamentary gradualism. While awaiting the arrival of hegemony, the PCI had to do more than support any and every working-class demand. The temptation to organize coherent state intervention recurred in the so-called new course of 1946 as well as in the CGIL's employment plan. The new course offered wage restraint in return for government planning and a role for the works councils. The 1949 plan called for the nationalization of the electrical industry and public works to create full employment. Both schemes presupposed a reformist, Keynesian state, which cannot be considered a facade for private capital. Yet in both cases the PCI failed to find a language that could present them other than as concessions wrung from a liberal state or as signs of working-class hegemony.

Such schemes might not have worked, but the attempt to make them work would have offered the model of a reformist state. It is probably illusory to imagine that alliances might have been forged with the Republicans or with DC planners such as Pasquale Saraceno and Ezio Vanoni. But at least Socialists such as Rodolfo Morandi would have been encouraged to develop their planning projects. After 1947 the PCI was excluded from power because of its ties with the USSR, but it also engaged in a "self-exclusion."[54] It turned away from the business of government.

This is the true form of duplicity practiced by Togliatti. It has been argued that he preached democracy but plotted revolution. Many Communist militants did not turn in their arms at the Liberation. They viewed the new party's commitment to democracy as a tactic and believed that the machine gun was needed to create socialism. The party kept a paramilitary structure intact that went into action after the attempt to assassinate Togliatti on July 14, 1948. Amid the wave of strikes, DC offices were attacked, and at Abbadia San Salvatore, the telephone center that controlled the North-South lines was occupied. Milan, Turin, and Genoa appeared on the brink of insurrection.

There was no plan by the leadership for an uprising, although for a day Luigi Longo and Pietro Secchia hesitated, allowed the disturbances to continue, and consulted the Soviets who offered them no help. As the strikes and occupations flagged, the PCI leadership called on the workers to cease all unlawful activity. Their duplicity lay in their hesitation, which provided the pretext for Scelba's repression.[55]

Togliatti, who on his way to the hospital had told his comrades not to lose their heads, never showed sympathy for illegal activity. When Giancarlo Pajetta occupied the Milan prefecture in November 1947 to protest the dismissal of the CLN-appointed prefect, Togliatti was furious. Ever afterward he mocked Pajetta for lusting after revolutions. When the Cominform criticized the PCI for allowing itself to be dismissed from the government, Togliatti was obliged to declare that the PCI was not limited to legal forms of retaliation. But this was no more than a gesture, which provided him with room for maneuver in his defense of the parliamentary road against critics like Secchia.

Togliatti's real duplicity lay in pretending that the PCI was considering revolution when in fact it was not. Probably this was necessary to draw into the new party and into parliamentary democracy the northern Italian militants who believed in the machine gun. But the price of preaching revolution was the shunning of reformism. This condemned the PCI to immobility. Secchia became the voice of an alternative policy that advocated working-class pressure, in the form of strikes, demonstrations, and occupations, in order to gain concessions. This seemed to Togliatti dangerous but, while he was probably right, there is truth in Secchia's outburst that "if we listen to you we'll never do anything."

The PCI's exclusion and self-exclusion from the state made it into an excellent party of local government in the regions it dominated. In Emilia-Romagna it set out to construct a model society with a broad class base and it succeeded in winning over segments of the middle class and some small entrepreneurs. The reformist and revolutionary strands were reconciled because the practice was Social Democratic—public investment in infrastructure and social services—while Communism acted as a utopian goal and as a moral code.[56]

Emilia-Romagna could not be transferred to Italy because it was constructed against Italy. The consequences of the PCI's (self-)exclusion for the party, for the state, and for the DC were profound. Having no representatives in the upper levels of the civil service or the nationalized industries, the PCI lacked knowledge, as the years of the historic compromise would reveal. Its culture was primarily one of opposition rather than of government and the organization it knew best was its own. The state suffered because there was no left-wing reformist party that would be obliged to use the state's instruments and consequently make them more efficient. Finally the DC was allowed to become the permanent party of government without having to demonstrate that it could represent the electorate or act efficiently.

Togliatti's achievement was to wean a radical working class away from illusory revolutions and toward the new state. His work complemented De Gasperi's distinction between the PCI as a party of government and the PCI as cofounder of the Republic. Togliatti set his party off on a road of heresy along which lay Berlinguer's appreciation of the value of the Republic's institutions.

However another pillar of the postwar settlement was the PCI's recognition of the DC's central role. By not challenging the DC's right to take the lead in governing, in return for a modest role in government before 1947, and for assuming the leadership of the opposition from 1947 to 1976, the PCI became an ally as well as an antagonist.

There are affinities between Communist and Catholic culture. Parallels, as well as major differences, exist between the way the PCI ran Emilia-Romagna and the way the DC ran the Veneto. The Catho-Communist Franco Rodano's quest to unite both faiths by setting the Marxist concept of history within a Christian metaphysics is emblematic. In the 1940s the Communists' defects complemented the Catholics. Both ally-antagonists created mass parties that were supposed to instill democratic values and yet the Church and the PCI had Leninist structures. Jealous and all-embracing, each saw itself as the pole of identity that the state is supposed to represent. Tacitly the two agreed the Italian state was best left weak.

For this reason the notion of Catholic hegemony is questionable. If the term *hegemony* is used to indicate not merely possession of power but the use of that power to guide the whole of society toward defined goals, then the Catholics were not hegemonic. A glance at Italy's role in the world reinforces this conclusion.

3

Italy and the World: Helpful Americans, Rich Europeans, and Resourceful Italians

Several recent events demonstrate how the intertwining of Italy with the outside world has changed. When the Ciampi government was formed in April 1993, it contained PDS ministers. They were from an ex-Communist rather than a Communist Party and they resigned after a day or so. Yet they evoked memories of 1947 and of the 40-year U.S. veto on PCI participation in the government. This time there were no anathemas from Washington. During the 1994 elections the anti-Communism was homegrown.

In the debate about foreign policy it has been argued that Italy must find a new framework. The end of the Cold War has deprived her of both automatic U.S. protection and of occasional, safe revolts against it.[1] Life may well be harder without the heavy-handed but easily exploited Americans. In 1993 Foreign Minister Beniamino Andreatta, warned Italians that it was no longer enough to follow other countries; Italy must act too.

In Europe the lira's departure from the EMS in September 1992 was a defeat for the Europeanist strategy, which was such an important part of the postwar settlement. Andreatta reacted by reaffirming Italy's belief in a federalist Europe, while the Amato and Ciampi governments pursued austerity policies designed to allow Italy to re-enter the EMS. However the Berlusconi government proclaimed its preference for a "Europe of the Fatherlands" EU, while its macroeconomic policy was weak.

The postwar settlement involved opening the Italian economy to the world economy, which created hardships that have returned in the present recession. Unemployment has given rise to demonstrations, which have a special bitterness rooted in the reconstruction years when the working class paid a high price and waited a long time for a prosperity that now seems menaced. The threat to the Bagnoli and Taranto steel plants has reawakened the Southern question, which had never really gone away but which Italy had made strenuous attempts to resolve. In October 1993, when national unemployment stood at 11.3 percent, it was 7.7 percent in the North and the Center, but 18.9 percent in the South, with Sicily, Calabria, and Campania with more than 20 percent unemployment.[2]

To adapt the economy to the international order, the state—once more playing catch-up—had struck a bargain with the northern industrialists. They received much aid but a large nationalized sector was created too. Now both sides are struggling: Fiat has cut workers and dividends, while Efim has gone bankrupt.

However, in support of the thesis that the years 1992-94 reflect, in part, a modernization crisis, the Italian economy has begun to recover. Adaptation to world trends, albeit following national traditions, is present in the Fiat restructuring plan as well as in the privatization program. In spring 1994 the stock market soared and more shares were traded than at any time since the mid-1980s, while the denationalizations of Credito Italiano and Comit proceeded smoothly.

World time, in the shape of the Cold War and the internationalization of the economy, did create extra difficulties for the weak Italian state. However, while the state was not able to dominate outside events, it could seize the opportunities they offered—such as membership in the EC. So it is correct to say that "Italy has been shaped by international conditions to an extent unknown in any other Western democratic country, with the exception of Germany,"[3] provided one acknowledges that Italians found ways to exploit those constraints. The PCI disappointed Stalin in the 1940s and irritated Brezhnev in the 1970s. The Americans did not want the DC to enjoy a monopoly on government, but the DC did. Similarly the Italian republic can not survive the end of the Cold War and the advent of the Internal Market without being re-founded, but both the spur and the obstacles to change come from within.

This chapter is divided into four parts: the influence of the East-West split on domestic politics, Italy's place in the world, her role in the EC, and the impact on her economy and society of the process of internationalization. In these discussions the unity is thematic rather than chronological.

HELPFUL AMERICANS

The Truman administration entered the battle of the 1948 elections in the fall of 1946.[4] In November the Republicans gained control of the Senate and House. The Democrats needed a cause and Stalin thoughtfully provided one. I have argued that the 1948 result was the conclusion of a long struggle in which the bloc that gathered around the DC was far stronger than the Left's supporters. But in 1947 the outcome of the elections was in doubt, while East-West relations were deteriorating.

This worked against the Left. Stalin's rejection of Marshall aid, his call for the Western Communist Parties to take a harder line, and above all the Prague coup of February 1948 undermined Togliatti's conciliatory strategy. By contrast the United States offered bread, money, a statement that the Western powers supported Italy's right to Trieste, and military assistance. The last of these affords insights into the Italian way of dealing with helpful foreigners. According to the peace treaty, Allied troops were to leave Italy by December 14, 1947. De Gasperi wanted a tough U.S. statement pledging military intervention if there were a Communist insurrection. Truman obliged and the United States also offered to send a military mission.[5] However, De Gasperi refused this, just as in March 1948 he refused a U.S. offer of massive reinforcements for the police and army.

Two issues are involved. The first is that De Gasperi and the Italian political elite had no objection to outside interference in domestic affairs, but they sought to shape it. De Gasperi maneuvered to gain autonomy from the United States as he did from the Vatican. The second is that he believed the threat of force was more useful than the reality of force, which might produce a backlash in a nation still suffering from war and defeat.

In the months before the election the United States combined covert funding of the DC with threats not to send Marshall aid if the Left won. Both actions were welcome to De Gasperi who continued, however, with Einaudi's deflationary policy despite American suggestions that increased government spending would be popular.

The pattern that the international situation would impose on Italian politics was taking shape. The Soviets damaged the PCI by their behavior but they also provided it with money. The United States ensured that the PCI was kept out of the government and had as little power as possible. The Catholic Church, the DC and its satellites, as well as the majority of Italian voters welcomed this help. To speak of American imperialism is absurd. However the forms that U.S. pressure took were often irksome and conversely the United States was often exasperated by its inability to get its way.

Usually American demands helped Italian leaders to do things that they would have done anyway, although perhaps in a different manner. When Clare Booth Luce prophesied there would be a civil war in 1954,[6] Italians flatly refused to comply. But when she reminded Fiat that the Pentagon was not awarding military contracts to companies in which the Confederazione generale italiana del lavoro (CGIL) organized the workforce, Valletta took action. In the 1955 shop-stewards elections the Communist metalworkers union dropped from 63 percent to 36 percent and in 1957 to a mere 21 percent.[7]

However, while Valletta may have been spurred by Luce's unsubtle reminders, he had been waging a long war against the PCI and the CGIL. In 1949 he had ceased dealing with the works council and in 1951 he had fired the Communist director of social services. Moreover the PCI contributed to the difficulties of its union by not updating its analysis of the working conditions in a modern, mass industry.

In general the United States set parameters: it could veto the PCI but it could not refashion the government. American interference damaged Italian political culture by blocking the alternation of parties in power—although at least until the 1970s and perhaps later, domestic opposition to any PCI presence in the government was overwhelming—by weakening the state's prestige in the eyes of its citizens through ostentatious interference (although the citizens had scant regard for the state anyway) and by subordinating economic and social issues to anti-Communism. Covert funding encouraged corruption. Funding the MSI, as Ambassador Graham Martin did in 1972,[8] encouraged a party that was not free of violence.

An unanswered question is whether the CIA participated in the plots and acts of terrorism perpetrated by the Far Right. The aim of such actions, insofar as they were not undertaken autonomously by right-wing groups who often emerged from the MSI and who traced their legitimacy to the Salò Republic, was to threaten the PCI with a Fascist takeover and to remind the DC that it might not be indispensable. Evidence of CIA participation exists in the proven complicity of segments of the CIA-trained Italian secret services.

The Solo Plan, orchestrated in 1964 when the Center-Left was in a delicate phase, was led by Giovanni de Lorenzo, an ex-head of SIFAR (Servizio informazioni forze armate), which had been financed and organized by the

CIA.[9] Vito Miceli, head of SID (Servizio informazioni difesa) and accused of participating in the subversive organization, the Rose of the Winds, was trained at NATO and had close ties to Graham Martin. There was SID involvement in the coverup of the 1969 Piazza Fontana bombings and perhaps in the bombings themselves, which raises the possibility of CIA knowledge or involvement. Certainly the CIA knew in 1974 that Edgardo Sogno was plotting a coup and yet it did not share the information with the Italian government.[10] One observer concludes that the student and worker movement "had to be beaten back. The Italian secret services, in all probability linked with the American, NATO secret services, thought the Greek solution might work: bombs, terror, a swing to the Right, if necessary some sort of coup."[11]

Similarly there is circumstantial, although not as yet concrete, evidence that the Italian secret services manipulated the left-wing terrorism of the 1970s in order to damage the PCI.[12] It is surprising that the Red Brigades were not broken up in 1976 when they were weak and infiltrated. Here again the question of CIA involvement is raised and no definite answer can be given.

Finally the CIA helped set up the Stay Behind or Gladio organization, which was first mooted in 1950 and took shape in 1956. Supposedly designed to provide resistance and intelligence in the event of a Soviet occupation, this illegal formation was probably used against the PCI.[13] If the CIA did participate in such actions, its role was to reinforce the U.S. veto. Here again there is no evidence to suggest that segments of the Italian secret services were dragged kicking and screaming into right-wing plotting. The United States probably played a formative role in providing money and training, especially during the late 1940s, but it never lacked recruits. However it conferred legitimacy on Italian participants. America guaranteed a political system that revolved around DC power. It did not invent or impose it, but it did help.

ATLANTICISM AND NEO-ATLANTICISM

The choice of Atlanticism was made with a certain reluctance. Later Italy flaunted her loyalty to NATO on many occasions: in the early 1980s she hosted the Cruise missiles at Comiso, with far fewer protesters than the installation of such missiles provoked in Germany, Holland, or even Britain. But Italy has her own worldview, which is often unshared and unloved by the United States. The 1993 clash over Somalia was the most recent example.

From September 8, 1943, Italy's prime foreign policy goal was to relegitimize the country. Like Konrad Adenauer, Carlo Sforza sought equal treatment. Italian objections to the peace treaty included the disappointment at being considered a conquered enemy, instead of an ally against the Nazis. The road to legitimacy lay in joining international organizations, which explains the instructions given by De Gasperi to Paolo-Emilio Taviani who led the Italian delegation to the meetings of the Schuman Plan. Taviani was to agree to anything, because what counted was to demonstrate Italian support for European integration.[14]

This did not prevent Italy from negotiating skillfully in the Coal and Steel Pool. Like the other European countries, Italy sought, in the new international world of NATO and the EC, to reinforce the power of the Italian state. When Italy's interests were not served by international organizations, the government dragged its feet. Conversely it sometimes persisted with policies that were internationally unpopular. The Einaudi line of austerity, as confirmed by Giuseppe Pella, was criticized by the Marshall Plan administrators, and the balance of payments surpluses it created irritated the Europeans. A case of foot-dragging came in early 1948, when Italy was invited to join the Brussels Pact. Ernie Bevin felt he was being generous and he was outraged when Italy declined. De Gasperi feared supporting military alliances, which were widely disliked, and driving voters into the arms of the Left. Moreover he detected a nationalist mood that was disappointed with the peace treaty and that wanted Trieste and the colonies given back.[15]

The next year Italy joined the Atlantic Alliance. The election was over and the government realized that by dragging its feet it was isolating itself. NATO offered security, and if the other members expected little from Italy, then so much the better. As an Italian and as a Christian Democrat De Gasperi knew that enlightened self-interest dictated joining. But although the change of policy was conducted with trumpet blasts of commitment to Western defense, the national concerns remained.

The first was for peace. Its constituency ran from the PCI via the PSI to Gronchi and to the Dossettiani, who accepted entry into the Western alliance with great reluctance.[16] Where Sforza identified the Italian nation with the tradition of the Western Enlightenment, many Catholics identified it with the Church and with a Mediterranean culture that was uncapitalist and populist. Pope Pius XII himself was lukewarm about the alliance. Forty-two years later the Catholic-Communist front would re-emerge during the Gulf War of 1991 when the PDS, at the Rimini Congress, where it was officially breaking with its Communist past, proclaimed its distaste for military action against Saddam Hussein and found common ground with Catholic protesters.

By now the Cold War was over and the position of orthodox Atlanticists was weaker because the enemy was no longer the mighty USSR. However the distaste for the Gulf War had deep roots. The neo-Atlanticist tendency that emerged in the 1950s was inspired in part by a Third Worldism, which led it to question both the bipolar structure of the Cold War and European colonialism. Amintore Fanfani's attempt to begin a dialogue with Egypt after the Suez conflict, Enrico Mattei's dealings with the Algerian rebels, and Giorgio La Pira's later attempt to mediate in the Vietnam conflict are examples. Behind all of them is the belief that Italy, having no colonies, was able to deal fairly with developing countries.

Students of continuity in foreign policy would see the neo-Atlanticist thesis, that Italy's culture and her geographical position on the Mediterranean offered her a sphere of influence in North Africa and the Middle East, as a revised form of Mussolini's dreams of empire. Certainly the idealistic vision of a fairer relationship with the Third World overlapped neatly with a reassertion of Italian nationalism against the dominant Western powers. Fanfani, who had supported the invasion of Abyssinia, was such a nationalist.

The economic dimension of the policy was provided by Enrico Mattei. Offers to Iran and Egypt of a better deal than the U.S. oil companies offered were designed to obtain a measure of independence in the domain of energy. Between 1948 and 1962 Mattei doubled Ente nazionale idrocarburi (ENI)'s share of the amount of petrol sold in Italy. His discovery and exploitation of the natural gas deposits in the Po Valley was one reason for the economic miracle. Meanwhile foreign companies were allowed to drill only in Sicily.[17]

Mattei's success in competing with the oil giants was limited; in 1962, before he was killed in a plane crash, he was in the process of compromising with them. The whole enterprise of neo-Atlanticism was dubious. Its protagonists were not united among themselves: Amintore Fanfani and Giovanni Gronchi were rivals, while Mattei founded a separate faction of the DC, the Base. The most likely candidate to lead such a movement was the PCI, which was barred by its illegitimacy and formed no more than temporary alliances with Mattei. The goals of neo-Atlanticism and its relationship with orthodox Atlanticism were unclear.

Yet most European countries—Britain as well as Gaullist France—have sought, each in its own way, a degree of independence from the United States. That Italy, too, should have a national vision of world affairs and should wish to pursue it is yet another proof that Italians sought some control over their destiny. Nor did this attempt cease with Mattei's death and Fanfani's defeats. Fiat bestrode the East-West divide when it founded its plant at Togliattigrad, and in the 1970s it incurred U.S. displeasure when it sold a block of its shares to Qadaffi.

In the 1980s Italian ties to the PLO were closer than the United States would have wished, and Italy opposed the U.S. readiness to use force in the

Middle East. A dramatic conflict flared up after the hijacking of the *Achille Lauro* in October 1985, when the U.S. navy forced a plane carrying a group of Arab terrorists to land at Sigonella. The United States wanted to take the men into custody but the Craxi government asserted Italy's control over her national territory. It took charge of the group and then released them. Andreotti, who was Foreign Minister in the Craxi years, persistently opposed U.S. initiatives in the Middle East. He sought to avoid the use of force, to work through the UN, and to establish Italy as a mediator.[18] There is no evidence that he was without public support and, among the political parties, objections from the PRI were outweighed by sympathy from the PCI.

Criticisms of the substance of this policy are legitimate but not overwhelmingly convincing. The Reagan administration was strong but inconsistent in its stands on the Middle East. The most telling objection to Italy's softer line is that the political will to promote it was lacking. When the Persian Gulf came up for debate at the G7 meeting in June 1987, Craxi had been forced out and the caretaker Fanfani led the Italian delegation. Once more there were various strands in Italian policy. Craxi supported the Palestinian aspiration toward a home state, but he distinguished between moderate and extremist Arab countries and he was very anxious—for domestic and party reasons—to remain on good terms with the United States. Andreotti sought rather to unite the Arab world so that it could find its own solutions to the Palestinian question. This offered Italy a special role as the Arabs' principal interlocutor at the risk of worsening relations with the United States.

In general the state behaved abroad rather better than it did at home, but with the same flaws. The DC-led coalitions excelled in mediation, but they could not lead. Nor could they pursue any heretical policy for long because of their internal divisions. This reduced much of Italian foreign policy to mere symbolism.

The aim of liberating the Third World did not extend to liberating it from Italian corruption. Craxi took pride in increasing foreign aid, which went from 0.24 percent in 1983 to 0.4 percent of GDP in 1986. However the Clean Hands operation has questioned the way aid was distributed. Officials in the cooperation program are under investigation, while money, allocated for projects in distant countries like Bangladesh, seems to have gone only as far as the pockets of Italian politicians and businessmen.[19] Even before he became Prime Minister, Craxi was accused of engaging in shady deals with the dictator, Siad Barre, and the Somalians remembered them when the Italian contingent of the UN force arrived in 1993. Of course, corruption in dealings with former colonies is not exactly unknown in France and Britain either.

Another criticism is that Italian heresy would not have been possible, if the United States had not been present to protect orthodoxy. This view leads to the conclusion that, since the United States is now withdrawing, Italy will be left with no policy at all. But such pessimism presupposes that the process of re-founding the state will collapse. It is legitimate to argue that a stronger state may be able to define and pursue a national vision, which the old regime perceived but sacrificed—to American strength and to its own weakness.

Ciampi and Andreatta made a start. Andreatta defined the new situation: "There are no more 'locomotives' or outside leaders."[20] He argued that Italy can only act through international organizations and he threw himself strongly behind the February 1994 NATO ultimatum in Bosnia. Ciampi has even spoken of the need to increase defense spending in order to improve Italy's deliberately neglected armed forces. In what seems a rebuke to neo-Atlanticism and to its roots in Catholic populism, Andreatta dismisses "any so-called special role" for Italy based on the notion that her culture is "closer to man." Yet it is hard to see how there can be a greater national effort in foreign affairs unless policy is grounded in national culture. Andreatta has defended the action of the Italian contingent in Somalia, emphasizing the knowledge of local conditions and negotiation against the American resort to force. He writes of the need for the UN "to give up an arbitrary and unilateral use of violence."

The cultural forces that steer Italy toward a Mediterranean role are still present. Recently *Il Manifesto* suggested that the Mediterranean countries might form a group that would bridge the gulf between wealthy Europe and the poor, overpopulated Moslem nations.[21] This is the kind of special role, which springs from left-wing populism and which Andreatta condemns. Yet the very realistic Ciampi has spoken of the central importance of the Mediterranean basin for Italy.[22] The end of bipolarity has left openings for regional groups and, conversely, the situation in Algeria is so desperate as to make any serious Mediterranean initiative welcome.

Andreatta stresses the need for Italy to be "reliable."[23] Synthesizing the argument between Sforza and Dossetti, he claims that in the West there is a universalism that stems from the Enlightenment, of which Italy is a part via her membership in the European Community. Then there are the re-emerging nationalisms in Central and Eastern Europe and the resort to fundamentalism in North Africa or the Middle East. Italy can play a role by engaging in a dialogue with the second and third groups as long as she remembers that she belongs to the first. This is an outline of what the foreign policy of a revitalized Italian state might be.

The Berlusconi government had too short a period in office to leave its mark on world affairs. The Prime Minister handled the G7 meeting at Naples well. During the Rwanda crisis Italy first offered to send troops to support the French contingent and then backed off, which is understandable but hardly a sign of reliability. The Berlusconi-Yeltsin meeting in October was overshadowed by the domestic problems that beset both leaders. The Italian government pursued the goal of increasing Italy's influence in the UN Security Council. But this task was bequeathed to future governments, in particular to Susanna Agnelli, Dini's Foreign Minister.

EUROPEAN UNITY: A NATIONAL STRATEGY

Like the other defeated power, Germany, Italy needed the friendship of all her Western conquerors. De Gasperi took care to link Atlanticism with European unity and the habit has persisted. Italy dislikes conflicts between the United States and Western Europe: during the 1991 defense debates she maintained that the Western European Union could be the arm of the EC and an integral part of NATO. Atlanticism bears the connotation of battles, whereas Europe is associated with prosperity. In the postwar years the common perception was that other European countries were richer than Italy and that association with them would make Italy rich. Even today a certain inferiority complex lingers. The reverse side of the Mediterranean vocation is what has been called the "Tonio Kroeger complex": small brown people cannot afford not to associate with tall, fair people.[24]

To the DC-led governments being European meant supporting federalism. Even after it became obvious that de Gaulle's vision of a Europe of the Fatherlands had won out in the EC, Italy proclaimed her willingness to surrender her national sovereignty to a European authority. One explanation is that the weak Italian state had less sovereignty to lose. Another is that the informal networks by which the various clans exercised power could flourish under a European government, whereas more formal national power systems could not. Italy's Europeanism is, according to one view, composed of "rhetorical fervor, indifference, craftiness and lots of quiet reservations."[25] I would add that it contains a healthy dose of national self-interest.

In the postwar years Italy helped try to turn the OEEC (Organization of European Economic Cooperation) and the Council of Europe into federalist forces. De Gasperi's government presented a plan whereby the OEEC would become permanent, would lead to social and cultural collaboration, would set up a political committee to discuss foreign affairs, and would settle internal disputes through its own Court of Justice. Neither Britain nor France had any interest in such a project and it is hard to imagine that De Gasperi and Sforza did not know this. But they were pursuing the national strategy of rehabilitating post-Fascist Italy.

Reality dawned with the ECSC (European Coal and Steel Community). It was a Franco-German scheme and Italy was not consulted. However the De Gasperi government emerged from the negotiations with several victories. There was to be international, free movement of labor, which might ease unemployment; the Sulcis coal mines in Sardinia received a special subsidy for modernization, which has allowed them to remain open—albeit barely—until today; a Community market in scrap would provide cheap metal for Italy's many steelworks that used electric furnaces. Most important, Italy was to have access to Algerian iron ore for her full-process plants and was allowed to continue tariffs on imported steel for up to five years.[26]

These concessions provoke three comments. The first is that Italy was able to parlay her weakness into an advantage. The second is that the Algerian iron ore was a present from France, which had sought to keep Algeria out of the ECSC but made an exception for Italy. In her bid to counterbalance Germany, France would repeatedly seek ties with Italy. Finally the five-year transition period meshed with domestic economic policy because it gave the Italian government time to implement the Sinigaglia Plan for a full-process, modern steel industry in the public sector.

The Italian state had demonstrated that its Europeanism was also a matter of hardheaded national bargaining. The next development in European unity revealed that when there was no advantage to Italy, Europeanism could be cast aside. After hesitating until June 1951, Italy was sympathetic to Dean Acheson's wish to re-arm Germany and to René Pleven's plan to do this via a European Defense Community (EDC). However, as the issue dragged on, old fears of military alliances resurfaced. De Gasperi, who did not wish to repeat what he perceived as his earlier errors in the sphere of security, namely his foot-dragging over the Brussels Pact, launched a campaign to present the Pleven Plan as a step toward European unity. He stressed Article 38, which set out the goal of a federation.

However, added to the concern for peace stressed by the Left and within the coalition by the Social Democrats and segments of the DC, was Prime Minister Pella's attempt to get concessions on Trieste in return for ratification of the EDC. Italy would not say no to a proposal backed by the United States and framed in the sacred language of European unity. Instead the government postponed ratification until after the French vote, which fortunately for Italy was negative.

De Gasperi, who had by now left power, believed this to be a defeat for Europeanism, but his party did not. Even De Gasperi had allowed the EDC to take a back seat to the 1953 elections and to the noisy confusion that surrounded his manipulation of the electoral rules. This interpretation of the ECSC and the EDC gives little credence to the myth of De Gasperi as a founder of Europe, but it reveals an Italian state that saw in European unity a means of legitimizing itself—provided this could be done without too many military risks—and of modernizing its economy. In general it found its neighbors, who were pursuing their own national strategies, helpful. When they were unhelpful, Italy was not strong enough to impose its view.

These strands run together in Italy's role in the founding of the EC. To its diplomats, especially to Gaetano Martino, goes much credit for relaunching Europe after the failure of the EDC. Messina, Venice, and Rome are the cities where the community was conceived and born. The removal of tariffs on industrial goods followed years of high growth and increased trade with the other members: Between 1948 and 1953 Italy's imports from them went from 23 percent to 48 percent of its total imports, and its exports from 46 percent to 57 percent. The economic results during the years that followed the Rome Treaty were even better: between 1958 and 1968 per capita annual income went from $805 to $1,358.[27]

Conversely Italy fared badly with the Common Agricultural Policy (CAP). In part this reflected the structural problems of its agriculture, but it also stemmed from political weakness. Italy was unable to prevent France from giving priority in the CAP to cereals, of which France was a major and Italy a minor producer. The high guaranteed price of wheat brought little money to Italy, but it made it harder for her to persuade her farmers to switch to crops that they could produce more efficiently. In general the north European bias in the CAP worked against Italy and especially against the South. Fruit and vegetables, of which Italy was a major producer, derived less benefit than cereals and dairy products. Any Italian government would have had difficulties, but the complex, lengthy negotiations on the CAP took place during the years of the Center-Left, when the political system was growing more inward-looking and fragmented, and when systemic clientelism was entering a new phase.

Although economic modernization was spurred rather than caused by entry to the EC, the popular association of Europe with wealth was strengthened. This had two effects on the political elites: they would lose prestige if Italy could not remain abreast of EC developments—hence the trauma of September 1992—but they could use the EC as a way of coaxing and bullying the electorate into accepting unpopular measures. Or at least they could try.

The EMS negotiations of 1978-79 provide a good example. The Bank of Italy was skeptical of the country's ability to give up the weapon of devaluation, but Guido Carli, by now head of the employers organization, declared that Italy must join the EMS even though (or because) membership would entail wage moderation and less public money to bail out lame ducks.[28] In this case the foreigners were not helpful. Italian negotiators were unable to obtain either a version of the EMS that would place pressure on strong currencies to prevent them from moving upward, or changes in the EC budget that would provide Italy with financial aid. The obvious ally, Britain, was not interested in forming a joint front. The political system was weaker than usual because the period of the historic compromise was drawing to a close, and many in the DC wanted to use entry to the EMS to get rid of the PCI.

They were successful, but with the PCI went any immediate hope of combating inflation. The austerity measures of the Pandolfi Plan were forgotten, inflation soared, and the lira was devalued by 6 percent in March 1981. Yet Italy survived entry to the EMS thanks to her wider band of 6 percent and to intervention by two nongovernmental actors. Fiat took the initiative and in a harsh confrontation in autumn 1980 laid off 20,000 workers. Meanwhile, as already stated, the small enterprises switched their exports to the United States. These two actions not merely improved the Italian economy but gave the state time to implement a deflationary policy, which was symbolized by Bettino Craxi's stand against wage indexation in 1984-85. Italy Inc. pointed the way and the state followed. That segments of Italian society move "ahead" of the state is a theme in the present regime crisis.

Another lesson of EMS entry was that the tall, fair-haired men were often no richer than Italy (as with Britain) and that they were not going to solve Italy's problems (Germany). Italy continued to press for greater European unity and at the 1985 Milan summit of the EC Council of Ministers the Craxi government was active in the process that led to the Single Europe Act. Similarly Italy backed the Delors report on monetary union and held the EC presidency in the second half of 1990, when preparations were made for what would become the Maastricht Treaty of December 1991. Some of the details of the changes that the Internal Market and Economic and Monetary Union (EMU) would demand of Italy will be discussed in chapters 7 and 8. The principles were, first, that the EC could be used by modernizers—such as the Partito republicano italiano (PRI), the Bank of Italy (despite its wariness over the EMS), and the Employers Association—to force the public to accept in the name of Europe an austerity that it would not accept in the name of Italy. The second principle was that the DC-led coalitions would not be able to oppose a modernization, which threatened their clientelistic base, because of the prestige they derived from "Europe." The events of September 1992 proved once again that the rich Europeans were not going to help Italy at the expense of their own interests. Germany would not lower its interest rates, while France would not agree to a general devaluation against the mark. This time modernization required the breakup of the postwar order.

Andreatta restated Italy's European policy in traditional language. There must be a "Federal hard core at the heart of Europe"[29] that will be strong enough to open to up to Central Europe and other countries on the periphery. This is the old Italian concern for parity with France and Germany and the belief that federalism offers the best chance of achieving it. By contrast Berlusconi's movement broke new ground in stating that "a European Union can and must be realized without conflicting with the political and cultural institutions of its nations."[30] Was this a historic shift to a Gaullist view of Europe? There were contradictory signs. Forza Italia ran in the European elections on the slogan of "counting more" in Europe, but the presence of Alleanza nazionale (AN) ministers weakened the government. At the Corfu summit of the EC Council of Ministers Berlusconi put up some opposition to the Franco-German attempt to impose Jean-Luc Dehaene as head of the Commission. But here again the laxity in macroeconomic policy was important. Since Berlusconi did not reduce the debt, he in effect took a third path, neither federalist nor Gaullist but away from the EU. By contrast the Dini government has spoken of austerity and a return to the EMS.

INTERNAL CONSEQUENCES
OF THE INTERNATIONALIST OPTION

If joining the movement toward European unity was also a way of strengthening the Italian nation state, then opening the economy to Europe and to the world changed the nation state. Both the decision to open and the way it was done created problems for the state, while also providing the means to alleviate them. I contend that internationalization brought a prosperity that is one of the greatest achievements of the postwar political order, even if the politicians did not so much create the economic miracle as help it along, allow it to happen, and mediate its effects. For internationalization also brought conflicts and hardship.

Struggling with the Allied occupation and the new constitution, the fledgling state never established itself as a dominant economic decision maker. The first battle came in 1946 when the harvest was good and production rose. Inflation rose too, fueled by free exchange of the lira for certain exports, lack of controls on bank lending and on the stock exchange in order to create some sort of capital market, and a government deficit that was not covered by a long-term loan for fear of crowding out private investment.

The Communist Minister of Finance, Mauro Scoccimarro, proposed to deal with this by a currency exchange along Belgian lines, which would have permitted taxation of war profits. The government would have taken control of the economy and could have deployed further measures such as selective credit and the long-term loan. The risk was that currency reform would damage private sector investment and confidence when exports were rising. Moreover the economy was modernizing: machinery, which in 1938 had represented 6 percent of exports, would reach 20 percent by 1947.

Economists have anguished over the decision not to adopt Scoccimarro's proposal,[31] but I would like to make two observations. Firstly the political will to opt for intervention was not present: Prime Minister De Gasperi left the key economic decisions to Liberals even after Treasury Minister Epicarmo Corbino resigned in September 1946, while Togliatti avoided pressing for currency exchange lest it alienate the middle classes and endanger the PCI-DC alliance. Secondly once the state lost—or rather did not fight—this battle, control over economic reconstruction fell to the private sector and its political allies. By early 1947 inflation had reached 50 percent per annum and the only way to cope with it was Einaudi's line of austerity. Interest rates were raised, thus causing a sharp decline in bank lending. As a result the lira, which had gone from 600 to the dollar in May 1946 to 900 to the dollar in May 1947, was stabilized.[32]

It cannot seriously be argued that opting for Scoccimarro's plan would have meant opting against the internationalization of the economy. Internationalization was both imposed on Italy by the United States and chosen by Italy as a reaction against an autarky, which was associated with poverty and war. However the example of France demonstrates that dirigisme is compatible with free trade. Nor did the refusal of currency exchange mean that the state was giving up its right to intervene. There would be all too much state intervention in the postwar economy. It did, however, mean that the state would not take control of the economy in what might be called the "Gaullist" manner: it would not set targets and allocate credit. Nor would it, because of the expulsion of the Left from the government in 1947 and because of the class conflicts in the country, adopt another classic method, which has been called "Austrian"[33] and seems to suit Christian Democracy: nudging the social partners toward agreements.

The DC did not possess the authority to do the first nor the breadth of support to do the second. Nor could it follow the "Erhard" method, in which the state sets the rules and then withdraws, allowing the market to function and intervening only in the sphere of welfare. By the 1970s the Italian state was intervening so much as to prevent the market from functioning. At no time in the postwar period did the state govern economic development and its social consequences.

However for the first 20 years after Mussolini's departure the economy was run in an updated version of the traditional alliance between a hyperactive state and a suspicious but energetic private sector. This worked better than some critics would admit.

Thus the attack on economic policy made in February 1949 by Paul Hoffmann, an ex-president of Studebaker who was the head of the European Cooperation Administration, was misplaced. Eager for quick increases in living standards as a way of combating Communism and inspired by Keynesian or New Deal ideas, Hoffmann criticized the Italian government for using Marshall aid to strengthen the lira rather than for job-creating public investment programs. However there is a convincing argument that such schemes work only in a developed economy where excess capacity is lying idle, whereas in Italy capacity needed to be created. The same reasoning may be used against the CGIL's employment plan proposed in 1949.[34]

By then there was a political will to intervene in the economy. It may be found specifically in the Dossettian wing of the DC—an early nationalization, the Nuovo Pignone factory in Florence, was undertaken at the request of the mayor, Giorgio La Pira—and more generally in the distrust of the market that runs through Catholic culture. This may be also be seen as the contemporary form of the old Italian view that the state should quite normally support the private sector.[35]

The coherence of this view lay in the notion that the state did what the private sector could not do. It was a continuation of pre-war intervention when Mussolini had stepped in to bail out the banking system. At the Liberation the three major banks—Comit, Credito italiano, and Banco di Roma—remained in public hands and a new merchant bank, Mediobanca, was created to provide long-term and venture capital for industry. Despite the aggressively liberal ideology of the postwar years, neither AGIP (Azienda generale italiana petroli) nor IRI was dismantled. AGIP was turned by Mattei into ENI, which was the clearest example of the state taking the lead in a vital sector. IRI received a new statute in 1948, while a fund to finance the engineering industry turned into EFIM (Ente partecipazioni e finanziamento industria manifatturiera) in the early 1960s.

The private steel companies held that Italy should not develop a full-process steel industry. Most of them—except Falck—limited themselves to reprocessing scrap metal. However IRI went ahead with the Sinigaglia Plan, also inherited from the 1930s, and built a modern steel industry that used Algerian iron ore. Sinigaglia was part of a group of technocrats headed by Alberto Beneduce, who had presided over IRI during the 1930s. Donato Menichella, who became governor of the Bank of Italy in 1947, Saraceno, who founded SVIMEZ (Associazione per lo sviluppo dell'industria nel Mezzogiorno), and Raffaele Mattioli of Comit were also part of that group. It is tempting to see these men as Italian dirigistes. They had enjoyed much freedom under Fascism and in the late 1940s they led the battle to use state power in order to internationalize the economy. However, unlike their French counterparts, they had no institutions like the Ecole nationale d'administration and they were not working within a cultural tradition that favored the civil service or cooperation between technocrats and politicians. They were influential now because their masters were busy saving the world from Communism, but from the 1960s onward most of the public sector would fall prey to systemic clientelism. The Bank of Italy escaped, but Saraceno lived to see the willful sabotage of his plans to transform the South.

The closest the Italian state came to drawing up a blueprint for economic development was Saraceno's outlines for a four-year plan, which he presented to the OEEC in 1948. Its title indicates that it could be no more than a summary and it played nothing like the role of the Monnet Plan. However, sketchy as they are, the outlines reveal that a series of choices were made in the postwar period, in harmony with the key decision to internationalize the economy. Saraceno called for productive investment to increase exports, while consumption and labor costs were held down. The strategy worked: In 1952 exports were 10 percent of Italian GDP; in 1980 they were 26 percent. In 1951 Italy had 2.2 percent of world trade; in 1987 she had 5 percent. Moreover the growth figures were spectacular: from 1948 to 1963 the economy grew at an annual rate of 5.5 percent and industry at 7 percent. Fixed investment grew by 10 percent per annum in the 1950s, rising to 26 percent in 1963. By now there was a consumer boom symbolized by the Fiat 600.

This miracle was the Republic's triumph and it makes nonsense of the theme that nothing changes in Italy. It created an economic self-confidence on which Silvio Berlusconi would play in his 1994 campaign, when he promised a new economic miracle and was believed. Yet there was a price to be paid.[36] The choice of exports was a choice in favor of northern Italy and against the South, which exported little. Although one may argue that living standards have risen steadily in the South too, the split in the country remains. Within the North this was a choice against the working class, since it gave priority to exports over employment and higher wages.

The opposite set of choices would have created greater ills, but these ills were real. Moreover they were far-reaching. A parliamentary report demonstrates how the Camorra grew by catering to an unemployed Naples underclass that found jobs in smuggling first tobacco and then arms or drugs.[37] The exclusion of the northern working class was apparent in the unemployment statistics: there were two million jobless in 1950 and many more underemployed. The decision not to emphasize consumption meant that in 1950 the average Italian ate 24 percent less meat than before the war. Nor was Valletta's view of labor relations untypical.

Here the price was exacted once unemployment declined in the 1960s. Worker militancy grew and the Hot Autumn of 1969 saw massive and bitter protest, which continued intermittently until 1980. This period, difficult for all European countries, was especially trying in Italy, where the unions were too strong to be defeated and too alienated—except during the years of the historic compromise—to cooperate. Growth remained higher than in other countries but so did inflation. It never went below 10 percent, while in 1974 and 1980, which were the years of the oil crises, prices rose by 20 percent. Increases in welfare fueled the deficit, which then fed on itself and created today's problem. Interest on the debt was 2.5 percent of GDP in 1973; by 1982 it was 8.4 percent.

A further problem was that too few choices were made and that rapid, uncontrolled development brought social and cultural tensions. Between 1958 and 1964 alone, a million newcomers took up residence in northern Italy.[38] Emigration weakened the fabric of southern society and created problems of housing and integration in northern cities. They are given epic form in Luchino Visconti's *Rocco and his Brothers*. Along with the optimism about the economy ran a renewed pessimism about Italian society's ability to organize itself. This too finds cultural expression in Pasolini's later writing where modernization is depicted as a blind, inhuman force. On the level of political economy the state's role, while it did not degenerate until the 1960s, contained in embryo two kinds of weaknesses.

The first is that the private sector is both aggressively anti-statist and dependent on the state. Valletta's policy, inherited from Giovanni Agnelli, was to deal with public power from a position of strength. His success in obtaining U.S. aid was only one example. Yet throughout the 1950s Fiat enjoyed a level of protection that was the envy of other industries: cars were protected by tariffs up to 45 percent of their value, whereas the average was 17 percent.[39] It is not a coincidence that Fiat has been less than successful in other developed countries. Two out of every three cars made in its Italian factories are sold in Italy.[40] To make this criticism is not, however to argue that Luigi Luzzatti was wrong, but that the state-private alliance should take more sophisticated forms.

The second weakness lay in the assumption that the public sector could turn its hand to anything. Not only did IRI gradually become a pond full of lame ducks—Fiat sold its steel plant Teksid to the state in 1982 just when the steel industry was being cut back all across Europe—but there were no logic or limits to the big holding companies. The absence of a charter left space for empire-building. Mattei, instructed to close AGIP, turned it into a vast, diversified company, which went from oil and gas to petrochemicals and along the way acquired a newspaper, *Il Giorno*. Mattei was independent, whereas his successors became mere tools of the political parties. But the danger lay in the inability to define what the public sector was supposed to be.

One of the state's defects became a virtue. Too intrusive to allow big companies to grow bigger, the state helped small companies by its neglect. Often this took the form of not making them pay taxes or observe labor laws.[41] But it also permitted local cultures to flourish. Where such cultures were weak, as in the South with its pattern of absentee landowners and constantly moving peasants, no industry could develop. Where, as in Emilia-Romagna, the Veneto, or parts of Lombardy, there were peasant owners, sharecropping, and extended families rooted in Socialism or Catholicism, a special brand of industrialization took place.[42]

In these areas the firm was modeled on the family, with the father as entrepreneur, the mother as bookkeeper, and children as workers. As the firm grew, it employed neighbors but it remained in the village. The Catholic-Communist value of solidarity encouraged cooperation with other local companies to create a production chain, rather than competition for market share. Such companies made traditional products like clothes or shoes, but from the 1960s on they moved into medium technology areas like machine tools or electronics. They entered the tertiary sector, setting up firms to provide services to industry, and they employed larger numbers of women.

Small industry was stimulated by the decentralization of production undertaken by big companies during the 1970s as a way to escape strong unions entrenched in old industrial areas. But this was not the main impulse: the little Emilian town of Carpi had exported hats at the turn of the century. Rather small companies were the fruit of the absent—because overworked—state and of strong family and local ties.

They were a resource that helped Italy overcome the traumas of the 1970s. Whereas the number of workers in factories with more than 500 employees went down by 13.5 percent, the number in factories with fewer than 100 employees went up by 11.5 percent.[43] Flexibility, the great virtue of such firms, was vital in such a troubled decade. Internationalization did not disturb them: Carpi's hats continued to travel light.

CONCLUSION

The Americans and the Europeans set the parameters within which the Italians had to work. Born into the postwar world and nurtured by the Cold War and by European unity, the Republic benefited from Marshall aid and the Common Market, even as it suffered from the Soviet threat and the need to catch up with France and Germany. However, the margins of space left to the Italians were greater than they often acknowledge and within this space they maneuvered better than they often acknowledge.

This becomes obvious if one considers the issue of Americanization. In the 1950s Italy seemed to be growing American in its culture: Hollywood, consumer goods, and sexual freedom were supposedly everywhere. In fact as one looks back, much of what was considered American was modernity as lived in other European countries—there is nothing uniquely American about dishwashers. Even here Italy developed its own brand of modernity.[44] Many symbols of Americanization are thoroughly local—the Vespa and the Fiat 600—while other symbols—canned foods—never caught on. At a deeper level Italian habits survived amidst the consumer society. Italians have never learned to buy and sell property with American nonchalance and they have a thoroughly un-American savings rate.

This is not to deny that the limits on the freedom of the Italian state are obvious in decisions ranging from entering NATO to joining the EMS. World affairs accentuated the distortions of national history. Catholic rule was more severe and the alienation of the northern working class deeper. Greater demands were made on the state and its inability to respond to some of them was more damaging. As we will see, the DC's attempt to establish itself as a government that could cope with the domestic repercussions of this difficult world took shape in the mid-1950s.

4

Clientelism as the Art of Government

Beginning in 1992 clientelism, the special kind of corruption that lay at the heart of the postwar regime, was exposed daily in the press and on TV. Of all the examples the one that aroused most passion was the practice of Francesco De Lorenzo, Minister of Health in the 1989-92 Andreotti governments. He had systematically taken bribes from drug companies that wished to have their medicines certified by the government and hence put on sale. He had also taken a 5 percent cut on contracts awarded to companies that built new facilities in hospitals intended for AIDS patients.

Although the bribery involving health care treatment aroused anger in the general population, the distinguishing feature of De Lorenzo's behavior was its organization. In addition to Duilio Poggiolini, he had among his helpers a battery of university professors—one of whom committed suicide when his role was exposed—who performed the tests and approved the medicines for the marketplace. The firms involved knew what was expected of them and paid accordingly. As for the 5 percent cut, it may be seen as a kind of tax. The money went not only into the pockets of the minister and his helpers, but into the coffers of the Liberal Party. Without it De Lorenzo would probably not have been elected nor appointed Minister.[1]

He had gained control of a sector. A more common arrangement was division by territory. Remo Gaspari, the DC chieftain in the Abruzzo, saw his capital, Chieti, fall to the MSI in the local elections of 1993. He too had been exposed: his method lay in using his position as a perennial minister to divert government money to his supporters. Their efforts at election time brought him victories, which enabled him to demand a ministry. His power in Rome depended on his local base and vice versa.

Sector and territory overlapped in the case of Gianni Prandini, the Minister of Public Works in the Andreotti government. He was accused of taking bribes from construction companies, using a set rate of 2.5 percent of the value of the contract. Other ministers were alleged to have looked after their constituencies. For example, Nino Cristofori, Andreotti's emissary in Emilia-Romagna, ensured that Ferrara received its share of Prandini's contracts.[2]

These examples offer us a definition of clientelism. It is the attainment and retention of power through the private expropriation of public resources, and through the use of the state to expropriate private resources. As practiced from the 1950s onward, it was a system. Although individuals in the DC and its allies may have been free of it, clientelism was a normal way of conducting business and without it the postwar order could not function. It is different from ordinary corruption, which is a mere by-product of wielding power.

Clientelism was not the only reason for the DC's 45-year rule. Catholicism was more important at the outset, while conservatism and interclassism remained significant. Clientelism worked against the DC becoming a valid conservative party, because such parties defend the free market whereas clientelism works apart from and against the free market system. But occupation of the state gave the DC significant control over the electorate, although it helped lead to a crisis in the 1970s and it triggered the Clean Hands investigation that terminated DC rule. I have divided clientelism into two categories that begin, roughly, at different moments. The more sophisticated form, which I call the "publicized" economy, is left for chapter 5.

Clientelism's origins are said to lie in the South. It belongs to a society that has remained a *Gemeinschaft*, a community that is regulated by vertical relationships and by personal ties rather than by notions of citizenship and rights.[3] An idealized example is found in *The Leopard* in which Don Ciccio votes for the old monarchy because the King of Naples has sent him gifts of money so that he can study music. A more cynical version of the same explanation is that "amoral familism"[4] permits no social contacts other than those based on short-term advantage. The exchange vote, in which the elector barters his possession (his vote) for a pension or a job, serves as an example.

However it is too comforting to tie clientelism to the South and to backwardness. The Clean Hands operation was centered in Italy's most modern city. It might be argued that clientelism in the North is less the diversion of government aid to selected groups than the imposition of a tax on the market. The auctioning of public contracts replaces the exchange vote. This is not an insignificant distinction but it does not appear fundamental, since each case involves abusing the state to retain and expand power.

Nor is it sufficient to note, as we have done, that clientelism has long been practiced in Italy. This is a description and not an explanation. One might come closer in linking clientelism with Catholicism. At its best Catholicism produces volunteer organizations such as Caritas, but they, while admirable, share with clientelism the emphasis on individual "people" rather than on citizenship, as well as a distrust of structures such as a public education system.

This leads us back to the state and to the explanation that the unusually rapid pace of economic growth led the state to undertake an unusual degree of mediation.[5] Italy's integration into the dynamic world economy placed special strains on the South, which needed help. Its need crossed with the DC's need for a power base after its failure to find either a philosophy or a specific set of policies. This would explain both why clientelism became widespread after the departures of De Gasperi and Dossetti, and why it grew and changed along with Italy, spreading, for example, through the public sector industries.

The prime aim of clientelism is to win votes and so a politician has to barter with whoever can deliver them. In Sicily this meant the Mafia. But there is a closer bond because the politician, engaged in bending the law, is drawn to groups that stand outside the law that, relieved of the burden of pretense, are efficient. So the alliance between the DC and the Mafia is not an aberration but rather a logical, if extreme, extension of clientelism. It also presents two kinds of risks. It cannot be publicly, and especially not internationally, acknowledged by the politician, while the Mafia may be unwilling to tolerate the compromises that he needs. Recently the Mafia has become exasperated with the unreliability of the DC-led governments and it has turned its violence against them and their agents.

I have already argued that, although the prime responsibility for corruption in Italy rests with the political parties, civil society put up no great opposition. Or rather opposition emerged as society changed, under the influence of international developments and of the modernization process itself. It is worth considering the evolution of one social group—the magistrates, who brought down the system of which they were formerly a part—for the interesting insights this example offers.

This chapter will deal with the political system of which clientelism was an integral part and with the mechanisms of clientelism itself. It will continue with a discussion of the Mafia and conclude with the example of the magistrates.

FANFANI'S IRONIC TRIUMPH

The years between De Gasperi's departure and the Center-Left coalitions are often considered inconclusive and the 1953-58 parliament has been dismissed as static.[6] But behind parliament's immobility, the political order that would last until the 1990s took shape. The key figure was Amintore Fanfani, heir to both Dossetti and De Gasperi.

In the 1930s Fanfani had attended the Catholic University in Milan where he developed a brand of corporatism. Economics depended on political cooperation, which in turn rested on Christian ethics. This was an activist view since it denied the existence of immutable economic laws. It was also a view that could overlap with Mussolini's economic doctrine and Fanfani supported Fascism, especially the Ethiopian War. However, as the regime stumbled toward collapse, he moved to the nascent Christian Democrat party and entered Dossetti's circle. This was logical because the two shared a belief in state intervention and in the mission of a Catholic party.

Fanfani, who did not inherit Dossetti's selflessness, became Minister of Labor in 1947 and campaigned for full employment. He had more success in 1949 when, as Minister of Housing, he launched a building program that produced jobs, popular housing, and speculation. He later became Minister of Agriculture where he formed an alliance with landowners who were resisting reform. His broad support within the party enabled him to become secretary at the 1954 Naples Congress.

From Dossetti Fanfani had learned the importance of the party and from De Gasperi he had inherited the need to distance it from the Vatican. He also wanted to gain independence from the northern industrial elite. Where De Gasperi had initially left them and their political spokesmen, the Liberals and the Republicans, to run the economy, Fanfani wanted the DC to run it. He agreed with Scelba's 1948 comment that Italians would have to get used to seeing Catholics running businesses and banks. The DC was to be endowed with a project that would be Catholic corporatism, with a solid organization— Fanfani increased the number of party officials from 37,000 to 200,000—and with funding of its own. There was a dash of de Gaulle in the Fanfani who took a pro-Arab stand in the aftermath of the Suez expedition. Neo-Atlanticism suited the DC, which was a strong party and believed in creating a strong Italy. Fanfani would not allow his party to slip into aimless pragmatism.

In 1957 he set up the Ministry of the Public Sector and IRI and ENI, the big state holding companies, were regrouped within it. It was designed to give the DC greater control over the nationalized industries, and retrospectively it may be seen as foreshadowing the end of the period when the public sector was run efficiently. At the time there were clashes with the Employers Association, which feared the rise of what has been called the "state bourgeoisie." Significantly the first Minister, Giorgio Bo, had been Enrico Mattei's henchman. In 1958 he created Intersind, a bargaining unit for public sector workers and management outside the auspices of the Employers Association. In 1957 ENI received the exclusive right to drill for oil and gas in all national territory except Sicily. Fanfani's aim was a larger, more democratic but still well-run public sector; his followers saw an opportunity for patronage.

They also perceived Fanfani merely as a leader who was seeking to discipline them. After he increased the party's share of the vote in the 1958 elections from 40 percent to 42.4 percent, he combined the offices of Party Secretary, Prime Minister, and Minister of Foreign Affairs, which proved unpopular with his followers. He was pushed out of his posts and his faction, Iniziativa Democratica, split. The larger group, which opposed him, took the name Dorotei.

The issues around which this battle was fought were revealingly confused. Fanfani was associated with the projected opening to the Socialists, while his opponents were to the Right of him. Yet they elected as party secretary Aldo Moro, who would lead the opening to the Left. Clearly policy mattered little. Fanfani's bid to instill into the DC some sense of the state had failed and "the moral basis of party discipline and unity had almost collapsed."[7] There is a link between Pius XII's death in October 1958 and Fanfani's ousting. The new Pope, John XXIII, would leave the DC somewhat freer and it had no wish to sacrifice that liberty to a strong leader.

Moro, who would remain one of the two or three most important DC figures until his death, had a very different political vision. He did not wish to lead Italy anywhere. He perceived his role as mediating first among the various factions within the party, next among the party's allies, and then between the party and the country. He was a master of intricate compromises couched in language that was impenetrable to all except those with whom he was bargaining. His most memorable phrase was about converging parallel lines. Imbued with Augustinian pessimism, Moro believed the DC could remain dominant only by embracing the PSI and the PCI and slowly stifling them.

The increasing importance of the factions is a parallel development to Moro's rise.[8] They can be set on a left to right line with Forze Nuove and Base on the left, the Andreottiani on the right, and the Dorotei in the middle. But such categories mean little, except that the Dorotei, which prevented the party from drifting too far left or right, constituted the compromise within the compromises. Political ideas are no guide to the factions. Andreotti became Prime Minister in the years of National Solidarity because, as a right-winger, he was supposed to counterbalance the Communists. Forze Nuove might be on the Left but its leader Carlo Donat Cattin loathed the PCI. People moved from faction to faction: Salvo Lima began as a Fanfaniano and ended as an Andreottiano, while Remo Gaspari was a Doroteo who left to join Paolo-Emilio Taviani when Taviani formed his own faction. The aim of most leaders was to create factions of their own: Moro ceased being a Doroteo to form the Morotei.

The best method of analyzing the factions is to perceive them as maximizing DC power, while simultaneously fragmenting it. The Andreottiani attracted voters from the MSI—conversely in the Rome municipal elections of 1993 they delivered many votes to Fini. Forze Nuove drew on the Confederazione italiana sindacati lavoratori (CISL). The factions had a local base—the Andreottiani in Rome, Forze Nuove in Turin—from which they spread out across the country; the Andreottiani, for example, grew strong in Sicily because of Lima. The factions conquered power centers that were outside but close to the party—the Base was funded by Mattei's ENI, while the Dorotei were allied with the small farmers association, the Coldiretti. In this way the factions were spearheads of the DC's penetration of society.

But as the DC infiltrated the farmers or the bureaucracy it neither steered them in any particular direction nor united them under a firm government. Rather it reinforced the historical and cultural fragmentation that was already present. The factions acted—as the Dorotei did with Fanfani—to prevent the emergence of dominant leaders or adventurous policies. Two examples would be President Giovanni Gronchi's unsuccessful attempt, in the years after his 1955 election, to increase the powers of his office, and Fernando Tambroni's abortive bid in 1960 to change the rules of the parliamentary game by governing with the avowed support of the MSI.

The political system that revolved around the faction-ridden DC was characterized by its capacity for maintaining and increasing its power at the expense of the state and of civil society. Proportional representation encouraged a plethora of small parties that were divided by ideologies both old—the anticlericalism of the Liberals and the Republicans, and new—the pro-Americanism of the Social Democrats. Seeking to differentiate themselves one from the other, they entered and abandoned coalitions, thus weakening the government.[9]

This strengthened the parties, which were freed from the responsibility of ruling. Since new coalitions were formed by agreement among party secretaries, the voters' power was also reduced. While it seemed fragile and chaotic the party system was virtually immune to attack. It was protected against internal antagonists by its fragmentation and it could accommodate anti-system parties such as the Radicals. It is no coincidence that in 1993 Marco Pannella helped to mobilize parliamentarians against the Clean Hands investigation.

Recently it has been argued that the PCI was an integral part of this system, ruling jointly with the DC.[10] Although I have maintained that there were deep cultural bonds between the two groups, it seems an exaggeration to speak of joint rule. One must distinguish periods: until the 1960s the PCI was rarely consulted and it did its best to block such initiatives as entry to the EC. It was consulted about and approved the creation of the regional governments in 1970, but the failure of the historic compromise showed the limits of PCI power. In 1984-85 it tried and failed to protect wage indexation. The PCI was the DC's ally as well as antagonist because it protected the party system from external antagonists. The Communists dominated the opposition but, since they were considered illegitimate by the U.S. government as well as by a majority of Italians, they provided the DC with permanent power.

On the Far Right the neo-Fascists played a stabilizing role, which Tambroni interrupted when he tried to legitimize them. Usually they protected the DC against the emergence of a conservative party that would have provided competition. The MSI acted as a safety valve: it was an annex in which the DC could lodge its right-wing voters, knowing that they would return. In 1972 the MSI won 8.7 percent as a protest against economic disturbances and the student-worker movement. But as the PCI vote grew, the MSI's voters went back to the DC and in 1976 support for the neo-Fascists slumped to 5.5 percent.

The final actor in the system was the Italian secret services, operating with or without the CIA. Their role consisted not merely in taking action against the PCI, but in lending a hand to right-wing violence, promoting it, protecting its perpetrators, and laying false trails. Such acts of terrorism, along with the threatened coups, were designed to unsettle the Left. The Solo Plan drove the PSI to weaken the conditions it had imposed on its entry into the Center-Left governments. The bomb at Piazza Fontana in December 1969 came as a counterblast to the powerful worker demonstrations of the Hot Autumn. Fear of a right-wing coup was one reason for Enrico Berlinguer's caution as the PCI's strength rose in the mid-1970s. The secret services' activities also served to warn the DC that it was not indispensable. Inevitably the factions used the services in their clan warfare: Andreotti's long periods as Defense Minister are thought to have given him useful contacts. Knowing the secrets of clientelism, the secret services could hardly resist participating.

The mystery surrounding such questions, and the string of massacres that have never been fully explained, also protected the system. They made, and continue to make, rational analysis more difficult, while providing the material for self-interested accusations, blackmail, and tales of intrigue masterminded by omniscient, occult forces—the CIA, the Free Masons, the Soviets, it barely matters.[11] But the effect was conservative: to maintain the existing order. The repeated government crises gave foreigners the impression that the system was unstable. In reality it was at least as stable as the French Third Republic.

This regime was in no sense wholly bad. Its most spirited defender notes that Italians, while always ready to castigate their politicians, also showered them with attention.[12] Another defense might be that this system—conservative, flexible, and seeking to draw people in—was needed at a time of rapid, economic change. The contrast between a centralized, hierarchical government in France and an Italian political order that responds to demands from below, is a third rationale.[13] Finally in 1992-94 the Republic passed the supreme test of allowing itself to be drastically modified without abandoning democracy. However, by its lack of accountability, by its negative strength, and by offering no alternatives to itself, the political system produced a caste that perpetuated itself through clientelism.

The irony of Fanfani's period as secretary is that his party did liberate itself from the Vatican and the northern industrialists—as well as from him. But it did so by exploiting instead of guiding the state. A second way to analyze the factions is to consider them as clans that fought for their share of public resources. The DC's fragmentation[14] sharpened the clientelistic competition. The factions and the DC's satellite parties conducted civil wars, even while they were united in their determination to maintain the system. In Italy, as in most European countries, the state expanded its role in the 1950s by taking on the responsibility for social welfare. So there was much for the clans to fight over.

GETTING AND SPENDING WE INCREASE OUR POWERS

A well-documented example of how a DC politician and his faction amassed power via clientelism is provided by Antonio Bisaglia and the Dorotei, who conquered the Veneto.[15] The DC owed its strength in the region to the Church, which had a popular appeal that it had lost in some parts of northern and central Italy. After the war the party in Rovigo was led by a former member of Sturzo's PPI, Umberto Merlin, but the young Bisaglia was one of a group that rebelled and dethroned Merlin in 1954. It was the local equivalent of Fanfani's success at the Naples Congress. Untouched by ideology or ideas, Bisaglia wanted to shift power away from local notables to the party organization. He and the older Mariano Rumor of Vicenza were members of Fanfani's faction, Democratic Initiative, but they deserted Fanfani in 1959 and became Dorotei.

By now Bisaglia had established his own power base. The Coldiretti had gone from 220,000 members in 1944 to nearly 8 million in 1958. They ran most of the consortiums that provided farmers with cheaper oil and fertilizer, stored their crops, and gave them loans. They also ran most of the mutual funds set up in 1954 to extend health insurance to self-employed farmers.[16] As such they were an important organization in the countryside and a farmer could suffer if he crossed them. They were a flanking organization for the DC and sponsored 85 of its members of parliament. Bisaglia succeeded in becoming President of the Rovigo Mutual Fund, a position from which the skillful direction of benefits brought votes.

In 1958 Enrico Mattei had Bisaglia appointed to the board of an ENI company called Snam. Mattei is often considered the founder of government by clientelism. He was said to own some 60 members of parliament, most but not all of them Christian Democrats. The appointment of Bisaglia was an early example of the publicized economy. It extended DC control over the nationalized industries and channeled some of their profits to the party. The private sector did not stand aloof from this process and in 1961, Bisaglia, who was devoid of experience in the field, was named Rovigo agent of the Generali, Italy's largest insurance company. He brought customers to the company and conversely his ability to offer insurance on favorable terms could be converted into political influence over businessmen.

As his influence extended through the Veneto in the 1960s Bisaglia formed links with the Grassetto family, who were in construction, and the Grosolis, who were meat importers. It is reasonable to suppose that he was helpful with public contracts and food regulations.[17] More important was his influence over the Development Consortiums, set up by the government, in the Veneto. Here clientelism followed two patterns: factories were allotted to villages with DC mayors, while the companies that received grants often turned out to have DC owners. Perhaps most important of all, the Dorotei installed their supporters as presidents and board members of the chain of local savings banks.

Such local power brought enough votes to send Bisaglia into parliament in 1963 and to make him an important member of his faction. When the Dorotei split in 1969 Bisaglia joined Flaminio Piccoli and Rumor in the Movement of Popular Initiative. The three men also collaborated to build one of the most useless motorways in Italy, which was to run from Trento, Piccoli's fief, via Vicenza to Rovigo. At the DC's 1973 Congress this was the largest faction and hence Rumor became Prime Minister. However fragmentation continued: Bisaglia and Piccoli were joined in a generational struggle to oust Rumor and were on opposite sides in the struggle to replace him as faction leader.

By now Bisaglia was a frequent member of the government. In 1970 he became Under-Secretary to the Treasury and was placed in charge of a Deposits and Loans Fund that advanced money to local authorities. In March 1974 he became Minister of Agriculture, a post perennially held by the DC and used to keep relations with the Coldiretti running smoothly. At the end of the year he was moved to the Ministry of the Public Sector, where we shall rediscover him in our next chapter.

Bisaglia's career illustrates the way that the DC held onto power, after De Gasperi's retirement, by channeling public resources to its supporters. It was a process that destroyed statesmen and citizens alike, while turning everyone into a politician. Each region where the DC held power had its chieftain who ran it like a city-state: Taviano ruled Liguria and Moro Puglia. Political power extended not merely to the economy, but to the judiciary system and the press. Bisaglia "owned" the Veneto newspaper, *Il Gazzettino* and kept an eye on *Il Resto del Carlino,* published in nearby Emilia-Romagna.

Counterpoint to the penetration of grassroots society was control of the national bureaucracy, which was packed with DC supporters and that had to remain weak and slow in order to permit and justify political intervention. During the 1950s the coalition parties colonized the social services.[18] Welfare agencies such as the Istituto nazionale della previdenza sociale (INPS) and the Istituto nazionale assicurazione malattia (INAM) mushroomed. Unlike welfare agencies in Britain, they served only certain categories of people—which explains why self-employed farmers had their own health insurance system— and the regulations governing the sums of money they paid out were intricate. This suited the politicians who were able to divert payments to the most grateful rather than the most needy. INPS was a source of uninterrupted Social Democratic patronage from 1949 to 1965, while INAM was run by the DC from the Liberation to the 1970s. Party organizers were able to offer disability pensions in return for votes. So the bureaucracy was not purely defensive and conversely its role in clientelism further alienated the public.

Unsurprisingly Andreotti invented the most ingenious brand of clientelism.[19] During his many spells as Minister of Defense he reduced the funding for weapons and training but he increased military salaries. He thus created obedient, if ineffective, soldiers who marched from their barracks at election time to do battle with his opponents.

By its very nature the clientelistic process slowly undermined itself. Because it created bad government it cost the DC and its satellites voter support. In turn this meant more clientelism to win back votes. When the international economy plunged downward in 1973, there were insufficient public resources for private exploitation and the DC plunged too. In the local elections of 1975 it lost such bastions as Rome and Naples. It was, however, saved by its ally-antagonist, the PCI. As Communist support grew, the DC was able to play its other roles as the anti-Communist and Conservative party. However, it could not cease to be clientelistic and in the 1980s the quest for resources and supporters grew ever more desperate. To study the spinning and the unraveling of a clientelistic web we need only turn to the Gava family as an example.

DON ANTONIO IS NOT PLEASED

The South was the key region in the DC's bid to become an autonomous mass party. Between the late 1940s and the mid-1960s the percentage of its membership that lived in the North declined from nearly 50 percent to 28 percent, whereas in the South the figures were 18 percent and 30 percent and in the Islands 7 percent and 17 percent.[20] The main reasons were northern irritation with inefficient public services and the battery of government agencies that steered money to the South. The plans for state intervention drawn up by Saraceno, Morandi, and their helpers were distorted, and the Cassa, which was supposed to be used for special government intervention, became a discretionary fund for politicians. At first it provided infrastructure and the alliance between the DC and northern industrialists was evident in the way that the machines to build roads and the fertilizer for the pilot agriculture programs were made in the North. This pattern continued after the Cassa had expanded into setting up industrial plants. However the distribution of Cassa funds and the locating of public sector plants were fought over by the rival political clans in the South.

Naples provides a well-studied example of government by clientelism.[21] In the early 1950s the DC gave it as a fief to the Monarchist, Achille Lauro, who in return split his own party. While denouncing the Christian Democrats locally, he helped them nationally. As mayor Lauro surrounded himself with builders, to whom he gave public contracts, notaries and lawyers, who fixed rateable values, and shopkeepers who were seeking licenses. It was a clique without an organization and it depended on its leader's ability to occupy the town hall.

In 1957 Lauro developed delusions of grandeur and ran hard against the DC in the regional elections, raising the Monarchist vote to 9 percent in Sardinia. Suddenly the Minister of the Interior learned of corruption in the Naples town hall and suspended Lauro. This was the beginning of the end for him and his power passed to the DC proper, in the shape of Silvio Gava.

More properly power was passed to the Gava family: to Silvio, who was a government minister in the mid-1950s, and his sons, the best known being Antonio, who was president of the provincial government from 1961 to 1969, and who went on to a national career in the 1980s. From his immediate family—a son-in-law held the Fiat franchise in Naples—Silvio Gava extended his network to friends who were members of the Consortium for Industrial Development and leaders in the Chamber of Commerce. Control of credit was obviously vital and in 1959 the Gava family gained control of the Istituto per lo sviluppo e l'industrializzazione del Meridione (Isveimer). Six years later the publicly owned Bank of Naples fell to them and they had already had much influence in the private Banca Popolare.

The difference between Lauro and the Gavas is that, instead of being a clique, they were the dominant force in the Naples DC. Their control over the local federation gave them power in both the city and regional government, which increased, and was increased by, their economic power. Their power base depended on their ability to appropriate the public money that flowed to the South. They were able to do so because of their positions in the national DC and in the government, which they obtained because they controlled the local DC. Theirs was a more ruthless version of the Gaspari syndrome and their defeat of Lauro marks the transition from unorganized to systemic clientelism.

One measure of their control was the number of preference votes they could accumulate. While proportional representation and the party list were designed to weaken the power that local notables had exerted in the pre-Fascist period, the presence of preference voting—expressing a preference for one or several names on the list—provided a measurement of the popularity of each of the party's leaders. Competition for preference votes sharpened the competition among the clans, required the distribution of public resources, and increased the victors' control over future resources. Unsurprisingly, preference voting was a target of the movement for electoral reform and in the 1991 referendum the number of preference votes was reduced to one. Equally unsurprisingly, Antonio Gava opposed the referendum and the word circulated in Naples that "Don Antonio is not pleased." The fairly high level of participation—53 percent—as well as the massive yes vote—97 percent—in Naples marked a defeat for him.

This was one milestone in the decline of Antonio Gava's power. He had survived feuds with Emilio Colombo, the DC leader in Basilicata, and with Ciriaco De Mita, the Avellino boss; these were nothing more than the usual clan wars. Gava seemed to have survived the more serious Ciro Cirillo affair, where he was accused of using the Camorra to obtain the release of his henchman who was kidnapped by the Red Brigades in 1981. That Gava was later to become a leader of the Dorotei (now rebaptized as the Grand Center), who imposed Arnaldo Forlani as party secretary in 1989, and that he was briefly Minister of the Interior, where he controlled the police force, is proof of the political system's ability to defend itself.

Gava's power waned because of three overlapping factors: the loss of his electoral influence, the Clean Hands investigation, and the anti-Mafia struggle. In 1992 a scandal in the health services at one of his strongholds, Castellammare di Stabia, provoked 53 arrests for bribery and an investigation into his lieutenant, Francesco Patriarca. Elections followed and the DC vote dropped by 22 percent.[22] The following year the Cirillo charge was pressed by Luciano Violante, the PDS president of the parliamentary anti-Mafia commission.

Unlike the Mafia, the Camorra is an amorphous collection of bands whose roots lie in the unemployed Naples proletariat. From here the Camorra extends through the rest of society, penetrating banks and influencing magistrates. A politician seeking to extend his clientelistic network will almost inevitably encounter the Camorristi and Gava had long-standing ties with them.

The Naples earthquake of 1980 unleashed a flood of government funds, and contracts for clearance or rebuilding were distributed with no proper controls. Some 30 percent of the $40 billion allotted went to Camorra-owned firms.[23] At the same time, two attempts were being made to organize the anarchical Camorra, one by Raffaele Cutolo and the other by Carmine Alfieri. When Ciro Cirillo, the President of the Reconstruction Committee, was kidnapped in April 1981, his mentor, Gava, who was probably worried about what Cirillo might reveal, turned to the stronger leader, Cutolo.

In July Cirillo was released after $1 million had been paid to the Red Brigades. Cutolo's price had three parts: improved treatment in prison and the prospect of release; lighter police controls in Naples because the increased surveillance after the kidnapping was interfering with Camorra business; and reconstruction contracts for firms linked with his organization. All three requests were granted after negotiations that featured other leading Christian Democrats, such as Flaminio Piccoli.

However President Sandro Pertini blocked the transfer of Cutolo to a more pleasant prison and instead shipped him off to Asinara in Sardinia. Cutolo made his disappointment known, but the DC switched sides and threw its weight behind Alfieri. His firms received the contracts and his men decimated Cutolo's band. The anti-Mafia commission concluded that, although the ties between politicians and Camorra were endemic, "the key figure, both for the positions he has held in the government and in his party as well as for the actions with which he has been associated, is Antonio Gava."[24] One can see that Gava's decision to turn to Cutolo and to strike the bargain was the logical conclusion of his method of conducting politics. In the Naples mayoral election of November 1993 the DC could not find a presentable candidate and the winner was Antonio Bassolino of the PDS.

THE MAFIA—A DANGEROUS CLIENT

In March 1992, during the election campaign, Salvo Lima was killed by the Mafia. An ex-mayor of Palermo and the head of Andreotti's faction in Sicily, Lima was viewed as one of the chief intermediaries between the DC and the Mafia. From 1968 to 1979 he had been in the Rome parliament, elected with around 100,000 preference votes, and in 1979 he became a member of the European Parliament. He had been mentioned approximately 150 times in the reports of the anti-Mafia commission, although never formally charged.[25]

In 1982 the Mafia had executed the PCI regional secretary, Pio La Torre, because he was an opponent. No attempt could be made to present Lima's murder in the same way. A slightly more plausible explanation was that Lima's ties had been mostly with Stefano Bontade, whose family had been defeated in the Mafia wars of the early 1980s. However it is more likely that Lima was killed because the relationship between the DC and the Mafia, which he had personified, had broken down. His friend and fellow Andreottian from Catania, Nino Drago, withdrew from politics after seeing a henchman, Paolo Arena, murdered.

The most likely reason for Lima's death was his—and by implication Andreotti's—failure to get the long prison sentences imposed on Mafia leaders in the mass trial of 1986 reduced. The Mafia wars of the 1960s had ended with the extremely lenient Catanzaro and Bari trials. The different outcome 20 years later poses questions of why Lima had failed and why the DC-Mafia relationship had broken down.

The split turned into a war between state and Mafia, which is arguably unique in post-Liberation history, and hence another sign that the old regime was ending. In the early 1980s the Mafia had dispatched isolated representatives of the state who had threatened it—the best-known example is Carlo-Alberto Dalla Chiesa—but in the 1990s it conducted a war. Giovanni Falcone and Paolo Borsellino who had spearheaded the campaign against the Mafia were killed in 1992 and bombs were placed in Rome, Florence, and Milan in the summer of 1993. However this time the state fought back not merely by arresting the head of the Mafia, Totò Riina, but by delving into the DC-Mafia links and lifting Andreotti's parliamentary immunity. Where Dalla Chiesa had complained in 1982 that the government had abandoned him, the Amato and Ciampi governments backed the pool of magistrates in Palermo. The Berlusconi government was more hesitant: it questioned the reliance on Mafiosi who turn state's evidence and was generally hostile to the magistrates.

To discover what the DC-Mafia links were, we must glance back at Lima's pre-1968 career and at the Sicilian version of Fanfani's bid to create an autonomous party. Lima's adult life was spent in the DC. He was a member of its youth movement before he was elected to the Palermo city council and placed in charge of public works. Along with Giovanni Gioia and Vito Ciancimino, he represented the DC of the 1954 Naples Congress. The Palermo branch had been led by right-wing notables, but now the party machine ousted them. Money was descending from Rome and Lima used it to rebuild Palermo.

Where patronage had been distributed by individual notables, Lima centralized it in his office.[26] He had a familiar array of gifts: building contracts, zoning licenses, access to credit, influence in the capital. Before and after he became mayor in 1958 he awarded thousands of contracts and permits, often to individuals without capital or qualifications, who were front men for his friends. To conquer the city the Fanfaniani destroyed it: Many of its baroque palaces were replaced by skyscrapers and planning was nonexistent.

Meanwhile the Mafia was undergoing its own evolution. The role it had played in aborting land reform to serve the interests of rich owners as well as its own, ended when the power of the owners waned. It was time to embrace the DC. Michele Navarra, who was the head of the Corleonesi in the 1950s, had stayed with the Liberals until the 1948 elections but had then deserted them. Giuseppe Genco Russo of Caltanisseta had preceded him into the DC. When a DC official, Pasquale Almerico, worried aloud about this trend, he was murdered. More important Christian Democrats, such as Bernardo Mattarella, had been encouraging it as early as 1944. Giovanni Gioia, a future government minister, told Almerico that "certain kinds of comprises could not be avoided."[27] The Mafia saw that the new rulers of Sicily were the party of government, which took over the extensive powers of the special region that was instituted in 1947. Its right to hire civil servants without using the normal criteria allowed politicians a freedom that criminals could exploit.

The shift from countryside to city came easily to an organization that had historic roots in Palermo, where in the post-Unity years it had protected the owners of market gardens in the fertile Conca d'Oro. This had been a period of rapid change in the city, which lost its role as capital of Sicily but benefited from the expansion of agriculture. Such moments suit the Mafia and in 1950 another was at hand. Moreover the Mafia was in one sense continuing its role as mediator. The new rulers needed popular consensus in the shape of votes and the Mafia could provide them.

At polling time instructions were sent by the families on whose territory the constituency was located. Votes were normally to be cast for the DC, occasionally for other parties—Aristide Gunnella of the PRI was sent in the same year as Lima to the Rome parliament, where he remained until his embarrassed party got rid of him before the 1992 elections—but never for the

PCI. Perhaps more important was the distribution of preference votes within the DC, as Lima's triumphant score demonstrates. In return, construction contracts and cheap credit were awarded to firms controlled by or allied with the Mafia.

In Sicily, too, clans were formed. In Catania Drago, the Mafia chieftain, Nitto Santapaola, and the Costanzo family, which owned a construction company, joined forces.[28] Clans needed lawyers to draft contracts, friendly policemen who turned a blind eye, friendly magistrates to slow down such investigations as did occur, and influential officials in Rome who could transfer unfriendly magistrates. Businessmen forced to pay protection money often opted to join the clan. The Mafia-DC presence pervaded every nook and cranny of Sicilian life, as Leonardo Sciascia has depicted in novels like *The Day of the Owl*.[29]

However the Mafia was neither a diffuse influence nor a DC satellite. It remained what it had always been: an independent force specializing in the use of violence. It also changed in that it acquired new forms of economic power. Agriculture was still important: in the wholesale market of Palermo, for which licenses were granted by the city, all 42 stalls were under Mafia control in 1960. But the families acquired interests in construction, transport, tourism, and finance. They were helped by northern firms that moved south. The Genovese company, Elettronica Sicula, formed an alliance with don Paolino Bontade who provided reliable, non-Communist labor in the 1950s. This set a pattern for northern firms, which bought a welcome in the South by giving subcontracts to companies controlled by the Mafia or the 'ndrangheta.

The mere presence of a northern firm was sufficient to attract the Mafia into an area where it had hitherto not operated. It arrived in Melfi along with the Fiat plant.[30] In the last decade the Mafia has invaded central and northern Italy, where it has penetrated the Adriatic tourist resorts as well as Milan and Turin. Its chieftains were keeping themselves busy during their periods of enforced residence in towns far from Sicily.

The Mafia is both a national and an international institution. Its American colonies increased its power in Italy by allowing it to enter the drug trade. In the 1920s it had shipped small quantities of opium and heroin to the United States, hidden in crates of food exports. During the 1950s, drug trafficking made its first great leap forward and found the Mafia ready. Unexpected allies were Fidel Castro and the French state. Raw heroin from the East was being processed in laboratories run by the Marseilles gangsters and shipped to Cuba, from where it could enter the United States more discreetly. Fulgenicio Batista's defeat and the French police's victory left a vacuum.

Special skills were needed to fill that vacuum. The Sicilians had the right American contacts: Gaetano Badalamenti had a brother in the Detroit mob, while the Bonanno family of New York had kept its ties with the men of honor in its home village of Castellammare del Golfo. Moreover the drug trade, which entails travel, unwritten transactions, and dealings with people of many nationalities and cultures, creates the need for a core group that is dependable. The Sicilian Mafia answered the need because of its "ability to constitute a *state*: to set rules, to control and to punish."[31]

The drug trade did not take away the need for the alliance with the DC. The money had to be invested and magistrates had to be blandished or transferred. But its success altered the Mafia's dealings with the DC in three ways. First, it became more difficult for the politicians to maintain the alliance because public opinion grew more hostile to the Mafia, especially after the second great leap forward in trafficking during the 1970s and the spread of drug addiction in northern Italy as well as in other EC countries. Second, the enormous profits—in 1965 a kilo of heroin cost $350 at its place of origin and had a street value of $225,000—caused rifts within the Mafia and were partly responsible for the war of the early 1980s. Finally the profits tilted the balance of power within the alliance away from the DC. The Mafia was less tied to a ruling class than ever before. When Lima was mayor of Palermo and awarding contracts, the Mafia needed him more than he needed them. By 1992 the reverse was true.

This is a case where clientelism undermined DC power. Discredited by its dangerous acquaintances, the party was successfully challenged in Palermo by the Rete. In 1993 Leoluca Orlando was elected mayor, while Claudio Fava, whose father was a crusading journalist whom the Mafia had executed in 1984, almost emulated him in Catania. One might argue that Lima created Orlando. In turn Mafia arrogance spurred the state to a counterattack, which includes the most serious attempt in the Republic's history to purge the politicians, magistrates, and policemen who collaborated with it. The outcome, however, is uncertain.

MAGISTRATES: FRIENDS TURNED ENEMIES

Although Antonio Di Pietro became the necessary hero in a tale where most of the characters are villainous politicians, the Italian legal system has not emerged unscathed from the recent upheaval. Ordinary corruption among magistrates has been uncovered: in Messina they took bribes in return for granting building permits. More serious have been the revelations of collusion with the Mafia and the Camorra. At Caltanissetta charges have been made that magistrates had informed Mafiosi that they were being investigated and had helped block the procedures. In Naples 11 magistrates have been accused of collusion with the

Camorra, and one of them appears to have demanded as payment a Camorra assault on his ex-wife's new lover.[32]

Magistrates do not stand outside politics. In Milan a split emerged over the issue of corruption within the PDS. An avowedly anti-Communist magistrate, Tiziana Parenti, wanted to press charges against PDS officials over the opposition of her pro-PDS colleagues like Gerardo D'Ambrosio. The charges were not pressed and she left the pool. She ran as a Forza Italia candidate in the elections and made speeches in which she claimed that the judiciary system was being manipulated by the Left. Her charges were repeated by Silvio Berlusconi when the Milan magistrates were investigating Fininvest in the days before the election.[33] After Berlusconi's victory open war broke out between the government and the Milan magistrates, who won a notable victory in forcing him to withdraw his July 13 decree, which would have released from prison the politicians implicated in the Clean Hands inquiry. Equally disturbing have been the cases where magistrates have acted as an integral part of the clientelistic system. In the Enimont affair Judge Diego Curtò was arrested for illegally sequestering shares bought by Gardini's supporters.

The question as to why Curtò had been appointed to the sensitive position he held, led to a debate about the Consiglio superiore della magistratura (CSM).[34] As the body governing the corps of magistrates, it is composed of 20 members elected from their ranks and ten chosen by parliament, which means by the party secretaries, with the President as its chairman. Since the corps was divided into factions that formed and abandoned alliances with one another and with the politicians, the CSM could lay no claims to neutrality. Indeed Cesare Previti, the Fininvest lawyer who almost became Minister of Justice in the new government but switched to Defense, has suggested that the CSM should be reshaped to reflect the election victory.[35]

The origins of this unhappy state go back yet again to the late 1950s.[36] They demonstrate yet again Italian society's tendency both to form clans and to seek out politicians. This was not new because in pre-Fascist Italy the judiciary system enjoyed only a limited autonomy from the government and was considered a specialized part of the public administration. Generally conservative, it adapted to Fascism, which did not seek to transform it. When he needed them, Mussolini set up special courts and for the rest he had no reason to be displeased with the magistrates.

Unpurged at the Liberation, they gained greater independence because of the Republic's distrust of executive power. The CSM was set up belatedly in 1959 and it liberated the magistrates from the Minister of Justice. Yet at precisely this juncture the magistrates turned to the politicians who were extending their power through civil society.

The reason lay in the magistrates' lack of identity as a corps. Discontented with the way they were regulating their own affairs in the key areas of promotion and salaries, they split into factions. Most factions sought allies in the parties. If the original issue had been the younger magistrates' resentment against the forms of selection imposed by their senior colleagues, and if they gained a more rapid and automatic mechanism of promotion, they also opened the door to selection by political affiliation.

Over the next two decades the intertwining of magistrates and politicians increased. The former were well represented in parliament, while the latter were allowed a role in legal decisions. This helps explain why political corruption was rarely investigated. Their statute compelled magistrates to open inquiries, but not to pursue them. Fragmentation was increased because each city office enjoyed much freedom. However this left each office vulnerable to local pressure: in Rome the office was regarded as sensitive to Andreotti's opinions. Overzealous magistrates might find the CSM transferring them to distant spots or conversely an inquiry could be moved to a city where the magistrates were more pliant. In 1981 the investigation of Licio Gelli was transferred from Milan to Rome.[37] Government by clientelism went ahead unrestrained and representatives of organized crime often escaped surprisingly lightly. In 1988 the Supreme Court Judge, Corrado Carnevale, annulled the trials in which 100 members of the 'ndrangheta family, the Piromalli, had been convicted.[38] The Mafiosi convicted in 1986 had high expectations of Carnevale.

Of the factions that the magistrates formed, Unità per la Costituzione looked to the Center-Right, Magistratura Independente was legally conservative and distrusted politicians, while Magistratura Democratica (MD) perceived the judiciary system as a force for social equality. This stance led MD to support the PCI, which had initially distrusted what it considered class-based justice, but which found itself on the same side as the magistrates during the terrorism of the 1970s. Although this alliance could potentially turn against the system, it represented a further intertwining.

During the 1980s the magistrates did not appear restive. Wars were frequent but they were mostly struggles that pitted one group of politicians and magistrates against another. Even President Francesco Cossiga's broadsides against the CSM may be interpreted as an onslaught less on the magistrates, than on the political-judiciary power that the CSM had accumulated. But two signs of change were present. The first was that Berlinguer had instilled into the PCI more respect for the democratic institutions of the Italian state, which meant that the PCI-PDS supported MD as it grew more critical of the magistrates' involvement in clientelistic politics. The second was that the PSI, having less support among the magistrates and determined to expand the frontiers of clientelism, displayed hostility toward the corps.

In 1981 Craxi attacked the magistrates who had jailed Roberto Calvi. He obtained Calvi's release, but the magistrates noted that Calvi had threatened to give details about money he had contributed to the PSI. In 1984, now Prime Minister, Craxi issued a decree setting aside a judge's decision that was unfavorable to his friend Berlusconi with the comment "these magistrates are making me furious."[39] Earlier Craxi, anticipating the Berlusconi of 1994, had declared that he was the victim of a conspiracy spearheaded by left-wing magistrates.[40] In 1987 the PSI led the battle for a referendum that extended the civil responsibility of the magistrates for their rulings. Moreover, while Socialist Minister of Justice Claudio Martelli's battle with the CSM in 1991 over his desire to appoint Giovanni Falcone as head of the anti-Mafia squad was a complex struggle pitting Falcone against the CSM, his attacks on Agostino Cordova, who was investigating PSI corruption in Calabria, was a defense of the political system against an inquiring magistrate.

So the Socialists undermined the cozy alliance between the political and judiciary systems. Once the weakness of the ruling politicians was demonstrated in the 1992 elections, the magistrates had every reason to jump ship. The result of the 1987 referendum had demonstrated that as a group they were not popular so they sought new forms of legitimacy. Their onslaught on clientelism brought enormous public support. Nor was it a coincidence that the Clean Hands investigation began in Milan. It was the PSI's showcase city, but the rise of the Northern League had demonstrated the electorate's discontent, while the pool of magistrates included representatives of MD.

Magistrates in other cities followed, as they realized that the 1992 elections marked the end of a power system set up in the 1950s. In towns like Avellino the politicians were strong enough to stifle the rebellion, but Rome, after some hesitation, sided with Milan.

Di Pietro "with his chubby Molisan peasant's face, a face straight out of the countryside and the past"[41] seemed a figure from another, purer Italy. He had worked with his hands and studied at night. He had been a policeman before qualifying as a magistrate, so he was the right kind of person to investigate political corruption. His language lacked the polish of others in the pool but it was easier for ordinary Italians to understand and they trusted him. However, without underestimating his personal contribution to an independent justice system, the truth is that the old regime was collapsing because of the contradictions of clientelism. A glance at the "publicized" economy reveals similar tensions.

5

The Publicization
of the Economy

Silvio Berlusconi launched his election campaign with a speech on January 26, 1994, and a rally on February 6. His main theme was that Italy must rely "less on the state and more on private initiative."[1] Offering yet another variant on populism, Berlusconi invoked the individual, the family, the small company, and the nation. The distinctive trait of his populism was his appeal not to the "howling piazzas" but to "decent people who are sensible and competent." Such language is Thatcherite. She had called for blood, sweat, and tears, however, whereas Berlusconi radiated optimism. Unemployment could be reduced by tax cuts; a new economic miracle was at hand. This was a reassuring, calm brand of populism, which relied on the cool medium of television. Although he used the language of soccer and spoke of "taking the field," the owner of AC Milan inhabited a different planet from his team's rowdier fans. His calm was the mark of his superiority: there must be no doubt of the leader's ability to create jobs.

The rejection of the state was categoric. The goal was to privatize not merely the economy but education and health care. Berlusconi called for a break with "an Italy that is so politicized, statist, corrupt and hyper-regulated." The appeal of this message, which came after a two-year saga of corruption where the main villains had been the politicians, was obvious. Yet there was a marvelous irony about the messenger. Berlusconi had epitomized the overlap between the public and private domains, which had been created by the DC and PSI occupation of the economy.

His first fortune was made in property development around Milan. It is hard to imagine that an activity so dependent on decisions about zoning could be conducted successfully without political allies, or that the loans that Berlusconi obtained from banks were miraculously free of politics. Paolo Berlusconi, Silvio's brother, has been charged with paying bribes to obtain zoning exemptions in the Milan hinterland and to persuade the state-owned bank, Cariplo, to buy his buildings.

More serious charges were made against Fininvest. Marcello Dell'Utri, the head of one of its companies, Publitalia, was accused of creating a slush fund, undeclared to the taxation authorities and designed to provide money for bribes. Fininvest admitted bribing the taxation police.[2] However our interest lies not in Fininvest's moral or legal status, but in using it as an example of that overlap between business and politics that developed out of DC and then PSI clientelism.

Berlusconi flaunted his friendship with Craxi, who contributed mightily to the creation of Fininvest's television empire. In 1981 the Constitutional Court ruled that only the state networks could operate over all the national territory and three years later a magistrate invoked this law against Berlusconi. At once Prime Minister Craxi issued a decree that allowed his friend's networks to continue operating. A 1990 law, which permitted Berlusconi to keep his three networks, was passed during the last, or CAF (Craxi-Andreotti-Forlani), phase of the old regime, and Fininvest was duly grateful. Its present acting President declared that "our news will reflect the view that Craxi, Forlani and Andreotti represent freedom."[3] Berlusconi's only concern was to improve his relations with the DC while not irritating Craxi: Andreotti exacted his price for the law.[4]

So Berlusconi incarnated what I am calling "the state bourgeoisie":[5] business groups that either run public enterprises, or else are in the private sector but use and seek political power; or entrepreneurs, financiers, and fixers who attach themselves to parties that use political power for economic gain. Berlusconi though could convincingly take the anti-statist stance, because he had spent some 15 years building a commercial TV empire that competed with the state service.

The ambiguity of the Berlusconi phenomenon lies here. Confronting debts of $2.2 billion, the owner of Fininvest had to enter politics because control of credit had been thoroughly politicized. One of the banks to which he owed money was the Banca nazionale del lavoro, which was until recently "owned" by the PSI. In the 1970s the bank was a fortress of the P2 of which Berlusconi was a member. His privileged position in television could have been undone by a left-wing government. In the past the state bourgeoisie worked with and behind the avowed politicians. The collapse of the CAF led Berlusconi to bid directly for control of the state.

Yet many of his voters and his parliamentarians supported him because they wished to use neoliberalism to drive back the invasion of the state into the economy. Two roads lay open to Berlusconi after his March 28 victory: to become the chieftain of a super-clan that would occupy the state, or to rid Italy of the publicized economy.

Our task is to examine how the economy was publicized. (*Publicized* is a word I have chosen to denote the often indirect but always improper invasion of the economy by the state bourgeoisie. It is quite different from the nationalization of strategic industries that is a direct and often legitimate takeover by the state.) I am not discussing the Italian economy as a whole; thousands of companies and entire sectors lived and mostly flourished heedless of the struggles I shall describe. Yet from the 1960s on the state section was expanded and made into an instrument of clientelism, as had happened earlier with the social services. This distorted the historically close relationship between the state and the private sector. The state extended its power not merely by placing a tax on public contracts in the form of bribes, but by influencing the context in which private industry and finance had to operate. As well as damaging the economy through interfering with the free play of the market and preventing private firms from growing, publicization provoked a defensive reaction.

This reaction took the form of a struggle by the lay, elite families of Milan and Turin to resist the onslaught of Catholic business and finance linked with the DC. The conflict was masked by the open war that pitted the DC and the private sector against the PCI and trade unions, which both grew stronger after the autumn of 1969. Meanwhile these struggles fostered and hid the development of small industry, which flourished because the state was busy elsewhere. These three developments require a triple reading of recent Italian history, beginning with the Center-Left government of 1963.

THE DANGERS OF ELECTRICAL POWER

By 1963 the DC had ruled for 16 years. In Britain and Germany where the Right had been in power for similar periods, alternation took place. The Labour Party won the 1964 elections and the SPD entered the government via a grand coalition in 1966 before it began ruling without the CDU in 1969. In Italy alternation of parties remained impossible because the PCI was illegitimate and the PSI was too small to form the core of a coalition that excluded the DC. The only solution was to bring the PSI into an expanded coalition. This would give a measure of representation to the hitherto excluded working class and would provide an impulse for reform. After inordinate ruminations among the parties and their international patrons, Washington and the Vatican, the Center-Left government was formed in December 1963 with Aldo Moro as Prime Minister.

Although some reforms were passed, such as the application of a hitherto ignored law that raised the school-leaving age, the Center-Left was a failure. The DC power system was in place and the Socialists were too weak to change it. On the contrary it changed them: the PSI was given a share of patronage spoils and the hold of the politicians on civil society was increased. Welfare continued to be awarded as a privilege rather than claimed as a right. Between 1960 and 1970 the number of disability pensions almost tripled, rising from 1.2 to 3.4 million.[6] For the PSI cooption proved electorally disastrous and by 1976 its share of the vote had fallen from nearly 14 percent to below 10 percent. The DC and its antagonist/ally the PCI remained dominant in their respective spheres, and their clash was delayed until 1976-79.

The PSI initiated the process that, while expanding public power over the economy, led to the distortion of the private sector that resisted and compromised, and to the growth of the state bourgeoisie. The price that the Socialists demanded for entering the Center-Left coalition, after the Piano Solo had caused them to give up the issue of the local authorities' control over land use, was the nationalization of the electrical industry.

The demand was logical enough. In a country poor in energy sources electricity was enormously important. During the pre-1939 years Edison was the bulwark of private capitalism and was constantly denounced for not producing more and cheaper electricity. By the 1960s electricity was publicly owned in many other European countries. Moreover the state sector was working well in Italy and indeed ENEL, the public electricity company, while unable to prevent the politicians from imposing bribes/taxes on firms that supplied it, has performed adequately. The nationalization of electricity did not serve, as the PSI hoped, as the model of planning and of a more rational society. But the real trouble lay with Edison.

Shareholder compensation took the form of payments not to individuals but to the electrical companies, which found themselves with around $2.5 billion to invest. This has been described as an enormous boost to private capitalism, but if so the companies largely wasted it. Of the five electrical firms two were predominantly owned by IRI and they flourished: SIP went ahead with the telephone business, while SME became a food company and by the 1980s was coveted by private industrialists. The Centrale, which had among its main shareholders the Pirellis and the Orlandos, tried desultory industrial ventures before concentrating on its financial component. This did well enough, but the Pirellis withdrew and the Centrale fell into Michele Sindona's grasp before passing to Roberto Calvi's Banco Ambrosiano. The fourth company, SADE, was owned by established Venetian families, the Cini and the Volpi—the family that had industrialized Porto Marghera earlier in the century—but they were happy to fuse with the petrochemical giant, Montecatini, at the price of losing control over their firm. Here was a sign that Italian capitalism had not overcome the fragility that it displayed in the years after Unification, and that the electrical dispute would sharpen the disputes in Italian society.[7]

This was dramatically demonstrated by the adventures of Edison, which has undergone four transformations, at least three of them disastrous. They illustrate the difficulty that the private sector encounters when it moves into a high value-added area such as chemicals, and the way it falls back on support from a state that is unable to help but eager to exploit.

Edison spent anything up to $100 million at first to avoid being nationalized and then to ensure ample compensation. Here again corruption is not in itself the issue. Rather it is a sign that a company needs to buy political support because it cannot or is not allowed to cope on its own. Such bribery undermines both the free play of the market, which is manipulated by political favors, and the capacity of the state to set the rules of the game dispassionately. It leads to further evils like the distortion of information. Eugenio Cefis, the chairman of Montedison in the 1970s, had learned much from Enrico Mattei. Cefis bought *Il Messaggero,* lavished money on *Il Corriere della Sera,* and with cavalier disregard for ideology gave smaller sums to the Catholic paper *Avvenire* and the Communist *Paese Sera.*[8] The history of Edison demonstrates how industrial entrepreneurship takes third place behind political intrigue and financial juggling. In 1991 this would be the lesson of Enimont. Instead of constructing a chemical company, Raul Gardini spent his time manipulating the stock market to gain control of the firm, and then bribing politicians to get rid of it.

In 1964 Edison had as its head Giorgio Valerio who had no clear strategy. He diversified with his compensation money, bought the Standa chain of shops, and developed the petrochemical side of his company. But competition was tough since he had to contend both with Montecatini and with ENI. The easy part of the industry is the conversion of oil into basic petrochemicals. So all companies wish to concentrate on this, which crowds the field and cuts profit margins. Profit is greater at the top of the industry where complex chemicals are synthesized. However this requires technological expertise, lots of research and development, and long-term investment planning. Moreover the Italian market was distorted by the generous government grants available for investment in the South. Since technical expertise and skilled labor were in especially short supply here, a string of oil-processing plants sprang up along the coast.

Ecologically risky, they provided few jobs because petrochemicals is not labor-intensive, and they further sharpened competition.

One obvious answer was merger and in December 1965 Edison and Montecatini came together in Montedison. It seemed sensible: Montecatini, run by Carlo Faina, had technical expertise but was in deep financial trouble, while Edison brought its compensation dowry. The new Montedison, while small in comparison with Du Pont or ICI, had 80 percent of the Italian chemical market and 15 percent of the EC market. Moreover its shareholder syndicate—the group of leading shareholders who come together to run the company—included a representative from IRI, which owned 16 percent of the shares, but also Gianni Agnelli and Leonardo Pirelli. They were a guarantee that the new company would remain private, as was the man who had engineered the merger, Enrico Cuccia.

Private industry had never liked Mattei, had accepted with ill-grace Fanfani's organization of the public sector, and distrusted the PSI's talk of planning. Like the pre-war Edison, Montedison was to be the bulwark of private capitalism against the increasing inroads made by a state that had long since abandoned the noninterventionist philosophy of the Liberation.

The best defense of a private enterprise is economic success, but Montedison had none. Faina had not wanted the merger, the two management teams never meshed and Valerio did not improve as an entrepreneur. Montedison's second adventure began in 1968 when Eugenio Cefis, the head of ENI, bought a block of its shares with the connivance of Enrico Cuccia. Cefis saw no reason to compete with Montedison when he could take it over. As the student protests of 1968 gave way to the Hot Autumn of 1969, Cefis strengthened his position. He sold bits of ENI's chemical sector to Montedison and in 1971 he moved across to become president. Montedison's second disaster was at hand. It had fallen victim to the most talented and dangerous representative of the state bourgeoisie. Agnelli protested that the agreement to leave Montedison private had been violated, but Cuccia supported Cefis.

ENRICO CUCCIA: A DIRIGIST AGAINST THE STATE

Cuccia has become a legend in Italy. Born in 1907 into a middle-class Sicilian family, he grew up in Rome where his father was a civil servant in the Ministry of Finance.[9] He married the daughter of Alberto Beneduce and was taken into Comit by Raffaele Mattioli. One cannot help thinking that Cuccia's bid in early 1994 to gain control of the privatized Comit was a deeply personal matter. In the 1930s Cuccia belonged to what I called a group of "French" dirigists without a French state. After the war Mattioli and others saw the need for a merchant bank that could acquire shares in, and make long-term loans to, companies. A 1936 law had separated banking from industry in order to avoid a repeat of the crash when the collapsing industries had brought the banks down with them. But this left a gap, which loomed all the larger because of the weakness of the stock market. It was partially filled by the banks rolling over short-term loans, but the need for a bank that would service industry remained. So Mediobanca was created and Cuccia was appointed president.

Mattioli's expectation was that Mediobanca would promote new industries and provide venture capital, but Cuccia did nothing of the kind. Instead he bought blocks of shares in the leading companies, arranged mergers and new share issues for them and acted as their consultant. He helped them put together the shareholder syndicates, which allow small groups of important people to control a company without owning more than a relatively small percentage of its stock. He set up the interlocking holdings, which permitted the Agnellis to defend the Pirellis and vice versa. If Ugo La Malfa, another Sicilian who came north, was the political voice of the northern lay business elite, Cuccia was its financial advisor and confessor. When Italian capitalism demonstrated its fragility, he was called in. Mediobanca would put up money in return for controlling the errant company's behavior. It would bully other banks into putting up much more money in return for much less control. It would stitch together new shareholders syndicates with the same famous old names. At present Cuccia is attending to Ferruzzi; Salvatore Ligresti's construction and insurance group is another patient; and Fiat seems settled.

The Ferruzzi family are suffering at Cuccia's hands for they have been profligate, while he admires thrift and austerity. However their small shareholders are suffering too. For their insurance company, the Fondiaria, Cuccia arranged a new injection of capital that only a few large investors can afford. The small shareholders would lose by it, whereas if Cuccia had arranged a takeover, they could have sold their shares at a profit.[10] But Cuccia does not care about small shareholders. He wanted to let them learn that the market is dangerous. Cuccia does not like the market either and he tries to restrict its play.

This is the Cuccia legend. A practicing Catholic, he defends the lay establishment. A believer in facts and figures, he admires James Joyce (another canny Catholic). When Michele Sindona allegedly told him he was planning the murder of the lawyer Giorgio Ambrosoli, Cuccia informed neither Ambrosoli nor the police.[11] What could have caused him to make such a decision? The belief that each man lives alone? Certainly whatever motivated him was informed by a scant sense of citizenship.

Another, less mythological way of understanding Cuccia is to look at him in our context of an invading state and a truculent but fragile private sector. His work now appears more important than the provision of venture capital. It is nothing less than the defense of a national capitalism. Here the constitution of Mediobanca is revealing. Until the 1980s the three public banks of national interest, Comit, Credito Italiano, and Banco di Roma, had a large majority of Mediobanca's shares. But in the shareholders syndicate they had only three out of six seats, whereas Cuccia's private sector supporters, like Pirelli or Lazard Frères, also had three seats, although they owned fewer than 10 percent of the shares. This was all the more ironic because the public banks collected the money with which Cuccia doctored the ills of the private sector.

The 1989 privatization regularized but did not change the balance of power. The state banks reduced their share to 25 percent and Cuccia's cronies increased theirs to 25 percent, while 50 percent was placed on the market. As Credito Italiano and Comit went private, the state's share of Mediobanca fell to half of what it was. It has been said, amusingly but incorrectly, that when Cuccia got ownership of Comit, he would also own himself through Comit's approximately 8 percent share of Mediobanca.[12] In reality Cuccia has always owned himself. If he supported Cefis's bid to take over Montedison, it is because he thought that Cefis, like him, would use public money to strengthen the private sector.

Cuccia's role has been to resist the inroads of the DC-PSI state into the economy. This is why his great battles have been fought since the 1960s when the state began its invasion. The most famous of them was against Sindona. It is too simple to see Sindona's rise merely as the challenge of DC-backed finance against the lay finance of northern Italy, if only because two of Sindona's targets were Italcementi and Bastogi, which belonged to the Catholic, Carlo Pesenti. One cannot escape the concept of clans and it is more correct to see Sindona as the expression of one Catholic clan made up of segments of the Mafia, segments of the Vatican (although not IOR), and segments of the DC led by Giulio Andreotti, who had much influence over the Banco di Roma. As usual, the clan looked outside Italy for allies and found them in the Hambro Bank of London and in the United States where segments of the Cosa Nostra were helpful. Nor can one forget that the clans form and reform; in the battle of Bastogi Sindona did not have DC support, while Cuccia was allied with Cefis, who epitomized the state bourgeoisie and whom Agnelli had excoriated.[13]

In 1971 the Centrale fell to Sindona, who wanted to fuse it with Bastogi to create a financial bloc. Bastogi contained in miniature the entire history of the Italian economy. It was a railroad company that used the indemnity it received when the railways were nationalized in 1905 to become a financial company. In the early decades of this century it was important in financing hydroelectric power. By the 1960s it had become a strongbox in which the northern families could deposit the shares of their companies. Only trusted friends were given keys to the box. Clearly Sindona did not qualify.

Just when the Sicilian financier was about to make his bid, the new president of Montedison cast his eyes on Bastogi. Having established himself as president with public money from ENI, Cefis wanted to privatize himself in order to weaken the politicians' control over him. Bastogi owned a chunk of Montedison shares and Cefis planned to merge it with Italpi, a company that—in a familiar pattern of interlocking share-ownership—was owned by Montedison, but itself owned a bloc of Montedison shares. By owning Italpi-Bastogi, Cefis would own himself.

It has been argued that the battle of Bastogi was a struggle between two intruding state bourgeois,[14] but this too is an oversimplification. Certainly Cefis could outbid Sindona in the quest for DC support, which is a sign that the DC did not believe that Cefis would be able to own himself, or that the steady steam of money that had flowed from Montedison to the politicians would dry up. It is also true that Sindona, playing on the splits within the northern clans, convinced Cesare Merzagora, who distrusted Cuccia, to sell him the Generali's shares in Bastogi. But the real struggle was between the northern establishment and Sindona. Cuccia backed Cefis because he was gambling that the DC was wrong and that Cefis would run Montedison as an efficient private company. Pesenti simply thought anyone would be better than Sindona.

The battle was fierce and the Cuccia-Cefis forces showed scant consideration for the small shareholders. Before merging Italpi with Bastogi they stripped it of worthwhile holdings, such as its participation in the Pavesi food company, and endowed it with a less valuable bloc of financial stock.[15] A reputation for neglecting small shareholders clung to Cuccia and was used in 1994 by Romano Prodi in the argument over the Comit privatization. In 1971 Sindona also raised the issue but it was lost in the fury of the takeover that he launched in September. His bid failed in part because Cuccia gained the support of the then Governor of the Bank of Italy, Guido Carli, which illustrates another aspect of the main power struggle. There is an alliance, subject to the usual shifts of loyalty, between the bank and the lay northern finance.

The Sindona saga continued. Sindona was able to sell some of his now useless Bastogi shares to Cefis by threatening legal action over the issue of the small shareholders. He had his Banca Privata and he began to build up a financial group, Finambro. He also acquired the Franklin Bank in the United States. From 1972 to June 1973, with Andreotti as Prime Minister, Sindona's affairs flourished. Amid the chaotic monetary instability he speculated on the lira and in December

1973 he was hailed as a noble patriot by Andreotti. Since he was no longer battling Cefis, Sindona had behind him the DC and the Banco di Roma.

However, in August 1973, Ugo La Malfa, then Treasury Minister, refused to allow Finambro to raise fresh capital on the market. Cuccia unconvincingly denied any role in the decision. The DC mobilized to save Sindona, and the Banco di Roma was ready. However Credito Italiano and Comit, which were historically lay, were not ready and the Banca Privata collapsed in the autumn of 1974. Sindona had no doubt who was responsible and he resorted to Mafia tactics, threatening Cuccia.

In April 1979 Cuccia went to New York and met Sindona at the Hotel Pierre. Informed that the Mafia had passed a death sentence on him, he still refused the demand that he help bail out Sindona with public money. Andreotti, who had lavished praise on Sindona, was once again Prime Minister, although his term was reaching an end. Cuccia returned to Milan where Giorgio Ambrosoli, who was unraveling the web of the Banca Privata's many illegalities, was killed in July. Meanwhile a top Bank of Italy official, Mario Sarcinelli, had been briefly thrown into prison by the Rome magistrates, proving their susceptibility to government pressure, because he too was unhelpful in bailing out Sindona and other DC-backed businessmen such as Nino Rovelli of SIR. The governor of the bank, Paolo Baffi, was saved from prison only by his age and fragile health. It is tempting to think that Andreotti was able to take such steps because of the prestige he had acquired as the man who could outmaneuver the PCI. As for Sindona, he died in prison, probably poisoned.

His case turned into a clear example of the struggle between entrepreneurs or financiers backed by the Christian Democrat state, and the lay, private businessmen of the North. It is, however, too Manichaean to be typical. In general, relations between the two alternated between hostility and uneasy cooperation. Cuccia distrusted Rome but was willing to gamble on Cefis; La Malfa's Republicans were a perennial coalition partner of the DC, while enjoying the support of the northern families. But the private industrialists were all too aware that the balance of power between Rome and the North was threatened by the creeping publicization of the economy. Against this trend Cuccia was a bulwark.

Inevitably he had the defects of his merits. He showed scant interest in developing his native South and he distrusted high technology. By his liking for shareholder syndicates formed behind closed doors Cuccia discouraged new entrants onto the stock market and the formation of new, powerful groups. Not coincidentally, an expanded stock market and a larger number of financial firms would have weakened Mediobanca's position.

In his favor one might suggest that Cuccia was/is not a defender merely of the mighty—the Agnellis and Pirellis. He was eager to welcome upstarts such as Salvatore Ligresti or Cefis, provided that they played by his rules, which were different from those of the state bourgeoisie. It is hard to imagine that he thinks highly of Fininvest. Berlusconi loves spending and publicity, both of which are anathema to Cuccia. It comes as no surprise that Cuccia's estimate of Berlusconi's debts is twice Berlusconi's estimate.[16] Cuccia is not just a clan chieftain for he believes in an establishment: an elite that behaves properly and sets an example of work and efficiency.

His achievement is to have protected Italy's handful of big, private companies against the intrusions of the state. The price is that they remain a handful and that they are not big enough. There is a causal connection between DC and PSI publicization of the economy and the exiguous, family-based private sector. A limited but strong state, which ran the public services well, would have provided space and encouragement for a larger private sector. In such a state Cuccia might have been a great dirigist. In Andreotti's Italy he could only fight with James Joyce's weapons of silence and cunning.

ABUSING THE PUBLIC SECTOR

While Cefis was consolidating his position at Montedison, he was helped by a new public holding company called Egam. Montecatini owned a mining firm called Monteponi-Montevecchio, which was a perennial money-loser; Cefis handed it over to Egam. He wanted to rid himself of a Montedison executive, Giampiero Cavalli; Cavalli was named to the board of Egam.[17]

This seeming boon to private industrialists was invented in 1970 by the Minister of the Public Sector, who was none other than Flaminio Piccoli. Antonio Bisaglia also approved of it and both men used it to pursue two forms of clientelism. Its charter was to take over failing mining companies, whose workers could be expected to show their gratitude in the voting booth. In itself this does no great harm, but Egam, directed by Mario Einaudi who was a faithful servant of the DC and belonged to the Doroteo faction, went further. It bought useless companies in other spheres like manufacturing and transport. As well as taking several companies off Cefis's hands, it bought companies that were already in the public sector, such as Monte Amiata that belonged to IRI.[18]

Einaudi created a large public holding that had no prospect of becoming profitable. In three years Egam acquired 40 companies with a turnover of $400 million. For this it received a parliamentary grant of $200 million and its companies were eligible for many other kinds of government subsidies. Clearly this is different from what I have hitherto called clientelism. It is likely that

Egam bought some of its companies at prices that were too high and that the lucky sellers kicked back some of their gains. But that is mere corruption. The most important issue is the use of public money to create a fictitious economic entity, which in turn spawned an all too real group of state bourgeois who exercised power and interfered with the market. In the long run this weakens the private sector, despite providing it with a rubbish bin.

Egam prospered until 1975 when it made a mistake, from which it never really recovered but which illustrates how it operated. It took over a Genoese group, Villain e Fassio, which owned ships, as well as insurance companies and two newspapers, *Il Corriere mercantile* and *La Gazzetta del Lunedi*. Insurance was a long way from Egam's charter and newspapers are politically sensitive.[19] Significantly Giorgio La Malfa led the charge in *La Stampa*, while the PCI joined in. Not only had Egam paid $11 million for 51 percent of a group whose real total worth was around $7 million, but it had borrowed the entire sum at an interest rate of 17 percent from a savings bank run by a Doroteo. The probable logic of the venture was not economic but political. The Dorotei wanted the two newspapers because the main Genoese paper, *Secolo XIX*, was anti-DC, but more particularly because the papers were to be used against the DC chieftain in Liguria. Paolo-Emilio Taviani had left the Doroteo current in 1967 and had later returned, but was, along with Mariano Rumor, a target of the younger leaders like Bisaglia, who was by now Minister of the Public Sector.

This is an extreme example of how the public sector was run by the rules of clan warfare. When the bill for the economic miracle had to be paid from the 1960s on, the burden of payment fell on the state. Even the nationalization of the electrical industry may be seen in this context: the PSI presented its bill for the 16 years it had been (self-)excluded from government. But the Christian Democrats were not at all unwilling to pay—provided they could use public money. The nationalization changed the Socialists from enemies into junior partners.

In general the need for the public to reinforce the private sector offered the opportunity to expand DC power in both sectors. IRI and ENI were well run until the 1960s, when the initial failure to define their role proved damaging. They were unable to move out of sunset industries like basic steel, they had to bail out the increasing number of lame ducks, and they had to be accommodating to worker demands. They continued to have their successes: Alfa Romeo made money and was sold to Fiat in 1986, while at the same moment the SME could have been sold to De Benedetti. But haphazard conglomerations of holdings such as IRI and ENI were unusually vulnerable to the vagaries of the world economy. So the 1970s were especially difficult, while the 1980s saw improvement. The downturn that became evident in 1991 was all the more difficult because the EC, moving inexorably toward the Internal Market, did its best to block Italian government subsidies.

The gravest weakness of the public sector lay in the political criteria that had become its scale of values. It existed to provide jobs and money for DC-PSI supporters; it was a resource with which to buy consensus and finance feuds. These values spread to the private sector. Bribes paid for public contracts were not just a tax, but also a subversion of entrepreneurial values. Efficiency vanished along with honesty because it too was useless. Once more corruption was a mere part of publicization: the battery of government subsidies and the selective control of credit were just as pernicious. Private capitalism produced its own state bourgeoisie because political influence replaced market competitiveness. Guido Carli concludes: "We have taken responsibility from the entrepreneur but we have not done away with him. We have opened the road to state intervention but we have not planned it. We have corrupted socialism and capitalism alike."[20] Carli distinguished between the 1950s when there was an establishment—Valletta, Mattei, Menichella—and the 1970s when, despite Cuccia's efforts, there was none.

When Romano Prodi returned to head IRI in 1993, he confronted a holding that had lost $3 billion the previous year. However Prodi had an advantage over his predecessors because the political criteria lapsed with the switch from the old regime to the Ciampi government. Whereas DC and PSI had resisted privatization because of the Egam syndrome, Prodi was able to sell off Credito Italiano and Comit, which brought IRI some cash. Many unsalable chunks of IRI are heading for liquidation.

The difference in the problems Prodi has inherited may be illustrated by two brief examples from Finmare. Its ferryboat section, Tirrenia, has large debts, but they stem in part from the burden of having to maintain a service to the small islands; this represents a public good, which may justify the financial loss; however, in Finmare's past lies the "golden ferryboats" scandal when it rented boats from a private shipping firm at an enormously inflated price.[21] This represents collusion between the two segments of the state bourgeoisie.

In the 1992 collapse of EFIM the world recession was a catalyst, but the causes were Italian. Founded in the postwar period as a fund to help the engineering sector, EFIM grew from the 1970s on. It acquired food companies in the South that soon showed enormous losses. It began selling bits of itself to other bits of itself in order to show paper profits, while real money passed to the politicians. Its financial section, Safim, was headed by Mauro Leone, son of President Giovanni Leone who resigned after corruption charges, and was himself implicated in the Clean Hands investigation.[22] For years EFIM had been an economic fiction. The world recession reintroduced reality.

The heart of the empire built by the state bourgeoisie lay in certain banks. Control of credit was indispensable both for simple clientelism and for the creation of vast financial fictions. Some 80 percent of Italy's banks are publicly owned: the savings banks are run by the central government, which chooses presidents using political criteria. Many banks are perfectly well run and even the usual criticism that there is too great a number of them should be treated with caution.[23] However, some banks in the South have been infiltrated by organized crime because of its need to launder money, while bank presidents chosen for political reasons tend to lend money for the same reasons. Moreover the secrecy that surrounds banking transactions fosters abuse.

That bankers should break the law, is unsurprising. However, when Roberto Mazzotta, the head of Cariplo, the largest savings bank in Italy, was arrested by the Milan magistrates, it did not appear coincidental that he had been appointed to his post without ever having worked for a bank, but with much experience in Christian Democrat politics. A week later the president of the Banca Nazionale del Lavoro, Giampiero Cantoni, a Socialist appointee, had to resign. This was ironic because he was appointed in 1989 after the previous president, Nerio Nesi (PSI), and his deputy, Giacomo Pedde (DC), had been forced to resign in the arms-for-Iraq scandal.

The BNL's role illustrates the dangers of a banking system that is shaped by the DC-PSI power structure. The Italian government, eager to please the United States but also pursuing its own pro-Iraq policy, wanted to help the U.S. government to break U.S. law. Some top BNL people considered it natural to lend a hand and the vehicle chosen was the BNL's Atlanta branch. When the bank's officials reported on the irregularity of the Atlanta operation, they were ignored. The Italian and American secret services knew all they wanted to know. When the scandal broke the Italian government made scapegoats of Nesi and Pedde, but protected the bank against prosecution by the U.S. Department of Justice. The BNL probably lost money but that barely mattered, since its finances depended not on its performance in the market but on the DC-PSI power structure.[24]

THE POLITICS OF THE PUBLICIZED ECONOMY

The Atlanta case is interesting precisely because it reveals the political context in which the state bourgeoisie operated. Sindona's links with the Mafia and the BNL's dealings with the secret services were not typical of the publicized economy, but neither were they coincidental. The development of entrepreneurship in the Mafia, Camorra, and 'ndrangheta was spurred by the state bourgeoisie. The Piromalli family was allowed to acquire a fleet of trucks and take over transport in Gioia Tauro by the companies and civil servants who ran industrial development in the South along clientelistic lines. Organized crime fit into the publicization process, which ignored the laws of state and market alike. The Mafia's need to launder drug money meshed with the onslaught launched by Catholic finance against the northern elite. After Sindona, Calvi was the point of contact. Carmine Alfieri was different from the non-Camorristi businessmen who won government contracts after the Naples earthquake because he used violence. But he shared with them the priority awarded to political connections over market efficiency.

The secret service, which protected and threatened the political system while taking sides in its feuds, performed the same functions for the publicized economy. Its role was most obvious in arms dealings like the BNL-Iraq venture or EFIM's attempts to sell its Agusta helicopter. In general international ventures required help from the secret service: it watched over trade with Qaddafi, which took the form of arms for oil, with bribes at both ends. The Magliana band in Rome provided a network for right-wing terrorists such as Valerio Fioravanti; members of the secret service like Pietro Musumeci, who drew on its arms supply for the explosive he helped place on the Milan-Taranto train; Mafiosi such as Pippo Calò who wanted to establish himself in Rome; and businessmen like Flavio Carboni who engaged in property speculation on the Sardinian coast and was Calvi's associate. One member of the band was even found to be in possession of a check made out to Andreotti by Nino Rovelli, owner of the SIR petrochemical company.[25]

A central role in the ideology of the state bourgeoisie was played by anti-Communism. The overlap with right-wing terrorism, the secret services, and the P2 heightened but did not create this anti-Communism, which animated respectable entrepreneurs like Silvio Berlusconi. The reason is not merely that there had to be a Communist threat to justify the DC's permanent hold on government, which made publicization possible. Rather the state-financed fictions and banks such as the Ambrosiano or the BNL, which frequently departed from market rules, could masquerade as champions of free enterprise by using the rhetoric of anti-Communism.

It was logical that the BNL should employ so many members of the P2 lodge, which was both a center for right-wing extremists contemplating a coup to save Italy from Communism and an association of members who helped one another make money. There was no contradiction between the two. Absent from the P2 were the members of the northern dynasties—Cesare

Romiti boasts that not a single Fiat employee was a member[26]—whereas the state bourgeoisie was well represented by Giorgio Mazzanti and Leonardo Di Donna of ENI, as well as Berlusconi. One of the P2's triumphs was to win control of what had been the voice of the lay elite, *Il Corriere della Sera*. Its editor, Angelo Rizzoli, who gained control of the paper in 1974 with backing from Cefis, was enlisted by Gelli. It is tempting to argue that the P2 was waging the war of the state bourgeoisie against the Cuccias and the Agnellis, rather than against the PCI.

However, this suggestion does not hold up, if we consider the relationship between the growth of publicization and the advance of the Left. It was precisely during the late 1960s and the 1970s, when the student/worker protest movement peaked and when the PCI's share of the vote grew, that the public sector expanded. Cefis took over Montedison. Sindona and Calvi rose to wealth and the taxpayer's money poured into the coffers of DC-backed entrepreneurs like Nino Rovelli. One reason is that anti-Communism was a particularly useful cover at this time. Another explanation is that the private sector was so weakened by worker militancy that it could not prevent the shift of power to the state bourgeoisie. Indeed left-wing anti-capitalism allowed the DC to expanded the state's power and hence its own.

Moreover the Left was culturally unprepared for the dispute between state and private capitalism. *Rinascita* published thoughtful articles on Montedison[27] and Egam, while the PCI toyed with the notion of a "producers' pact" between the enlightened, efficient capitalists and the trade unions. This was at the core of the PDS's election program of 1994, but in 1975 the PCI was both too anti-capitalist and too eager to strike a deal with the DC. Giorgio Amendola might have been the man to bargain with the northern industrialists, but he grew increasingly more isolated in the PCI. The New Left was too generically and too virulently anti-capitalist to tolerate any producers' pact.

The first sign of such an agreement was the 1975 deal between the Employers Association and the trade unions for wage indexation, a deal that turned out badly for both sides. The austerity of the historic compromise and the so-called EUR line should have pleased employers, but the union leadership did not control the shopfloor and Romiti was planning as early as 1976 to defeat, rather than negotiate with, the workforce.[28] His strongest supporter was Cuccia. Agnelli had previously struck a bargain with Cefis, which allowed him to become President of the Employers Association with Cefis as Vice-President. Fiat was worried that the DC might use the 1973 oil crisis to weaken it.[29] The old dislike of, but dependence on, the Italian state reemerged at the moment of world economic crisis. The northern elite and the state bourgeoisie united against the working class.

CHEMICAL WARFARE

Montedison, which was engaged in a difficult, competitive industrial sector, but was also a honey pot for politicians, remained at the center of the power struggles, which went on both during the common war against the Left and after the Left's defeat in the autumn of 1980. Various threads run through the struggles: the would-be establishment's attempt to put down two different rebellions, the demise of a proud family firm, further inroads by the state bourgeoisie, and shifts of power within that bourgeoisie.

Cefis proved a disappointment to Cuccia because he was less an entrepreneur than a politician. Cuccia's gamble failed: Cefis was not able to turn Montedison into a successful, private chemical company. However Cefis's position within the state bourgeoisie was weakened by the decline of Fanfani, who was blamed for the DC's defeat in the 1974 divorce referendum. By the 1976 elections the two dominant figures in the party were Moro and Andreotti, who had Nino Rovelli in his clan. The next year Cefis resigned. His exit marked the end of the period when heads of the public sector conglomerates exercised great power in their own right. Where Mattei had run ENI, conducted his own foreign policy, and exerted more influence over the DC than its leaders, Gabriele Cagliari knew that he owed his position at the head of ENI to the Socialists and throughout the Enimont affair he did their bidding.

After Cefis left, the third adventure of Montedison began. The Mario Schimberni reign would not be a disaster, but it would represent a rebellion, in the name of popular capitalism, against the Cuccia model of interlocking family holdings.[30] It began, however, with an alliance between the two men who set about further reprivatizing Montedison. Cuccia enlisted the Agnellis, the Bonomis, and others to buy a block of publicly owned Montedison shares in 1981. This was the period of the P2 revelations and the state bourgeoisie was temporarily weakened. The next year Schimberni fulfilled his part of the bargain by following in Romiti's path and laying off 40,000 workers. The declining price of oil in the mid-1980s helped Montedison achieve a stronger position.

The improvement, along with the stock market rally, triggered a rift within the family-based private sector. Schimberni raided Fondiaria (1986) and the Bonomi family's financial company Bi-Invest (1985). The establishment abandoned Carlo Bonomi but it bitterly resented losing the Florence-based insurance company, Fondiaria. To Cuccia it was both his territory and territory shared by the families. By conquering it Schimberni had upset the balance of power essential to the establishment and Cuccia did not forgive him.

Schimberni, who came from a poor Roman family, had already alienated the elite. He then challenged it directly when he announced a huge share issue in

1987. His aim was to dilute the ownership of his company and leave its president with greater power. For this, Schimberni has been praised as a forerunner of the broad-based, Anglo-Saxon capitalism to which Romano Prodi tried to lead Italy with the privatizations of Credito Italiano (1993) and Comit (1994). Certainly Schimberni was challenging Cuccia, who feared that a company without a "hard core" of wealthy owners united in a shareholders' syndicate would be too weak to resist the inroads of the state bourgeoisie.

The second half of the 1980s was a difficult period for Cuccia because general prosperity and a broadened stock market were jeopardizing Mediobanca's role as a source of capital and the center of shareholder syndicates. However the Wall Street crash of October 1987 ended Schimberni's hopes of a share issue. In the meantime the families had found a new champion in the Ferruzzi group and its chairman, Raul Gardini. The Ravenna family had built an empire out of grain shipping and food. Serafino Ferruzzi had taken over Eridania, which had traditionally refined and marketed the sugar beet grown in the Po Valley. He and his son-in-law, Gardini, who became president in 1980, turned Ferruzzi into the second-largest company in Italy. Determined to diversify and to grow Gardini launched a successful takeover of Montedison in 1987. With a company that had a turnover of $4 billion, he gained ownership of a company that had a turnover of $9 billion. He blocked the new share issue and dispatched Schimberni, which pleased Cuccia, but he kept Fondiaria, which did not. The fourth adventure of Montedison was starting.

It unfolded between 1987 and 1993 and offers themes that are characteristic of the Italian private sector. The secrecy of family capitalism, the way decisions were made without consulting shareholders, its close relationship—despite the 1936 law—with banks are all present. If Gardini's energy and ambition were also typical—he reminds one of Carlo De Benedetti who tried to take over a company that represented one third of Belgium's GDP—so, albeit in exaggerated form, was the social fragmentation he created. Alien to any notion of an establishment or of a balance of power, he rejected the alliance with Cuccia. Even the Ferruzzi family itself broke up. Finally Enimont reveals the struggle but also the symbiotic relationship between family capitalism and an ever stronger state bourgeoisie.

In 1989 Gardini made two attempts at expansion. He tried to corner the soy market on the Chicago exchange and incurred losses estimated at $300 million. Of these $200 million were charged to Montedison, which was hardly fair to the other shareholders.[31] Like most family holdings, the Ferruzzi group was a maze of different companies—Montedison, Ferfin (Ferruzzi-Finanziaria), which was the group's financial arm, Serafino-Ferruzzi, which was the family's own financial center, and many others. This allowed great freedom in moving money and shares around. It made a true evaluation of the financial situation difficult, and this was compounded by the lax Italian laws about disclosure of information even in publicly quoted companies. Gardini took full advantage of such freedom, indulging in ill-named "back to back" operations. Funds transferred from some companies (especially those that were publicly owned) to other companies (usually those owned only by the family) were never transferred back.[32] There was also a Group Services Consortium, which undertook tasks like security or publicity for the various companies and drained them of money.

Gardini's second venture of 1989 was a return to the Cefis strategy of mixing private and public. In yet another attempt to form an advanced chemical group in Italy, Montedison and ENI set up Enimont, where 40 percent of the shares were owned by each partner and the remaining 20 percent were placed on the market, with Montedison and ENI pledging not to buy them in order to secure outright control. Such an initiative seemed implausible. By 1989 ENI was securely under the control of the PSI, and the chemical industry's historic role of providing slush funds for the parties made it unlikely that they would simply watch from a distance. In 1990 Gardini went on the attack and along with his associates he bought just over 10 percent of the remaining Enimont shares and gained outright control.

Again it is hard to imagine Gardini's plans. Did he seriously want to succeed where Cefis and so many others had failed and build a chemical company that could compete with Du Pont or ICI? Did he think the state bourgeoisie, reinforced by 14 years of Craxi's leadership of the PSI, would simply accept its defeat? Gardini is alleged to have previously paid the politicians $10 million to obtain a tax concession for Enimont, which never materialized. Surely that was a warning. Or was he planning from the outset to sell his shares to ENI at a profit?

ENI and its political mentors responded by obtaining from Judge Diego Curtò a decision that the shares acquired by Gardini and his associates (just over 10 percent) be sequestered. Gardini, who had scant faith in the fairness of the judicial system, took this as a sign that the state bourgeoisie would not permit him to take over Enimont. He now sought only to sell back his shares to ENI at the maximum profit, which meant paying the maximum in bribes. In January 1991 the taxpayer bought back Gardini's shares for $1.9 billion, in return for which Gardini allegedly paid $90 million to the politicians, the largest sum supposedly going to Bettino Craxi as the "owner" of ENI.[33]

Once more Italy was without a major chemical company. Once more the parties and a family cooperated to make a profit. However in June 1991 Gardini broke with the Ferruzzi. In June 1993 came a dual crisis: the debts which the Ferruzzi group had incurred in its race to expand became unsustainable and the Milan magistrates turned their attention to Enimont. Gardini committed suicide and a victorious Cuccia was called in to stitch together a family firm without a family.

CONCLUSION

The Ferruzzi saga is a tale about the relationship between public and private in the Italian economy. The size of the bribe as well as the politicians' ability to control ENI and to dictate to Montedison marked the conclusion of a process that began with the nationalization of Edison and the distortion of a public sector, which had worked well in the postwar years. The characteristics of this process were the use of public ownership not merely to protect otherwise uncompetitive industries, but also to create fictional companies that had no economic reason to exist but that expanded the power of the state bourgeoisie. In turn this weakened the private sector, limited its room for growth, and left in place the nucleus of family-owned big companies that were strong enough to face the marauding Roman hordes.

These two made a tacit agreement, which each tried to change to its advantage. The state did not create a free market by extensive antitrust legislation, did not protect the small shareholder, and watched while publicly owned banks made dangerous loans. In return the companies paid bribes/taxes on public contracts and did not foster opposition to DC-PSI rule. The struggle between Catholic finance and the northern lay elite took place within the framework of this agreement, although it also threatened it. Mediobanca defended the northern establishment both against the state and against pressure for wider share-ownership. The state bourgeoisie gained ground but overextended itself.

This struggle, riddled with internal factional disputes and stabilized during temporary truces, has been overtaken by developments inside and outside of Italy. Increased international competition has left the family dynasties uncertain that they can compete without modifying their structure: as an example, Fiat has gone through a year of change. The collapse of Ferruzzi should not, however, be seen as the symbolic death of family capitalism. Pirelli recovered from its catastrophe: its bid for the German company Continental. The battle between Cuccia and Prodi has been won by Cuccia but it was far from a simple struggle between old and new forms of capitalism. One of the best developments of the Clean Hands operation is the pressure to regulate the stock market by providing more information on shareholder syndicates.[34]

In 1974 Eugenio Scalfari perceived the emergence of the state bourgeoisie as marking the decline of the private entrepreneur. The fate of the Volpis was sealed and even Fiat seemed to him weak.[35] His pessimism was, however, unwarranted. New entrepreneurs have emerged in recent years: Callisto Tanzi of Parmalat, Benetton, Stefanel, and many others. Indeed the private sector, while it still contains too few big companies, does not lack dynamism. Small firms have developed, blissfully indifferent to Cuccia as to Sindona.

What of the state bourgeoisie? It has been the prime target of the Clean Hands investigation and Italian opinion is aware of the need to separate public and private enterprise. Yet the Right's victory in the 1994 elections remains ambiguous.

There was an ominous ring in the Lega Nord's response to the arrest of the Cariplo president, Mazzotta: The leadership of the Milan bank must be changed "to take account of the new expression of the will of the people."[36] Is this Lega clientelism? It would appear so.

6

Enrico Berlinguer and the
Historic Compromise

In the present Italian debates the name Berlinguer is rarely invoked. The commemorations that marked the tenth anniversary of his death seemed perfunctory, which is odd since his death triggered a genuine outburst of emotion. All Italy stopped for his funeral, and sympathy took political form a week later in the European elections when, for the first and last time, the PCI gained more votes than the DC—33.3 percent to 33 percent. It was a funeral wreath for the man, rather than for his party or policies. Still Berlinguer deserves attention today because he was the only leader who made "the moral question," which was his forthright way of referring to systemic clientelism, into the central issue of Italian politics. He did so clumsily, but he may be said to have anticipated the Clean Hands investigation.

Moreover in the years after 1979 he struggled to face up to the failure of Italian Communism. He remained a Communist, seeking to give a fresh meaning to the creed but also to preserve what he considered its values—rigor and self-sacrifice. If he is neglected, it is partly because such an effort seems hopeless today. However both then and earlier Berlinguer helped instill into the PCI the sense that Italian public institutions were precious and must be defended. He himself defended them against the terrorism of the Red Brigades, at a cost to his party.

The main reason Berlinguer is neglected is that his great adventure, the historic compromise, the meeting of Communist and Catholic culture that took concrete form in the governments of National Solidarity of 1976-79, was a failure.[1] It is important because it marks the postwar order's only serious attempt to reform itself. When it failed, that order began its decline. After 1979 neither the PCI nor its ally/adversary the DC was ever again as strong as it had been. Part of the failure was the short-lived attempt to reconcile the working class and the industrialists in an Italian version of the "Austrian" solution.

The situation out of which the historic compromise emerged has already been described. The international economic crisis triggered by the 1973 increase in oil prices was especially grave in Italy. One reason for this was the vulnerability of an economy that had grown so quickly: Italy imported 75 percent of her energy. The second reason was that the price for postwar decisions now had to be paid: the working class was stronger and more aggressive. It resisted deflation and in 1975 obtained wage indexation. Yet another reason lay in growing discontent with the DC. Bisaglia was lucid: "the country is tired of us."[2] The DC had too many factions and too few new faces or policies. There was anger with clientelism and anger because there was no longer money for clientelism. Two decades of prosperity had brought a demand for social reforms, which was expressed in the victory for the supporters of divorce at the 1974 referendum. Space was opening up for the PCI.

This chapter is divided into four parts. The first updates my analysis of the Communists, the second deals with the domestic issues of the historic compromise, and the third with the international dimension. The fourth sections treats Berlinguer's last years. The aim throughout is to see the PCI's bid for power from the viewpoint of 1994.

A COMMUNIST PARTY TRIES TO REFORM

Berlinguer and Henry Kissinger agreed that the oil crisis would push Italy to the Left, but in retrospect they were wrong. The protest movements of the late 1960s were subsiding, and even before the Arab-Israeli War the unions were concentrating on salary increases and job protection rather than on worker control. After 1974 the need for deflation shifted power back to the employers. Cesare Romiti claims he began to plan the restructuring of Fiat as early as 1976.[3]

So the PCI's 1975 Congress took place at a delicate moment. The political tide was running strongly for the Communists but the long-term economic trend was not. In July 1975 their vote in the local elections would jump 6 percent to 33.4 percent, which was only 2 percent below the DC. They needed to make a modest reform proposal, of which one ingredient was wage restraint.

Such things are not, however, the stuff of congresses. In September 1973 Berlinguer had launched the historic compromise supposedly "in the light of events in Chile."[4] In fact he had relaunched a policy that was rooted in postwar Italian Communist history. Although he would make the cover of *Time* the following year,[5] Berlinguer was shy and had spent his entire adult life in the party organization. Like so many other university-educated young men he had been attracted by Togliatti's Salerno project. Too young to have ties with the Third International, Berlinguer was steeped in the culture of the postwar PCI. Ascetic and disciplined, he believed in the mystique of the Communist militant who has more duties than rights. He had also studied Gramsci and agreed with Togliatti about the importance of collaborating with the Catholics.

Berlinguer's ancestors were Sardinian landowners and minor nobility. His grandfather moved to the Left and became a supporter of Giuseppe Mazzini, while his father, who was elected to parliament in 1924, took part in the Aventino breakaway. Berlinguer inherited the need to prevent any return of Fascism and the sense that Italian democracy was precious but fragile. He was close to his uncle, Stefano Siglienti, who was an economist and banker and an acquaintance of Ugo La Malfa. Berlinguer became the PCI secretary in 1972 and held the post until his death. If Italians admired him, it is quite simply because they considered him more honest than other politicians.

In his Congress address Berlinguer analyzed the international economic situation in language that used but updated traditional Communism. Lenin's theory of imperialism was being vindicated and capitalism was running out of markets. The OPEC countries had demonstrated that the Third World could no longer be easily exploited. More important, the working class had learned to defend itself and so "the traditional sort of deflation is no longer a valid solution."[6] This was a warning that the Italian government must not expect to run the economy as Einaudi did after 1947. Tight monetary policy and low wages would encounter tough resistance.

Berlinguer accepted the need for deflation, but not the Christian Democrats' version because "they did not try to make choices and set priorities," and because nothing was done "to reduce waste, profiteering, luxury and speculation." The PCI would use deflation to create "new economic and social structures that are more productive and rational." Berlinguer called for "forms of consumption and life-style . . . which are better and also less expensive for the national community."[7] This view, a blend of traditional Socialist collectivism, Club of Rome end-of-growthism, and Berlinguer's own form of asceticism, would be a key ingredient in the culture of the historic compromise.

Berlinguer, who knew little about economics, stressed that the real issue was political. He called for "a process which will gradually allow us to emerge from the logic of the capitalist system, and which leads the working class to take up its role of governing the nation." He linked the Gramscian notion of hegemony with the theme of collaboration between Communists and Catholics. His aim was not merely to create a left-wing coalition and to govern with 51 percent of the vote. Rather he stated that "all our proposals tend and must tend towards unity."[8]

Unity was one attribute of the historic compromise, an extremely difficult concept that Berlinguer had trouble clarifying. In its simplest sense it means nothing more than the coalition governments from 1976 to 1979 where the Christian Democrats had the support of the PCI, although there were no Communist ministers. However, that is not how Berlinguer saw the historic compromise. To him it was the meeting of the Communist and Catholic cultures, the twin forces that were shaping modern Italy. Their dialogue and the values they shared provided the framework for a political agreement. Berlinguer sought a conflictual but cooperative relationship with the DC that he accepted as the legitimate party of the Catholics.

The link with the postwar PCI is clear. Berlinguer was building on the Togliatti-De Gasperi notion that the two mass parties would consolidate democracy in Italy. The time had come to emphasize the "alliance" component of the adversary/ally relationship. The Communists would participate in the government along with the Catholics, which would unblock the political system and resolve the problem of the unrepresentative Italian state.

That is the aspect of the historic compromise that is most relevant to this study. There were other aspects, such as preventing the economic difficulties from causing a dangerous drift toward an authoritarian right-wing regime. Here, too, Berlinguer was demonstrating his sense of the need to reform the state. The trouble was that few non-Communists saw the historic compromise in this way, while few Communists could reconcile it with the rest of their beliefs. Berlinguer was unable to explain how the historic compromise would allow Italy "to emerge from the logic of the capitalist system." Many non-Communist Italians feared it would indeed have that consequence.

Support for Berlinguer came from the union leaders, Luciano Lama and Bruno Trentin. Lama offered the CGIL as a responsible bargaining partner, willing to accept deflation in return for economic planning. Trentin went further and admitted a link between high wages and "a strike of productive investment."[9] Although he was then to the left of Lama, Trentin's speech at the 1975 Congress anticipated the conciliatory line he has taken in the present economic crisis, where he has traded wage restraint for defense of employment. In 1975 he could not do so openly, which introduced into the historic compromise the first of two ambiguities. The PCI saw in the oil price increase a crisis of capitalism and an opportunity to seize hegemony.

As I have argued in chapter 1, hegemony was "an act of faith."[10] It led the PCI to neglect pragmatic reforms—as it had done at the Liberation—and to give priority to any and every increase in its own power. The belief that the Socialist society was waiting in the future shaped the party's policy in the present.[11] During the three years of National Solidarity it failed to achieve the reforms that would have justified to its electorate its support of deflationary measures.

The second ambiguity lay in the method chosen to strengthen the party and achieve hegemony, namely, the alliance with the DC. The PCI base was frequently anti-clerical and it viewed the DC as the arch enemy. This dislike was—and is—reciprocated by the Catholics. In the late 1960s the relationship between votes for the PCI and attendance at mass was revealing: where the Communist vote was 10 percent or less, mass attendance stood at 58 percent; where it was 40 percent to 50 percent mass attendance was down to 30 percent.[12] The Catho-Communist Franco Rodano had influenced the PCI leadership but not the rank and file, and he had not influenced the DC at all.

In 1975 conflict took precedence over collaboration and at the Congress Berlinguer declared that "the essential thing today is to defeat the line taken by the present DC leadership."[13] As secretary Fanfani served as the incarnation of the "bad" DC, which both placated the Communist base and pleased the increasing number of voters who were looking to the PCI as an agent of reform.

There had, however, to be a "good" DC, which was popular and anti-Fascist. Berlinguer allotted this role to Aldo Moro who had shown some understanding of the 1968 upheaval. One doubts whether the theory of the two DCs had much validity and whether Moro's aims, as distinct from his tactics, were different from Fanfani's. It is difficult to speculate about what Moro would have done had he not been murdered, but from 1976 to 1978 he stranded the Communists in the area of government without decisive governmental power, which eroded their support in the country. My conclusion is that he sought to maintain the DC's central role in political life.[14]

Missing from Berlinguer's endless speeches about the DC's two souls is any serious analysis of the way it ran the Italian state and economy. He did attack clientelism, but he neglected its systemic character and the way that the DC had become inseparable from the state apparatus and the nationalized industries. Only later did he see how deep the moral question went. When he dealt with the Church, he appealed to its ethical sense and ignored its desire simply to maintain its power. When the Council of Bishops called on the faithful to vote DC, Berlinguer responded by pointing out DC corruption. He was forgetting that the DC was the party that offered the Church the greatest share of power.[15] It is hard not to conclude that Berlinguer was worried by the shift to the Right in the early 1970s: the increase in the MSI vote in 1972, the bombs at Brescia and on the Italicus train, and the Chilean coup. Like Togliatti, he felt the PCI had no choice but to ally with the Catholics to legitimize itself and to prevent the return of Fascism.

The historic compromise was attacked by two very different writers. Leonardo Sciascia saw rulers and opposition merging to bring about change without change. In 1971 Sciascia had published *Il Contesto,* in which a Christian Democrat minister declares that "my party, which has been misgoverning for 30 years, has now decided that it would misgovern better in an alliance with the International Revolutionary Party."[16] In *Candido* (1977) the Palermo Communists turn into a mirror image of the Christian Democrats.

In an oblique way Pier Paolo Pasolini's work reflects the two dominant strands of the postwar settlement. His ideals are a pre-capitalist, rural Catholicism and an anarchical, urban subproletariat. For the DC he had no use, but in the early 1970s he exalted the PCI as the only pure force in Italy. The historic compromise, he felt, was nothing more than a sellout, less to Catholic culture, which had also lost its authenticity, than to modernity. Technology and consumerism were stifling the very awareness that society could be different. Bologna, the PCI's model city where Pasolini had attended university, was better run than cities where the DC was in power, but it was a city "where precisely there is nothing different."[17]

Varying arguments came to the same conclusion. Far from establishing hegemony, the PCI would be drawn into the web of Christian Democrat power. Italy was looking for an alternative to the DC, but the only candidate was a party that wanted to ally with the DC. It needed the alliance because it was determined to remain a Communist party, pledged to overthrow both the DC and capitalism. Its bargaining power lay in its ability to control labor, but a Communist party could not endorse the Austrian solution. So wage restraint had to be masked as "sacrifices without compensation,"[18] made by a working class that had already assumed its hegemonic role. Or else austerity had to be presented as a working-class value, superior to the waste and selfishness of consumer capitalism.

Berlinguer's language was vivid: key words were "decadence" and "decline"; Italy was menaced by "fragmentation." Decadence took the form of an "exasperated individualism," which left Italians "ridden with anxiety" and prone to "self-denigration." By contrast, the PCI offered "new human values" based on work, which would create unity.[19] In this moral discourse lies the vision of a reborn Italian state, but the political means of creating it were absent. At the moment of its greatest electoral success, when it gained 34.4 percent in the 1976 vote, the PCI was weaker than it seemed and the DC stronger.

If we turn to the more concrete matter of voters and members, we discover similar weaknesses. PCI spokesmen liked to point to an unbroken increase in votes from the Liberation on but this is misleading. Between the Constituent Assembly elections of June 1946 and the 1968 elections the PCI went from 18.9 percent to 26.9 percent, which amounts to 8 percent in 22 years. Between 1972 and 1976 the party's share jumped over 7 percent, from 27.2 percent to 34.4 percent; previously its largest gain had been 2.6 percent, between 1958 and 1963. A 7 percent increase was abnormal.

Nor was the earlier electoral progress unmitigated by failure. In a party that took such pride in being a mass party the fall in membership was seen as a defeat. In 1947 at its highest point the PCI had 2,252,446 members, but with the departure from government and the Cold War, decline set in. In 1948 there were 2,115,232 members and by 1955 there were 2,090,006. The Khrushchev revelations and the invasion of Hungary reduced the army to below 2 million. Then the slide continued. It was briefly halted in 1964 but then began again despite the revival of worker militancy. In 1968 there were 1,495,662 members. Still more worrying was the slump of the Federazione dei Giovani Comunisti Italiani (FGCI). Its membership in 1968 was less than half of what it had been in 1948.[20]

The PCI's achievement was to have survived as a Communist party in Western Europe and to have rooted itself in such organizations as the unions and the cooperatives. By 1970 it was the largest party in Emilia-Romagna, Tuscany, and Umbria (regions won by the Progressisti—along with the Marche—in the 1994 elections). In the most advanced industrial areas—Piedmont, Lombardy, and Liguria—it was the second party, as it was in the northeast where the Catholic influence was stronger and the DC's lead greater. In the South, despite its Gramscian strategy of bringing together Northern workers and Southern peasants, the PCI lagged. Even the electoral growth was unsatisfactory. It had come largely at the expense of the Socialists and the high price the PCI would later pay came in the form of Bettino Craxi. The new recruits were predominantly working-class voters drawn from the subculture of the Left.[21] The PCI was not yet able to draw many Center-Right or Catholic votes. So there was no inexorable movement toward hegemony.

So the 1970s mark a break in the party's history. There was no inexorable Hegelian progression but rather an opportunity furnished by the wave of protest in Italian society. Yet despite the oil crisis, there was nothing in the voting patterns or in the general behavior of the Italian people to indicate that they had despaired of capitalism, much less that they discerned any alternative. The revolutionaries "remained a small minority" and their ideals of "social and economic equality, a collectivist way of life and direct democracy" were antithetical to the fundamental desire of modern Italians, which was and is for "each nuclear family to improve its standard of living."[22] Many people were becoming convinced that the DC was unable to help them in this task so they looked toward the PCI. Initially the historic compromise was appealing because it offered reform without risk. In this sense too it was a defensive strategy.[23]

As such it met with electoral success. In the divorce referendum Berlinguer was too prudent and, having done everything possible to avoid it, he was surprised at his margin of victory: 59.26 percent to 40.74 percent. However Pasolini was right in arguing that the victory was not for any kind of Communism but for modernization.[24] The PCI was attracting support from people who sought less religious authority over civil society. Next the local elections of 1975 left the PCI as the largest party in most of Italy's big cities—Rome, Milan, Turin, Florence, Venice, and Naples. Here the Communists were rewarded as the party of honest, efficient administration.

A discrepancy was arising between what the PCI was and why it was attracting people. Twelve years earlier Italo Calvino had written that the PCI "had taken on the burden, among its many other burdens, of being the ideal liberal party that had never existed in Italy."[25] He was prophetic because people were not voting for working-class hegemony or for austerity, but rather for reforms. It seems impossible that they were not voting for the Historic Compromise that had become the PCI's banner; but they perceived it less as the Rodanian fusing of the Catholic and Communist traditions than as a cautious brand of reformism.

This would explain the PCI's success in 1976 when it gained 3.5 million votes, of which 1.5 million were new voters, 1 million came from other left-wing parties, and 1 million from the Center-Right.[26] Many of these were probably working-class Catholics, a natural target of the historic compromise. But a further discrepancy arose between the PCI's old electorate and its new supporters who were "more critical, more voluble and more unstable."[27] Once the reforms did not come they would be more likely to desert. Moreover the speed with which this happened reinforces the view that the increase in PCI support in the mid-1970s was fragile.

The same is true of membership. Immediately after 1968 growth was slow and 1969 saw an increase of around a thousand members. However by 1972 the party had grown to 1,584,659, foreshadowing the electoral rise. After 1972 growth was faster and in 1976 there were 1,814,317 members. But then decline set in again and by 1979 there were only 1,761,297. Still more revealing was the number of new members. In 1977 the PCI attracted fewer than 100,000 new members, whereas in 1976 the figure had been 174,473. In retrospect the years from 1972 to 1976 represent an exceptional period in the party's history.

The first to depart were the young. In 1976 the party gained 38 percent of the new voters. They wanted change because unemployment in the age group 16-25 was running at 14.4 percent. However the most radical of the young came together in the 1977 Movement, whose protest was directed primarily against the PCI. In February Lama was driven out of Rome University, while in September the movement took over Bologna. The PCI found itself in an impossible position. Although the movement was too extremist and too prone to violence to represent a valid political option, its culture "of our own needs"—of forcing shops to reduce their prices and of creating "free spaces" inside capitalism—struck a chord among young people.[28] At the very least it was more appealing than cooperation with the DC. In 1979 the PCI won less than 33 percent of the new voters, and the problem grew worse in the 1980s.

The PCI's success also disintegrated rapidly in the South. It had won 23.7 percent of the southern vote in 1972, 26.6 percent in the local elections of 1975, and 31.4 percent in 1976. But the Communists could offer nothing to replace DC clientelism and in 1979 their losses were higher than in the country as a whole: 7.4 percent in Campania, 6.3 percent in Calabria, and 6.4 percent in Sicily, compared with 4 percent nationally.[29]

These two examples indicate the difficulties that the PCI faced. It could hardly be expected to find instant remedies for youth unemployment or southern backwardness. Still these were two of the sources of discontent that accounted for its success in 1976. Moreover Berlinguer's prudence was justified because the DC vote held at 38.7 percent. It gained votes from the Right—MSI and PLI—in its role as a bulwark against Communism. This confirmed Berlinguer in his view that only the Catholics could confer legitimacy. The country was saying that it did not want the PCI as an alternative to the DC, but it was also saying that it did not want the DC. It probably wanted Calvino's ideal liberal party that it could not have. The postwar political system was showing that it could not reform itself. Next we shall see that it could not reform society either.

FROM 1976 TO 1979:
WAGE RESTRAINT AND DEFENSE OF THE REPUBLIC

Berlinguer's decision to offer negative support to the post-election government by not voting against it was an attempt to strike a balance between antagonism toward and cooperation with the DC. The government was headed by Giulio Andreotti, the DC's most brilliantly devious representative, the incarnation of the postwar order. Berlinguer's conversations with Andreotti were deliberately vague. The reality of the historic compromise lay in the detailed discussions that took place among the government, the employers, the PCI, and the unions. Two aspects are crucial: the trade deficit caused by the oil price increase for which the solution was deflation, and high wage costs in a rigid labor market.[30] As the wage indexation agreement of 1975 had shown, there was a narrow strip of common ground between the employers who were willing to recognize—at least temporarily—the fact of union power, and the union leaders, who were concerned about investment and unemployment and who were regaining control over the shopfloor militants.

The framework was set by a series of austerity measures, imposed by the Andreotti government in the autumn of 1976 and backed by the PCI. Interest rates went from 12 percent to 15 percent, tighter limits were placed on the acquisition of foreign currency, prices of government-controlled items such as tobacco, petrol, telephone services, and electricity were increased and modifications were made in the wage-indexation system. The result of these measures was "a success that has few precedents in the history of Italian economic policy."[31] Domestic demand was reduced by around 3 percent of GNP; by mid-1977 the balance of payments was in the black, by mid-1979 the foreign debts accumulated between 1973 and 1976 were paid off, and there was an investment boom. The "Austrian" solution was working.

On wage costs the three-year contracts had already been signed at the national level so the government and employers wanted measures to improve labor productivity and moderation in company and plant level bargaining. On December 9, 1977, a law amended the wage indexation system for workers earning more than 8 and 6 million lira: their cost of living increases for the period September 1976 to April 1978 were to be paid wholly or partly in the form of treasury bonds to be redeemed in five years. On January 26, 1977, the unions agreed to exclude cost of living increases from retirement bonuses.

Further agreements were signed on flexibility that permitted increased shift work, greater use of overtime, and greater internal mobility. In February, one month after Berlinguer set out the philosophy of austerity, the government asked for further union sacrifices. To help employers, some of their social security costs were to be paid out of general taxation and this was to be financed by an increase in VAT, which was not to affect the cost of living increases.

This proposal, which had the backing of the International Monetary Fund, outraged the shopfloor militants and embarrassed the union leaders. It was also a case in which the PCI, obsessed with the quest for international legitimacy, found itself caught between its base and the IMF, the symbol of Western economic orthodoxy. A compromise was reached so that the VAT increases were included in the cost of living calculations, but other items such as electricity tariffs were not.

After these measures the union leaders kept trying to moderate the salary demands at company and plant levels and met with success. During the years from 1976 to 1979 real wages increased by only 2.6 percent annually in comparison with 11.4 percent annually for the previous three years. Man-hours lost by strikes dropped from 177 million in 1976 to 15 million in 1977 and 71 million in 1978. Although unemployment went up in 1977 from 1.4 million to 1.9 million, it is reasonable to suppose that the unions' choice of defending jobs through salary moderation prevented a greater increase. None of this went beyond the rearguard action that Social Democrats put up in periods of recession, and the parallels with the British Labour Party's social contract are obvious. The difference was that the Communists were fighting on two other fronts. The political struggle to get into government took a new turn as the PCI, mindful of the services it was rendering Italian capitalism and the risks it was running with its own constituency, demanded greater power. It succeeded in June 1977 in obtaining a formula of "policy agreements" where the party secretaries and their advisors met with the government to establish policy.

The second front was a series of legislative projects designed to introduce a degree of governmental control into the economic and social area. Judgments on these projects are mostly negative: a typical comment is that they were "massive, confused and ineffective."[32] Moreover they were frequently voided by legislative delays and bureaucratic shortcomings. Fernando Di Giulio, the leader of the Communist group in the House, concluded that "the state apparatus was quite unable to carry out any serious acts of reform quickly."[33]

This was the intentional result of Christian Democrat rule. That the PCI should only now discover it seems naive. De Giulio concludes that the Communists "having been for too many years outside the area of government, were not able fully to appreciate the damage that had been done to the state structure."[34] Their long (self-) exclusion from the workings of the state had taken its toll.

Not that the legislative record of the years 1976 to 1979 is unimpressive. An abortion law was passed. A decree on regional government fixed the transference of financial resources from the state to local authorities, even if it did not give to the regions the power of taxation. A law to limit sharecropping and transfer land to the farmers working it was delayed; but this went through in 1982.

Most disappointing was the law on industrial reconversion (Law 675), which was the closest the PCI came to giving the state a new role in planning.

It was designed to allow governments to reorganize by sector, and to avoid being stranded with lame ducks and economic fictions. Unsurprisingly, DC ministers managed to circumvent Law 675. The state bourgeoisie survived the historic compromise unscathed.

A batch of laws dealing with territorial planning, construction of homes, and rents was similarly thwarted. The law that regulated construction was struck down by the Constitutional Court and the plan for building homes failed to meet its targets. Without new homes rent control was bound to create shortages, especially because landlords in big cities preferred to keep their apartments off the market.

PCI proposals for health reform foundered on poor state structures. An innovative plan to move mental patients out of institutions and help them live in the general community failed, because the systems for help were inadequate and the patients were thrown back on overburdened families. The December 1978 law creating a unified health service run by local bodies called the Unità sanitaria locale (USL) was bound to stand or fall by the quality of its administrators. Mostly it fell. The USLs became organs of clientelism and helped corrupt the PCI.[35]

The historic compromise was doing precisely what the PCI had accused Social Democrats of doing. It had imposed wage restraints, while leaving existing social structures intact. The PCI ran into the difficulties with which the British Labour Party was familiar. The autumn of 1977 saw a series of demonstrations and strikes that the party tried to orchestrate in support of its policies of increased investment, but which it feared because they were expressions of impatience with austerity. The climax was reached when the metalworkers marched through Rome on December 2.

The PCI could not ignore *its* metalworkers so it pressed ahead. It called for a government of National Solidarity and on January 16 Andreotti resigned. At the EUR congress on February 13 the union leaders reiterated their support for wage restraint in return for investment to create jobs. EUR was a symbolic triumph for Lama and for the policy of bargaining, but it marked an end rather than a beginning. In 1978 wage restraint was falling apart and along with it the historic compromise. High inflation, which came down only as far as 12 percent at the end of the year, made it difficult for the union leaders to control the shopstewards. In October came the strike of nurses and hospital workers. When the issue of entry into the European Monetary System was posed in November, the PCI feared it would mean further deflation, while the employers, worried at losing the weapon of devaluation, wanted greater freedom to lay workers off. The common ground between unions and management was shrinking and the PCI had exhausted its role as broker.

In March the compromise between Communists and Catholics reached its peak when the PCI moved into the governmental coalition although not into the government. As if to demonstrate that the DC had the upper hand, Andreotti submitted a list of ministers who were all Christian Democrats and some of whom—Antonio Bisaglia and Carlo Donat Cattin—were fervent opponents of collaboration with the PCI. Whether or not the PCI would have endorsed such a government became irrelevant when, on March 16, the day of the confidence vote, the Red Brigades kidnapped Moro. Now the PCI and the occasionally reluctant DC joined together to defend the Italian state.

It is impossible to fault Berlinguer's decision to throw the PCI into the front line against terrorism and to oppose negotiations with the Red Brigades. This represented the best aspect of the Gramscian tradition, and in the long run it helped save the PCI from the fate that befell so many Communist parties. It demonstrated the party's sense of the state. But in the short term it was damaging.

During the months of the kidnapping the PCI suspended all criticism of the DC and neglected other issues in order to organize an endless round of meetings denouncing the Red Brigades. Here again the fear of illegitimacy was lurking: a Communist Party could not run the risk of being soft on left-wing terrorists, who also called themselves Communists. The Red Brigades traced their actions back to the same partisan struggle that was a source of PCI legitimacy.[36]

However, Turin workers could not understand why the issue of the Moro kidnapping should be kept separate from the 30 years of DC misrule that had helped create an environment in which terrorism could flourish.[37] Leonardo Sciascia's argument that the PCI was defending the state "as it was,"[38] convinced some young people, who helped the Radical Party to its relatively high 3.5 percent in the 1979 election. The PCI did not succeed in balancing its firmness toward the Red Brigades with a concern for individual freedom. Its reaction was correct, perhaps all too correct.[39]

Sciascia was wrong in prophesying that the Moro affair would strengthen the historic compromise. The DC hid behind PCI firmness while not forgetting to point out the Red Brigades' links with Communist tradition. There was no electoral reward for the Communists. In partial local elections of May 14 they slipped from 35.5 percent in 1976 to 26.4 percent, whereas the DC climbed from 39 percent to 42.6 percent. In January 1979 Berlinguer called the two-and-a-half year experiment to a close.

During the historic compromise the PCI rendered Italy two major services. It helped defeat the terrorist onslaught and it left the economy in better shape than it found it. The PCI failed in the task that it undertook, again without admitting it, of bringing Social Democracy to Italy. The late 1970s saw the crisis of Social Democracy, and it is no coincidence that the PCI departed mere months before Thatcher arrived. A specifically Italian criticism is that the PCI failed to guide the reformist movement that grew out of the events of 1968.[40] It remained a Communist Party, unwilling to change itself and hence unable to change the political system or society. The problems of the state remained. In 1981 the DC negotiated with the Red Brigades to get Ciro Cirillo released. In autumn 1980 Romiti went into battle with the unions and crushed them. Berlinguerian austerity gave way to the irresponsibility of steadily rising deficits. Systemic clientelism entered its most exuberant phase.

NO BRIDGE-BUILDERS REQUIRED

The historic compromise affords an opportunity to study the international constraints within which the postwar order operated. The 1975 Congress set out the PCI's view of East-West relations. It would remain in NATO because leaving would impede the process of detente and divide Italy. Neither reason could be expected to gladden the hearts of NATO supporters. The PCI did not acknowledge any Soviet threat. It considered "anti-sovietism, whoever is proposing it, as harmful and as an obstacle to the general struggle against imperialism and reaction."[41]

Of course the matter was not so simple. The PCI had sought an increasing independence from the USSR ever since Togliatti's return in 1944. However it had never envisaged, and it did not now envisage, a complete break. The Yalta memorandum and the invasion of Czechoslovakia were landmarks in the PCI's evolution, but its condemnation of the Czech invasion did not imply a condemnation of the Soviet system as a whole. So during the 1970s Moscow and the Italian Communists engaged in "mutual, if reluctant attempts at forbearance."[42]

Nor was this merely Berlinguer's reluctance to break with the Togliattian past. At the 1975 Congress Berlinguer stated that, while Eastern Europe's political institutions were not those that the PCI envisioned for Italy, its economies had survived the early 1970s better because they were planned. He added that, whereas the West had lapsed into "corruption and fragmentation," Eastern Europe possessed "a moral climate that was superior."[43]

Behind these statements lay the uncertainty that pervaded other aspects of PCI political culture. Berlinguer stated that the PCI had "solid international traditions to which we intend to remain faithful."[44] But what were they? A

Rinascita article tried unsuccessfully to spell them out: the Czech invasion must not be forgotten but the USSR is now changing and moving toward detente; the PCI looks toward the non-Communist Western European Left, but it is critical of the Italian Socialists. Anyway, it must not be Eurocentric, because there are also the liberation movements in the Third World.[45] Two themes emerge from this confusion: the trust the party placed in detente and the growing attention for the non-Communist world. Each reflected the PCI's desire to bridge the gap between East and West, without, however, abandoning the East.

As it drew closer to government the PCI tilted ever further westward. In a much publicized interview of June 15, 1976, Berlinguer stated that NATO was a shield that protected the Historic Compromise from ending up like the Prague Spring—"I feel safer on this side."[46] Surely this was anti-Sovietism? At the Soviet Communist Party's XXV Congress of February 1976 Berlinguer affirmed that the Italian brand of Socialism was based on an expansion of previous democratic conquests—no longer dismissed as formal or bourgeois— and would take place in a pluralist system. In November 1977 he went further when, at the sixtieth anniversary of the Russian Revolution, he declared that democracy was a "historically universal" value, thus undermining the validity of the Soviet brand of Socialism. The Italian brand was no longer separate and equal; it was superior.[47]

To what extent Berlinguer had the party behind him is hard to assess. It has been estimated that the base was generally anti-U.S. and anti-NATO and that it was divided about the USSR, with as many as 25 to 30 percent of the members opposing Berlinguer's clear break with Moscow in December 1981.[48] This would explain why Berlinguer, obliged between 1976 and 1979 to impose domestic policies that displeased the base, took care periodically to praise the Soviet Union. His speech defending the Russian Revolution, delivered appropriately at the Festa de l' *Unità* in September 1978, was one example.[49]

The PCI made increasingly desperate attempts to resurrect Lenin. Admitting that Russian Marxism was "a closed body of doctrine," Berlinguer argued that Lenin must be reread critically.[50] But what did this mean? Well, the Lenin of left-wing infantilism could be invoked against the 1977 Movement, or the Lenin of Brest-Litovsk could justify compromises with one's opponents. In return the Lenin of the one-party state could be forgotten.

How did the Soviets perceive the Italian comrades? They disliked PCI heresies but admired PCI success. The PCI was becoming less of a pro-Moscow, opposition party, but it might become an anti-Washington government party. Alternatively it has been suggested that the Red Brigades received help from Eastern Europe because their terrorism embarrassed the PCI.[51] In retrospect it is clear that the PCI was engaged in a long slow movement out of the Soviet orbit. As long as detente lasted forbearance could continue. The invasion of Afghanistan and the imposition of military rule in Poland would lead to a clear break. But in the late 1970s the PCI wanted to remain a Communist party and thus wanted the Soviet connection.

It also wanted to be tolerated by the United States. During the postwar period the United States could not control who won in Italy but it could control who lost. The PCI needed to remove the American veto on its entry into government. As already stated, Kissinger and Berlinguer were in partial agreement about the economic problems of the 1970s. They stemmed from a crisis of capitalism that might create a shift to the Left throughout Europe. Kissinger envisaged chaos in Italy, the Communists forcing their way into power, offers of Soviet aid, and an end to Italian democracy. In turn this would have repercussions in other countries like France, where conventional wisdom held that the Communists would prove the dominant partner in the Union of the Left. The EC would be weakened and the United States would retreat into isolation.[52]

Moreover Kissinger was under pressure in the United States because his policy of detente seemed to be working in favor of the Soviets. The SALT agreement supposedly gave them a military advantage, while the Helsinki accords provided them with political legitimacy. Weakened at home by Watergate and abroad by the flight from Saigon, the United States no longer appeared the dominant world power. This helped trigger the current of U.S. neoconservatism that viewed Kissinger as a traitor.

In particular the New Right disliked Kissinger's acceptance of the fact of Soviet power and of the division of the world into blocs. Small wonder that it viewed the rising Communist influence in Western Europe as a proof that it was right. But even without this pressure Kissinger would have been intransigent toward Eurocommunism, because his view of the world as two blocs presupposed that the Soviets should have no influence in the Western bloc.

To Kissinger the PCI's professions of pluralism were a fiction. Communists might make a pretense of democracy or they might be sincerely democratic, but once they attained power, they would follow the logic of Communism in terminating pluralism and bidding for absolute control.[53] This view of the PCI seems doubly wrong. First, because the PCI's worldview was not a mask for traditional Communism, but rather the form that Communism had assumed in the Italy of the 1970s. Second, Kissinger overestimated the PCI's strength, refusing to admit that a party with 34 percent of the vote in a country teaming with NATO soldiers would simply be unable to take over the government. The probable reason for this error is that, to Kissinger, the PCI was a pawn in the larger chess game he was conducting with the Soviets and the American neoconservatives. Any victory for the PCI could be used against him.

After the June 1976 elections the United States and its allies moved immediately. At a Group of Seven meeting in Puerto Rico it was decided that if Communists entered the government, Italy would be isolated and there would be no more international loans. The Social Democrats, Helmut Schmidt and Jim Callaghan, supported this stand.[54] Indeed Schmidt took the decision to make it public.

The arrival of the Carter administration in 1976 seemed to announce a change of policy. During the campaign Jimmy Carter had attacked Gerald Ford for excessive interference in the affairs of allies, while Zbigniew Brzezinski substituted the notion of the polycentric world for Kissinger's two blocs. This might mean that the United States would cease to make its views felt in Italy, or that it would consider the economic issues and accept a Communist presence in the government in return for wage restraint.

Either of these developments would have represented an enormous change in U.S. foreign policy and neither took place. Although there were differences of opinion within the administration—Cyrus Vance was relatively soft and Brzezinski hard—the Carter people endorsed the Kissinger line. Carter's foreign policy, while erratic, was in no sense left-wing and his *Americanismo*—his belief in America's mission to bring democracy to the world—lent itself to anti-Communism.[55]

In 1977-78 the parallels with the postwar period were clear. The United States used and was used by the DC. Each time the United States wanted a reformist government and the PCI in opposition, it obtained the second but not the first. The State Department pressed Andreotti to introduce reforms but, predictably, although he did precisely the opposite, he was applauded as a new De Gasperi when he visited Washington in July 1977, because he was keeping the PCI outside the government.[56] Christian Democrats encouraged Washington to make its views known and then used those views as a reason for not admitting PCI ministers. Ambassador Richard Gardner complied by reiterating traditional U.S. policy: "we do not want Communist Parties to be influential or dominating in Western European governments."[57]

In his memoirs Brzezinski claims that U.S. efforts were a "distinct help" in ending the historic compromise and that this was "one of the less-known success stories of the Carter years."[58] The only criticism one might make of this statement is that the United States slew a dragon that it had itself invented. In no sense can the Italian case serve as an example of how the United States hurled back the Brezhnev onslaught of the post-detente years.

The PCI used such influence as it possessed to project a moderate image. Its spokesmen sped across the Atlantic bearing brand new visas and promising to leave power if defeated in an election. But anti-Communism was a necessary part of American political culture and the United States had invented *its* PCI which was quite separate from Berlinguer's. The only criticism to be made of the PCI is that if it had discarded its obsolete cultural baggage it might have made Kissinger and Brzezinski work harder.

The veto remained. The PCI wanted to build bridges between East and West but world time was working against the historic compromise. Detente was giving way to the last phase of the Cold War.

U.S. opposition was probably less important in the failure of the Historic Compromise than the DC opposition or the PCI's own weaknesses. The former recovered its old role as a bulwark against the Eastern hordes, while the latter paid the price for its determination to remain a Communist party without really knowing why. During the years 1976 to 1979 the PCI almost lost "any sense of where it stood in society."[59]

Its decline dates from 1979. It never again came close to power and by 1987 its share of the vote had fallen to 26.6 percent. The Christian Democrats did not benefit in the long run from their victory. As Communist influence diminished, they declined too. The antagonists had fought each other to a standstill and they could not resume their tacit alliance afterward. The historic compromise is significant because the attempt to reform the political system left the system bankrupt. In turn this accounts for the fascination of Berlinguer's last years.

BERLINGUER FROM 1979 TO 1984: THE TWILIGHT OF THE PCI

Berlinguer's position as secretary was not seriously threatened by the failure of the historic compromise. Indeed he was allowed to make major decisions, such as the December 1981 break with the Soviet Union, in isolation. This stand and the choice of the alternative government in November 1980 helped Occhetto transform the PCI into the PDS between 1989 and 1991.

The party's verdict on Berlinguer's last years is unfavorable.[60] The Right, which looked to Giorgio Napolitano, felt that Berlinguer, reacting against the historic compromise, was too extreme. Critics cited his speech at the Mirafiori gates in September 1980, which offered PCI support to the Fiat workers if they and their unions decided to occupy the factory. Berlinguer was equally intransigent in opposing the modification of the wage indexation system in 1984, a stand that led to the PCI's defeat in the referendum of 1985. The same critics disliked the theme of Communist "difference," which isolated the party. In an Italy where terrorism was being beaten back, where a recovery from the economic traumas of the 1970s was underway, and where the working class was declining in numbers and in power, Berlinguer stranded the party in the sterile purity of opposition, while Craxi's PSI was growing in importance.[61]

One reason for discussing Berlinguer's last years is precisely his awareness that Communism in Italy, though masked by victories like the overthrow of the Cossiga government in 1980 and the 29.9 percent vote won in the 1983 elections, was approaching a crisis. Berlinguer watched the rise of neoliberalism, in which he saw an exasperation of the individualism he had denounced. He felt that Craxi was turning the PSI into the bulwark of a new Right. Eastern Europe provided no solutions. So Berlinguer made a desperate attempt to redefine Italian Communism. He emphasized the old distinction between Social Democrats who accepted capitalism and Communists who fought to transcend it. Now, however, he transformed this difference into a moral stance: a refusal of the values of consumer capitalism. This reaffirmation of Communism as self-sacrifice must be seen as a bid to revitalize a dying creed by invoking the energies of its youth. The ideal of a Gramsci who died in prison for his beliefs haunted Berlinguer. It is all too easy to understand how absurd it seemed to Emilia-Romagna Communists who had made their party strong by creating wealth and a stable government. Berlinguer remained "faithful to a teleological project which, although it had lost its dynamism, lived on."[62]

Yet while draped in cultural pessimism and unable to find a coherent political outlet, the discourse of Communist difference pointed to Italy's real problems: the occupation of the state by the parties, systemic clientelism, and the growing alienation of the citizens. Until 1979 Berlinguer had believed in the Togliatti-De Gasperi vision of the Republic, where the major parties—especially the DC and the PCI—would spread democracy by involving the masses in government. Belatedly realizing that the postwar settlement had turned into systemic clientelism, Berlinguer abandoned this vision.

His concept of difference was yet another service to his party because Occhetto could invoke it during the Clean Hands investigation. Its weakness lay in its sparse political content. Berlinguer knew that it involved an alternative government but he did not envision alternation of parties in power. He did not give up the belief in a "good" DC, although he did know that the existing DC could not help to reform the state. He failed to form an alliance with the PSI (although this probably would have been impossible anyhow). He did not take up the issue of electoral reform. He placed too much hope in new forms of protest like the women's movement.

Yet Berlinguer's last intuitions were correct. He realized—unhappily—that he was living in the twilight of the PCI and he knew that the postwar order was breaking down. In 1980 he stated that "today the moral question has become the most important national issue."[63] In his attacks on the state bourgeoisie, there was a sense of what the Italian state might and should be. Even in the 1970s he had tried to ensure that the men nominated by the PCI as heads of banks were chosen for their ability rather than for their party affiliation.[64] Spurred by the revelation of the P2 lodge and the Calvi affair in 1981, Berlinguer uttered a cry of protest: "the parties have occupied . . . the structures of local government, the welfare agencies, the banks, the nationalized industries, cultural institutions and hospitals."[65] His words almost foreshadow the outcry of 1992.

7

From Craxi the Exacter to Bossi the Spoilsport

If the DC received its most severe punishment from the electorate in 1983, and if Berlinguer's sense of Communist difference was the PCI's last intellectual upsurge, then essentially the Republic had run its course by 1979. One is left with the problems of explaining why the crisis did not come until the elections of 1992 and how and why it came then. One obvious answer lies in world time: Italy could not change until the Cold War ended even though the East-West split only conditioned but did not determine the Italian situation.

Another reason lies in the domestic political developments. The PSI first gave the postwar settlement a reprieve by promising to modernize Italy and then undermined the clientelistic order by its greed. Into the opening—literally into Craxi's Milan—stepped the Lega, which not only took away the DC's Northern votes, threatening its role as the linchpin of the postwar order, but proposed to solve the problem of the Italian state by terminating it.

These political developments are inseparable from economic and social trends: the Lega gave voice to the small companies of the Milan hinterland, the kind of companies that had dragged Italy through the 1970s, but which were underrepresented politically.[1] This chapter is divided into three parts, the first dealing with the PSI, the second with the Lega, and the third with the years before 1992. Running through each section is an analysis of economic and social processes that the political system finally proved unable to manage.

BETTINO CRAXI: THE SYSTEM DEVOURS ITSELF

In the 1994 elections the PSI simply disappeared. Ottaviano Del Turco, its recently installed leader, won a seat in Emilia-Romagna, but his party gained a mere 2.2 percent of the vote and so failed to reach the 4 percent minimum, above which a party was eligible for seats in the proportional representation segment. A few ex-leaders ran in other formations—Giorgio Ruffolo with Alleanza democratica (AD)—while ex–Prime Minister Giuliano Amato did not run at all. In Bettino Craxi's Lombardy the PSI won only 1.5 percent. Deprived of their parliamentary immunity, ex-leaders like Claudio Martelli had their passports taken away and are awaiting trial. Craxi has not waited, but has fled to his country house in Tunisia. The Clean Hands investigation decimated the Socialists, who had accumulated power during the last years of the old regime and have now gone down with it.

In 1972, roughly a decade after the Center-Left governments began, the PSI polled at 9.6 percent. In 1976, despite the surge of the Left, it remained at 9.6 percent. The electorate had not forgiven it for its failure to implement reforms and for its emulation of DC clientelism. In a generational coup Craxi became party secretary with the support of Claudio Signorile. The two belonged to different currents in the PSI, Craxi stressing autonomy and Signorile cooperation with the PCI. They agreed that the PSI had been punished for its subordination to the DC, but, whereas Signorile saw the solution in improved relations with the Communists, Craxi believed that greater self-assertion would bring the party new support. The two views were compatible as long as the PCI sought a privileged relationship with the DC, but after the end of the historic compromise Craxi and Signorile clashed and Craxi won out.

Much attention has been paid to Craxi's personality and style of leadership, but one wonders whether he deserves it.[2] Blustering and bullying, he ran the PSI from 1980 to 1992 like a minor Stalin, while during his four years as Prime Minister he made ostentatiously bold decisions, some of which disintegrate when examined closely. It is not incorrect to argue that this would-be strongman was the first postwar politician to readopt a style reminiscent of Crispi and even of Mussolini. However, Craxi reflected the decadence of an aging regime rather than the birth of a new authoritarianism.

His strategy rested on the perpetuation of Communist illegitimacy. Anti-Communism came naturally to Craxi, who remembered from his youth Socialist subordination to the Communists between 1948 and 1956. Moreover the PCI furnished him with a pretext by snubbing the PSI during the historic compromise.[3] Communist illegitimacy provided the PSI with its goal of creating an autonomous left-wing party of government, while in the meantime it justified coalitions with the DC. The mistake of the Center-Left would be corrected by tougher bargaining with the Christian Democrats. However the twin pillars of the postwar settlement would remain in place for the foreseeable future, even if they were less massive. Craxi's gamble was that PCI and DC would emerge weakened from the historic compromise—which they did—and that space would open up for the more modern and pragmatic party that he said he would create but did not.

Sociological trends were indeed running for the PSI and against the PCI. A glance at the Communist Party in the Veneto reveals that in 1982 47.7 percent of its members were workers, whereas in 1988 the number had dropped to 43.3 percent. Conversely the number of pensioners had increased by nearly the same amount—16.7 percent to 20.6 percent. The working class was growing older and with it the PCI. However the postwar barriers were breaking down: of the delegates to the Federation congresses of 1990 22 percent had belonged to Catholic organizations. Moreover 30 percent had been active in parish activities in their childhood and 40 percent had mothers who were practicing Catholics.[4] Although these figures may exaggerate the degree of openness extended by the mass of Catholics to the PCI, they are a sign that political loyalties could change more easily than in the immediate postwar years.

One reason was that class divisions were less sharp. In 1960 the average salary was three times the average wage. In 1970 the average salary was twice as much as the average wage and by 1983 it was only 1.3 times as much. Like other European societies Italy was turning into a constellation of social groups, of which an underclass—11 percent of the working population—was clearly left out, while others were clustered together. The general prosperity turned workers into consumers whose tastes were similar to those of other consumers. The changing roles of women made their political attitudes more diverse.

It became a cliché to contrast the activism of the early 1970s with the concentration on private life in the 1980s. Amoral familism was supposedly back.[5] But the 1970s had not really marked a break with the attempt by the family to improve its economic status, while the 1980s demonstrated no wish to go back on social reforms like the right to divorce. The major change was in the size and nature of the working class and of the urban middle class. Working-class growth had peaked in 1971 when it represented 47.1 percent of the working population, 6 percent more than in 1951. But by 1983 it had decreased to 42.7 percent, which was another reason why the PCI's difficulties could only increase. Meanwhile the urban middle class, which had also grown from 1951 to 1971—26.5 percent to 38.5 percent—went on growing and in 1983 reached 46.4 percent. An intriguing statistic is that the category of "artisans" declined from 6 percent in 1951 to 5.3 percent in 1971, which was predictable, but then rose to 5.8 percent in 1981. Since this category includes owners of small businesses, it is probable that they grew by more than 0.5 percent, while conventional artisans continued to decline. Certainly the number of self-employed increased from 24 percent in 1980 to 29 percent in 1988.[6]

As in other European countries, industry employed a smaller percentage of the labor force. In 1971 the figure was 42 percent, up 7 percent from 1951, but in 1983 it was back at 35 percent. Unlike other European countries, 40.3 percent of industrial workers were in plants with fewer than ten employees; the corresponding figures for France and Germany were 22.3 percent and 18.2 percent. Agriculture had long lost its army, declining from 43 percent in 1951 to 18 percent in 1971 and 13 percent in 1981. But the service sector was growing from 15 percent in 1951 to 30 percent in 1971 and 37 percent in 1983. The percentage of government employees rose with it from 7 percent to 10 percent and then to 15 percent.[7]

If the final set of figures hints at the lasting problem of the state bureaucracy, the other statistics show the transition to a society based less on the division between capital and labor. Moreover at precisely the moment when the march of the 40,000 who protested against the 1980 strike appeared to mark the split between the white-collar and blue-collar workers at Fiat, that distinction was being eroded. Continuing a process that had been noted during Valletta's reign, the upper levels of the industrial workers were turning into technicians.

The development was not uniform, for in the early 1980s the robotization of the workplace also de-skilled Fiat workers.[8] But, as the Fordist working class broke up, it also lost its power to attract other social groups. To oversimplify, the common sense of society was represented by a better-educated group, less influenced by the PCI or by the Church, and less unionized, more flexible in its political behavior, without any vision of an order outside Western capitalism, but displeased with DC rule. Small business, with its particular culture of self-reliance and distrust of the state on which it nonetheless makes demands, was especially important.

The weakened working class faced employers who had reacquired their self-confidence after the defeat suffered by the PCI. Cesare Romiti's bold stand, which rather frightened the coalition government, reshaped not just Fiat but all Fiat suppliers. The worker militancy of the 1970s disappeared and management regained control of the shopfloor. Eventually this would lead—in the 1992 and 1993 wage agreements—to a tripartite consultation process, which marked a reconciliation between the working class and the state, albeit on terms that the CGIL of the 1950s or the 1970s would have judged unacceptable.

The old difference between North and South was blurred but unchanged by the development of small industry in the Center. In the 1970s private-sector white-collar workers were 15.9 percent of the working population in the northwest and 12.6 percent in the Center and northeast, but they were only 8.4 percent in the South. The figures for public-sector white-collar workers were 7 percent, 8.1 percent, and 13 percent.[9] Whoever ruled in the South, whether Christian Democrats, Socialists or, as today, the National Alliance, was doomed to support a large role for the state.

The postwar problem of finding a policy blend that suited North and South remained. The change was that a party that challenged the DC should be Center-Left and interclass. Was Italo Calvino's ideal liberal party about to be called into existence by Craxi?

The answer was no, but we must briefly consider the first three periods of his leadership, leaving the fourth for later. The first, from 1976 to 1979, saw the PSI wait, terrorized at the prospect of its demise, until the PCI was weakened. Then it struck at Berlinguer's strategy. During the Moro kidnapping the PSI called for concessions to the Red Brigades, played on the emotions of the DC rank and file, and tried to split the DC and the PCI, which had refused to negotiate. The contrast with Berlinguer's sense of the state was glaring. Next Craxi, switching tactics, tried to delegitimize the PCI by publishing an essay where he set the PSI in the tradition of Proudhon and denounced the PCI's Marxist heritage.[10] This was one of many attacks on the Communists' collective memory. Others would include onslaughts on Gramsci or, alternatively, on Togliatti's neglect of the imprisoned Gramsci. Intellectually crude, these broadsides exposed the excessively subtle way that the PCI reconstructed its past. They were accompanied by a celebration of the PSI's ties with other western European Socialists, although in reality the party had little in common with either the Labour Party or the French Socialists.[11]

In the 1979 elections the PSI gained some votes from the PCI in the South. This began a long march in the South that involved clientelism and ties with organized crime. Overall the PSI increased its vote by only 0.2 percent. Craxi's conclusion was that the party must return to government, which would isolate the Communists in opposition and allow the Socialists to undertake reform. After the DC congress of February 1980, he took advantage of the victory of the groups that opposed cooperation with the PCI and forced his way into the government. To underline the difference with the Center-Left, he insisted on obtaining nine ministries, including Finance, Public Sector, and Defense.

To appeal to the growing urban middle class, the PSI took a libertarian stand on social issues such as abortion. It talked vaguely of electoral reform, but feared a British or French voting system that would greatly reduce the number of seats it held in parliament. Instead it called for the direct election of the president, which suited Craxi's image but had no chance of being implemented. It succeeded, through individuals like Giorgio Ruffolo, in attracting intellectuals who wanted to reform Italy, but it gave them scant power in the party. The PSI was caught in a vicious circle of its own making. By governing with the DC, it dissipated its reformist energies. The only way it could assert itself was in the war for spoils. As the voters perceived this, they refused to reward the PSI with the increased support it needed to bring pressure on the DC.

The only solution Craxi could devise was to win the war for spoils. The PSI wrestled for control of ENI, a larger chunk of state television, the BNL, and local government agencies. Inevitably scandals resulted. The ENI-Petromin bribery hit the press in September 1979, although Craxi manipulated it into a weapon to defeat Signorile. In May 1981 the published list of P2 members included such well-known Socialists as Enrico Manca and the party chief in Liguria, Alberto Teardo. In July the jailed Roberto Calvi claimed that he had lavished money on the PSI, which prompted Craxi, who presumably feared further revelations, to attack the magistrates for imprisoning Calvi. This sparked the long war between the PSI and the magistrates, which contributed to the Clean Hands investigation. The public grew accustomed to seeing Socialists carted off to prison. Teardo and his associates were jailed in 1983, while Giuseppe la Ganga somehow avoided a similar fate in Turin.[12]

Unsurprisingly the PSI vote went up by only 1.6 percent in 1983, despite the sharp fall of the DC and the stagnation of the PCI. Craxi was right in thinking that many voters wanted change, but the PSI offered only the trappings of modernity through slick, expensive party congresses designed for TV. Not without reason Berlusconi was drawn to the Socialists. Craxi's quest for power was rewarded when he took advantage of the DC's defeat to become Prime Minister.

To understand his economic policy we must review the events of previous years. The ending of the temporary Austrian solution, provided by the historic compromise, and the second increase in oil prices, which raised the cost of oil imports by 70 percent in 1980 and by 49 percent in 1981, left Italy with a $20 billion trade deficit in 1980 and with an inflation rate that was around 20 percent.[13] However by 1983 economic improvement was in full swing, led by the restructuring and labor-shedding of big industry and by the export flair of small business.[14] In 1983 growth ran at 2.9 percent and it continued at this level for the next two years. By including the black or untaxed economy Craxi could proudly announce in 1987 that Italy had overtaken Britain in per capita GDP. He was also fortunate that he was in power when oil prices and the dollar dropped in 1986.

This was a boon to the anti-inflation struggle, in which Craxi played his part. In 1984 he cut back the mechanization of wage-indexation to meet the government's target of reducing inflation to 10 percent for the year. He did so with a decree that enhanced his image as a leader willing to take bold decisions. Politically this was genuinely bold, and Berlinguer, who was in his mood of hard-line opposition, helped Craxi by launching the Communist majority of the CGIL into a crusade of opposition. The battle went on long after Berlinguer's death and culminated in a 1985 referendum, which Craxi won by 54 percent to 46 percent.

This victory established Craxi as one of the two or three dominant figures in Italian politics. His role in pressing for the Single Europe Act at the Milan summit of 1985, and the way he refused to hand over the *Achille Lauro* terrorists to the Americans, helped make him indispensable to the formation of a government. If he did not lead it, he had at least to bless it. De Mita's government of 1988-89 went unblessed and did not last. The wage indexation victory was won despite the PCI, and thus contributed to the Communists' decline to 26.6 percent in the 1987 elections.

The economic effect of the decree was slight, if only because the government offered concessions such as holding down prices it controlled. Inflation fell to 10.6 percent in 1984 and to below 10 percent in 1985. Probably the international factors, the Bank of Italy's tight money policy, and the victories won by management over labor played as much of a role as the government. Moreover Italian inflation was still running 4 percent above the EC average, and Craxi was unable to gain a lasting disinflation, as Mitterrand did in France.

On another, even more vital issue Craxi made no impact. The government debt had grown rapidly, spurred by spending on social programs—such as health care—in the 1970s. By 1981 it stood at 55 percent of GDP and Craxi could do nothing to halt it. When he left power in 1987 it had reached 92 percent of GDP, and was fueled by interest payments.[15] In 1981 the Bank of Italy ceased financing the deficit because of its obligation to maintain the value of the lira. The government turned to massive issues of Buoni Ordinari del Tesoro (BOT), which drove interest rates up and created a powerful pressure group that resisted attempts to tax the bonds, thus increasing the debt.

So the rosy glow of prosperity that accompanied the later years of Craxi's premiership and that suited the Socialists' image as modernizers was short-lived. It faded as soon as the world economy turned sour in 1990. Italy's old strengths and weaknesses remained. Her entrepreneurs were dynamic—Berlusconi's TV empire was thriving and in 1986 he acquired AC Milan. However, industry remained weak in the areas of high technology. The big companies like Fiat expanded their financial operations, which made money and helped them avoid high interest rates. But small firms were damaged by interest rates, and the attempt to enlarge the stock market caused only brief worries for Cuccia. The state bourgeoisie did well under Craxi, as the example of Berlusconi demonstrates. The economic factors that contributed to the 1992 upheaval were left untouched.

To say this is not to condemn Craxi's prime ministership. The 1984 Visentini law, which forced shopkeepers and artisans to pay more—although not all—of their share of taxes, was another achievement. In substance although not in style, the PSI governed much like the DC. It was no coincidence that Craxi formed a wary alliance with his Foreign Minister, Andreotti. In the 1987 elections the electorate rewarded the PSI, increasing its share of the vote to 14.3 percent. This convinced Craxi that his methods were correct, but in fact his attempt to dominate the political system was undermining it, since unknowingly he had helped call its enemy into being.

THE BARBARIANS MARCH ON ROME

In the 1994 elections the Lega won 8.4 percent of the vote, which with the help of the mostly winner-take-all system turned into 122 seats in the House. Umberto Bossi's triumph was overshadowed by two problems. The first was that he had been obliged to form an alliance with Forza Italia, which had threatened to take over his policies and his supporters. The free market, the family business, the contempt for the old regime were Berlusconi's themes, and his ability to frame them in a language that was populist but governmental rather than populist and protesting, appealed to the Lega's more sophisticated supporters. Bossi's share of the vote went down from 9.2 percent in 1992 and it dropped by 2 percent in Milan to 16 percent. The Lega ran ahead of FI in its strongholds of Varese, Brescia, and Bergamo, but it was overtaken in Como and Pavia and it ran behind Berlusconi's army in the Veneto. Around 19 percent of the Lega's 1992 voters deserted to Forza Italia.[16]

The second and overlapping difficulty was that the Lega would have to become a party of government, whereas it was designed for opposition. It had been all too successful: it had helped bring down the old regime and prepare the way for the new one, but it risked losing the political space it had won.

A brief glance at Lega history reveals its destructive power. It began as a regionalist movement in 1984, modeled in part on the Unione Valdotaine. There was a small upsurge of regionalism and in the 1983 elections the Liga Veneta gained over 5 percent of the vote. While seeking the special status awarded to the Val d'Aosta, Bossi tried to present Lombardy as a cultural unit. The son of a poor family of farmers, he had seen his rural region transformed by industry and he fought for its traditions, especially its dialect. However he gained scant support. Lombardy was not Sardinia, voters did not care about the dialect, and in any case there was no overt mood of protest. Bossi's career is counterpoint to Craxi's, and in the mid-1980s Craxi, who was Prime Minister, was successfully leading the attack on wage indexation. All that remained of Bossi's first phase was the sense of a strong "them" and a rebellious "us."

The way in which the "us" was redefined is indicated by the Lega's language. Without money to buy TV time, Bossi stuck up posters and scribbled on walls. While spray-painting graffiti, he got into fights. All this confirmed his view of language as transgression.[17] However, he abandoned the dialect for a language characterized by its crudeness. Allusions to the virility of Lega supporters and to the impotence or sexual preference of their opponents, slogans like "Roman robbers," attacks on the physical appearance of other politicians, and the deformation of their names—Berlusconi becomes Berluskaiser—established the Lega as the incarnation of the swaggering males of the small bars around Milan.[18] Italy had produced yet another brand of populism.

The "us" took economic and social shape. "We" were the working class, the self-employed, and the small businessmen of Lombardy, the unappreciated wealth creators. Culture was replaced by common interests: the industrious North as opposed to immigrants with other customs or to idle Southerners. The real "them" became the Rome government, which redistributed money to the South and placed bureaucratic obstacles in the path of northern wealth creation.

One manifestation of the economic component in the Lega's regionalism came in 1994 with its attempt to prevent Cariplo from forming ties with its counterpart in Puglia.[19] An example of the Lega's economic populism is its hostility to the Cuccia-Agnelli establishment. The Lega backed privatization, but it objected strongly to the way that Credito Italiano and Comit fell into Cuccia's grasp, even if it did ironically strengthen Cuccia by helping destroy the DC and its dubious financiers. In general, small businesses resent having to borrow money at interest rates that may be almost double the prime rate. The Lega's link with them was reflected in the statement of Vito Gnutti, the new Minister of Industry, that "their interests would be a central preoccupation" of the Berlusconi government.[20]

With its reshaped identity the Lega grew. In the general elections of 1987 it won 3 percent in Lombardy. By the European elections of 1989, it had risen to 8 percent and in the local elections of 1990 it leapt to 19 percent. The size of the second increase indicates that a protest, which had been latent, had suddenly taken form. Geographically the protest was strongest in the small- and medium-sized towns: the Lega won only 12.9 percent in Milan but it reached 20.8 percent in Varese and 20.1 percent in the DC stronghold of Brescia. In the province of Milan it gained 2.3 percent more than in the city itself, while in Como the difference was greater—22.9 percent compared with 18.2 percent. The Lega even invaded red Emilia, reaching 6.7 percent in Parma, while the Liga Veneta achieved scores that offered hope to the future Lega Nord—7.2 percent in Verona and 5.9 percent in Rumor's old stronghold of Vicenza.

The social and economic factors lay in the mixture of achievement and malaise present in a predominantly DC electorate. As early as 1982 the astute Bisaglia explained—but did not correct—the phenomenon. The DC state had concentrated, he maintained, on the South and on the big northern cities, but it was perceived in Varese or Brescia as a taxing, inefficient bureaucracy.[21] The inhabitants of the Lombardy periphery were sophisticated enough to grasp the way in which the government worked, but they were unable to turn it to their advantage. The expansion of the state bourgeoisie damaged them, while the Austrian solution promised by the historic compromise was irrelevant to them. Prosperous but only recently so, they tolerated the regime until the situation changed. By 1990 the economy was starting to decline.

The political situation had changed too. Craxi was both out of power and very much a part of government by clientelism. The DC, far from renewing itself, offered in Andreotti and Forlani its most devious and its weariest leaders. The transformation of the PCI into the PDS was so painful as to provoke desertions rather than converts.

The long-delayed crisis of politics had arrived.[22] Some elements were common to all western European countries: economic specialization and decentralization broke up the red subculture based on the Fordist working class, while Pius XII's nightmare came true as prosperity undermined religion and the white subculture. The population was more mobile: 33 percent of Italians now live in places where they were not born. The percentage of the electorate voting for the two major parties declined from more than 66 percent in 1975 to around 45 percent in 1990. Both the leading parties of the governmental coalition suffered in the 1992 elections: the DC dropped 4.4 percent to below 30 percent and the PSI slipped 0.7 percent. In Italy as in other countries skepticism about government grew: whereas in 1967 only 33 percent of people surveyed felt that the government was not honest, 85 percent held this view in 1980. But the level of disillusionment in Italy was far higher than elsewhere: In a 1989 comparative survey 29 percent of people felt that the government was competent and 49 percent felt it was not. The equivalent figures for West Germany were 51 percent and 16 percent.[23]

The expressions of the crisis of politics were various and contradictory. One form was the demand for a kind of militancy, which took more account of the individual's needs. The Verdi, the Partito radicale, and the women's movement sought to provide new forms of participation. Another form was the decreasing significance of the Left-Right split; this was a complex phenomenon because the memory of Fascism had faded, which permitted a revival of the MSI. Yet another form was the re-creation of the traditional mass party on a new basis: the Lega brought people together around the theme of regional identity. People voted out of opinion rather than out of belief and hence switched their vote more easily. Yet the need for identification created— especially among less educated voters—parties like the Lega that divided the world into good and evil. Irene Pivetti's opinions on religion and Fascism are not typical of the Lega, but their intensity is. The myths that depict the citizens of Lombardy towns driving back Emperor Barbarossa and rapturous meetings at Pontide are designed to answer this need. Similarly the structure of the party, which discourages factions and grants authority to the charismatic leader, stems from the Lega's role as a *Gemeinschaft*.

Such uniformity masked political and social differences. By 1992 the Lega drew 60 percent to 70 percent of its voters from the ex-parties of government, but a substantial minority came from the former PCI. Socially the interests of working-class supporters were frequently in contradiction with those of the self-employed. The Amato government's decision to impose a minimum tax on the latter suited the former. There was a fundamental clash between Lega supporters who were voting primarily as a protest against Rome and those who were voting for the free market. The second group was tempted by Berlusconi, while the first saw in him the personification of the old regime. Diversity increased with success. When Milan fell to the Lega in the mayoral elections of 1993, the Lega voter was likely to be better educated than before, to be middle-class, and to have voted PSI in the past rather than DC.[24] He or she—Marco Formentini gained 57 percent of the male vote but only 43 percent of the female vote—was also more likely to abandon the Lega.

Despite mistakes of strategy, such as ignoring the 1991 referendum on reform of the voting system, the barbarian hordes continued to grow between 1990 and 1992. They marched out of Lombardy, incorporated the other northern leagues, and proclaimed the Northern Republic at Pontide in 1991. In the 1992 elections they won 20 percent of the vote in Lombardy and 17 percent in the North. They were halted, albeit with difficulty, at the frontier of Emilia.[25] Then the Clean Hands revelations provided fresh impetus. The Lega and the magistrates reinforced each other. There is truth in Bossi's claim that "without our electoral victories the politicians would have sent Di Pietro to break stones in some Sardinian mine."[26] Conversely the magistrates gave credence to the Lega's tirades against Roman robbers. In 1993 Bossi himself was accused of taking money from Montedison, but still the Lega could claim victory for the politics of protest. Craxi's capital of Milan had been conquered by Formentini and the reprieve granted to the political system was over.

As the prospect of power drew closer, the Lega set out its plan for a federal Italy. The term *federation* is probably incorrect and should be replaced by *confederation* because there was to be no more Italy but rather an Italian Union.[27] There would be three republics: Padania in the North, Etruria in the Center, and a southern republic, which has not earned the dignity of a name. Associated with them would be the autonomous regions of the Valle d'Aosta, Trentino-Alto-Adige, Friuli-Venezia Giulia, Sicily, and Sardinia. Most of the power would be held by the republics, which were to have their own parliaments. Power over foreign and defense policy, justice, and money were left to the Union, which was to have an elected legislative body and a directly elected prime minister. However economic power would be the prerogative of the republics.

This vision is consistent with the Lega's history. It offers freedom from Rome and a Padania government that can implement free market policies. From our perspective it may be viewed as an extreme attempt to solve the problem of the Italian state. It consigns to the scrap heap both the DC project of finding a mass Southern base to support the interests of northern industry and the PCI dream of a Gramscian alliance between a southern peasantry and a northern working class. It would simply do away with the bureaucracy, which it considers unreformable. Since the Lega gained power less has been heard of the independent republic of Padania and perhaps the Lega's confederation will serve merely—but this would be important—as a catalyst for fiscal federalism. As a vision it is an indication of, rather than a solution to, the breakdown of the postwar order.

THINGS FALL APART AND THE CENTER DOES NOT HOLD

Craxi's image as a bold decision maker was designed to appeal to the modern segments of Italian society, which admired efficiency.[28] However between 1987 and 1989 he played an obstructive role. The government crisis of 1987 lasted four months and was so bitter as to make DC and PSI implausible coalition partners. Craxi was equally bitter in his onslaught on President Cossiga.[29] The republic's institutions were further discredited two years later when De Mita's government fell in another long crisis, artificially prolonged by the PSI, which wanted to use the European elections as a test of PCI strength in order to decide whether to force national elections. Cossiga cooperated, allowing Giovanni Spadolini to waste several days in an "exploratory" mission, which had no reason for existence. PSI manipulation was clear when the objections, which it had made to De Mita, vanished as soon as Andreotti become the DC candidate.[30]

The CAF (Craxi-Andreotti-Forlani) period began with the all too obvious agreement that Craxi would become Prime Minister after the 1992 elections, while Andreotti piled up power to bid for the presidency, and Forlani maneuvered to defeat him. In 1991 Cossiga joined in the discrediting of the institutions by issuing diatribes against the magistrates, his own party, or whomsoever his fancy indicated. There was a logic to Cossiga's behavior. He was worried that the Gladio investigation might lead to him and he was demonstrating his ability to fight back. Cossiga was also protesting the attacks on the president's institutional role, which he himself damaged by his harangues. In this he was supported by Gianfranco Fini and thus helped the revival of the MSI.

Meanwhile the revelations of corruption grew more frequent. In 1987 Rocco Trane, Signorile's secretary, was arrested, while Craxi's friend, Salvatore Ligresti, a builder of Sicilian origin who seemed able to raise surprising amounts of money from unknown sources, was involved in the first of many Milan investigations. Meanwhile the Craxi clan exacted enormous tribute: a brother-in-law, Paolo Pillitteri, was the mayor, while the post of party secretary went to Craxi's son, Bobo, who was also named by Berlusconi to the board of AC Milan. Other Socialist clans occupied Salerno, where Carmelo Conte established a clientelistic network, and Naples, where Giulio Di Donato had to battle mighty DC champions like Don Antonio or Andreotti's ambassador, Paolo Cirino Pomicino, and Bari. The PSI replaced the PCI as the second party in the South by thoroughly unmodern methods.

The DC-PSI rivalry rendered intolerable what the political system had long tolerated. Internal rebellions broke out: Mario Segni's plan for constitutional reform and his use of referenda to allow the electorate to speak directly; Leoluca Orlando's protest against DC-Mafia ties; and especially the revolt of the magistrates. Whereas in the 1960s the system had been sealed off from outside attack thanks to the United States and the PCI, now it was vulnerable.

The end of the Cold War released DC voters who turned to the Lega. In their move toward unity the EC countries began to wonder aloud what closer ties with Italy might bring. They noted that funds allotted for vocational training vanished into the pockets of DC politicians. They discovered they were paying CAP money to nonexistent Southern farmers. Helmut Kohl asked rhetorically whether there was a risk that organized crime could spread out into neighboring states.[31] The need to hold the value of the lira against the mark introduced tension into the Italian economy.

Growth held up well in 1989 at 3.2 percent, but inflation ran at 7 percent, double the French rate. In January 1990 the lira entered the narrow band of the EMS, but as the world economy declined, growth for 1990 went down to 2 percent, while inflation remained at 6.1 percent. Macroeconomic policy was contradictory because Andreotti did not cut public spending lest unpopularity should damage his presidential hopes, while the Bank of Italy protected the lira with high interest rates. The deficit could only increase, financed and worsened by the BOT.

By the summer of 1991 the EC had joined the IMF in calling for deficit reduction, but the fall budget showed no political courage. The Employers Association, fearful of the 1992 deadline, was louder than usual in its criticism of the way public sector wages were pushing up labor costs in the private sector. The association backed the June 1991 referendum because it considered that a more efficient Italian state was a prerequisite for competing with French and German industrialists.

The referendum was the clearest sign of discontent with the political system. It started as Segni's revolt from within the DC, and then it received PDS backing. A modest proposal to reduce the number of preference votes to one, it became the litmus test of faith in the regime because Craxi advised the electorate "to go to the beach." 62.5 percent of voters disobeyed and 95.6 percent of them voted as Segni and Occhetto indicated. This manifestation of disaffection foreshadowed the defeat of the CAF in the 1992 elections.

Another early signal was the growing demand for reform of the state apparatus. In 1990 a law was passed that limited the secrecy of decisions, allowed more controls, and increased the accountability of civil servants (Law 241). Parallel to the rise of the Lega went the move toward decentralization. In the same year a new law gave greater power to local officials, made possible privatization of some services, and introduced local referenda (Law 142). Both trends were accelerated after 1992 and the innovation of the direct election of the mayor came in 1993. Although such changes increased citizen power, it is hard to see how they can make a decisive difference without a more radical reform of the central state apparatus.[32]

Of all the overlapping reasons for the regime crisis that the 1992 elections exemplified—the end of the Cold War, EC pressure, the defections from within the DC, the disaffection of the magistrates, and the rise of the Lega—the one I would like to stress is the change in Italian society. The Censis survey for 1990 detected a widespread frustration with the social services and with the self-perpetuating, directionless rule of the DC-PSI coalitions, but also a "waiting stage,"[33] during which people were reluctant to act. In 1991 it reported the same massive distrust of the parties, a concern about the spread of organized crime to the North, and a coolness toward Europe that was linked with doubts about Italy's ability to compete. However, now the mood was active and Italians were eager for change.

The strong protest vote in the 1992 elections stemmed from this mood, which was, however, complex. The "new" culture in Italian society distrusted intermediaries and sought a greater role for itself. It favored decentralization and privatization. It was proud of its professionalism and tended to associate politics with competence. This made it dissatisfied with the "old" culture of ideological parties and a cumbersome state bureaucracy. The wealthier supporters of the Lega could be attracted by technocratic and neoliberal solutions. However the opposite problem was also present: the new was inseparable from the old.[34] As Vito Gnutti's remark, quoted earlier, indicates, the emerging small businesses did not wish to do without the state, even if they distrusted it. The two trends could overlap in creating a new and different state. But if unsuccessful they could fall back, each in its own way, on the time-honored methods of forming clans to reallocate the resources of the weak state and of withdrawing to fresh forms of traditional allegiance—the family and local networks. The Clean Hands investigation was about justice and citizenship, but it was inseparable from a struggle for wealth and power. In 1992 the fourth attempt to (re-)found the Italian state began.

8

February 1992 to March 1994: Revolution and Restoration? Or Change?

Certainly these two years often seemed like a revolution. The postwar political order collapsed and Giulio Andreotti's career ended. Clearly the Berlusconi government can be seen as a restoration: the Prime Minister is a former member of the Craxi clan and the overlap between political and economic power is more apparent than ever. However the downfall of the DC-led state was a process of change: it was both a regime crisis and a crisis of modernization. To oversimplify, the urban middle classes of Northern Italy decided that the DC-PSI governments no longer served their interests. So they decided to change the political system.

This view implies that the old regime was not all bad and that Italy is capable of achieving incremental change. The privatization of Comit and Credito Italiano is the culmination of a series of banking and financial reforms, begun after Italy entered the EMS in 1979. Similarly there is no reason to perceive the Berlusconi phenomenon merely as a restoration. One reason why Forza Italia won the 1994 elections was that a bloc of voters felt it would provide the leaner, more efficient state that a modern economy needs. This does not mean those voters were right: I shall argue in chapter 9 that they were mistaken.

At the core of the debates lies the familiar but thorny problem of the Italian state. From the 1950s on, the state had changed from a besieged to an overbearing force, and the PDS and Forza Italia could agree that its invasion of civil society must be beaten back. Privatization and decentralization were pillars in the programs of Left and Right alike. Yet countries find it hard to correct their historic distortions and it is far from clear that Italy is doing away with the overworked state.

Change took many overlapping and oblique forms in the two-year span. One may argue that the year between the 1992 elections and the April 1993 referendum was a period dominated by a tearing-down process, while the next year was a time of reconstruction. Yet economic policy was consistent at least up to the 1994 elections. The various strands in the tale began to intertwine. The murders of Falcone and Borsellino heightened public anger with the political class, but in the 1994 elections economic issues were more important than either the anti-Mafia struggle or the Clean Hands inquiry. This chapter takes the form of a story, whose main but often hidden protagonist is the state.

THROW THE RASCALS OUT

The Clean Hands operation began on February 17, 1992, when Mario Chiesa, a PSI official and head of an old people's home, La Biaggina, was arrested in Milan. However he did not turn state's evidence until Antonio Di Pietro had left him to languish in jail for a few weeks. Then there was a small spate of further arrests and newspaper articles. These were overshadowed, however, by the March 12 murder of Salvo Lima in Palermo. In Milan the magistrates were moving cautiously, fearful that they would be accused of interfering with the April 5 elections.[1] Afterward they quickened their pace and by mid-June, 16 PSI, 14 Christian Democrat, and 7 PDS politicians were informed that the magistrates considered them suspects. The prime target was the Craxi clan, but by September 1993, 2,600 people were under investigation, including 325 parliamentarians.

The first questions that the arrests and revelations pose are: Why did they come as such a shock? and Why did they come at this point? After all bribery was endemic, ranging from micro-illegality to systemic corruption. It had been discussed in sources available to the general public. To take only one example, Adriano Zampino, a surveyor whose confessions had helped bring down the Turin city council some ten years earlier, had declared to *La Repubblica* that "I am no different from 90 percent of businessmen who work on public contracts." The politician was "like an addict in search of drugs, he always needs money."

Dismissing any distinction between the political class and civil society, Zampino added that "the system works in the private sector too."[2]

To say that most Italians "knew" of corruption is to underestimate the complexity of the verb "to know." An occasional newspaper article is different from the flood of details that deluged Italy from April 1992 onward. However the previous awareness suggests that corruption was not the cause but the catalyst of a greater anger. The De Lorenzo scandal unleashed pent-up wrath with the public health service; the real issue was the low level of care.

Since the health service was no worse than it had been ten years earlier, why were its deficiencies exposed in 1992 rather than in 1982? A full answer involves all the themes already discussed, but clues to the immediate reasons lie in the Milan magistrates' initially slow pace in investigating abuses and in Bossi's statement about De Pietro breaking stones in Sardinia. In addition, the April 1992 elections weakened the DC-PSI power system.

Initially, voter irritation was still muted. The four parties of the governing coalition had a majority of seats in the House—331 out of 624. However the margin was too small to permit the traditional clan warfare. Moreover the coalition won only 47.1 percent of the vote, the DC's share went down by 4.6 percent, and the PSI's record of improving in each election was broken, as its share declined from 14.3 to 13.6 percent. The parties of responsible opposition also fared badly. The Republicans increased their share of the vote by a mere 0.7 percent to 4.4 percent, which was a poor reward for their withdrawal from the Andreotti government in 1991. It was a hint that the electorate was seeking parties that were more clearly new or different.

The PDS's 16.1 percent was a disappointment to Achille Occhetto. That the party had survived the collapse of world Communism was testimony to his courage in changing its name and symbol, as well as to Berlinguer's sense of the state and to Togliatti's heresies. The 5.6 percent lost to Rifondazione Comunista was evidence of the PCI's orthodoxy. The criticism that could be leveled against Occhetto is that he made the change so hesitantly that he lost the chance—if it ever existed—to create a broader Left around the PDS.[3] This problem recurred two years later.

By contrast the parties of protest, such as RC, fared well. Best of all was the Lega, whose performance was a death blow to the DC in northern Italy. The MSI's share went down by 0.5 percent, which demonstrates that the causes of its 1994 success were not yet present. But these three parties, along with the Rete, the Verdi, and the remnants of the Partito radicale gained 25.3 percent of the vote.

Voter irritation was heightened by the state of the economy. To return to the "why now?" question, the specific reason for the anger with the social services was that their cost was much greater. Government revenue as a percentage of

GDP had risen from 33.3 percent in 1980 to 43.3 percent in 1991. In general the contradictions of Andreotti's government had grown sharper. The debt had increased over 20 years and by 1992 it stood at 103 percent of GDP. One of the effects was pressure on the lira, which had to be defended with special care because in December 1991 Italy had signed the Maastricht agreement with its commitment to monetary union. This required austerity, yet Andreotti allowed domestic spending to continue, which drove up inflation. It reached 6.2 percent in 1991, which was 3.5 percent higher than the Maastricht guidelines. However, despite domestic demand, because of the world recession, exports were declining, which caused rising unemployment in the northern industries.[4]

It was growing harder to find room to maneuver within the confines of the EC requirements. In harmony with the trend toward independent central banks, the government gave the Bank of Italy freedom to set the discount rate in January 1992. In the previous October it had given the banks greater control over the use of their required reserves. This was part of a package to enable Italian banks to compete once free trade in services was introduced by the Internal Market. However both innovations reduced the government's ability to finance its debt. Here again public concern about the economy was muted and the financial crisis came only in the summer.

In the meantime the old regime demonstrated the blows it was receiving in the election of the President and the choice of Prime Minister. The CAF arrangement that Craxi should take the second post and either Forlani or Andreotti the former, was undermined by three factors. The parliamentary majority was too exiguous to tolerate the clan divisions. The Milan magistrates were undermining the position of the DC and the PSI. The Mafia strategy of confronting the state, which took the form of murdering Giovanni Falcone on May 23, forced the regime to change.

As if to demonstrate that the order could no longer function, President Cossiga resigned after the election. This disturbed the plan that he would ask Craxi to form a government, after which the Socialists would concede the presidency to the DC. So the presidential voting took place before the trade-offs had been made. The splits within the DC, where Forlani's leadership was contested by the reformist Segni, by the "left-wing" faction of De Mita and, more discreetly, by Andreotti's supporters, dragged out the process, which was not in itself unusual. But the revelations of corruption created a demand for that elusive creature, a clean candidate. Oscar Luigi Scalfaro's election became possible. The Mafia promoted it when they killed Falcone; his murder triggered a moral revulsion that made further intrigues appear scandalous.

It is unlikely that the Mafia sought to influence the presidential choice. The murder was part of a war with the state that stemmed from the breakdown of complicity. Over the next two years this strategy would provoke an energetic response from segments of the judicial and political class. Its effects would be to further damage the DC, as evidence of its former complicity emerged, and to drive the state toward reform. The Mafia has also suffered severe defeats. However the outcome of this war, as of so many other matters discussed in this chapter, remains uncertain.

The reasons for the decline of complicity may be sought in the behavior of both the Mafia and the DC. Until the 1980s the Mafia had lived by the rule that it "should not make war on the state."[5] Then the overlapping factors of the huge sums of money brought by the drug trade and the coming to power of the militaristic Corleonesi, led by Totò Riina, made the rule obsolete. The Mafia had always sought to deal with the state as an equal; now if equality were refused, there would be war.

The very ferocity of the Corleonesi made it difficult for the government to grant what they wanted—impunity or at least light sentences. Other obstacles were Italian public opinion, especially after organized crime moved north, and pressure from the EC. Helmut Kohl's rhetorical question was typical, while the Maastricht plan for closer cooperation among Ministries of the Interior and police forces reduced the space for delicate compromises.

For these and other reasons the convictions at the mass trial of 1986 were not overturned in the appeals courts and Salvo Lima was killed. This was a warning. Falcone, who knew so much about the Mafia, was killed next and then came Paolo Borsellino. The bombings in Florence, Rome, and Milan during the summer of 1993 were committed by the Mafia. Riina has been nothing if not consistent: in May 1994 he indicated Luciano Violante, Giancarlo Caselli, who replaced Borsellino in Palermo, and Pino Arlacchi as Communists and as enemies to be dispatched.[6] The resort to warfare does not mean that the Mafia has given up the quest for allies within the political and legal system. It is pursuing both strategies, believing that fear will spur complicity.

Meanwhile a furious Craxi was forced to recognize that the Milan scandals were an insuperable obstacle to his being designated Prime Minister. He made way for his advisor, Giuliano Amato, at the head of the four-party coalition. Although the new government looked like so many old governments, it was different. First, there was no alternative to it. Throughout the postwar years governing coalitions had been made and unmade but the principles on which they rested—DC leadership, PCI exclusion, proportional representation—remained inviolate. Now these were vanishing, but the elections had brought no new potential rulers. The PRI and the PDS had no desire to be branded by the Lega or RC as the saviors of a discredited regime. Within the coalition the clans had to expend all their energy on trying to escape prison, so they had none left to challenge Amato. This liberated the government in its economic policy.

The second novelty was the Prime Minister himself. Amato was an intelligent reformist, the author of a 1990 law on banking that opened the way to privatization and reversed the 1936 law that forbade banks to hold shares in industry. He was also Craxi's collaborator for whom Socialist corruption held no secrets. From June 1992 to April 1993 Amato watched as the men with whom he had worked were politically destroyed. Within his own party alone De Michelis, Andò, and Di Donato were placed under investigation. The PSI's deputy leader, Claudio Martelli, made a doomed attempt to reform the party before suddenly abandoning politics in February. Craxi was allowed to hang on far too long as Secretary and, even after he resigned, parliament voted in April not to remove his immunity. Five party secretaries had to be replaced in the lifetime of the Amato government, and ministers—De Lorenzo was only the most serious case—departed regularly at the behest of magistrates.

Yet even as he presided over the death throes of postwar Italy, Amato made a brave attempt to tackle the economic crisis. In the summer of 1992 the contradictions of Andreotti's policy exploded: the projected deficit stood at $120 billion and the lira was exposed. Amato responded with measures to cut the deficit by $20 billion. Some of his fiscal maneuvers were one-off, as opposed to structural, and of dubious legality, such as the tax imposed on bank accounts. However Amato also attempted structural reforms. In a July 31 agreement the government endorsed an employer-union plan to scrap wage indexation. This prepared the way for the July 1993 agreement, which outlined a new framework for collective bargaining.

In September Amato produced a package that included severe cuts in social spending, especially in health care and pensions. Although attacked by the PDS, RC, and the unions as unjust, the package and the follow-up 1993 budget both limited the financial damage and at least tackled underlying Italian problems. Health care was to be administered by the local and regional authorities but financed by the central government; Amato transferred the responsibility for controlling costs to the regions. Budgetary overruns were to be financed from their resources, but they were granted some increased autonomy in taxation. This was a step toward uniting the functions of administration and finance and toward a more real decentralization. In the sphere of pensions Amato raised the general retirement age, cut back indexation, and tried to reduce the opportunity for early retirement. He took a tiny step toward abolishing the special pensions that the DC had used for clientelistic purposes. To deal with income tax evasion, rampant among self-employed professionals, Amato imposed a minimum tax on the self-employed.[7]

In September he froze public sector salaries, which in 1991 had risen by 8 percent and in 1990 by 18 percent. In the 1993 budget he changed the structure of public sector pay. He reduced parliament's power to grant increases, subjected pay to civil not administrative law, set up an autonomous body to negotiate with the public sector unions, encouraged the kind of contracts used in the private sector, and tried to link wages to productivity. The budget also contained a clause requiring parliament to provide financial coverage for any new expenditure it passed.

The principles of financial responsibility and of disciplining the public sector, which underlay these measures, mark an attempt to reform the over-worked state and to give more responsibility to civil society. Amato was unfortunate in that such principles, which signaled a break with DC rule and would guide the Ciampi government, were overshadowed by popular resentment of austerity that inevitably hit poor people hardest. To the demonstrators who thronged the piazzas the rewards were all the less clear because financial problems continued. Thus while government spending excluding interest on the debt did not exceed revenue for the first time in 30 years, interest payments were so high that the 1992 deficit was 10.7 percent of GDP, the same figure as 1991, while the debt rose from 103 percent to 108 percent of GDP. Nor did the austerity measures save the lira, which was first devalued by 7 percent and then forced out of the EMS in September 1992.

The total devaluation amounted to around 20 percent and it was the start of a long-term, export-fueled revival, in which small companies demonstrated the same dynamism as in the 1970s. For this Amato can take no credit, although his reforms of the public sector must in the long run help private employers. He was tough enough to terminate the economic fiction of EFIM, even if a plan to repay creditors with long-term government bonds paying submarket rates caused outrage in the international financial world and had to be withdrawn. His government drafted a plan for extensive privatization of banks and industrial companies; this continued his 1990 law and was in part enacted by Ciampi.

The rewards of austerity were present if not evident. By October 1993 inflation was running at 4.2 percent, 1 percent below the pre-devaluation rate, while the increase in unit labor costs declined steadily from 7.6 percent in 1991 to 3 percent in the first half of 1993. The discount rate, which had been raised to 15 percent in September 1992, stood at 11 percent when Amato left office. The price of austerity was a worsened recession: in the second half of 1992 GDP dropped by an annualized rate of 1.2 percent, the first decline in a decade.

The immediate political consequences of the crisis and Amato's handling of it were to reinforce the Clean Hands revelations by increasing popular anger with the political class. Another result was to make unemployment a central concern: between mid-1992 and mid-1993 the unemployment percentage rose from 11.1 to 13.1. In companies employing more than 500 people employment was reduced by 6 percent and the number of hours covered by the Cassa Integrazione Guadagni (CIG), which provides compensation for the temporarily unemployed, was increased by 23 percent.[8] While unemployment heightened political protest, it marked a more significant shift. Economic issues rather than corruption or institutional reform would decide the 1994 elections.

In the winter of 1992-93 Italy was living through the destruction of the old political order. Local elections made clear the fate of the DC and the PSI. In September support for the DC went down by 7.7 percent in Mantua and in December it dropped by 6.1 percent in Monza. Even more ominous was its 7.3 percent decline in Reggio Calabria, which revealed that its southern bastion was crumbling. The MSI's share of the vote leaped from 8.4 percent to 16.6 percent, a harbinger of its success the next year.

The DC attempted reform and Mino Martinazzoli, who was untouched by the Clean Hands investigation, became party Secretary on October 12, 1992. But the old leaders were tainted by more than bribery. In March 1993 Gava's ties to the Camorra were exposed, while in April Andreotti's parliamentary immunity was removed so that the investigation into his links with the Mafia could go ahead. Forlani's Secretary was dragged off to prison in chains and Forlani himself would reappear, reluctantly, in the Enimont trial. Clientelism had turned against the DC. However, the party retained two assets. The first was the Church, which continued to see the DC as the main instrument of its power. The second was Mario Segni, who was leading the battle for institutional reform. To the chagrin of the Council of Bishops, Segni left the DC on March 29, 1993, declaring that it could not be reformed; however, the Church hoped Segni might repent and acted to ensure that he did.

The PSI had no such assets so it simply disintegrated. In the local elections it lost 25 percent of its previous vote and was severely punished in Lombardy. In Varese its share plunged from 10.6 percent to 4.2 percent and in Monza from 12.9 percent to 5.5 percent. It too attempted reform with first Giorgio Benvenuto and then Ottaviano del Turco as Secretary, but its attempt to use union leaders to revive popular support failed.

Once more the PDS, which presented itself as the party of responsible opposition, was unable to win the mass of DC or PSI votes. It did, however, suffer far less than its rivals, losing only 2 percent in Mantua. Occhetto's task was to demonstrate that the PDS-PCI, while it had been tainted with corruption, stood outside the DC power system. In general he was successful. The Milan branch had sinned, but this could be blamed on the Right of the party, one of whose leaders, Gianni Cervetti, was placed under investigation. The role of the PCI-PDS in obtaining public contracts for the red cooperatives and of the co-ops in steering profits back to the party was frequently cited, but did not become a major issue until December 1994. The Ferruzzi group had paid a large bribe to a PCI official, Primo Greganti, but he swore he had kept the money for himself; he was either a rogue or the model Communist militant. The PDS leaders had not enriched themselves personally. The memory of Berlinguer counted for something and Occhetto never failed publicly to praise the magistrates.

So the PDS became by default the only strong party in Italy. It had the opportunity, which it had been seeking since its 1989-91 transformation, to become the cutting edge of a Left-Center coalition. Conversely the prospect of a PDS-led government would galvanize the Right. 1993 was Occhetto's year, 1994 would be Berlusconi's.

In the local elections of late 1992 protest continued to dominate. In Varese the Lega, whose share jumped 9 percent to 37 percent, had more votes than the DC, PSI, and PDS combined. RC and the Rete also performed well. In March 1993 the Amato government discovered how strong the mood of anger was. The magistrates were methodically mowing down Italy's elites and it seemed they might never stop. Whether in a desperate attempt to halt them, or because genuine problems had arisen, such as the backlog of trials and the unemployment in the construction industry that stemmed from the blocked public contracts, the Minister of Justice, Giovanni Conso, produced a decree. It transformed the illegal financing of parties from a crime, punishable according to the usual procedures, into a an offense that could be canceled by repayment, a fine, and a five-year ban on holding office. The PDS and the Lega did not need to organize opposition. An outraged public understood only that the politicians were granting themselves an amnesty. Fury ran so high that the decree was swiftly forgotten, while Amato offered to resign.[9]

He stayed until April 18. As in 1991 the referendum was the means of making the changes that the parliamentary majority sought to block, and institutional reform was the road to political reform. The author of the referendum, which called for senate elections to use the British, winner-take-all system for 75 percent of the seats with the remaining 25 percent left to proportional representation, was once more Mario Segni, who was backed again by the PDS. Their goal was to create something like the two-party system, to bring about a clear electoral victor, and to give the voter rather than the party secretaries the power to choose the government. The electorate understood this: The turnout was high—77 percent—and the yes vote won by 83 percent to 17 percent. It was accepted that the method of voting for the House would be altered too and with the end of full proportional representation (PR) another pillar of the old regime came crashing down.

The series of events in April—the referendum, Amato's resignation, and the disgrace of Andreotti—marked the end of the first period within the 1992 to 1994 years. Already in 1992 Censis saw "a growing need for leadership."[10] People wanted *organization,* a word that Berlusconi would use frequently.

OCCHETTO RULES!

The demise of the old regime was reflected in the choice of Carlo Azeglio Ciampi as Prime Minister. Ciampi was not a politician and as President of the Bank of Italy he was the leader of almost the only elite that had not been mown down. The bank was historically suspicious of the political class, which it considered uneducated and spendthrift. So Ciampi brought economists into his government who moved in the bank's orbit, like Luigi Spaventa, or who had been marginalized by their parties, like Beniamino Andreatta. Romano Prodi returned to head up IRI. This was supposed to be a transitional government, which would supervise the change of voting procedures and organize elections to renew a delegitimized parliament. In fact it remained in office nearly a year and took significant action. Its transitional character freed it from the parties, which were now preoccupied not just with staying out of jail but with the elections.

In June local elections were held in Milan, Turin, Catania, and many smaller towns. They used the new electoral method—direct election of the mayor and two rounds of voting—that the parliament had passed in March. As well as marking a shift of power from center to periphery, this new method offered a trial run for the parliamentary elections because it entailed coalition-building. Since the Lega sought no allies and could not have found them and since the DC was in chaos, coalition-building was the prerogative of the Left—RC, the Rete, and the PDS—of the Center-Left—the Republicans and Alleanza Democratica (AD)—and of Segni's dissident Christian Democrats.

The campaign demonstrated that the key alliance of the referenda, that between Segni and Occhetto, was fragile. The two came together in Catania behind the Republican who won, Enzo Bianco, but more often they disagreed, as in Milan where both lost. This failure, which would help shape the 1994 elections, was not just another example of the fragmentation of Italian culture. Some of the problems were inherent in coalition-building: Segni had a wider following as an individual, while the PDS had a more powerful organization. If the two were to come together in a structure such as the AD, then Segni wanted the dissolution of existing party organizations into a broad movement that he would head. Occhetto, however, having spent two years persuading his rank and file to transform the PCI into the PDS, could hardly now ask them to give up their new home.

But the breakup of the referenda alliance, which did not occur officially until the fall, was caused by such factors as Occhetto's refusal to break with the RC and the pressure that the Church placed on Segni. These were signs of a deeper incompatibility that continued to separate the ex-Communists from the post–Vatican II Catholics. If they were to shape the new regime as they had shaped the old—by their co-operative antagonism—the heirs of Togliatti and De Gasperi, and of Berlinguer and Moro, would this time have to work together. But they could not, and their failure would open the door to Berlusconi. Their old differences took new forms: abortion replaced atheism.

Still, the PDS emerged as the chief winner in the June elections. In its traditional territory it swept the towns of Ravenna, Ancona, and Siena, while in the South it once again became the second party and surprised itself by its performance in Campania. It spearheaded the coalition that won Turin for Valentino Castellani after he had run 16 percent behind Diego Novelli of the Rete on the first round. Turin and Catania proved that Occhetto was a talented alliance-builder.

However the victory masked weaknesses. In Milan and Turin the PDS won only 9.5 percent and 8.8 percent of the vote, running behind RC to which it lost much of its working-class support. Then too the successful candidates it supported were well to the right: Castellani was a Catholic who was also endorsed by Agnelli. The collapse of the DC had left a huge space that centrist, PDS-backed candidates could occupy. That did not mean the PDS itself could occupy this space, or that a Center-Right party would not emerge to compete for it.

The mood in the country was changing, perhaps in response to institutional reform. Able to cast a "real" vote, the electorate rewarded competence as well as protest. This was evident in Milan, where Marco Formentini won in part because he was challenged from what was perceived as the Far Left, the Rete's Nando dalla Chiesa, and in part because he projected a practical image. The Lega swept across the North. It was the largest party in Vercelli, Novara, Pavia, and many smaller towns, as well as in the region of Friuli-Venezia Giulia. Its anti-statist discourse was all the more popular because of the corruption revelations. However the Lega faced difficulties: the local elections revealed that it too needed allies—in Novara its 26.8 percent was nearly 10 percent ahead of any other party but it was 5 percent behind the Left coalition—and it had to now demonstrate that it could govern.

For the DC the elections were a disaster outside the South. Another warning came in Trieste as the party's share dropped from 22.4 percent to 14 percent, while the MSI's rose to 17.1 percent from 12.2 percent. In Sicily, however, the DC held on to Agrigento and remained the largest party in Catania. Although its share of the vote declined, the DC remained strong south of Rome with around 30 percent of the electorate. However as corruption revelations merged with reports of ties to organized crime and as sources of clientelism dried up, the DC faced the greatest difficulties of the three parties.

The November-December round of local elections confirmed this. Over the summer the Church had made it clear to Segni that it was backing Martinazzoli and that it would do its utmost to prevent him from gathering Catholic support.[11] The result of Segni's painful meditations was that he broke with Occhetto and with AD, but he did not rejoin the DC. Thus he weakened the Left, isolated himself, and did not help his old party.

Martinazzoli soldiered on, but in the local elections the DC collapsed in the South. In Remo Gaspari's stronghold of Chieti the MSI, whose share jumped from 25 percent to 36 percent, took over the council. The neo-Fascists won four provincial capitals—the others being Benevento, Latina, and Caltanissetta—and became with 16.4 percent the fourth largest party in Italy. Not only were the DC's losses in the South severe—in Caserta its share dropped by 30 percent—but in the mayoral races of Rome and Naples it could not present serious candidates. In Naples it ended up endorsing Togliatti's ex-Secretary, Massimo Caprara, while in both cities it was eliminated on the first round. On the second round its votes were split evenly between the MSI and left-wing candidates. Gianfranco Fini's 47 percent in Rome and Alessandra Mussolini's 43 percent in Naples marked the MSI's success in supplanting the DC.

The Left not only won both cities but also swept Venice, Trieste, Genova, and Palermo, where Leoluca Orlando was elected on the first round. Genova reinforced the lesson of alliances to the Lega because its vote rose 15 percent to 29 percent and it became the largest party, yet it lost the mayoral race to the Left's candidate, Adriano Sansa. These elections were Occhetto's triumph and yet they revealed the PDS's weaknesses. Of all the new mayors only Antonio Bassolino was a leading PDS exponent, while in Trieste Riccardo Illy was an entrepreneur—an example for Berlusconi? Both he and Sansa were Centrist candidates operating with scant opposition from the Center-Right. Moreover the specter of a Left-Center government hegemonized by the ex-Communists would and did galvanize Berlusconi. He understood that many Italians were voting for clean faces and competence, that they were not quite ready to vote Lega or MSI, but that they were unenthusiastic about the PDS. Finally the size of the voting swings revealed how mobile the electorate was. Occhetto's rule would be short-lived.

STATE VERSUS MAFIA

Throughout 1993 the war on the Mafia continued under both the Amato and Ciampi governments. In January Totò Riina was arrested after long years "on the run." In fact many Mafiosi who were fugitives from justice had simply gone on living in their home neighborhoods. Like other citizens, they sent their children to state schools. When they met policemen, each looked the other way; a policeman who hunted down fugitives was likely to be murdered.[12] Those glances of nonrecognition were the mark that the state in fact recognized the Mafia's role in the postwar order.

Riina's arrest after long years of tranquil existence in Palermo marked a break. It did not change Mafia strategy, which continued, under Bernardo Provenzano, the new Corleonese leader, to emphasize military struggle. Tommaso Buscetta considered this an error and argued with unconscious irony that Riina was destroying Cosa Nostra. The chairman of the Anti-Mafia Commission, Luciano Violante, agreed, stating that the campaign against the Mafia was going well because "institutions and civil society have now grown very aware" of the Mafia threat.[13] Citizen support in Sicily and more efficient work by police and magistrates who were sure of government backing were the marks of a state that was no longer absent and did not inspire in its population merely distrust.

The state's victories over organized crime took several forms. The most obvious was the wave of arrests, which led to the jailing of Nitto Santapaola, the Catania chieftain, and Carmine Alfieri, who decided to collaborate with the authorities. Then too a blitz in January 1994 led to the arrest of 62 members of the 'ndrangheta who were operating in Lombardy, and, significantly, the first initiative taken by the Lega Minister of the Interior, Roberto Maroni, was another onslaught on the Lombardy 'ndrangheta in June 1994.

Just as important has been the peeling away of the Mafia's allies. The trial of Bruno Contrada drew attention to the overlap between segments of the secret service and the Mafia. Violante's report dealt with Mafia infiltration of Free Masonry, while the issue of the Church and the Mafia was posed dramatically in the autumn of 1993. A priest working in a poor parish of Palermo was murdered and, conversely, allegations of complicity were leveled against Bishop Salvatore Cassisa of Monreale, who was called a close friend of Salvo Lima. Nor did magistrates escape. A dramatic moment occurred in the revelations of the Camorrista who turned state's evidence, Pasquale Galasso, when he told the Campania magistrates, "Gentlemen, many of you are not cops, many of you are on our side."[14]

The most controversial subject of the investigation has been the Mafia's links with the DC and in particular with Giulio Andreotti. This includes the allegations that the Mafia may have murdered two men as favors to Andreotti: Mino Pecorelli, who ran a blackmailing newsletter, and Alberto Dalla Chiesa, who supposedly had compromising evidence on Andreotti's behavior during the Moro kidnapping—although the Mafia had ample reasons of its own to want Dalla Chiesa dead. The Andreotti faction in Sicily has been described as "polluting political, social and institutional life," and Andreotti has been called the political leader who "for a long period assured the continuation of Mafia power."[15] According to this view Andreotti was trapped in his 1989-92 prime ministership by anti-Mafia opinion and obliged to take such measures as sending 41 Mafiosi back to prison whom Corrado Carnevale had released on appeal.

Although the state's sudden success was the result of new tactics, like the encouragement offered to arrested Mafiosi to collaborate with justice and the choice of good personnel (including Giancarlo Caselli), the real difference was public opinion. Violante notes that the state cannot maintain its effort simply by relying on its servants—the police and magistrates—but needs a strong public opinion to keep ministers' focussed and to outweigh the political forces that encourage complicity. Thus two dangers lay in wait for the Berlusconi government.

The first was that by reacting against left-wingers like Violante, Forza Italia would seize on errors made by the present anti-Mafia apparatus and weaken the campaign. Berlusconi's Minister of Justice, Alfredo Biondi, was both a lawyer, accustomed to seeing the plaintiff's viewpoint, and a survivor of the old regime that had indulged in complicity. Tiziana Parenti, who became head of the Anti-Mafia Commission, offered legitimate criticism of the reliance on the Mafiosi who repent. When they attacked Violante as a Communist, Berlusconi's supporters were, however unwittingly, following Riina who, when he named Violante, Caselli, and Pino Arlacchi as targets, also branded them as Communists.[16]

The second danger was that the Mafia would succeed in infiltrating Forza Italia. That it was trying to do so was certain, given its history. FI's ally, the Centro Cristiano Democratico, sent to parliament two ex-followers of Andreotti from Messina, while at least one of Lima's acquaintances was elected directly by FI.[17] This does not mean FI members supported the Mafia, merely that, as Tiziana Parenti stated, the danger of infiltration was very real.[18] Fresh evidence of Mafia help for FI and AN candidates emerged in January 1995. Conversely threats were made against local, left-wing officials. Although the Mafia's political alliances are grounded in pure self-interest, its history as an organization that defended the landowners makes it inclined to favor the Right, while political opposition has in recent years come more from the Left, notably from the Rete and the PDS. I shall return to this topic in chapter 9.

THE CHANGING ITALIAN ECONOMY

The economic policy of the Ciampi government continued Amato's policy and was based on the same principle—that austerity must be accompanied by structural change. Priority went to cutting government spending, which was scheduled to produce a 1994 deficit of less than 10 percent of GDP. If interest costs are taken out, spending ran at 1.8 percent below revenue. To deal with the interest payments Ciampi concentrated on reducing rates: the interest on a five-year government bond went down from 11.7 percent to 7.5 percent during his year in office.

The recession had bottomed out and in 1993 Italy ran a balance of payments surplus of $12 billion, as opposed to a deficit of $22 billion in 1992. In the last quarter GDP was running at +3.2 percent, as opposed to -1.8 percent in the first quarter. However unemployment remained high with the historic regional differences: a national figure of 11.3 percent broke down into 7.7 percent for the Center-North and 18.9 percent for the South. The working class continued to change and to shrink as there was a 7.1 percent decline in blue-collar employment, compared with a 3.6 percent decline in white-collar jobs. The overall figure of -5.5 percent explains why Berlusconi's promise of a million jobs was so seductive.[19]

The Ciampi government's greatest achievement was the July agreement on incomes policy and bargaining, which set up a new tripartite structure for collective bargaining. Employers gained concessions in labor market flexibility, such as greater freedom to use temporary workers and lower entry wages for jobs in which training was given. Unions gained stronger representation rights at the plant level, although local pay increases were to be awarded only when they were in step with profits. Most important, a bienniel meeting of government, employers, and employees is to set a low target of inflation with provisions for reducing public indebtedness and maintaining employment levels. In this context a national incomes policy will be designed.[20]

It is tempting, although premature and exaggerated, to see in the July 1993 agreement the model of a national community. Premature because the new system was strained in the fall of 1994, and exaggerated because, as already argued, the bargaining power of unions was weak. However, the "Austrian" solution had come to Italy.

As the large companies have been recovering from the recession and taking fresh shape, Enrico Cuccia's role has been significant once more . He attracted the magistrates' interest for his handling of the Ferruzzi collapse but nothing came of this inquiry. Cuccia benefited from the extinction of DC-backed finance, from the recession, which has compelled companies to turn back to him, and from the privatization program. He has used these boons to outline a financial and industrial order that is recognizably his and is designed to enable northern Italian companies to survive in the world economy.

The ills of the elite were not all the same. Ferruzzi suffered from Gardini's megalomania, family knavery, and too much diversification. Many of its component companies were solid, including Eridania Béghin-Say and Himont. Pirelli needed time to recover from its failed invasion of Germany. Salvatore Ligresti's property empire was tottering, while his dealings with ENI and with Craxi brought him a spell in prison in 1992. But here again Ligresti's insurance company, SAI, was solid.

Fiat was hit by the international slump in demand for cars and exhibited the special fragility of Italian capitalism. Traditionally too dependent on the Italian market, its share of that market dropped from 60 percent to 40 percent over four years. In the first half of 1993 its sales of cars declined by 11.7 percent, while industrial vehicles plummeted 15.9 percent. Losses for the year ran to more than $1 billion and the prospect of future Japanese competition was ominous.

With Cuccia's advice, Fiat devised a strategy that left it a family firm, but slightly less so. Meanwhile it obtained all the help it could from the Italian state, but became more independent of it. In September 1993 came the announcement that Gianni Agnelli and Romiti, who had been expected to retire, were staying on to reassure the markets. Into the shareholders pact came two newcomers, Alcatel and Deutsche Bank, while existing Italian partners, like Mediobanca itself and the Generali, reinforced their position. The reshuffle was important because, while Fiat remained a family firm, the family no longer ruled alone. On the board it had seven votes out of 11, but nine were required for a majority. The entry of Alcatel and Deutsche Bank marked a strengthening of foreign alliances.[21]

Next Fiat announced a capital increase of $3.5 billion, the largest ever by an Italian company. Part of the money was to be put up by existing shareholders, but a large chunk came from the market. In a rather dubious maneuver Rinascente shares were offered to Fiat shareholders, while the holding company's financial arm, IFIL, launched a takeover of Rinascente. This meant that without being asked IFIL shareholders were pumping money into Fiat and being saddled with Rinascente (which is, however, in good health).

Then in January 1994 Fiat announced plans to lay off 14,000 workers, 6,000 permanently and 8,000 because of the decline in demand. The Church criticized the company but Fiat responded that at its Melfi plant it was creating 7,000 jobs directly and 4,000 more among its suppliers. With increasing unemployment and with an election at hand, the government had to intervene.

The tripartite agreement provided a package of early retirement, solidarity contracts, and CIG, which protected most of the jobs. Some of the provisions looked feeble: the Arese plant in Milan was kept open to work on ecologically safer, primarily electrical, cars. Arese's chances of remaining open appear slight, while the Naples plant is to do nothing but process worn-out cars. Even in Turin, where jobs were saved at Mirafiori, Fiat looks less central.[22]

Of Fiat's 261,000 workers, 100,000 are employed outside Italy, especially in low-wage countries like Poland. Does this mean that Fiat is bent on abandoning Italy or on becoming a nomad multinational? Far from it. The Italian state has once more proved generous. Its share of the job-saving packet runs at about $100 million; it is putting up money for the electric cars and local authorities are likely buyers. Moreover total aid for Melfi is expected to come to more than $1 billion. Yet Fiat can respond that its investment program comes to around $7.5 billion.[23]

Luigi Luzzatti would have understood this cooperation between company and government. Combined with a strong, if less dominant family presence, it is the Italian way of confronting the world economy. The entry of Alcatel and Deutsche Bank will push Fiat toward greater internationalization, perhaps toward a joint venture or even a merger with Renault. Fiat's goal is to diminish its reliance on the Italian market by selling half of its new cars, the Puntos, abroad. Cogefar has been separated from the group, which is a signal—although not a proof—that illicit relations with the political class are to be discouraged.

The Italian road toward internationalization is being mapped out by Enrico Cuccia, who stitched together the new Fiat shareholders pact. The disappearance of the DC could have brought the decline of Cuccia if, as countless Anglo-Saxons have observed,[24] he and the DC had complemented each other and worked together to prevent the emergence of a broader capitalism. Cuccia's power may yet decline because forces pressing for an Anglo-Saxon system are strong, but this has not happened yet. As with Fiat it seems that Cuccia is helping strengthen Italy in a more open financial world.

The end of the DC-PSI coalitions damaged the publicized economy and made possible the privatizations. Some companies, like the Nuovo Pignone, were sold to suitable bidders, in this case General Electric. Others, like the Credito Italiano, were placed on the market, with a block of shares reserved for institutional investors and the rest for the general public.

This provoked an enormous and misleading dispute that pitted Romano Prodi, the DC Left with which he is associated, the PDS, and most Anglo-Saxon commentators against Cuccia, the Milan-Turin families, and Giorgio La Malfa. The former group called for popular capitalism with the widest possible distribution of shares, while the latter preferred "hard cores" that would control the banks. Prodi tried to achieve his ends by restricting the number of shares that any group could buy in Credito or Comit to 3 percent. When the dust had settled, it was discovered that Cuccia had put together a web of interlocking companies that, by buying 10 to 15 percent of the shares, controlled the banks.[25]

Supporters of popular capitalism pointed out that in Italy only 6 percent of families owned shares, whereas in France the figure was 14 percent. They noted that only 5 percent of Italian companies were quoted on the stock market, while the French figure was 15 percent. However this was misleading because, while it would be advisable for Italy to have many more small shareholders, Credito and Comit had plenty. The government should take and has taken steps to encourage popular investment, such as pushing the Consob to improve the flow of information and passing the January 1992 law that regulates the Società di Intermediazione Mobiliare or multifunctional investment firms. But small investors could not run Comit.

Prodi was on safer ground when he spoke of creating more big companies and more merchant banks to resolve Italy's historic problem of having too many dwarfs and not enough giants. Of the world's 500 largest companies Britain has 43 and Italy only 7. But to achieve the goal of strengthening Cuccia's rivals, Prodi should have had alternative bidders for Comit and Credito who represented powerful financial interests. None emerged. In the Anglo-Saxon world such interests are frequently pension funds that entrust the companies, in which they hold blocks of shares, to professional managers. This system has its defects, but arguably it makes for greater financial power and a more intense search for profits. So the law of April 22, 1993, which sets up and regulates private pension programs, may be the most important move Italy has made toward widening its financial markets.[26]

Here may be the future, alternative sources of power to Mediobanca. However Cuccia can hardly be blamed for taking control of Credito and Comit when no rivals challenged him. As for pension funds, Cuccia is busy tightening his links with the Generali and regaining control of Fondiaria. If insurance companies become even more important, then he will be ready. His aim in gaining control of Comit and staffing it with his protégés, such as Enrico Beneduce, the grandson of Alberto Beneduce, is to form a vast financial bloc that can play a role in world finance and in the new industries. Cuccia is watching the privatization of Stet, IRI's profitable telecommunications company.[27]

In forming his bloc he has foreign allies like the Deutsche Bank, Lazard Frères, Commerzbank, which bought into Comit, and Allianz, which bought into Credito Italiano. He continues to reach outside his traditional circle of friends to the medium-sized entrepreneurs like Luciano Benetton, Diego Della Valle (of Tod's shoes), and Achille Maramotti (of Max Mara), whom he wishes to bring into Gemina, Credito, or Comit.[28] The sons of Romiti and Cefis work in Mediobanca. Is this merely another example of the tyranny of the family or a renewed attempt to create an establishment?

Once more there is no need to overestimate Cuccia's importance, since the vast majority of Italian companies flourish outside his empire, or to create the counter-myth of Cuccia as a selfless patriot. In order to preserve the dominance of Mediobanca, Cuccia has limited the power of Fincomit, Comit's merchant bank, which is a potential rival.[29] Prodi and the PDS were right to insert into the new privatization projects regulations that allow minority shareholders to be represented. The Lega is right to grumble that Cuccia pays scant attention to small business. But it remains true that Cuccia, the dirigist without a state, is using traditional methods to modernize Italian finance.

His relationship with Prime Minister Berlusconi is intriguing. In what seemed the start of an alliance Mediobanca was asked to usher Mondadori onto the stock market, but in mid-1994 the old coolness between the two very different men seemed to return.[30]

THE 1994 ELECTIONS: A DEBATE ABOUT THE STATE

Behind the intricate struggles among the political parties lay several visions of how the Italian state ought to work. To oversimplify, the doomed Centrists of the PPI–Patto Segni offered a clean version of the DC state mediating between the market and the populace. The left-wing Progressisti axed their entire campaign on a reform that would create a state that administers less and governs more; they also offered economic continuity with Ciampi. As already explained, the Lega sought to terminate the overworked state by forming an Italian union. Alleanza Nazionale (AN) called generically for a stronger Italy. Forza Italia (FI) offered a neoliberal critique of the state combined with an appeal to entrepreneurial creativity. Although all these projects were full of gaps and contradictions, all demanded an end to the overbearing state and the publicized economy. Moreover the electorate was offered a choice, albeit highly distorted, between the principal options of the Progressisti and FI.

After a final flirt with the Lega in January 1994, Segni returned not to Martinazzoli's rebaptized Partito Popolare Italiano, but to an alliance with it. The Church blessed the PPI–Patto Segni formation, but its help was a shadow of its 1948 effort. The DC past and the new electoral system spelled doom for the Catholics. They retained only 53 percent of the people who had voted DC in 1992,[31] while Segni suffered the extra humiliation of losing his Sassari constituency. The winner-take-all method squeezed the Centrists in a way all too familiar to Paddy Ashdown: with 15.7 percent of the votes, they gained approximately 7 percent of the seats. In Toni Bisaglia's Veneto they were left with four seats, the once white region with its small entrepreneurs going over to Forza Italia. In Remo Gaspari's Abruzzo the PPI-Patto was reduced to 15.4 percent of the vote, while in Western Sicily it won only 14 percent, once more outdistanced by Forza Italia.

This electoral result along with the virtual disappearance of the PSI marked the transformation of Italian politics. The postwar order had begun under Catholic rule and it was ending with Catholic defeat. Martinazzoli resigned and was replaced by Rocco Buttiglione. Cardinal Ruini did not resign. Paradoxically, in a time of recession, the Church's voluntary organizations are more valuable than ever .

If the PPI's downfall was inevitable, the Left's defeat was more surprising. There was a spurious logic in the proposition that the crisis of the DC state would bring to power the DC's antagonist, the Progressisti. However if we accept that the 1993 triumphs were too easily won, then there is not much evidence of PDS or Progressisti strength. The PDS gained 4 percent more votes than in 1992 and remained the core of the Left. Its coalition partners were no great help. RC seemed to run its own campaign and Fausto Bertinotti played into the hands of the Right by calling for the taxation of government bonds and questioning NATO. At least RC existed and won 6 percent, whereas the Rete's 1.9 percent must surely lead to its demise. Alleanza Democratica had lost its reason for existence when Segni spurned it, and Ottaviano Del Turco's Socialists barely survived Craxi's disgrace. In total the PDS's smaller allies reached a mere 8 percent. The Right-Left split—Rete and RC against AD and PSI—and the Verdi's solo performance meant that the Progressisti spoke with many voices. Left-wing fragmentation therefore survived the end of the Cold War.

Another reason for the Left's defeat was the re-emergence of anti-Communism. In this supposedly de-ideologized age only the PDS had given up ideology. Silvio Berlusconi resorted to 1930s' language when he explained that he had entered politics to block a left-wing dictatorship. He offered this portrait of Massimo D'Alema: "He wore an unpleasant, threatening grimace. His thin moustache trembled with a hideous joy. I understood that he cared nothing for this country . . . nothing for the Italian family."[32] That Berlusconi should use such language is understandable, but why did it work?

One answer lies in the continuity between the new and the old—and even the older—regimes. Italian leaders from Mussolini to Craxi had disseminated anti-Communism. The PCI had ceased to exist only three years before and to many Italians Occhetto and D'Alema were tainted by their past. Moreover in the years 1993 to 1994 fear of chaos, inspired by the deteriorating economy and the disappearing elites, was at least as strong as the anger that had dominated in 1992 and 1993. Anti-Communism, which in a country that lacks the strong non-Communist, left-wing traditions present in France swiftly turned into hostility to the entire Left, offered security.

More important, the regime crisis was caused by a state that had expanded into all areas of society. At least in Northern Italy the electorate wished to repulse and punish the invading state. FI and the Lega could be trusted to do this, whereas the Left could not.

Herein lies a great irony. The PDS's program offers an excellent critique of the overbearing state. It diagnoses the real significance of corruption, which it defines as "a perverse mechanism that, on the one hand, has destroyed the state as regulator and guarantor of the general interest and, on the other, has strangled the forces of work and production."[33] It gives priority to the reconstruction of the state, which must be an arbiter—just and efficient but modest. In its promised war on unemployment, the PDS would not use public works or expansion of demand, but would seek, for example, to help the private sector grow by developing financial markets.

This is certainly the road Italy must take, but the PDS never succeeded in making its message credible. Its campaign was lackluster, partly because deficit reduction is not a theme that makes left-wing hearts beat faster. Occhetto spent much time reassuring the City of London and NATO, forgetting that British merchant bankers and Turkish colonels do not vote in Italian elections. Perhaps he had not lost the old PCI sense of illegitimacy. But the main reason for the Left's defeat was not its uninspired campaign, it was its inability to compete with Silvio Berlusconi's message. Both sides told the electorate that the state had failed them. The PDS offered to reform the state, Berlusconi offered also to substitute for it the dynamism of the entrepreneur. The PDS offered difficulty, whereas Berlusconi was optimistic. In the Italy of 1994 his message was more appealing.

The red belt felt differently. In Emilia-Romagna the PDS alone gained more votes than the entire Right—36.6 percent to 31.9 percent. The same was true of Tuscany where the Progressisti took 50.1 percent to the Right's 29.5 percent. The Left had mixed results in the South, carrying Campania, where the PDS was the largest party in Naples with 23 percent, but losing Puglia and also Sicily, where the anti-Mafia campaign did not carry over into the elections. Even more troubling to the Progressisti was the heavy defeat suffered in the "modern" regions of Lombardy and Piedmont.

The PDS proved unable to convince the discontented supporters of the old regime, winning fewer than 15 percent of the 1992 PSI voters and a mere

2.5 percent of DC voters. Its gain of roughly 4 percent seems to have come at the expense of its coalition partners: it won 16 percent of 1992 RC voters, 14 percent of Verdi's, and 16 percent of Rete's.

The result brought cries for Occhetto's resignation, which did not come until the European elections, when the PDS's share of the vote dropped 1 percent, while FI's rose by 10 percent. The choice of Massimo D'Alema marked a shift of style, but the problems of the PDS remained: how to cease being an ex-Communist Party, whether to ally with the Catholics, and how to project convincingly its vision of the reformed state. The questions would re-emerge in the governmental crisis of December 1994.

The MSI seemed an unlikely candidate for a major role in the new order. In the 1970s, when it achieved the 8.7 percent that so worried Berlinguer, it failed to capitalize on its success.[34] Old dilemmas were exacerbated: it was still torn between its roles as a southern, conservative party and as a radical spokesman for popular protest in areas like the outskirts of Rome. It continued to resolve the contradiction by remaining a Fascist party. In the 1980s it changed in two ways, neither of them decisive. The calmer mood both of Italian politics and of the study of Fascism made the MSI less of a pariah. The first sign that it might be accepted as a legitimate party came in 1983, when Craxi declared that it was not unconstitutional and that he was ready to bargain with it.

However, while this opened the door that had remained closed to Arturo Michelini, the MSI did not know how to respond. As the crisis of politics drew closer, the party felt that its Fascist identity was more valuable because it was the badge of its estrangement from the flagging DC-PSI system. So as before the MSI remained static, even when in the 1987 elections its vote dropped by nearly 1 percent to 5.9 percent. It ignored the obvious fact that Fascism was not seen by most of the electorate as a valid form of protest against, much less as an alternative to, the existing regime.

At the Sorrento Congress of December 1987 Gianfranco Fini was elected as successor to the ailing Giorgio Almirante in the name of continuity. In Fascism "there is everything," stated Fini's congress motion. Fascism was not a period or creed to be consigned to history or to be viewed with nostalgia; it was both universal and Italian and it could renew itself without help from outside.[35]

Decline continued: membership had dropped from 383,000 in 1984 to 120,000 in 1987, while in the European elections of 1989 the MSI vote went down by 0.4 percent. This at last gave Pino Rauti his chance and he ousted Fini in January 1990. But Rauti's spell as Secretary proved that his brand of left-wing radicalism—anti-capitalist, anti-American, and in quest of an ideal community—could neither retain the MSI's conservative voters nor profit from the now evident crisis of politics. In the 1990 local elections the MSI's share of the vote fell to 4 percent and the next year Fini returned as Secretary. He threw the party behind Cossiga's attacks on the existing system and the notion of a presidential republic. Perhaps because of this Fini limited the party's losses: in 1992 its share of the vote fell by only 0.5 percent.

It is logical to deduce that the MSI's success in 1993 and 1994 stemmed primarily not from what it was or did, but from outside causes. Its long exclusion from government enabled it to benefit from the Clean Hands investigation, but the decisive factor was the collapse of the DC vote in the South. Next in importance was the legitimacy it derived from Berlusconi's statement, made between the two rounds of the Rome mayoral election, that he would vote for Fini. The process begun by Craxi was completed and Berlusconi then moved from endorsing the MSI to accepting it as a coalition partner: "There is no reason to discriminate against Alleanza Nazionale (AN) . . . we are following its evolution with interest."[36]

This time the MSI leadership seized the opportunity. Fini understood the power that the DC had unwittingly bequeathed to him—"No one can do without us."[37] In the summer he had founded AN, which was a front organization, not very different from organizations proposed by Michelini in the 1950s and by Almirante in the 1970s. It was to be "a great center-right pole bringing together people from the MSI, from the Catholic party and from the lay parties."[38] But a more determined effort was made—at least superficially— to separate AN from Fascism, one spokesman comparing it implausibly with the historic Right that had governed Italy after Unification.[39]

The all-important negotiations with Forza Italia were helped by the presence of Domenico Mennitti, who was among Berlusconi's advisors. As a member of the MSI, Mennitti had proposed in the 1987 Congress a reform that would have broken with Fascist continuity. Now Fini had moved far enough to proclaim that "Fascism is irrevocably consigned to history. We are post-Fascists."[40] Fini also performed well on TV, kept his distance from the nostalgic populism of Alessandra Mussolini, and ignored Rauti's sniping.

He did not, however, steer his party through the painful self-scrutiny that Occhetto had imposed on the PCI. Fini waited until the election was won before asserting that Mussolini was the greatest Italian statesman of the century and that until 1938 Fascism had many positive features. Yet in MSI minds there is no contradiction between such statements and protestations of the party's commitment to democracy. Fini would admit a break with Fascism but not a complete denial of it, and he wanted the other parties to make a similar break with anti-Fascism. There may then be a national reconciliation, which is the way AN interprets the fiftieth anniversary of the liberation of Rome.

As already argued, given Fini's strategy and its success, the strength of anti-Fascism in the country is questionable. The elements of continuity between AN and Mussolini's regime do not attract many voters, but nor do they deter as many as might be expected. However the loss of 1 percent in the European elections caused partly by the foreign criticism of the "Fascist ministers" as well as the logic of his evolution made it likely that Fini would continue to move away from Mussolini toward some sort of Italian Gaullism. Electoral success and a role in the government would make this more palatable to the MSI base than it was in the 1970s or 1950s. This explains why Fini fought so hard to preserve the Berlusconi government in January 1995. His greatest fear is that AN will be sent back to the MSI's ghetto. In the run up to the January 1995 congress it looks as if any schism will be small.

Running against the Left and in favor of a break with the DC-PSI coalitions, AN performed well in the elections. It gained 13.5 percent of the vote with peaks of 27.5 percent in Puglia and 27 percent in Rome. The Roman bureaucracy was seeking protection in the new order and the defection to AN of a group of Christian Democrats, notably the Andreottian, Publio Fiori, who became Minister of Transport in the new government, was revealing. Throughout the South voters saw in AN a happy blend of protest and reassurance. An interclass cluster of shopkeepers, free professionals, and young unemployed voted for the continuation of the government's traditional role, which the DC could no longer guarantee. In Molise as in the Abruzzo, AN was the largest party. Nationally it gained 9.8 percent of the DC's 1992 electorate.

If success in the South was predictable, AN performed relatively well in the more difficult Center-North. Running without FI support it achieved 5.9 percent and 6.4 percent in two of the Lombardy colleges, while in red Emilia-Romagna and Tuscany its share reached 9 percent and 11 percent. Here Fini's success in projecting a TV image of responsibility may have been important.

AN talks a great deal about the need for a strong state. Law and order and anti-Communism are leitmotifs. In the 1980s it ran a campaign for the reintroduction of the death penalty. Fini has called for a reassertion of Italy in Europe by citing Italian claims on the former Yugoslavia and condemned the Maastricht agreement as "a match that cannot be won."[41] However AN's residual illegitimacy tends to weaken any government in which it participates. Similarly, it accepts the privatization program—even if Rauti has declared that "talk of the free market makes me reach for a machine gun"[42]—but its southern base makes it support interventionism with the attendant danger of clientelism.

The key to the Right's success was not the Lega nor AN, but the movement that brought them together in the Freedom Pole: Forza Italia, its creator Silvio Berlusconi, and his company, Fininvest. FI is a complex phenomenon and should not be explained away too simply. Berlusconi does not owe his victory solely to TV. Certainly he could not have won without the TV blitz he launched in January 1994, but he initiated his political activity in the late spring of 1993, while in his TV commercials and appearances the medium was not the sole message. Nor is the "Berlusconi phenomenon" an example of naked economic power replacing political power because Fininvest is a special and untypical company, better suited than most others to run a political operation. My thesis is, first, that Forza Italia is a particular kind of populism that emerged from a country rich in—or burdened with—many brands of populism, and that suited the historical moment of 1994. Second, FI is an ambiguous movement that reopens the debate about the overlap between state and market.

One more characteristic of any populist movement is its charismatic leader. In a country where businessmen are also celebrities, Berlusconi had the advantage of being involved in two newsworthy activities, soccer and TV. It was his good fortune that as he advanced toward becoming Prime Minister, his team AC Milan was marching to victory in both the Italian championship and the European Champions Cup. In England soccer is labeled working-class, whereas in Italy it is followed by all social classes. AC Milan brought Berlusconi not merely mass enthusiasm but an aura of patriotism, which he exploited in the name he gave his movement. Forza Italia, or "Let's go Italy," is chanted at international soccer matches. Meanwhile his ownership of three TV stations offered him free publicity as well as the endorsement of his popular performers like quizmaster Mike Buongiorno. In a period when politics as spectacle was important, the creator of spectacles had an advantage.

Another advantage Berlusconi enjoyed over other businessmen was that he had created, not inherited, his empire. He was not a friend of Cuccia and he spoke of the "rarefied air" of the Employers Association.[43] Much of his money came from selling TV time to small businesses and he was able to empathize with their owners. Indeed he had long depicted his networks as the voice of the people: "I think we can be against the TV of the palaces of power . . . we can be a positive TV . . . one with which people can feel at home."[44]

The linking of "people" with "positive" implies an optimism that was facile but answered the worries of the electorate. Of course, Berlusconi was not ideally suited to his new role. Fininvest's debts hardly seemed to qualify him to take charge of the vast national debt. More important, he was identified with the old regime as a member of the Craxi clan who had been tainted during the Clean Hands investigation. His opponents were quick to suggest that he had entered politics to gain control over the state-owned banks to which he owed money and over the magistrates who were harassing him.

Although he was an integral part of the publicized economy, Berlusconi had another side to him. He was the plucky David who challenged the Goliath of state TV. He had dared to start up commercial television in the late 1970s when the PCI supposedly exercised hegemony and his networks did not merely sell goods but spread the values of the market economy such as "freedom, individualism and meritocracy."[45]

So at a moment when the state was struggling and the politicians were discredited, people looked for a savior. One may make the comparison with the period after July 25, 1943. Then Italians turned to the Pope, "the man in white," the "angelic pastor." That they should now turn to an entrepreneur who specialized in consumer goods would have seemed to Pasolini definitive proof that his nightmarish vision of modernity had come true. But in fact, while projecting the image of the modern manager, Berlusconi appealed to such robust Italian traditions as distrust of the state, anti-Communism, and the family firm. He harked back to the postwar economic miracle and promised to repeat it. He would create a million jobs: the round number seemed more like a parable than an item of economic policy.

Already we see the ambiguity of his victory. Since he still owned his TV networks, his publishing companies Mondadori and Silvio Berlusconi editions, magazines like *Panorama* and the newspaper, *Il Giornale*, he worsened the overlap that helped bring about the 1992 crisis. Significantly one of his many lawyers was defeated in his bid to become regional president of Sardinia in June 1994. The wary voters suspected that Berlusconi, the construction tycoon, had designs on their coastline.

The opposite interpretation is that Berlusconi was not Craxi's successor and that he understood the need to reform the state. Populism is frequently a way of appealing to a particular segment of the electorate that feels itself neglected. Berlusconi sought the support of the small- and medium-sized entrepreneurs of Northern Italy and, more generally, of the urban, educated middle class. FI's Program speaks of removing "the bureaucratic muddles and the innumerable obstacles which prevent the creation of wealth."[46] The Thatcherite language is characteristic of his manner. Berlusconi wanted to cut back the welfare state and reduce taxes on individuals and companies. He went part of the way with the Lega in calling for the transfer of power to the regions. However it is unclear from the program whether Berlusconi appreciated that the market requires rules and that only a modest but strong state can provide them.

Another trait of populism is its use of a simple, frequently emotive language that appeals to the people over the heads of the elites. As his onslaught on D'Alema demonstrates, Berlusconi is passionately anti-Communist. If the people are to be defined as good, there must be an evil villain whom they defeat before they enter the promised land. However emotional outbursts were fairly rare in Berlusconi's public appearances because he was vying with Bossi for the right-wing vote. He left slang, invective, and sexual allusions to his rival and used the language of calm reason: *moderation* and *balance* are terms that recur in his speeches.[47]

Still more frequent is the verb "to organize." Berlusconi made few references to technology, which is a theme ill-suited to populism, but he pitted the order of the business world against the chaos and ideology of politics. Implicit was the contrast between the state services and the private sector. Organization was never dull or mechanical, but was associated with creativity, which was the mark of the entrepreneur.

Fininvest's creativity produced the political movement Forza Italia. Three branches of the holding company were especially important. Publitalia, which sells TV time, used its contacts all across Italy to win the support of local business leaders, to set up Forza Italia clubs, and to find candidates. Programma Italia, a financial firm, worked through the broader circle of its investment clients to set up clubs and generate an electoral base. Diakron conducted public opinion polls to discover the issues that most troubled the electorate. Fininvest's TV journalists tested the potential candidates and trained the best of them in public speaking and TV performance.[48]

Tensions emerged in the FI clubs. Clubs were formed by ex-Socialists and ex-Christian Democrats looking to disguise their pasts. In Sicily there were fears of Mafia infiltration. Conversely club members resented the weight of Fininvest and the way Publitalia, led by Marcello Dell'Utri, reserved safe seats for its own managers. In some cities, such as Bologna, Publitalia and Programma Italia were at each other's throats. No one, not even Berlusconi, knew how many clubs or members there were. In February FI claimed there were 10,000 clubs and 1 million members, which was less a statement of fact than a boast.

One aspect of these maneuvers concerns us. Berlusconi had not decided what he wanted FI to be. Certainly it could not and should not become a traditional party apparatus, bureaucratic and bent on extending its power over civil society. But should it be merely an electoral machine, while political power was reserved for Berlusconi? This would lead to plebiscitary democracy, to the charismatic leader who instinctively understands and interprets the desires of "his" people. Or it would lead just as easily to the usurpation of power by the new super-clan of Fininvest. Alternatively FI could become the transmission belt between civil society and the government, whose decisions it would influence. It could be the Center-Right, modern capitalist party that Italy has never had. This was, in essence, the issue that underlay the seven-month Berlusconi government.

9

Clan Rule

Forza Italia emerged from the elections as the largest party, with 21 percent of the vote. In the industrialized, modern northwest it gained 25.7 percent, which was more than the PDS and RC together. It swept Sicily, eclipsed the PPI in the Veneto, and trounced the Lega in Milan by 28.6 percent to 16 percent. It demonstrated its appeal to the working class by winning the Lingotto-Mirafiori constituency in south Turin, where many Fiat workers lived and where the PDS's candidate was the secretary of its Turin federation. FI pulverized its opponents among young voters, winning 39.6 percent of those under the age of 25. It drew voters from the old and new parties: it gained 25.8 percent of DC voters and nearly 15 percent of PSI voters; it also seduced 18.6 percent of Lega voters and, had the two parties not formed an electoral alliance, that figure would surely have been higher.

As it was, the Lega with a mere 8.4 percent of the vote won 122 seats and was the largest component in the Freedom Pole's House group. FI had 95 seats and AN 109. With a total of 266 seats the pole had an outright majority over the Left, which had 202 seats, and the Center, which won 46 seats. In the senate the pole had only a relative majority: 151 seats to the Left's 122 and the Center's 31.[1] So the British system of voting, accompanied by the residual 25 percent proportional representation, had not functioned perfectly, but it had produced a dominant coalition. However, the question of the coalition's internal consistency remained.

On May 11, after a surprisingly long period of preparation, Berlusconi presented his government. It was surprising because such tardiness was characteristic of the old regime, with which Berlusconi was ostentatiously breaking, and because the delay stemmed from the same familiar causes, namely, the battle among the coalition partners for jobs. Yet Italy's first "new" government was unlike its predecessors. As already argued, the Amato and Ciampi governments had marked a break because they had functioned without the safety net of DC domination, PCI exclusion, and PR. But they had been merely temporary governments of transition, whereas the Berlusconi government possessed the legitimacy of having been elected under the British system that allowed the voters to make a more direct choice. Two further innovations were the preeminence of the Prime Minister and the lack of a hegemonic party. So the government possessed various kinds of strength along with a clear vulnerability.

Five ministries went to AN, including the Ministry of Agriculture, the source of so much DC clientelism. That the environment was given to Altero Matteoli, who had run the MSI organization and who liked hunters and motorways, indicated where the new government's priorities did not lie. Giuseppe Tatarella became both Minister of the Post, a position that oversees television, and deputy Prime Minister. President Scalfaro insisted that the AN ministers not have participated directly in the Salò Republic, but their presence still caused an international backlash as some of their foreign counterparts refused to meet them.

The Lega gained the important post of the Ministry of the Interior, which oversees much of the regional government apparatus. It also obtained the Ministry of Industry, which Vito Gnutti could use to help small companies. However the Lega was both within and without the government. As Minister of the Interior, Roberto Maroni incarnated the responsible party that understood the need to compromise, while Umberto Bossi roamed free and demonstrated the Lega's purity by attacking FI and AN.

The choice of Lamberto Dini, a high official in the Bank of Italy, as Treasury Minister demonstrated that Berlusconi understood the need to offer the international financial markets a reassuring symbol. From symbol to reality the road would be long. Berlusconi brought into the government his Fininvest loyalists, by one count ten in all.[2] The most important was Cesare Previti, a lawyer who was initially destined for the Ministry of Justice (an amazing idea!) but was switched to Defense, a post that he combined from October on with the job of leading FI. Berlusconi installed a non-Fininvest lawyer, Domenico Contestabile, as Undersecretary of Justice, but he gave the sensitive post of Undersecretary to the Prime Minister to Gianni Letta, who had been in charge of government relations for Fininvest. Another sensitive position, the Ministry for Relations with Parliament, went to Giuliano Ferrara, a regular performer on Berlusconi's TV networks and a man not renowned for his tact. Publitalia had its own voices in the government: the Undersecretaries for the Interior and for Transport, Domenico Lo Jucco and Gianfranco Miccichè.

Although Fininvest had introduced into the campaign both marketing techniques and the myth of management's ability to solve all problems, and although entrepreneurs and managers made up 51 percent of its parliamentary group, it made no attempt to adapt business methods to government. Indeed Berlusconi complained that he could not impose his decisions on the government as he had done in his entrepreneurial career, but had to spend his days mediating. There was a paradoxical contrast between the image of a charismatic leader and a government that demonstrated that it was weak rather than authoritarian in the key areas of justice and the economy. This weakness sprang from two main sources. The first was that FI turned out to be a clan rather than an agent of reform, which was the real significance of the Fininvest contingent. The second was that Berlusconi had no party to rally support behind him once his charisma was tarnished.

Examples of the first weakness were the enduring conflicts between the owner of Fininvest and the Prime Minister. A company as large as Fininvest was affected by a battery of government decisions. Did the Prime Minister wish to cut state pensions? It could be argued that this favored the private pension funds run by Fininvest. If the budget increased taxes on the co-ops, then Standa could only benefit. Moreover Berlusconi sharpened the conflicts through his purge of state television and his war on the Milan magistrates.

Weakened by these troubles, he was unable—as well as unwilling—to conduct a policy of economic austerity. Caught between the financial markets and grassroots protest, he found that his lack of a majority in the Senate and—more importantly—his dependence on the Lega in the House made him an easy target. The confident narcissism of the campaign was strained: Berlusconi's allusions to himself as Christ carrying his cross grew more frequent and Bossi was transformed into Judas.[3] Then, when his governing coalition fell apart, the charismatic leader appealed over the head of parliament to "his" people.

This merely masked the reality that the problem of the Italian state had not been solved. The Berlusconi government was unable to act as arbiter. Its budget was criticized as class-based in that the pension cuts fell most heavily on the working class and were not balanced by sacrifices from the self-employed.[4] But even this might have been accepted from a genuinely strong government that was less obviously using public resources to serve private ends. The campaigns conducted to silence the magistrates and to purge state television took away the government's prestige.

Not that the other political actors were blameless. Perhaps it was inevitable that the Left paid lip service to reducing the public debt while it whittled away the budget cuts. The PPI flirted shamelessly with Right and Left alike. Alleanza

Nazionale obstructed the separation of state and market by slowing down the privatizations and by trying to extend the power of the parties over the Bank of Italy. This was more serious as it hampered the reform movement begun in 1992. The parties had not completed the task of reforming themselves. The Lega had not made the transition from a protest movement to a partner in government. Most serious of all, FI remained a virtual party, devoid of organization and of goals. Berlusconi opted to keep it powerless. These were the parties of a political system in transition.

Alternatively it is tempting to see in their behavior the triumph of change-without-change. A new alliance was taking shape between the Northern small- and medium-sized industrialists, who benefited from the income tax amnesty and voted Forza Italia or Lega, and the South, which relied on AN to keep public money flowing. Yet the impulse to reform the state was present in the protest against the decree of July 13, 1994, as well as in the confused attempt by both the unions and the Employers Association to maintain the agreement of July 1993.

The Berlusconi government's record is not, however, entirely unimpressive. Lamberto Dini began to reduce state ownership of the savings banks by prodding them to put 50 percent of their capital on the market. The privatization program made some progress: SME's supermarket chain was sold off, as was a half share in the Istituto Nazionale delle Assicurazioni (INA). The Finance Minister, Giulio Tremonti, launched a plan to simplify the income tax system, which represents the best chance of combating evasion. Fresh blows were struck at the Mafia. In general, however, citizenship did not flourish between May and December 1994. The Berlusconi government cannot be considered to have advanced the reform of the state, even if it may represent a pseudo-solution that Italy could not but try out. Clans and populism were rooted in Italian history; they were bound to re-emerge during a crisis. We certainly have not, even now, seen the last of Berlusconi.

POLICY: BATTLING THE MAGISTRATES NOT THE DEFICIT

The government's first economic measures blended coherence with facility. Tax cuts were offered to employers who were young, who were starting up for the first time, who reinvested their profits, and above all who hired new workers. The last group received a tax credit equal to 25 percent of the starting salary of each new employee. Labor law was changed very slightly to make it easier for small business to hire, although nothing was done to promote temporary or part-time employment.[5] Nor was it clear how the tax cuts were to be financed, which was an example of Berlusconi's conviction that confidence could be a substitute for thrift.

In foreign policy national assertiveness found expression in the demand that Slovenia settle its differences with Italy before it could apply for EU membership. Inevitably Slovenia responded with allusions to Mussolini's invasion, which were embarrassing to a government with AN ministers.[6]

On June 12 the electorate demonstrated its desire to be governed by Berlusconi when it increased FI's share of the vote to 30.6 percent in the European elections. This huge jump not only forced Occhetto's resignation but it awakened in Berlusconi the dream of triumphant fall elections and of a coalition without the meddlesome Bossi, whose Lega lost 20 percent of its vote.

In retrospect it is clear that such dreams were one reason why Berlusconi squandered the opportunity to use his popularity in order to push through an early, tough budget. Another reason was his desire to seduce the electorate rather than to convince it of the need for sacrifices. During the election campaign he had proclaimed that higher taxes were unnecessary, thus flattering the voters and indirectly benefiting his own Fininvest, a company dependent on domestic consumer spending, but relatively unaffected by the state of the lira. Berlusconi, hostile to the Bank of Italy because his predecessor, Ciampi, had been its president, simply underestimated the speed and the force with which financial markets would react. However, it is hard not to conclude that Berlusconi gave priority to clan interests.

Thus he postponed financial measures until the fall, although the Constitutional Court still managed to add approximately $15 billion to the debt through a retrospective decision about pension rights. The markets took note and were further alarmed by a squabble between the government and the Bank of Italy over Dini's successor. Berlusconi blocked the nomination of Tommaso Padoa Schioppa, whom he considered a Ciampi protégé. This was interpreted by the markets as an attempt to interfere with the bank's independence, which was the very last thing that foreign financiers—perhaps naively—expected of a government of businessmen.

Two months after Berlusconi had taken office the lira had declined by 4.2 percent against the mark, while the stock market—in part for reasons unconnected with Italy—had lost 7.7 percent of its worth. Banks began to raise their interest rates and foreigners started to withdraw their money. In the second quarter of 1994 there was a negative capital flow of $14 billion.[7] Berlusconi made a proposal to cut the 1995 deficit by $29 billion without, however, saying what was to be cut or how fresh revenues were to be raised.[8] On August 11, in order to protect the lira, the Bank of Italy raised the discount rate by 0.5 percent.

This provoked fresh accusations from the governing coalition about a supposed plot, in which Ciampi, the bank, foreign financiers, and even American Jews allegedly were active. The attacks on the bank were led by AN. The issue of Dini's successor was allowed to drag on until October, when a compromise candidate, Vincenzo Desario, was appointed. Meanwhile AN spokesmen kept up their sniping in a bid to gain greater control over the bank. One of their proposals was that the Governor be appointed for a fixed period rather than for life.[9]

This went directly against the thrust of reform, which had sought to resolve the twin problems of the overworked state and the publicized economy. The same may be said of the government's campaign against public television. One of the indirect consequences of the Clean Hands operation had been an attempt to diminish political interference with television. Under the old regime the three main channels were "owned" by the DC, the PSI, and the PCI-PDS respectively and their nightly news bulletins reflected this. A new team, led by Claudio Demattè and Gianni Locatelli, had been installed to clean up these audiovisual Augean stables as well as to cut costs.

However on June 30 the government forced both men to resign and installed as the public television supremo Letizia Moratti, whose family had ties with Berlusconi. An attempt to create balance was made when Alfio Marchini, whose father had had close ties to the PCI, was also named to the governing board. As an entrepreneur Berlusconi had always felt that the state television had an unfair advantage over his channels because it received, via the government, the money people paid for their TV licenses. Now he could try to cut state television's budget, which was indeed bloated. In turn this would reduce the service offered and make it more difficult for state television to sell its advertising slots. Naturally extra money would flow into the Fininvest coffers.

As a politician Berlusconi was concerned about the political slant of the news broadcasts and of the talk shows on state television. In September Moratti changed the heads of the three networks and also the people in charge of the news broadcasts. She appointed as the heads of Channel 1 and 2 news a man who had worked for Fininvest and was regarded as close to AN and a man who was thought to be a follower of Craxi before he went over to Berlusconi.[10] Channel 3 was allowed to remain in opposition, with left-wingers in charge of the news and the network. However the new network head, the well-respected Sergio Zavoli, turned the job down, fearing that Channel 3 would be gutted.

The battle over state TV, which saw the resignation of Alfio Marchini, took up enormous space in the media. One doubts, however, whether the average Italian cared: TV had always been politicized and only the bias was being altered. Even that was not certain. Berlusconi continued to complain bitterly about the antigovernmental prejudice in the news coverage and Channel 3 was alive and well when he left office. The key issue is not that Berlusconi succeeded in taking over or in crippling state TV, but that the governmental coalition spent so much time trying to do so. One consequence was the damage done to relations with the Lega, which felt that it had lost out in the struggle to place supporters in key positions.

Of greater moment was the war between the government and the magistrates. Relations were tense from the start, if only because Forza Italia contained so many lawyers accustomed to defending clients against prosecuting magistrates. But the real issue was Fininvest's role in corruption and how much Berlusconi knew of it. Here the government showed none of the sloth it revealed in dealing with the economy. Cesare Previti spoke frankly of wishing to win the magistrates over to the government. Alfredo Biondi had to be more reticent but he suggested separating the investigating magistrates from the rest of the corps, which raised the suspicion that he thought they would be more easily controlled if they were isolated.[11]

On July 13, while Italy was playing Bulgaria in the semifinal of the World Cup, the government issued a decree that allowed De Lorenzo, Diulio Poggiolini's wife, and hundreds of others jailed in the Clean Hands operation to leave prison. It also limited to three months the length of time the magistrates could investigate a suspect without informing her or him, and it banned newspaper coverage until the decision to put the suspect on trial.

Like the Amato decree, Biondi's initiative provoked a flood of protest that was in no way mollified by Italy's victory over Bulgaria and that reached its climax before the heartbreaking loss to Brazil in the final. In a new form of the "everybody-in-the-piazza" syndrome, newspapers and radio stations were bombarded with fax messages denouncing the decree. One poll showed that 83 percent of those contacted were opposed.[12] On July 14 the Milan Pool resigned and Antonio Di Pietro read their statement on TV.

It was a moment when Berlusconi's emphasis on the media was used against him. Di Pietro's blazing emotion was felt by the viewers to be authentic and the "cool" men of the Fininvest networks were unable to counter the impact he made. One might speculate that the collapse of political structures in Italy has left space for three charismatic figures—Berlusconi, Bossi, and Di Pietro. They are very different in their personalities and in their roles but their clashes have been key scenes in the drama of the 1994 government. After his TV performance Di Pietro was hailed as the voice of a peasant Italy that had survived the economic transformation. He was "an emigrant from Molise," broad-shouldered and hardheaded but "gentle."[13]

Berlusconi took a tough stand on July 14 and capitulated on July 19. The decree was withdrawn but the war went on. The Milan Pool continued its investigation into the bribes offered by, or exacted from, companies whose tax records were being examined. Prominent among firms that had bribed the tax police was Fininvest and on July 26 a warrant was issued for the arrest of Paolo Berlusconi, who had authorized the payments.

Two days before this, a meeting was held at Arcore, Silvio Berlusconi's mansion outside Milan. Present along with the Prime Minister were two other members of the government, one of whom was Previti. The acting president of Fininvest, Fedele Confalonieri, and the lawyers of the accused executives also took part. Nothing could better symbolize Berlusconi's lack of any sense of the state's role as arbiter and the way he confused the private and public spheres.

Although the conflict between the owner of Fininvest and the Prime Minister was now apparent, Berlusconi did little to resolve it. Perhaps there was not much he could do. Had he so wished, he could not have sold such a large and diverse holding company. Divesting himself of bits and taking some companies onto the stock market were at best palliatives. To buy time Berlusconi had set up a committee of three wise men to study possible solutions and on October 8 they recommended a blind trust. But this made little sense since the Prime Minister and all his government knew what the activities of Fininvest were.

Meanwhile the Clean Hands investigation drew ever closer. On September 3 Di Pietro had suggested a political solution: companies that had paid bribes would be given three months to confess and provide information; in return for their cooperation they would be immune from criminal prosecution. Ironically this would have suited all businessmen except Berlusconi, who could hardly avail himself of such an opportunity after protesting his innocence so volubly.

On October 5 Francesco Borrelli, the head of the Pool, made the oblique statement that "we are drawing close to the highest levels of finance and politics."[14] This was widely interpreted as meaning that Berlusconi would be charged and Borelli was widely condemned for issuing a threat. Berlusconi retaliated by asking the CSM to discipline him, but, although the Council discussed the case, it took no action.

Borrelli's unwise statement reflected the pressure under which the magistrates were working. They were vulnerable because they had used preventive detention in ways that went beyond the intent of the law. It was legitimate to feel that the balance between the claims of society and the rights of the accused had swung too far against the latter. Moreover, whether they sought it or not, the magistrates had acquired political power because, as I have argued throughout, clientelism was less a matter of individual morality than a pillar of the postwar order. So now the Milan Pool was generally supported by the PDS and, albeit more discreetly, by AN, because these parties had stood largely outside that system.

As rumors that Berlusconi would be charged grew ever more frequent, the war grew more ferocious. Charges were made that Di Pietro had mishandled evidence and he was investigated. In November Biondi dispatched inspectors to the Milan office, which was interpreted as an attempt to discredit the Pool. In a dangerous development the war spread to Sicily and to the anti-Mafia campaign. Defenders of the rights of the accused argued that the Mafiosi who turned state's evidence were treated too favorably and the imprisoned Mafia chieftains too harshly.[15]

The anti-Mafia struggle continued under the Berlusconi government. In September Antonio Gava was arrested on charges of collaborating with the Camorra, while the investigation into Andreotti's ties with the Mafia went ahead. Nitto Santapaola's deputy was arrested and decided to tell all he knew about the Catania crime family. In Palermo Michelangelo La Barbera was arrested and accused of helping to organize the murders of Falcone and Borsellino.

Yet the fears that the campaign against organized crime would be damaged by the government's war with the magistrates persisted. They were expressed forcibly by Giancarlo Caselli, the head of the Palermo Pool,[16] who once more drew attention to the parallels between the language that Berlusconi's supporters used to attack the magistrates and the anathemas uttered by Totò Riina. Moreover the charges that FI and AN candidates in Sicily had, knowingly or not, received help from the Corleonesi, were revived in January 1995 when Riina's financial advisor was arrested.[17]

On November 22 the long-awaited letter from the Milan Pool was delivered to the Prime Minister. It was severe in that it did not merely notify him that he was being investigated but also summoned him to appear with his lawyer before the magistrates. Berlusconi had already declared that he would not resign and he won sympathy because the news was leaked in advance to the press and because the letter was delivered while he was hosting an international conference on crime in Naples.

Previti was characteristically blunt: "a Prime Minister should not be interrogated."[18] Berlusconi was slightly more subtle but he made it clear that he considered the accusations against him not merely groundless but politically motivated. In a logical but dangerous extension of his populist worldview he began to claim both that the magistrates had no authority over him because they had not been elected and that parliament could not overthrow him because the voters had chosen him to lead the country. Using his religious language, he declared the people's representatives to be "anointed by the Lord."[19]

Behind such extravagances a troubled Berlusconi could not hide the fear that he, the creator of spectacles, was now unsure of the type or reality of the image he was projecting. He felt that he had become both Jekyll and Hyde. This modern entrepreneur sounded like a caricature of the traditional Italian male—like a character from an Alberto Sordi film—when he swore on the heads of his children that he was innocent. Meanwhile AC Milan had started to lose matches.[20]

The Prime Minister fought back. Ferrara and the other hired guns kept blazing away at the magistrates. An appeals court decision transferred the first of the tax police cases from Milan to Brescia. To transfer political cases to small towns that had fewer and less experienced magistrates had been a tactic of the old regime. Amid a storm of protest, the judge who had made the decision resigned and was hailed by the Berlusconi camp as a martyr.

Then on December 6 Antonio Di Pietro resigned. He explained that his work and he himself had become so politicized that he felt unable to perform his duties as a magistrate. At this time we can only speculate about his other motives, but a profound weariness with the entire situation must have played a part. The hired guns blamed tensions within the Milan Pool and sought to annex Di Pietro as a chief martyr. The resignation was a political victory for Berlusconi in that it deprived the Pool of the member who was best able to gain the support of public opinion. Borrelli came from the traditional Milan bourgeoisie and Gherardo Colombo was an intellectual, but Di Pietro belonged "body and soul to a peasant culture which is alien to our ignorant urbanized country."[21] He too was a man of tradition and a man who could be draped in the mantle of a very different populism. His sayings were much quoted: "Idle chatter is carried on the wind but documents sing."[22] Di Pietro will surely be heard from again.

Berlusconi appeared before the magistrates on December 13. It was the first time in postwar Italy that a Prime Minister had undergone such a humiliation, which reflected the change in the country. On two occasions Andreotti had been summoned before the magistrates while he was Prime Minister and each time he had evaded them.[23] Berlusconi remained in the Milan law offices for seven hours and he left without giving the promised press conference. The media master was unable to project any image at all. He recovered, though, and struck back using videos, his TV networks, and—for the first time—street demonstrations.

It is probable that the magistrates questioned him chiefly about an attempt to cover up a bribe paid by Fininvest to the tax police. But there were also the issues of how much Berlusconi knew of the Swiss payment in the Gigi Lentini transfer, of Publitalia's alleged creation of secret funds to pay bribes, and of whether Berlusconi owned more than the 10 percent to which he was limited by law of the pay-TV company Telepiù.

To his supporters it was quite simply clan warfare: "We're going to the mattresses . . . everyone against everyone else" (Domenico Contestabile); "there's a general war, the magistrates have joined in, it's everybody fighting everybody" (Marcello Dell'Utri).[24] Berlusconi's strategy was fixed. He was not going to resign even if, as he expected, the magistrates sent him to trial. Elected by the people to lead Italy, he could not be deposed without fresh elections. His roles as savior of the nation and as clan chieftain were complementary in that both excluded his role as Prime Minister in a parliamentary democracy.

Throughout the fall the possibility that Berlusconi would be arrested had hung over the financial markets, depressing the lira and government bonds. The traditional contradiction of the Italian economy had returned. Spurred by a lira that in the lifetime of the Berlusconi government lost 10 percent of its value against the mark, Italian exports soared. Fiat's sales in Europe were 28 percent higher than a year earlier, while the small companies throve and modernized, lowering their distribution costs.[25] However Italian government bonds had to offer yields 4.5 percent higher than German bonds[26] and the debt hovered around 120 percent of GDP.

In 1992 and 1993 government spending would have been in the black without interest payments, so it was vital not only to make cuts but to be seen making them. Only a demonstration of government resolve in imposing austerity would convince investors to keep lira and buy treasury bonds, which would in turn reduce interest rates and the deficit. World time in the shape of free movement of capital was pressing on Italy. Without the capital controls, which the EU had eliminated, the old contradiction between a dynamic industry and a wasteful public finance had become untenable. A display of austerity was essential.

Much hung on the budget that had to atone for the missed opportunity before the summer. Yet Berlusconi remained bound by his promise not to increase taxes, by his view that Italy could expand its way out of its problems, and by his desire to break with Ciampi's methods. To this must be added the objective weakness created by Fininvest's legal problems and the consequent reluctance to open up a new hostile front.

The government set the target of a $30 billion cut in the 1995 deficit.[27] Increased revenue was to come from three sources: an amnesty on nonpayment of income tax for people who now paid up, a similar amnesty on penalties for construction that infringed on the building code, and special taxes or rather closure of loopholes. Here already were the budget's first defects. The two amnesties, instruments of the old regime, simply rewarded the traditional fiscal evasion that was one sign of a lack of citizenship. Since they favored the self-employed they provoked the criticism that the budget was class-based, although the difference between self-employed and salaried did not correspond to the difference between middle and working class. Meanwhile the amnesty on abuses of the building codes infuriated environmentalists. The special taxes were less controversial, although the proposal to reduce the tax immunity of the cooperatives annoyed red and white co-ops alike. A tax on dummy companies set up to avoid taxes was an anticipation of Tremonti's proposed simplification of the entire taxation system. The financial markets also noted that the amnesties were "one-off" measures rather than structural improvements in the government's capacity to raise money.

So the other component of the budget—the cuts in government spending—assumed greater importance. A minor clash took place over the subsidy for Alto Adige-Süd Tirol. The proposal to cut it infuriated the German-speaking minority who were already worried by AN's presence in the government. Since the subsidy formed part of the international agreement with Austria, it had eventually to be restored. A more significant issue was the cut in the health budget, which involved closing some hospitals as well as reducing the number of people who obtained free medicines. But even this was overshadowed by the problem of pensions.

Far from representing the Berlusconi government's neoliberalism, which was in practice nonexistent, the attempt to reduce spending on pensions was necessary and Amato had begun it. The deficit of the state pension fund accounted for 22 percent of public spending and would reach 40 percent in 2025.[28] Pensions represented in miniature the flaws of the postwar settlement. As argued in chapter 4, the system had been left in a haphazard state to permit special government intervention in the form of clientelism. In the 1970s, when the "bill" fell due, spending on pensions rose along with other social measures. Costs were further increased by the decision to upgrade low pensions, by the so-called baby pensions, which allowed people to retire from their jobs after a relatively short time—say 15 years—and obtain a percentage of their full pensions, and by the concessions won by public-sector workers who were allowed to retire far earlier than in the private sector, where 35 years were needed for a full pension.

In this context the government's proposals were not harsh. At first it attempted a structural reform but, faced with strong opposition, it settled for cutting costs. Of the approximately $30 billion involved in the budget, about half was to come from extra revenues. Of the other half the cuts in pensions represented the major item but amounted to no more than $6 to 7 billion, which was approximately 4 percent of planned spending on state pensions in 1995. These savings were to be achieved by blocking for the year retirement based on years worked, as opposed to age, and by reducing future pensions through a change in the methods used to calculate them.

Since pensions were such a sacred cow, reaction to the government's proposals was rapid. That the figures were approximate and the administrative details complex added to concern. Berlusconi could legitimately state on September 9 that "nothing will be taken away from pensioners,"[29] but he did not allay fears. Indeed he proved unable to explain the changes in a convincing manner, revealing once more that his skill lay in seduction rather than in reasoning. The trade unions saw an opportunity to reaffirm their role as the champions of social solidarity and on October 14 a national strike took place.

It has been argued that adoption of the British electoral system would produce clearer political debates among the various socioeconomic actors and would lead to firmer choices.[30] Governments would no longer have to pander to all interest groups but would cater to their own electorates. In turn this would put an end to the overworked state. Such a development is both probable and desirable but Berlusconi's government lacked the authority to impose its policy. Like the old DC-led governments, it had undermined its legitimacy by using its power to serve private interests. Unlike them, it was branded as right-wing, which made cooperation with the unions more difficult.

The other actors did little to help. At a dinner in Agnelli's house in Rome on September 23 the Northern industrialist elite made its peace with the upstart Berlusconi and urged him to be firm. However employers simultaneously wanted social peace and above all they did not wish to see the agreement of July 1993 endangered. The unions, though, regarded the change in the right to retire as a violation of that agreement and they threatened to withdraw from it. They knew that pension cuts were necessary but felt they should have been consulted. Whether they could have agreed to and supported cuts, whether the Austrian method would have worked, remains unknown. It is clear that the attempted firmness of a spuriously strong government using the Gaullist method did not work.

On November 12 1.5 million people demonstrated against the budget in Rome. Once more Berlusconi talked tough and then gave way. He had little choice as his supporters abandoned him. AN remembered its heritage of social concern (which went back to Salò), the Lega saw an opportunity to attack the Prime Minister, and the CCD reverted to DC-style mediation. Berlusconi came to an agreement with the unions in time to avert another strike planned for December 2. Early pensions would be blocked only until June 30, 1995, while a general reform was negotiated. The proposed change in calculating the amount of money in a pension was forgotten.

The budget was passed by parliament in the last days of the Berlusconi government. The general pension reform was bequeathed to the Dini government. Meanwhile the budget figures had been overtaken by fresh expenditures that resulted from the November floods and from the high interest rates. The government's aim had been to reduce the deficit from 10 percent of GDP to 8 percent but the financial markets were skeptical. The IMF declared that a supplementary budget would be needed in February 1995 to save a further $12 billion.

Judgments on the Berlusconi government's handling of public finance are mostly negative. The stock market had lost 25 percent of its value, while the lira stood at a record 1,050 to the mark, and the debt was around 125 percent of GDP.[31] Inflation, a product of the weak lira, was at last surfacing: in December it went above 4 percent and, since the price of raw material imports has risen by 15 to 20 percent, it may well go higher.[32] The million jobs that Berlusconi had promised in the election campaign were never more than a parable: unemployment between November 1993 and November 1994 went up from 11.3 percent to 12 percent, which was higher than in France.[33]

The budget saga prompts two general considerations. The first is that Berlusconi was guilty of not concentrating his attention on this vital issue and that he expended all too much energy as a clan chieftain. The second consideration is that all the political actors failed to provide leadership on the pension issue, demonstrating that the March 27 elections had not brought a positive transformation. The old regime's habit of avoiding social clashes by postponing decisions lived on. The state was still overworked and weak.

POLITICS WORSE THAN USUAL?

It has been argued that the attempt to create a new regime has relied too much on referenda, on tinkering with electoral systems, and on using simple methods to make complex decisions. Parties and other associations have not changed their behavior.[34] If anything, they have been weakened by the electorate's distrust and are less capable than ever of providing leadership. This view, while substantially correct, may be unduly pessimistic. It ignores the fact that, despite much recycling of old Christian Democrats and Socialists, these are new parties. The governing coalition contained two parties that had never been a part of the postwar order and a third whose role had been marginal. FI and the Lega have not had the time to turn themselves into parties of government, although AN has made the change all too successfully! Meanwhile the PDS has a new leader who is trying out a strategy that cannot yet be considered a success or a failure, while the PPI's new secretary must adapt his strategy to the still changing electoral system as well as redefine his relationship with the Church, which is redefining its own role.

So this is not a case of change-without-change. That old habits, such as fragmentation, lived on does not mean that they could be indulged in as before. Before 1992, the collapse of a government less than one year after an election would have meant nothing more than a reshuffle of the old ministers, with the process to be repeated several times over. Now it has meant that the political class has had to step aside to make way for neutral technicians. It may also mean fresh elections and the destruction of a party—the Lega. This is not politics as usual, although politics may be worse than usual. There is some hope but no guarantee that a new order will emerge. The "new" Berlusconi government may in fact be part of the transition from the old regime to an as yet undefined future regime. A review of the parties' behavior between May and December 1994 illustrates the problems they faced as well as possible future developments.

Forza Italia's existence was virtual until the fall. At the time of the elections it had been made up of three components: its charismatic leader, his company, and a plethora of clubs that served as an electoral machine. The clubs had no say in the organization of the campaign and they remained separate from the political movement, which itself was run from the top.

After the March 28 elections there was a period of conflict as the clubs struggled to achieve some power but Berlusconi and his lieutenants distrusted them. One reason for this was that the crisis of politics and the reaction against the mass parties were strong in Italy. Overlapping with this was Berlusconi's desire to avoid having an organization with its own bureaucracy and interests come between him and "his people." He could make policy decisions more quickly without a structured movement and to win support he relied on his TV channels, Gianni Pilo's polls, and his own flair for seduction. The clubs reported to a senior Fininvest manager, Angelo Codignoni, who had been appointed by Berlusconi as the head of the clubs and who gave them nothing to do. Members who asked questions were simply expelled and after the June elections the clubs were left dormant until such time as they would be needed again. The political movement, which numbered about 4,000, fared no better, and its activist leader, Domenico Mennitti, was forced out in June.

After the elections, though, there was a fourth component in FI: the parliamentarians. Inexperienced, owing their election to Berlusconi, they nonetheless began to criticize—Tiziana Parenti's warnings about Mafia infiltration are an example—and to take sides. By the fall a split had developed between the segment that was close to AN and that looked toward Previti, and the segment that wanted closer ties with the PPI. At the same time the clubs were reactivated because of the need to fight local elections in 1995.

These twin developments could have signaled—and may still signal—the transformation of FI into an agent of reform. The parliamentarians have no direct interest in furthering Fininvest's fortunes, while the clubs, which Berlusconi envisaged rooted in, but confined to, civil society, could transmit the demands of that society to the FI leadership. To do this, they must be given political power and the vertical structure of FI—which has been described as Europe's last Stalinist party[35]—would have to be turned upside-down.

Since this would present a risk to Berlusconi's authority, he was reluctant. He preferred a presidential council, composed of men chosen by him and dominated by Fininvest executives. Even this had no regular meetings, for best of all Berlusconi liked to summon a long-standing loyalist, like a king summoning a courtier, and entrust him with a particular task. Thus Dell'Utri, who had officially returned to Publitalia, remained politically influential.

In October Previti was named coordinator of FI and proclaimed that "it is necessary to go ahead with the movement from the center to the periphery in order to arrive as quickly as possible at the reverse movement."[36] This does not sound convincing and Previti is rarely viewed as an advocate of grassroots power. Still his remark shows that the leadership is aware of the need for FI to be present in political as well as civil society. At the same moment Vittorio Dotti was named head of the FI group in the House. Yet another Fininvest lawyer, Dotti distanced himself from Previti and called for cooperation with the PPI. Significantly he also promised a freer debate within the group.[37]

The defeat in the partial local elections of November 20, when the FI vote dropped by approximately 10 percent from the European elections, spurred the trend toward rebuilding the clubs. Then, on December 19, confronted with the governmental crisis, Berlusconi told a Milan meeting (which took place appropriately in a theater) that "a tide of ordinary people, a great freedom march will make the high priests of the Palace understand whose side the Italy of work and justice is on."[38]

The appeal to the piazza against the palace marked another milestone in Berlusconi's populism. It embarrassed the doves in the parliamentary group and damaged FI's bid for autonomy since the movement was being ordered to mobilize on behalf of its leader, rather than invited to share in his decisions. At least initially FI did not take kindly to the piazza: the Turin clubs managed to turn out approximately 7,000 people on December 20, but the Milan demonstration was a flop. Moreover it was embarrassing to be outnumbered and outchanted by more practiced AN militants wearing Celtic crosses.

Berlusconi has not resolved the problem of what to do with his movement, but his experience as Prime Minister has surely taught him that he cannot dispense with it. FI's structure remains vertical: below Previti are the regional and local coordinators, who may indeed have been elected to parliament or to regional councils but who have been appointed to their party jobs. Supposedly this system is to be stood on its head and power will emanate from the clubs who are the base. One remains skeptical. There is a chance that FI could turn into the modern capitalist party that Italy has never had. But this requires that it not remain a mere appendage of its leader.[39]

AN is the segment of the victorious coalition that fared best during the Berlusconi government. It defined its goals simply and pursued them unremittingly. Gianfranco Fini understood that he had been offered legitimacy, a role in government and the chance to grow. All these gifts came from Berlusconi, without whom they might disappear. The first pillar of Fini's strategy was loyalty, to which Bossi's flagrant disloyalty gave added luster.

During the formation of the government AN was modest in its demands. In some of Berlusconi's campaigns, such as the struggle with the Bank of Italy, AN provided the shock troops and, when the government fell, AN fully endorsed Berlusconi's plan for immediate elections. Linked with loyalty was the display of responsibility, which once more contrasted with Bossi's fecklessness. Fini abandoned all traces of Fascist mythology—doublebreasted suits replacing black shirts—and of Fascist populism, which he abandoned to his critic, Teodoro Buontempo, the self-styled voice of the Roman subproletariat and Rauti's ally in the January 1995 congress. Fini's language was serious and solemn; it was a self-conscious attempt to demonstrate statesmanship.

Loyalty to Berlusconi did not exclude marking out different positions. On the July 13 decree, AN, which had been greatly helped by the Clean Hands operation, took a softer stand than FI. During the budget dispute it never forgot its heritage of social reform. But disagreement was kept low-key. AN might harbor hopes of replacing FI, for its organization was certainly better, but for the foreseeable future it needed Berlusconi. The 1 percent decline in its vote at the European elections, which followed the foreign criticism, was a warning.

The second pillar of AN's strategy was a penetration of the state apparatus. Masked as a defense of the strong nation-state, this mobilization to put supporters into key jobs revealed that AN had inherited DC clientelism. The example of state TV has already been noted. The Minister of Agriculture, Adriana Poli Bortone, who demonstrated a tenacity worthy of Bisaglia, moved her supporters into key posts in the farmers' organizations.[40] If the privatization program slowed down, one of several reasons was AN's desire to preserve the economic and political power associated with Enel or Stet. If it stayed in government AN would create its own state bourgeoisie.

In turn this overlapped with the party's defense of its southern base. AN feared that privatization would play into the hands of Cuccia, whom it greatly distrusted. It disliked the splitting up of Enel, favored by the Lega, lest the South be left behind. Although Cariplo is state-owned, AN was wary of the Milan-based bank's incursions into the South.[41] Similarly AN's Minister of Transport, a former member of the Andreotti clan, protected Bari's role as a center of the rail network.

Attention has been given to whether or not AN remains Fascist. It has been noted that AN is nothing more than the old MSI.[42] Certainly the planned congress of January 1995, after which the MSI will cease to exist, seems a cosmetic operation. Fini, who formerly claimed that in Fascism there was everything, now wishes to retain virtually nothing of it.[43] This is equally unconvincing and Rauti[44] is right to note the cultural void. But the real issue may be AN's role as a new DC and a champion of the resistance to change in Italian society.

The Lega emerged from the 1994 elections with its dilemma sharpened. The mayoral elections of 1993 had taught Bossi that he needed allies and he found one in FI. The anti-Southern strand in the Lega and the anti-Fascist tradition in Northern Italy ruled out an extension of the alliance to AN. Indeed the epithet "Fascist pigs" became part of Bossi's stream of invective. The alliance between FI and the Lega worked and the Lega duly won its 122 seats. Yet Bossi attacked Berlusconi throughout the campaign. After his victory he declared candidly that he had formed the alliance only because "otherwise we would have been torn to shreds."[45]

His fears were understandable. As the linchpin of the three-party Freedom Pole, FI would gain the leadership of the coalition and Berlusconi would become Prime Minister. His appeal to a large segment of Bossi's electorate, already strong, was enhanced by the mood in the country. The new voting system had produced a majority that must now go to work. The moment when the Lega must cease to be a party of protest and become a party of government had arrived. This would have been difficult anyway, but it would be even more difficult because it entailed working for Berlusconi. The distinctive trait of Lega thinking was federalism but Bossi probably had few illusions about the average voter's interest in the independent republic of Padania. Fiscal decentralization, which was—and remains—an issue, could be undertaken by Forza Italia. As a junior partner in the government the Lega would fall under Berlusconi's control and next election there would not even be any need to tear it to shreds.

The solution Bossi derived was to send Roberto Maroni into the government as the head of the Lega delegation, while he himself remained outside to assert the Lega's autonomy. One should not, however, overemphasize the rational nature of this choice. Maroni explains: "the truth is that Bossi does not trust, has never trusted, Berlusconi. He is suspicious of everything Berlusconi does, he can't help it, it's stronger than he is."[46] Behind the personal clash between two charismatic leaders lies a cultural conflict that reveals much about the last three hectic years in Italy.

Where Berlusconi was rich, Bossi was poor, and while Berlusconi had three TV channels, Bossi had spent years writing slogans on walls. But even more dangerous than the differences were the parallels. Each considered himself a sacred vessel: Berlusconi's mission was to save Italy from Communism, Bossi's was to save Lombardy from Italy. In August the two were supposedly reconciled and were photographed eating incongruous plates of spaghetti in Sardinia. But their rivalry went too deep. Bossi's role had been to undermine the old regime, but he had nothing to put in its place. Berlusconi sought to incarnate a new Italy, but to Bossi he was still a member of the Craxi clan.

While Maroni participated loyally in the government and pleased Lega voters with measures like the attempt to block the Mafia's advance in the North, Bossi denounced "Emperor Berlusconi" and watched him grow weaker. In December he decided that the moment had come to withdraw from the government and restore the Lega's purity. However the segment of the Lega that admired Berlusconi thought otherwise. Bossi's charisma no longer exerted the influence it had before the 1994 elections and the long-awaited Lega split took place.

It is hardly surprising that the three parties, so different and so unsure of their identities, failed to form a coherent coalition. One might imagine that Maroni's wing of the Lega could govern comfortably with a Forza Italia that possessed some autonomy. Such a coalition could include the PPI once it had chosen between Right and Left. The alternative right-wing coalition of a Berlusconi in his Christ role, a Forza Italia ruled by Previti, and a clientelistic AN appears less suited to a modernized Italy.

On July 29 the PPI elected Rocco Buttiglione as party secretary. The elections had demonstrated that the Center could not survive on its own in the winner-take-all system but also that the percentage of votes it had obtained— 15.7 percent if one adds the 4.6 percent of Segni's Pact to the PPI's 11.1 percent—could bestow victory on the Left or the Right. There was, however, no guarantee that the Center could maintain that share because its supporters might well decide that their votes were wasted. Buttiglione's task was to form an alliance that would offer his party a place in government. An overlapping question was what the Church's role would be in the changed political order.

Buttiglione was faced with a right wing of his party—of which Roberto Formigoni was a spokesman—that wished to ally with Berlusconi, and a left—Rosy Bindi—that looked to the PDS. Buttiglione's contradictory solution, which he pursued coherently, was to adopt as a goal an alliance with FI from which AN was excluded; however the way to attain such a goal was to demonstrate the PPI's power by forming alliances with the PDS on specific issues and in certain places. In the local elections of November 20 such an alliance enabled Mino Martinazzoli to be elected mayor of Brescia.

Buttiglione was regarded as being close to Pope John-Paul II and the Church's support was vital to the PPI. Although its political influence was much reduced, the Church still provided "its" party with a structure. Moreover it enjoyed what one might call institutional power since President Scalfaro and House Speaker Irene Pivetti were devout Catholics. Although the Church had been obliged to give up the doctrine of Catholic unity, it replaced it with the more modest goal of promoting cooperation among Catholics in the various parties. "The seeds are to be found in many fields," said the Vatican Secretary of State, Cardinal Angelo Sodano.[47]

However, as argued earlier, the Church hierarchy lacked the vision and determination it had shown in the postwar period. When Berlusconi was summoned before the magistrates, *Avvenire* first warned the PPI against allying with the PDS[48] and then, as if realizing that this constituted a defense of the Prime Minister's conduct, Cardinal Sodano declared that the PPI was free to make its own decisions. In doing so, however, he still took time to warn Catholics of the importance of abortion as a political issue.

Berlusconi's brand of consumerism and his habit of comparing himself to Christ irritated the hierarchy. However the money allotted in the budget to large families and the promise of funding for Catholic schools were forms of seduction that the Church could not ignore. Nor was the Church united. The red Bishop of Ivrea, who had been Berlinguer's ally, denounced Berlusconi, while the conservative Opus Dei supported him.

Both the PPI and the hierarchy probably realized that most Catholics would prefer to ally with FI rather than with the PDS. In 1994 the hierarchy did not have the power to persuade them to take a different path, even if it had one to offer. When Berlusconi grew weaker the PPI offered its own vote of no confidence and yet it did not exclude a future alliance with FI. Ambiguity reigned.

The PPI-PDS alliance was one option for Buttiglione but it was the cornerstone of D'Alema's policy. Elected to replace Occhetto by the PDS national council, which gave him 249 votes to Walter Veltroni's 173, D'Alema was perceived as the candidate of Communist tradition—his father had been an important PCI official and he himself had been head of the Young Communists— and of the party bureaucracy. By contrast Veltroni, an expert on the media and an admirer of Bobby Kennedy, was considered better able to overcome the anti-Communism that Berlusconi had exploited and to appeal to Centrist voters.

D'Alema, however, followed a double-pronged strategy. He defended the PDS apparatus, especially by leaving it alone. Where Occhetto called for daily transformations of the party, D'Alema said that the PDS must "become what it is," namely, a Social Democratic party with a strong organization.[49] The second part of his strategy was that the PDS must form an alliance with the Center. The November 20 local elections were a triumph for D'Alema, who used them as proof that the PPI could win votes by forming joint lists with the PDS.

Both D'Alema and Veltroni believe that the March defeat stemmed from the failure to ally with the Center. To remove the obstacle cited then by Segni, D'Alema decided that the PDS would not give priority to its relationship with RC.[50] The risk D'Alema is running in his bid to convince the voters that he and his party have abandoned all traces of sectarianism is that the Catholics may still spurn his embrace. Meanwhile RC with its 40 parliamentary seats remained in proud but sterile isolation, able to organize opposition to the budget but not to help offer an alternative.

In the fall of 1994 the magistrates deepened their investigation into the ways in which the red co-ops may have illicitly financed the PCI-PDS. Although the detective work was difficult because of the historic and organic relationship between the cooperative movement and the Left, this seemed to be a scandal waiting to be unearthed. It consisted of alleged cases in which the PCI-PDS obtained public contracts for co-ops, cases in which co-ops paid the salaries or social security contributions of people who in fact worked for the party, and cases in which co-ops were born, received grants from the Italian or EU authorities, and then died, having turned the grants over to the party.[51] In January 1995 accusations were made against the co-op national president, Giancarlo Pasquini, and the scandal may reach the PDS leadership.

Despite this the Left has probably gained popularity because of the Berlusconi government's errors, and yet two problems remain. The first is summed up in the accusation that the Left has "yet again no positive proposals."[52] In one sense this is unfair to the PDS's 1994 election program, to its anti-Mafia stand, and to its support of the Clean Hands investigation. However it remains true that the Left has not linked its proposals for reform of the state with a vision of social change. This leads to the second problem of the Left's intrinsic electoral weakness and its resultant reliance on the highly dubious alliance with the Catholics. Both aspects of this problem have existed throughout the history of postwar Italy as a legacy of the PCI's (self-)exclusion from government. They led Berlinguer to the historic compromise and they survived Occhetto's innovations. The PCI-PDS has changed a great deal but it has not been able to spawn a broad Left-Center coalition that can win elections. Occhetto's victories in 1993 were short-lived.

The parties of opposition have not then reshaped themselves into a credible alternative to the barely credible coalitions of the Right. Until the Left comes to power with or without the Center, the reform of the Italian state cannot be completed. But the disarray of almost all the parties became clear when the government collapsed on December 21, 1994.

THE FALL OF BERLUSCONI

The Lega's defection brought Berlusconi down but Bossi could not have withdrawn from the government if it had not lost credibility. The July 13 decree, the summons by the magistrates, and the budget fiasco were the real causes of its disintegration. FI's defeat in the November 20 local elections demonstrated that Berlusconi was vulnerable.

Yet during the battle that followed his fall he demonstrated his populist's skills and the weakness of his opponents. On December 19, two days before he announced his resignation, he set out his case in the Milan theater. He had been elected by the people and, if parliament overthrew him, it delegitimized itself and the people must make its choice again via fresh elections. Berlusconi resorted to emotional language: Bossi was a Judas who had to be "massacred";[53] he himself was a victim whose only crime was that he would not hand Italy over to the Communists. He hammered home this message on "his" state TV as well as on the Fininvest channels. On December 19 he was on TV live from the theater and on another channel in a specially prepared video: he competed with himself for the nation's attention.

Although he did not forget his other weapons, such as polls that showed his enemies reduced to a handful of votes and allusions to soccer in which he cast himself as "an attacker capable of scoring 30 goals . . . whose opponents are breaking his legs,"[54] Berlusconi stuck to his strategy of excoriating his political rivals and appealing over their evil heads to the good TV-watching Italian people. In this Manichaean world there was room for only the tiniest of compromises. Equally, such mundane issues as the deficit and the plunging lira became irrelevant.

Berlusconi's resignation speech on December 21 was a diatribe against Bossi. On December 30 he issued a fresh blast in which he declared parliament to be illegitimate and called again for elections. An outraged President Scalfaro invited him to step aside for the nation's sake. Berlusconi had the full support of AN and of the Previti wing of FI, but the Dotti wing, disturbed by the bitter polarization of politics, began suggesting that he give way to another member of his government, such as Urbani or Dini. Although Berlusconi quashed this promising demonstration of FI's autonomy, he allowed Dell'Utri to suggest on

January 6 that an Urbani or Dini government might be acceptable, if it were strictly limited in time and guaranteed early elections.

This governmental crisis in no sense resembled the innumerable crises of the postwar order. However long they lasted and however frequent they were, their parameters were clear. Berlusconi, by appealing to the people, was now undermining the legitimacy of their representatives who, in turn, did not possess the resilience of the old DC. Berlusconi laid bare their fragility, which may in the long run be a useful service.

The Lega split into a majority that backed Bossi, a handful that supported a new pro-Berlusconi formation called the Federalisti liberaldemocratici,[55] and a minority led by Maroni that was not prepared to vote for anything other than a Freedom Pole government. The first and third groups were held together by a dread of fresh elections, in which they would be annihilated. However Bossi, like Berlusconi, lived through the government crisis as if it were a great myth in which he, a dying King Arthur, was destined to defeat the Knight of the Golden Mask, the Prime Minister.[56] One cannot help but share the Lega's doubts about its future, although Bossi continues to fascinate.

The Lega's divisions meant that neither Berlusconi nor the opposition had a reliable majority in the House. This created a further novelty: President Scalfaro played a more active role than presidents had done when the DC was strong. His goal was to defend the parliamentary rather than the plebiscitary view of democracy and to avoid new elections. Meanwhile Buttiglione held the PPI together on a position of supporting a non-Berlusconi government, whether led by FI or a Catholic like Romano Prodi, provided that it be a real government and not simply one that would collapse on command and provoke elections. Behind this facade of unity lay a seething confusion about whether the PPI should go into elections—if they were held— in alliance with the PDS, and whether its long-term future did not lie in a coalition with FI, and even with an AN that would renounce Fascism at its January congress.

The PDS stood compact behind D'Alema, who opted for the cautious policy of calling for a government of "truce" and of "rules." Determined to show that the PDS was not conspiring to reverse the verdict of the March 28 elections, D'Alema wanted to include FI and even AN in such a government, provided again that it would not collapse on demand. By "truce" D'Alema also meant an end to polarization; by "rules" he meant a change in the electoral law to eliminate the 25 percent proportional representation, the establishment of tighter regulations on TV campaign advertising, and the enactment of economic measures to calm the financial markets and of antitrust legislation.

Although such "rules" marked a sensible contribution toward the reform of the Italian state, one cannot help suspecting that D'Alema's ecumenism masked the PDS's residual fear of illegitimacy. Such timidity left the initiative with Berlusconi. In general his opponents were able to agree on little except their desire to get rid of him and they seemed to have no project of their own. One may agree that Berlusconi's blend of clan warfare and (in practice weak) authoritarian populism offers Italy less hope than the politics of cooperation. But cooperation must not slip back into the endless mediation of the old regime; it must take active forms. Post–Cold War Italy should be able to tolerate and use sharp conflicts, it should not fear them.

On January 12 a delicate compromise surfaced. One of Berlusconi's ex-ministers would form a government of technicians. It would not guarantee early elections, but would have a specific, limited program to be executed in a few months.[57] This would allow both sides to claim victory. The next day Lamberto Dini was invited by Scalfaro to undertake the task. Dini announced a four-point program: a supplementary budget, pension reform, a switch from PR to winner-take-all in the regional elections, scheduled for June 1995, and equal access to TV during campaigns. Significantly absent was antitrust legislation. But the formula worked initially, for Berlusconi claimed he had a gentleman's agreement that there would be elections in June, while the Lega wished the government long life.

Dini announced his team of ministers on January 17. His personal triumph was founded on two political failures. The first was that Berlusconi had been unable to resolve the crisis of the state with a blend of charisma and populism. The second was that the political class was turning over power to a government of supposedly neutral technocrats.

Did this mean that the broader reform movement had lost its way? One indication that it might have was the arrest of several Lega, PPI, and Socialist politicians. They were accused of dividing up the jobs in the local health centers by party affiliation. Nearly three years after Di Pietro had begun his investigation, clientelism was alive and well in Milan. As argued in chapter 7, the social groups pressing for reform of the state had had the option of giving up and concentrating on the defence of their own interests. It seemed they might have done so in Italy's most modern city. But in fact 1995 would offer a mixture of innovation and paralysis.

10

1995: Dini Endures and Italy Changes—Quietly

The Censis report for 1994 stated that the "discourse of change is going out of fashion." But it added that Italy "has no genetic flaw and is not condemned to collective tragedy."[1] The following year, Censis made a sharp distinction. The political class was bent on suicide but Italian society was continuing to change.[2] While Lamberto Dini, who was a good technocrat but an even better politician, exploited the failings of his colleagues to remain at the head of the government for over a year, some Italians got on with the job of modernizing their society and economy. The Milan magistrates continued their investigation, although they were no longer the main agents of the process of reform that they had helped initiate in distant 1992.

Andreotti's trial on charges of collaborating with the Mafia began in February 1995, but it moved slowly and with long adjournments. (In February 1996 no end was in sight.) Also in February 1995, Calogero Mannino, the most powerful politician in the Sicilian DC, was arrested for his ties with the Mafia. The Palermo pool won other battles too, such as the arrest of Riina's lieutenant, Leoluca Bagarella. The Corleonesi were on the ropes, but as a whole the Mafia was not defeated.

Dini was supposed to provide the "real" politicians with a calm interlude that would enable them to undertake fresh reforms. Instead he became a key figure in a political struggle that had other new protagonists like Romano Prodi but that repeated stale, old mistakes. Dini endured as Prime Minister until the parties, which failed to agree on institutional changes to promote lasting majorities and stable governments, stumbled into an April 1996 election that almost no one wanted. 1995 was an aimless, gloomy year in which Lampedusa's many disciples seemed vindicated. However changes were taking place at the grassroots. Some of them were in the key area of state-citizen relations. Others were economic, such as an improved banking system and a glimmer of hope in the South.

PERIPHERY AND CENTER AS PARTNERS

Certainly the years since 1992 had deepened people's skepticism about national politicians. In 1995, 19 percent of the population felt that no one represented them, up from 16 percent in 1992. The decline of trust in government and parliament was steeper: In 1992, 14 percent felt that the government represented them, and 17 percent felt that parliament did so; in 1995 the figures were 4.5 percent and 6.7 percent.[3] By contrast 93 percent thought that the direct election of the mayor was an improvement.

The mayors elected since 1993 have been mostly popular and one of them, Antonio Bassolino, has been credited with bringing about a renaissance in Naples. He defeated Mussolini's granddaughter, cleaned up the palace of the former Kings, devised a plan for turning the obsolete steel plant at Bagnoli into museums and gardens, and brought a flood of tourists to the city. In reality Bassolino's renaissance is fragile: He lacks the power to attack Naples's chronic unemployment, and the Camorra is too deeply rooted in the daily life of Naples and the surrounding area to be eliminated by the arrest of its leader, Carmine Alfieri. Other mayors have achieved less than Bassolino: Marco Formentini has not been able to gain control over the bureaucracy in Milan. Yet the elected mayors have succeeded in restoring some of the confidence in local government that the Clean Hands investigation had destroyed.

Moreover they have spearheaded a trend that had begun with Law 142 of 1990. This law, which is yet further proof that the movement for change in Italy has its roots in the pre-1992 period, increased the power of the city councils, made local government more professional and permitted the privatization of some services.[4] In 1992 the cities received over half their funds in grants from Rome and raised a third themselves; by 1995 these figures were reversed. The mayors chose the heads of the various branches of city government, who are thus liberated from the parties and more directly responsible to the electorate. Competence rather than ideology has become the criterion for selection, and a mayor tends to be judged by his ability to attract good collaborators.

In the context of Italian history it is natural that political reform should flourish in the cities. Moreover as the big cities reach the limits set by an aging population and by increasing pollution, smaller cities develop alongside them. The expansion of Bologna university into Forlì and Cesena is one sign that Italy is no longer the land of "a hundred cities," as it was at Unification. The number is now much higher. However, while it is also a trait of Italian history that change comes from below, it is incorrect to imagine that it comes solely from below or that the problem of the state can be solved merely by shifting power to local government. The introduction of the British, constituency-based electoral system, which was supposed to create a bond between each member of parliament and her/his constituency, has not increased the importance of the local member. Instead the national leaders of the parties and coalitions have, albeit for other reasons, gained in stature.

The correct lesson to be drawn from Italian history is that power, whether used well or badly, lies in the alliances formed between segments of the periphery and segments of the center. The DC currents ran Italy in this way, as Giolitti had done. So now quiet change took place as reforms made at the center were taken up at the periphery.

Reshaping the state remains the metanarrative of the 1990s. The Rome civil service has created Offices of Public Information—which are spread throughout the country—that inform the citizen of her/his rights and explain how the apparatus of the central government works.[5] The North has more than its share of these offices and while 35 percent of them are closed on Saturdays, when it is easiest for working people to come, 96 percent also give information via the telephone.

If the Rome bureaucracy is starting to think that it exists to provide services to the citizen rather than to protect the government against its subjects, that is no small innovation. Italians remain unconvinced. A mere 19 percent are satisfied with the local branches of the national government, whereas 45 percent express satisfaction with the branches of regional government. Yet the intention is clear. In 1995 it became obligatory for each school to set out its educational choices, requirements, and practices in a Charter of Services.

Reform of a welfare system undermined by systemic clientelism has been a theme of post-1992 governments. Amato made a brave attempt not merely to control spending on health, but to unite the functions of financing and administering care at local and regional levels. Another goal has been to impose order on the Unità sanitarie locali, an unfortunate product of the historic compromise. Some of the Unità have been rebaptized Aziende sanitarie locali, which indicates that they are to be run with private sector managerial methods. Health-care establishments sell their services to the ASL on the basis of prices fixed for each diagnosis or operation.

This is a process of rationalization undertaken by experts rather than a move to end or reduce the alienation that the subject feels towards government. Moreover, as in all European countries, public opinion correctly links the verb "to rationalize" with the verb "to reduce." But the Ministry of Health has created a Charter of Public Health Services that explains to the citizen how the system operates and what the costs are. Moreover since the inefficiency of state services is a cause of alienation, improved efficiency should help create trust.

Organizations that check the quality of health care are to be established, and representatives of the users, which means the public, are to participate. This serves as a reminder that reshaping the state involves greater civic effort—a challenge for Italians, who do not rank a sense of citizenship high on the list of values that parents should instil in their children.[6] As if to demonstrate the challenge, Massimo Cacciari, a philosopher and the Mayor of Venice, chose the end of 1995 to write an essay on "democratic man," who is intolerant of restraint, dogmatically convinced of his own goodness, but perpetually in need of protection.[7]

Cacciari wonders how any community can be formed out of "democratic men." Still reaction against the penetration of society and the economy by political power is so strong that many public bodies are trying to relegitimize themselves by appealing to civil society. The trade unions, hitherto centralized and linked with the parties of the left, have followed the trend. As part of the July 1993 agreement workers in factories now elect their works councils or Rappresentanze sindacali unitarie (RSU). Although one third of the seats are reserved for the established unions, CGIL, CISL, and UIL, the RSU are selected from lists that are open to all groups. Union spokespersons emphasize that such councils are "voted by the workers and hence answer to the workers." If the council votes to accept a wage increase that the regional or national union rejects, then the council's view prevails.[8]

The council members no longer derive their power from the union bureaucracy or its associated party. In turn this demands that the unions take a "lay" view of the worker who is neither a slave of capitalism nor a model communist militant but rather an individual who also has a life outside the factory.[9]

In the very long run these changes should improve the relationship between state and citizen. However in the meantime exasperation with the slow pace of change is increasing distrust and could lead to more protest voting and more demonstrations like the rallies against Berlusconi's proposed pension reform. According to one estimate government spending now represents 53 percent of GDP. Although this is 18 percent higher than in the United States, it is only 1.5 percent higher than in France.[10] What counts is whether or not the citizen feels she is getting value for her money. A particularly sensitive group is the self-employed, among whom tax evasion is high and on whom successive governments have tried to crack down. Increased regulation has led to exasperation, as Prodi discovered when he was shouted down by an audience of Turin shopkeepers in March 1996.[11] Whatever the political and economic developments, the near future is likely to be turbulent in Italy. But this is a manifestation of unfinished change rather than of stasis.

THE ECONOMY: TRADITIONS AND NOVELTY

The Italian economy performed well in 1995, spurred by the same combination of decisions already made at the center and by initiative at the periphery. The major impulse from Rome continued to be the devaluation of the lira, undertaken wittingly by Amato in 1992 and unwittingly by Berlusconi in 1994. The second boost came from the most significant change yet made: the tripartite agreement of July 1993 to limit wage increases. Spurred by these advantages entrepreneurs, who also profited from the precarious international revival, sent exports soaring to 15 percent above the 1994 level. Italy was unable to avoid the problem that plagued the European economies: unemployment remained around a stubborn 12 percent. The downside of devaluation finally made itself felt when, despite wage moderation, inflation rose to 5.8 percent at the end of 1995. But growth was still high by EU standards: 3.4 percent to Germany's 1.5 percent.[12]

Neither the growth and export figures nor the performance of the fabled small companies have come as any surprise. Novelty springs from the geographical variations. The North West, the cradle of Italian industry, fared less well than the North East, which now exports much to Central Europe and is the wealthiest area in Italy. However, scattered all across Northern Italy are cities like Porto Marghera and Genoa that are fighting industrial decline. Meanwhile regions like Emilia-Romagna, where small, modern industries dominate, are running out of skilled labor.

Here again there is scant truth in the notion that the small entrepreneurs can thrive without reform of the state. Although they display an increasing ability to cooperate and to undertake in-house job training, they need help from the state in the shape of improved infrastructure, such as railways and telecommunications, and advanced scientific research.[13] As Vito Gnutti kept saying, perhaps the greatest need is for lower interest rates and a capital market tailored to the needs of the small entrepreneur. An Italian version of "Nasdaq" is scheduled for 1996, although it will not, like its American model, be a separate exchange.

The real novelty, although it is no more than a glimmer of hope, lies in the data from the South. Some $50 billion, much of it from the EU, is earmarked for investment between 1995 and 1999. In itself this means little to anyone who remembers the "cathedrals in the desert" and the Cassa grants that were squandered in clientelism. However there are signs that this money may be better used. Southern productivity has been increasing at rates comparable to the Center-North: 2.7 percent to 1.7 percent in 1993 and 3.1 percent to 3.6 percent in 1994.

Behind these figures lies an increasing split within the area. If the per capita GDP figure in the South for 1994 be taken as 100, then the Abruzzo stands at 127 and Sardinia at 112, whereas Sicily is 97, Campania is 95, and Calabria is 80. Between 1980 and 1994 per capita GDP increased by 22 percent in the Abruzzo and by 25 percent in Sardinia, whereas it rose by only 13 percent in Sicily, by 15 percent in Campania, and by 10 percent in Calabria.[14] It cannot be coincidental that the last three regions are the strongholds of organized crime.

To the very many students of Italian history who attribute the South's difficulties to the lack of an entrepreneurial culture, there are encouraging signs. Surveys indicate a greater willingness to move in order to find work, although unwillingness to move is a recent rather than a traditional obstacle. Perhaps more revealing is a survey taken in the area around Melfi which shows a positive view of the entrepreneur. Of those interviewed, 30.5 percent considered him a man of ability, as opposed to 12 percent who felt he was just lucky. Only 3.5 percent attributed his success to lack of ethics, while 33.5 percent credited him with the willingness to take risks.

Here again more positive attitudes will not enable the South to dispense with state intervention. But the forms it takes must not resemble the clientelistic or crudely productivist practices of the old DC. Present plans to improve rail service in Sardinia are more promising than the chemical plant constructed outside Nuoro by the unlamented SIR.

In 1995 the banking sector lived through a period of agonizingly slow evolution towards privatization. More rapid was the emergence of German-style universal banks and of new financial groups that will, in the future, be able to compete with Mediobanca. Change began with the 1990 Amato Law which turned the very large number of state-owned banks into joint-stock companies. This was a necessary step to privatization, although parliament wrote into the Amato law the obligation that 51 percent of the shares should remain in public hands. The banks were run by Foundations whose members were chosen by the government. Here, as so often, the EC provided a spur to change with its Second Banking Directive. In September 1993 Law 385, promulgated by the Ciampi government, turned these banks into universal banks and reversed the 1936 law that prevented them from holding shares in industry.[15]

As Treasury Minister, Dini issued the Directive of 18 November 1994, which recommended that the Foundations sell their shares in the banks and devote themselves to investing in socially useful projects like hospitals and low-cost housing. The Directive was not binding, but the legal road to privatization was now open. 1995 revealed, however, that the men who ran the banks had less interest in privatization, which might threaten their power, than in forming alliances. Conversely some members of the Foundations suspected that the real aim of the Directive was to steer them towards investing in government bonds!

Progress has been made: The Cariplo Foundation has begun to separate itself from the bank. However opposition to privatization of the banks has come from AN and RC at the opposite ends of the political spectrum. Nor has FI been enthusiastic and it cannot be mere coincidence that Berlusconi's enterprises are financed by state-owned banks like the BNL or the Banco di Roma. If they were privatized, banks might find it easier to say no to an ex- and perhaps future prime minister. Just as important is the opposition from the present heads of the banks. The collapse of the DC has left them room to manoeuvre, and they have no reason to seek new masters in the shape of shareholders.

However they have eagerly been jockeying for power in a struggle that should leave Italy with a wider banking-system in which competition is stronger. The Banco di Roma, which had already swallowed up the Banco di Santo Spirito and the Cassa di Risparmio, took over the Banca nazionale d'Agricoltura. Its owner, Count Auletta, had been close to Andreotti and now felt vulnerable. The new Banca di Roma represents one of several powerful financial blocs. Other banks seeking to expand are Cariplo, San Paolo di Torino, and Ambroveneto, which are rivals in the rich North East although allies against Mediobanca.

Southern banks like the Banca di Sicilia and the Banco di Napoli have still not recovered from the decades when control of credit was a political weapon. Dini and the Bank of Italy installed a tough executive, Federico Pepe, to clean up the Banco di Napoli but in 1995 it reported a half-year loss of $1 billion. The Treasury Ministry did persuade a group of banks to help out but restructuring and a large dose of fresh capital are still needed.[16] Most Sicilian banks were forced to make bad loans by the hegemonic alliance of the Mafia,

DC politicians, and local businessmen. Sicilcassa has been taken under the direct control of the Bank of Italy, and leading members of its staff have been suspended.[17]

Pepe wants to cut the branch network of the Banco di Napoli and to reduce the number of workers. Other large banks will probably have to do the same. Credito Italiano and Cariplo showed unimpressive profit margins in 1995, while Comit is trading at nearly 40 percent below its privatization price. However these troubles may be caused in part by the transition.

There is a good chance that groups of strong, sophisticated banks will emerge from the present upheaval. Ambroveneto has had to fight off a take-over bid by Comit and its victory is a sign that Enrico Cuccia may soon have rivals. Credito Italiano succeeded in taking over Credito Romagnolo. It campaigned openly, and the struggle was widely reported in both the national and local press, which increases public understanding of financial affairs. One result was that Credito was obliged to recognize the strong, local backing for Rolo. Then Credito fused Rolo with another Emilia-Romagna bank, Carimont. The Carimont leaders fought hard and obtained positions of power in the new bank. This too may be seen as a case of the periphery resisting the center, and here again intermediaries were found. Achille Maramotti, an Emilian entrepreneur but also Cuccia's ally in the privatization of Credito, joined the Board. It was never in Credito's interest to alienate the Emilian bankers who ran Rolo and Carimont as profit margins in 1995 were higher in smaller, provincial banks.

The solution to the dominance of Mediobanca lies in the emergence of several financial coalitions. Another organization in transition is the Istituto Nazionale delle Assicurazioni (INA). Founded in pre-Fascist Italy to provide workers with insurance against sickness, it is headed by Sergio Siglienti, formerly with Comit and also a cousin of Enrico Berlinguer. INA is being privatized, but at least three of the banks that have bought its shares are still publicly owned: IMI, Saint Paolo di Torino, and Cariplo. However IMI has been almost completely privatized, and the other two banks should follow. In 1995 approximately 20 percent of INA and IMI were sold to institutional investors, both Italian and foreign, in order to form a "hard core." As an insurance company, INA is well suited to forming part of a powerful financial block. Although such blocs lack the experience and specialized knowledge of Cuccia's merchant bank, they should in time become leading actors in a broader Italian economy.

It is hard to see how this can happen without privatization. Financial groups owned by the state would be more strongly tempted to cut deals with one another and more subject to political pressure. Bank presidents might yet find shareholders easier taskmasters than AN. If the Center-Left wins the upcoming elections, the chances of privatization are high, whereas a victory for the Center-Right means longer delays. In the meantime one might argue that the emergence of several powerful financial groups has been facilitated by the freedom leading bankers have enjoyed.

Enrico Cuccia has fought and won the battle for control of Montedison. The episode, which includes a subplot in the form of Supergemina, provides arguments for the prophets of change without change, and yet it contains novel elements. Cuccia had nursed Montedison back to health by bringing in other banks like San Paolo di Torino. His task was made easier by Eridania Béghin-Say, which had never been in trouble, had reported excellent results in 1995, and had taken over American Maize. To gain control of Montedison, Cuccia announced a plan to fuse it with the establishment's holding company, Gemina. The plan had a spurious industrial logic in that Gemina possessed, via Agnelli, a chemical fiber company, Snia. But Cuccia's real goal, aside from repossessing Fondiaria, was to take over the historically important Montedison.

He was thwarted when Gemina's shares collapsed as the losses of the Rizzoli group became apparent. This brought a rift in the would-be establishment as Carlo Pesenti, the head of Gemina, began wondering aloud why the Agnelli, who had sold Rizzoli to Gemina, had not known of these losses. Such disputes were/are not unusual but timid signs of a changing Italy appeared when both the Consob and the magistrates announced they were making enquiries. These unusually indiscreet gazes brought the transaction to a halt.

Undaunted, Cuccia changed strategy. He announced a large new issue of Montedison shares, knowing that his rival, San Paolo di Torino, had reached its legal limit of 15 percent, whereas his battalions, Comit, Credito, and Mediobanca, could increase their holdings. They duly did so and Montedison fell to Cuccia, who won a retrospective victory over Schimberni and Gardini.

Here again the nascent movement to bring transparency and consistency to the stock market made his task more difficult. Critics charged that, since he was gaining control of Montedison, he should have been obliged to launch a takeover. This would give the small shareholders the opportunity to sell their shares at a profit. Showing more energy than in the past, the Consob agreed at least in part. It limited the number of shares Cuccia had to buy to the equivalent of the 10.7 percent he had just bought. However the notion that the change of ownership of a major company should not be carried out in the secrecy of an establishment drawing-room is gaining ground.[18]

In February 1996 the stock market, which is now fully computerized, took another step towards fairness and transparency when it reduced the period within which a transaction must be cleared from forty-five days to five. This measure limits the chance that a large investor will manipulate the price of a share he has bought or sold before the deal is concluded.

1995 was in general a good year for the leading Italian companies. Fiat continued its successful bid to increase foreign sales: In 1995 it had 13.5 percent of the European market, 1 percent more than in 1994 and second only to Volkswagen. The group also announced plans to expand in Latin America. Even as it became more of a world company, Fiat reemphasized its identity as a family firm. Gianni Agnelli retired in early 1996 and his nephew is being groomed to succeed him. In the meantime Cesare Romiti will head the company, although the Clean Hands investigation is drawing ever closer to Romiti.[19]

Another sign that Italian companies are improving their performance abroad comes from the Generali. Blocked in its attempt to take over the French insurance company Midi in 1989, the Generali, which now has a French chief executive, Antoine Bernheim, has reached an agreement with Midi's other main shareholder, the French company Aja, to launch a joint venture.

Not all big companies fared well. Olivetti began 1996 with sharp drops in the price of its shares and rumors that Carlo De Benedetti's position was growing difficult. His proud boast that he has taken Olivetti from typewriters to computers rings a trifle hollow as the computer market grows ever tougher. Olivetti is gambling heavily on the portable telephone business, where it confronts IRI.

IRI, caught between segments of the political class that hold the old view of the public sector as a source of clientelism and the difficulties of privatizing such a large holding company, had debts amounting to $40 billion in September 1995.[20] Speculation that it will meet the fate of Egam and Efim is rife. One of its main problems is Alitalia, which appears about to collapse in a welter of debts and strikes. Here again the impetus of change, while strongly resisted, makes privatization the solitary, albeit difficult, solution.

Finally 1995 provides mixed evidence for my argument that Italy is growing richer in medium-sized companies and has no shortage of entrepreneurial talent. Stefanel has encountered difficulties and is being tended to by Cuccia,[21] but Leonardo Del Vecchio's Luxottica, which has expanded in the United States, reported excellent earnings for the year. Del Vecchio is an example of the new entrepreneurs. Of modest background, he started a business in Milan. Then the good labor and the sense of community attracted him to a village near Belluno. He became a leading maker of spectacles and collaborated with fashion designers. In a joint venture with Benetton he bought the chain of motorway restaurants, Autogrill, from the government and the Euromarkets from Berlusconi. With Cuccia's blessing he became a shareholder in Credito Italiano. His greatest coup came in 1995: He bought a U.S. chain that sold shoes but could also distribute his spectacles.[22]

1995 does confirm that the Italian economy has used elements of the 1992 crisis, such as the collapse of the aggressive, clientelistic state and the departure from the EMS, to bring about a revival and—up to a point—to make structural changes. The surge of exports that followed the forced deval- uation of the lira was traditional. In other periods such success has been swallowed up by inflation, loss of the newly-acquired competitiveness, and the persistence of underlying weaknesses such as the huge, inefficient public sector and Southern backwardness.

This time the crisis was graver and the opportunities it offered the economic actors were greater. It is too soon to decide whether or not the economy is being transformed. There is much evidence that it is not. There are still too few giants, too little high tech, and too much secrecy. Yet novelty is present in the developments in the South, while the banking system is certainly very different. The old political order helped the economy by collapsing, but the economy needs a new political order. This need is most obvious in the way that political failings bring retribution on the currency, on interest-rates, and on share-prices. But the need for stable, innovative government is demonstrated by the very internationalization process that Fiat, Generali, and the small firms of the North East are undergoing. In the global economy Italy is competing as one entity. There is need for a state that does not merely provide improved infrastructure and better labor but that can help the market work by maintain- ing a stable currency or by regulating industry and finance without preying off them. Such a state must also bargain well for its citizens in international fora like the EU or the GATT. We must now consider whether the politics of 1995 improved the Italian state's performance.

LAMBERTO DINI: A SHREWD POLITICIAN

Another difference between Ciampi and Dini is that Ciampi was content to govern during an interlude, whereas Dini manoeuvred to make his interlude last as long as possible and to remain in politics after it ended. Dini had never been aloof from the old regime: He owed his job as Director General of the Bank of Italy in part to the backing of Bisaglia and Andreotti.[23] At the bank he was considered too much of a politician and, when Ciampi departed, the post of Governor went to Antonio Fazio. Dini drew the logical conclusion and joined Berlusconi's government. He and Fazio clashed over his 1996 budget, which, in the Bank's opinion, made too many concessions to his Center-Left majority and was short on rigor.

As a practicing politician Dini lacks the good looks of Bologna's Pierserdinando Casini, the flamboyance of Bossi, and the cold professionalism of D'Alema. However he does not shrink from clichés: His contribution to the language of sport now favored by politicians is a very banal "when the going gets tough, the tough get going."[24] Dini's short, quietly spoken sentences are full of ostentatious understatement. He was aware that the public's skepticism about politicians made it respect technocrats. On such respect a political career could be built.

Dini's government was devoid of politicians. Aside from Susanna Agnelli, few of its members were well-known to the public. Some like the Minister of Labor, Tiziano Treu, came from the universities, but more were civil servants.[25] The new Minister of Justice, Filippo Mancuso was a magistrate, while the Minister of Defence, Domenico Corcione, was a general.[26] Ciampi had chosen ministers, like Beniamino Andreatta, whose stature equalled his. Dini's government was competent but grey. The presence of the Roman civil servants gave it an Andreottian flavor. This flavor continued to hang around Dini and when he presented his new party in 1996 it contained several ex-Andreottiani.[27] However, Dini's culture, based on economics, is very different from Andreotti's, and he does not share Andreotti's sense of original sin.

When the vote of confidence took place in the House, Berlusconi was already convinced he had been tricked. He understood or claimed to have understood that Dini would either carry out his program or fail to carry it out, but that in either case Dini's rule would be quick and that elections were near. In reality Dini had, if he so wished, an excellent opportunity to remain in power. On the Center Right the Dotti wing of FI continued to entertain doubts about Berlusconi's violent language, while the CCD wanted time to allow some of their ex-DC companions to join them on the right. All segments of the ex-DC were alive to President Scalfaro's determination to avoid early elections.

Rocco Buttiglione also needed time to carry out his plan to lead his battalions over to the right. The PDS thought its own vote would hold up in elections but that the Center Right would be the overall winners. Berlusconi's only ally—aside from AN and even AN needed time, after its January congress, to demonstrate that it was responsible—was RC, which thought it would benefit from an increased protest vote. Neither the Employers Association nor the unions wanted Berlusconi back. The financial markets simply wanted continuity. The Church had learned to distrust elections.

Few of these reasons were edifying, but taken together they were compelling. The elasticity of Dini's four points, and the diffuse but widely-shared notion that part of his mandate was to allow tempers to cool, worked against Berlusconi, whose temper had clearly not cooled.

Propelled by a weak dollar, the lira continued to fall against the mark, and on February 16 it reached a new low of 1,078. Since the EU was calling for financial discipline, the mini-budget was Dini's first preoccupation. He sought to cut the deficit by around $12 billion, of which one third was to come from reduced spending and two thirds from extra revenue. This involved delicate political juggling because the classic rightwinger abhors tax increases, while the left is allergic to cuts in social spending.

Dini's solution was to make small cuts in many areas of spending, while avoiding as much as he could areas, like health care, where the left is especially sensitive. A cut in the budget for the secret services went through unchallenged but it was tiny. The bulk of the money raised came from an increase in VAT on a wide range of items from clothes to coffee. To protect himself against the argument that VAT increases fall most heavily on the poor, Dini provided help for large families.

In reality it was a traditional mini-budget. It obeyed the electoral logic that people, whether wealthy or poor, do not notice moderate price increases as much as they notice extra deductions from their salary checks. Anyway the economic niceties were forgotten as Berlusconi, enraged that there was no sign of imminent elections, called for a vote against the budget. On March 4, he formally broke with Dini—claiming "he has slammed the door on us"[28]—and forced a vote of confidence on the mini-budget.

As was obvious to one and all, the vote was about the continued existence of the Dini government. The balance in the House was held by RC, which split between party leader Fausto Bertinotti's call for rigorous opposition and parliamentary leader Famiano Crucianelli's appeal not to vote with the right. Crucianelli and 16 of his comrades voted for the Dini government. Since the RC organization stood firm behind Bertinotti, Crucianelli's band later left to form the Communists for Unity. *La Voce's* headline drew the obvious conclusion of the House vote: "Dini wins. Slap in the face for Silvio."[29] The image of a responsible, non-political government hounded by self-interested demagogues jostled with the previous image of a democratically-elected leader brought down by intriguers and traitors. The names had changed but the political class remained the villain.

The issue of pension reform revealed the two principal traits of Dini's government. The first was that it was trying to follow the policy of rigor and reform of the state undertaken by the Amato and Ciampi governments. The second was that, where his predecessors had been freed from political pressure by the Milan magistrates, Dini was kept in power by the Center-Left whose worldview he had to consider.

So the pension agreement, which was signed on May 9 and went through parliament on August 8 after another vote of confidence, was a compromise between rigor and the unions' struggle to protect what they perceived to be their constituency. The unions had submitted a proposal, which the government accepted as a basis for discussion. Dini defied them on a key point: they wanted to maintain the right of people to retire at any age provided they had paid 35 years of contributions. The government demanded 40 years of contributions and held firm. However the agreement as a whole was attacked by the Employers Association and by the right, which claimed it would take effect too slowly and would not save enough money. Probably Berlusconi's plan would have saved more money. Anyway the representatives of the Employers Association refused to join the government and unions in signing the final document. Dini avoided a wave of social protest, but the price of consensus was a certain laxity. The debate demonstrated that the Center-Left accepts the need for rigor but—like left-wing parties elsewhere in Europe—has not come to love it.

The agreement severs the pension system from other forms of social spending, which will make it more transparent. A unified plan, albeit with many exceptions, has been drawn up for public and private sector workers as well as for the self-employed. People are to retire between the ages of 57 and 65: The average worker is expected to retire at 62 after paying 37 years of contribution; there are penalties for retiring sooner and rewards for working longer. There are also incentives to contribute to top-up private pension funds, which will in turn help the stockmarket to grow.

The principle of rationalization is to base the size of a pension not, as now, on the salary earned in the last ten years but on the contributions made throughout a worklife. Critics argue that for the next ten years only $6.5 billion will be cut from a total pension bill that reaches $190 billion. The long transition from the present to the new system means that most of the sacrifices will be made by the next generation.[30] It was not long before the plan incurred the wrath of the self-employed. In February 1996 they were called on to pay 10 percent of their year's salary into the pension fund. Their irate reaction came during the election campaign and the politicians made frantic efforts to pin the blame for the 10 percent tax on their opponents. This was another example of the "turbulence" discussed above.

Dini had also made progress on his other two points. In March the government issued a decree on the use of TV in electoral campaigns. No political advertising was allowed in the last thirty days before the vote and no polls were to be published in the last twenty. Political advertising was to be allowed from the forty-fifth to the thirtieth day. The various parties were to be allowed equal access to TV, a rule that applied to talk-shows as well as news programs. A guarantor was appointed to oversee the application of the rules. He could impose penalties, but the culprits had the right to appeal to the TAR, the Lazio Supreme Court, which would give a ruling in forty-eight hours.[31]

Dini announced that the decree was based on input from all parties, although the House Constitutional Committee had failed to reach agreement. Berlusconi declared that the decree marked a return to the Middle Ages and that it worked against FI, which had most of the daily newspapers as enemies and lacked the PDS's network of militants.[32] Since it was a decree not a law it had to be renewed before each election. It was not a substitute for comprehensive legislation.

The new voting system to be used in the regional elections represented a compromise between the popularity of direct election of the mayor and the political class's lasting love of proportional representation.[33] Eighty percent of the councilors were to be elected by PR, but the president of the region was to be chosen directly. To ensure that he would not find himself in the minority, his list was to receive extra seats on the council to assure that he had around 60 percent of the total number.

Dini ignored the regional elections of April 23, informing journalists that he was working on the pension legislation and flying off to Washington for a G7 meeting, held on April 25. In reality he understood that Berlusconi's defeat in the elections meant a new lease on life for his government. He pointed out "there are lots of ideas and programs that could be carried out, if parliament wanted to."[34] By now Prodi was also pressing for elections, but his own party, the PPI, was dragging its feet. In early May, Filippo Mancuso called for disciplinary action against the Milan magistrates, which marked the start of a dispute between Dini and "his" Center-Left majority. But the pensions debate overshadowed it, while Berlusconi was further damaged in late May by the arrest of Marcello Dell'Utri.

The June referenda weakened Dini because they marked public displeasure with the unions, which were his interlocutors in the pensions debate. Conversely Berlusconi regained stature when the electorate demonstrated its support for his TV networks. The announcement in June of his plan to go public and to sell more than 50 percent of the shares in his TV holdings seemed a step towards ending the conflict of interest accusations that had plagued his term as prime minister. Berlusconi once more began demanding elections. However Scalfaro continued to feel that another election without a clear outcome would set Italy firmly on the path followed by the Weimar Republic. Moreover D'Alema still had no confidence in the Center-Left's ability to win elections, and he too dragged his feet. D'Alema seemed to be seeking a broad agreement with Berlusconi on constitutional reform. He may have had the Togliatti–De Gaspari accord as a model, although a more cynical, equally Togliattian, interpretation was that he wanted to prop up a weak opponent. However his attempt was genuine because these summer overtures foreshadowed D'Alema's determined attempt to reach agreement with the Center-Right in January 1996.

In this context there was no alternative to Dini, whose poll ratings rose. In an August interview[35] he spoke of the 1996 budget and the Italian presidency of the EU Council of Ministers. He promised more action on privatization and blamed parliament for the stasis. His approval ratings were the highest among leading politicians: He stood at 52 percent with Fini second at 46 percent, D'Alema at 41 percent and Berlusconi at a distant 37 percent.[36] Dini talked, albeit in general terms, of creating a center, which could help form a stable majority. In embryo his 1996 plan was already present. As if sensing it, both the Freedom Pole and the Olive began to court him.

Dini's promise of action on privatization was only in one respect fulfilled. The selling off of public utilities, once again forced on Italy by the EU but fostered by the reaction against the overworked state, had been held up in 1993 by a parliamentary vote that decreed that "authorities," on the British model, should be set up to oversee the privatized agencies. On November 14, 1995, Law 481 set up such an authority for the electricity industry. This cleared the way for the privatization of Enel, which is, however, opposed by AN in the name of protecting electricity supplies to the South. The legislation did not apply to telecommunications so Stet is still waiting.[37]

It is tempting to attribute Dini's failure to privatize to his cultural background. He has never worked in the private sector, while both he and his government have more experience of the civil service. However such considerations are not decisive in Italy where Romano Prodi, a manager in the state sector, is more enthusiastic about privatization than Berlusconi. Resistance within the public sector—from unions fearful of lay-offs and managers liberated from their political bosses by the Milan magistrates—within parties that hope to revive the old practice of clientelism, and within private sector firms that supply the public sector is more important.

Dini did succeed in launching the privatization of ENI, although only 15 percent of the holding was put up for sale. Once again a private placing was used to create a "hard core," while the government retained a "golden share," as is normal in a company dealing in oil. ENI inserted into its by-laws clauses to protect small shareholders. It was also listed on both the New York and the Milan markets. ENI's shares rose in the months after privatization, and the operation may be considered a success. But a coherent program of privatization can be carried out only by a government with a solid parliamentary majority and the prospect of several years in office. The Dini government lived from confidence vote to confidence vote.

A dramatic vote of confidence was part of the Filippo Mancuso incident. As Minister of Justice, Mancuso waged a guerrilla war against the magistrates. He launched no fewer than 217 inspections and his favorite target was the Milan pool. Whatever his motives—eccentricity, Kantian moral rigor, or a belief that the magistrates had grown too powerful—the result of his actions was to reinforce Berlusconi's stand. In September the PDS was informed that Mancuso was opening up a new front against the Palermo anti-Mafia pool, and Luciano Violante was only one figure who recommended that Mancuso be reined in.[38]

There was an irony in the PDS's stand. The party had come around to the view that the magistrates too had to be reined in. The investigations of the red coops and of left-wing municipal governments—such as in Genoa where the mayor, D'Alema's supporter Claudio Burlando, had been accused of corruption on very flimsy evidence—had left their mark. D'Alema felt that it was time to redress the balance between legal and political power.

The PDS was following a mood in Italy. Even as fresh areas of corruption—in the armed forces and in the universities—were unveiled in the autumn of 1995, so public opinion grew less enthusiastic about the Clean Hands investigation. The departure of Di Pietro and the charges of corruption brought against him probably created confusion. There was still support for the Milan magistrates and opposition to letting the guilty politicians go free. But the support was not as strong as it had been. It was galvanized by Craxi's outrageous faxes from Hammamet, but the country simply could not go on rooting out a corruption that seemed, Hydra-like, to sprout multiple new heads for each head that was chopped off.

For the PDS, however, the gulf between weariness and deserting the Palermo pool was wide. Dini had adopted Fabian tactics after D'Alema's first conversation with him but by October the Center-Left parliamentary group wanted action. Mancuso saw matters differently: He felt that Dini had supported him in his attempt to root out improper action by investigating magistrates but had then abandoned him in order to maintain his position as prime minister.[39] It was true that Dini was losing his aura of neutrality and that over pensions, Mancuso, and the budget his government took a Center-Left stance.

Since Mancuso would not resign the only way to get rid of him was by a vote of no-confidence. In his speech of October 19, Mancuso did not merely defend himself but launched attacks on Dini, whom he depicted as a traitor, and on Scalfaro, against whom he made grave accusations. Mancuso maintained that Scalfaro had pressured him to bring charges against Berlusconi and Fini for calumniating the head of state and that in 1993, when Mancuso headed a commission of inquiry into the Sisde slush funds, Scalfaro and his staff had tried to persuade him to whitewash the president. The drama of the speech was heightened when Mancuso omitted these accusations from his oral version, threw onto the Senate floor the pages that listed them, including one blank page—was it a threat, a piece of blackmail, or a touch of melodrama?—and then declared that the oral version was the only authentic one.

Il Manifesto called for Mancuso, Dini, and Scalfaro to resign. None of them did but Mancuso received only 3 votes in his favor, while the Center-Right did not vote and the Center-Left voted him out of office. The plight of a gallant warrior punished for combatting the Milan magistrates was too much for Berlusconi, who had been sent for trial by those same magistrates earlier in the month. He called another confidence vote on the Dini government.

Once more, RC held the balance, and Bertinotti announced that his party would vote against the government. However he was overwhelmed with protests from his base, which rejected cooperation with the ex-Fascists. He abruptly changed his mind, Dini was saved and Berlusconi was left muttering about Communist treachery.

In all this, Dini had done little except endure, but he had endured well. He had taken no clear stand on the issue of the magistrates and he had postponed the decision on Mancuso as long as possible. He acquiesced to the Center-Left's policy, survived the onslaught of his former friends, and was rescued by people whose opinions were the antithesis of his. He also acquired a third job as Minister of Justice. Although he repeated that he would resign in December, he called for a grand coalition for which—and he left this unsaid—Lamberto Dini would make an excellent prime minister.[40]

The government was now safe until the budget came to a vote. Dini set out to reduce government borrowing by around $20 billion. Just less than half was to come from spending cuts and just more than half from new taxes.[41] Once more, employers were disappointed: the tax break on reinvested profits was cut drastically; the wealth tax was to be continued for another two years; and the sum of money allotted for public sector pay increases was suspiciously large. Meanwhile the Center-Left was aggrieved about a brand of federalism that cut the grants to regional and local governments, but allowed them to raise property taxes by 10 percent. Tax amnesties were proclaimed and the amount of money they were to bring in seemed suspiciously high.

When the budget came up for debate in December, it was found to contain a large tax break for Berlusconi, who was taking his TV networks onto the stock market in a company called Mediaset. The Center-Left removed the tax break and it can hardly have been a complete coincidence that Berlusconi resorted to another no-confidence vote.[42] Once more, playing the European card, Dini left for an EU summit in Spain and the no-confidence vote failed.

A conspicuous number of FI parliamentarians did not turn up. This made Berlusconi seem weak or, conversely, spawned a malicious rumor that their absence was to with the presence of state-owned banks among the financial backers of Mediaset.

Dini's government came to a natural end, and on December 30 he offered his resignation to Scalfaro. The budget had been passed but it represented the "Austrian" solution at its worst. Social tensions were avoided by financial compromises. Perhaps it was the best possible result and the markets seemed to recognize it as such, but the Bank of Italy called for a mini-budget in the Spring. At first Dini denied the need and the April elections ended the possibility. But the familiar rift between Dini and Fazio was reopened and the new government's first task would be to pass a mini-budget.

Perhaps if the Center-Left had had a firm majority in the House, it would have acquired more enthusiasm for rigor. By then inflation had broken through the barrier of wage restraint. Although growth stood at 3.4 percent, compared with 1.5 percent in Germany, the prime rate was 5.25 percent higher than in Germany, and the yield on a ten-year government bond was nearly 5 percent higher.[43]

Dini's government had made some but not much progress towards the Maastricht criterion. In 1995 the deficit was reduced to 7.4 percent of GDP but the total outstanding debt still hovered around 124 percent.[44] This was all the more damaging because, after the spluttering "nationalism" of Berlusconi, the Dini government had returned to traditional Europeanism. It consisted first of asking Italians to make sacrifices in the name of Europe. Thus Dini's pensions and budget proposals were presented as steps towards rejoining the EMS and the movement towards monetary union.

As Foreign Minister, Susanna Agnelli was regarded outside Italy with a confused reverence and was considered a vast improvement on Martino. She made progress in the dispute over the property rights of the Istrian refugees, and she bullied Slovenia less. She also asserted Italy's role in the Mediterranean without extolling the special harmony of Mediterranean man in the manner that had so irritated Andreatta.[45]

Agnelli also adopted an attitude of benign tolerance towards Jacques Chirac's repeated attacks on Italy. These began in June at the EU's Cannes summit. Chirac complained that the devaluation of the lira prevented his home region, the Corrèze, from exporting a single veal escallop to Italy. Italian agricultural experts displayed much ingenuity in refuting the accusation, and they discovered Corrèze escallops in every Italian city. Unappeased, Chirac denounced the Italian government for voting in the UN to condemn the French nuclear tests. Aside from the merits of the government's stand, it was prompted by a vote in the Rome parliament, and it reflected Italian opinion. When Agnelli deserted the Bastille Day celebration at the French embassy in Rome, there was no evidence the public objected, while anti-nuclear demonstrations organized by the Verdi drew large if not passionate crowds.

Dini stood up well to Chirac at Cannes and later. The French president canceled a visit to Italy in the Autumn, threatened not to attend the EU Intergovernmental Conference at Turin in March 1996 and suggested that Italy receive its EU grants in devalued lira rather than in écus. Dini countered by refusing to appear with Chirac at the EU's Madrid summit in December and by explaining away the effect of the lira devaluation in economic jargon that made the issue utterly incomprehensible. Chirac's touchiness was a parody rather than a continuation of de Gaulle's bold initiatives, and Italy's self-assertion was admirable.

It was not, however, accompanied by a serious reflection on the state of post-Maastricht Europe and the consequences for Italy. The Italian press reported the disarray in France, the record unemployment in Germany, and the strains in the Franco-German relationship. But the government continued to behave as if "Europe" were a paradise that sinful Italians could re-enter after repentance, fasting, and genuflections. If, as I argued in Chapter 3, a refounded Italian state could conduct an independent foreign policy, there was little sign that this was happening. The most useful service any Italian government could have rendered the EU and Italy was to use the Italian presidency to conduct a critical review of post-Maastricht Europe, which would include proposing alternatives to the present plan for monetary union or at least a sketch of the relationship between countries in the core group with countries outside it. But this chance was lost.

Nor is there much evidence that the Dini year saw any new departures in Italo-American relations. Italy sent troops to Bosnia as part of the NATO–UN intervention. Susanna Agnelli emphasized that it was a peace-keeping operation, the PDS and FI supported the action, and even RC agreed, provided it was more a UN and less a NATO intervention.[46] No one pretended to be enthusiastic or explained how the cost would be met. In September, Italy refused a request to allow a Stealth aircraft, the F 117A, to use the Aviano base for its Bosnian missions. The reason was Italy's exclusion from the core group of countries making decisions about Bosnia—the United States, Russia, Germany, Britain, and France. "They were accustomed to our saying an automatic yes to their every request," said Susanna Agnelli, who renewed an old Andreotti habit when she asserted independence of the United States at the Festa dell' *Unità*.[47]

Actually Italy's exclusion from the core group was less a U.S. than a French initiative. But here again no serious review of Italy's relationship with the United

States was made during Dini's year. If, as seems likely, the United States comes to play less of a role in Europe, then Italy will have to do more to ensure her own security.[48] The long-awaited age of neo-Atlanticism may have dawned as Atlanticism wanes. The opportunity for Italy to play a greater role in the Middle East may be at hand. Central Europe is another region where the Italian flag could follow trade. But until a government with a stable majority and a prospect for five years in office emerges, long term foreign policy planning is unlikely.

The judgment on Dini's year as prime minister must be positive as far as his performance is concerned. He ran the economy fairly well and he offered the financial markets an image of stability. He succeeded in maintaining social consensus. He nudged the banks down the road of modernization, and, if he did little to promote privatization and decentralization, he allowed them to proceed, albeit at a snail's pace. One can hardly expect more from a novice government supported by the Prime Minister's former foes. However, Dini's impact on the process of political reform is more dubious. Posing as a technocrat, he reinforced the public's belief that politicians do not know how to govern, whereas in reality Dini could have achieved nothing without the backing of the PDS. Finally, Dini's ambition led him to create a center party of his own. In my opinion there are few things Italy needs less than yet another small centrist party dominated by one individual.

A WASTED YEAR?

At the end of 1994 two observers of Italian politics wrote: "As yet we have not succeeded in achieving that minimum of political agreement without which no serious process of reform can be undertaken."[49] The view that the fault lay in the nature of Italian parties—and implicitly in the kind of groups that Italian society produced—was gaining ground. Perhaps the parties simply did not wish, and did not know how, to undertake institutional reforms that would permit clear majorities and stable governments. How does their behavior in 1995 support or contradict this judgment?

In January one party knew clearly what it wanted. AN was heading into the Fiuggi Congress, which was to mark its break with its Fascist past. According to *Il Manifesto* this was a classic case of change without change. The congressional document did not include the standard reference to the "continuity of ideals" with Fascism. Other familiar points of reference, such as corporatism, were missing.[50] But the delegates had no doubt what the real issue was: "the weight of the prejudices which had shamefully confined the right to a remote corner is falling away."⁵¹ AN was taking advantage of the DC's collapse to emerge from the ghetto.

Fini did put his followers to one test. A sentence in the congressional document spoke of the essential role of anti-Fascism in reestablishing democracy in Italy. This proved too much for Pino Rauti who led a small band of followers out of AN. At the time, Fini was probably pleased because Rauti was implying that AN really was different from the MSI. To anyone who had lived through the tortured and tortuous process by which the PCI became the PDS, the striking feature was how little self-criticism the electorate demanded of the ex-Fascists. Once more, one wondered retrospectively about the importance of anti-Fascism.

Fini did not allow the Congress to interfere with AN's daily business. In the confidence vote on the Dini government he joined Berlusconi in abstaining. In general, AN supported the Previti wing of FI, which backed Berlusconi's hard line. The polite candidate of the 1994 elections, who had held aloof from the "howling piazzas" of the left, was a remote memory. Berlusconi kept repeating that Italy was not a democracy and that he had been betrayed first by Bossi, and then by Scalfaro and Dini, who had promised early elections. Berlusconi talked less and less to his fellow-politicians and more and more to *la gente,* his mythical other self. He forced and lost the confidence vote over the mini-budget, and then he made the graver error of trying to turn the April regional elections into a referendum on his December ousting.

Not only do local and regional elections have a pattern of their own, but this time the voters were being allowed directly to choose the president of their region. So they were unlikely to vote for or against Berlusconi. Moreover FI was still a "virtual" party that lacked roots in local life. Finally the PDS was allied with the PPI.

Berlusconi was soundly defeated. The Center-Right carried Lombardy, Piedmont, Veneto, Campania, Calabria, and Puglia. It could take comfort from its victories in the most modern parts of Italy, but it lost not only in the red Center but in much of the South. Within the coalition, AN did not the make the expected gains, and FI remained the dominant party with 22.4 percent. But it ran behind the PDS, which with 25 percent became the largest party.

Although Berlusconi did not stop demanding national elections, his cries were growing shrill. In May his legal problems resurfaced and could not be conjured away by denunciations of Communist magistrates. The Gigi Lentini transfer fee was resurrected, but more serious were the arrest of Marcello Dell'Utri and the accusation that Fininvest had created massive slush funds on which no tax had been paid and that were used to bribe politicians.

By now Berlusconi seemed to have become a liability to the Center-Right. Certainly the contrast between his self-indulgence and Dini's image as the champion of rigor worked to the Prime Minister's advantage. Yet Berlusconi was saved by the referenda of June 12. There was a strong current of protest voting, but it was directed against the unions either for the concessions they had made in the pensions debate or for the negotiating power they seemed to possess. The electorate demonstrated that it wanted the Fininvest channels. The referenda that would have stripped Berlusconi of one or two of his channels or would have limited the activity of Publitalia became a vote for or against the Fininvest programs, some of which were extremely popular. Thirty-five percent of RC supporters voted to protect them.

The fluid nature of Italian politics in a period of transition was revealed: Dini was weakened by the vote against his interlocutors, the unions, while the PDS was associated with the onslaught on Fininvest, which it had, in reality, done little to foster. Popular support for Mike Buongiorno and the teenage idol, Ambra, rubbed off on Berlusconi. However in the Autumn his legal difficulties and his passion for no-confidence votes damaged him again.

The Lega survived its pyrrhic victory over Berlusconi in December 1994, but only just. It dropped to around 6 percent in the polls, lost many of its parliamentary representatives, and was cut off from its more plausible coalition partners on the right. In 1995 the Lega's main goal was survival, which meant keeping Dini in power and avoiding elections. It held the hard core of its electorate because of discontent in Northern Italy with the lack of political reform. Unimpressed by the steady but slow changes taking place at the grassroots, Lega militants from the heartland around Milan pointed to high interest rates, government instability, and, above all, a state that was more interventionist in combatting tax evasion among the self-employed, but incapable of offering the help small business needed. The Lega became ever more a vehicle of protest, and Bossi's language grew ever more radical and mythological. Autonomy not federalism was the watchword.

The Lega's future seemed in ever greater doubt, and it was widely felt that its decline would allow AN to penetrate Northern Italy. The Center-Left made various attempts to convert the parliamentary alliance with the Lega into an electoral alliance, but the rhetoric of autonomy and the history of betrayal made the Lega an unlikely ally.

Bossi incorporated the film *Braveheart* into his personal legend: He was no longer King Arthur but rather Wallace, who was defending Scotland—or was it Ireland?—against the Roman robbers who had adopted the winner-take-all electoral system invented by "the English pigs." Wallace was hanged, drawn and quartered because he clung to his principles; Bossi warned D'Alema that he was equally intransigent, but that he did not intend to meet the same fate.[52] As a proof, Bossi inaugurated a Northern parliament at Mantua. The Lega members of the Rome parliament helped pass a decree allowing the government greater freedom in expelling immigrants. But Bossi denounced it as wholly inadequate and returned to Mantua. Reverting to his original legend of the victory over Frederick Barbarossa, he told his followers, who were assembled at Pontide, that the Lega's only interest in Roman politics was the creation of a Constituent Assembly to work out the division of Italy. This was Bossi's most difficult hour, and yet he would survive it because his flamboyant brand of political theater corresponded to a genuine, if more sober, demand.

Meanwhile the situation on the left had changed. As leader of the PDS, D'Alema first concentrated on rebuilding his party's self-confidence and on reassuring its organization, which had been bewildered by the unpredictable Occhetto. D'Alema interpreted the defeat of March 1994 as a demonstration of the need to form an alliance with the center rather than as a spur to transform the PDS into a party that could attract centrist voters. His deputy, Walter Veltroni, who had inherited the PCI fascination with "the other America," had a different view of the PDS. His model was the Democratic Party of John Kennedy. However he shared the conclusion that an alliance with the center was vital and he was more willing than D'Alema to merge the PDS into a Center-Left coalition.

In February the providential coalition partner turned up in the shape of Romano Prodi. In reality Prodi, who offered himself as the leader of the Center-Left, mostly PDS-PPI, alliance, was part of a campaign led by Andreatta and the old DC left against Rocco Buttiglione's plan to lead the PPI into an alliance with Forza Italia. Buttiglione had the support of Cardinal Sodano, the Vatican secretary of state, and of Cardinal Ruini, the head of the Council of Italian Bishops.

Andreatta's strategy worked, for the alternative offered by Prodi railroaded Buttiglione into Berlusconi's camp, but robbed him of many followers. An unedifying battle ensued as the PPI's National Council ousted Buttiglione as party secretary by three votes; in turn he appealed to the courts and was reinstated. Legal battles were fought over the DC emblem, while the battles for office space in Piazza del Gesu were almost physical. The Comunione e Liberazione current sided with Buttiglione, and Rosy Bindi, the Joan of Arc from the Veneto, backed Prodi. The PPI's businessmen divided—Calisto Tanzi opting for the right and Vittorio Merloni for the left. The leaders of the Catholic voluntary organizations went with Prodi, while the bishops divided.

However the Church leadership was cool to Prodi. It did not treat him as harshly as it had treated Segni, but the inextinguishable distrust of the ex-PCI persisted. Abortion was the burning issue, but along with it came a concern for Catholic schools and an attempt to place limits on the state in social policy. The Soviet Union having collapsed, the PDS had no alternative focus of loyalty. From Berlinguer it had inherited the ideal of a democratic and fair Italian state. The Catholics, whether because the Vatican has not collapsed or because of their belief in their version of civil society—the family and the voluntary organizations—considered the PDS too statist on social issues.

This nagging dispute reveals how complex the problem of the state can be in Italy. It was not, however, crucial to the alliance that went through an initially good phase before encountering difficulties. Prodi presented himself as the antithesis of the new Berlusconi and as a leader who somewhat resembled the Berlusconi of March 1994. He talked little of his stint at IRI, claimed never to have been a member of the old DC, and stressed that he wanted to bring into politics people from the professions and industry. To the glory of AC Milan, Prodi opposed the freedom of his Sunday cycling rambles in the hills around Bologna. He declared his admiration for Gino Bartali, the great post-war Catholic cyclist, but remembered, as an ally of the PDS, to say a kind word about his rival, Fausto Coppi, who was considered to be a left-winger. Where Berlusconi's TV networks had centralized Italy, Prodi set out in a camper to visit the Italy of the hundred cities.[53]

This brand of Catholic populism was refreshing after Berlusconi's maniacal monologues of betrayal. However doubts were soon raised about Prodi's TV performance and, more important, about his ability to pull together the Center-Left alliance. These problems lie at the core of the political system's inability to reform itself.

On the PDS's right lies an area that includes left-wing parties, like the former PSI; the Verdi, who are a new group; the remnants of the PRI, who are centrist but lay; Segni's shrunken band; and the PPI. In 1995 these and other groups were small, but some of them were large enough to survive on their own, while the others preferred to form electoral alliances rather than to merge into a new, strong party. All were conscious of representing cultural, social, and geographical currents that ran deep in Italian history.

The new, "British" voting system encouraged but did not compel them to unite. Disunity would cost votes, but might be preferable to the sacrifice of historical identity. The problem was compounded by the size of the PDS and by its Communist past, which clung to it. To the PDS's coalition partners, both factors were spurs to unite but they also had the opposite effect of making the parties stress their own identities while at the same time looking for other coalitions. Meanwhile the PDS's residual illegitimacy made it seek any and every coalition partner—Dini after Prodi and Amato after Dini—even as its good organization worried its existing partners.

All these effects are so perverse that one cannot help seeing in the divided, weak Center-Left the historic fragility and divisions of Italian society. Meanwhile the burden of creating unity fell onto Prodi, who was unable to shoulder it. He could not create a party of his own without breaking with the PPI. He had no power over the other parties that belonged to his Olive Tree coalition, but did not wish to be absorbed into it. They could depart, as the Verdi threatened to do and as Segni did. The PDS dispatched Veltroni to become deputy leader of the Olive Tree, but D'Alema remained cool.[54]

Prodi proved to have little talent for knocking heads together. His only power lay in his role as the Center-Left's candidate for Prime Minister, but, as elections receded, criticism of his performance mounted. The Center-Left limped along until Dini's resignation and D'Alema's attempt to strike a bargain with Fini and Berlusconi.

In 1985, the third attempt at cooperation between the now ex-Communists and the Catholics was no great success. Unlike the first two attempts, it was not stymied because of a clash between strong, conflicting identities. The comparisons between Prodi and Dossetti are silly: Prodi is an efficient manager untroubled by visions of a Catholic Italy. Similarly, no PDS leader shares Berlinguer's admiration for the ascetic Communist militant who has more duties than rights.

This time the cause lay in the general inability of the political system to reorganize itself into large, stable units. The PPI with 6 percent in the regional elections and the Lega with 6.4 percent lived on. So did a plethora of smaller groups on the left and right. Charismatic leaders emerged. Their charisma was used up quickly but they remained. Pannella was a ghost from the past, and Di Pietro was a promise or an illusion of the future. The utterly uncharismatic Dini was the present. As already argued, politics can bring about change: Action by Amato and Dini fostered improvements in banking. But politics cannot impose a general shape on change because it cannot impose such a shape on itself.

It is not surprising that societal and economic innovations run ahead of politics. This was true in France from 1945 to 1958. But politics has to catch up. 1995 did not witness any catching up. Instead it demonstrated how a shrewd individual could exploit the system to remain in power. The main hope remains institutional reform. Certainly the problems lie deep in Italian society and history and, as I shall argue in the brief conclusion, they are closely linked with Italy's merits, which makes it all the harder to resolve them. But, while cultural change is required, and flawed societal relationships lie beneath the teeming, squabbling parties, one must start somewhere—and institutional reform has made an impact. Two kinds of reform are worth cultivating: The elimination of the residual 25 percent of seats awarded by PR and a shift of power from the legislative to the executive branch. In early 1986, I felt that perhaps the best result that could emerge from the April elections would be a hung parliament that would promote such changes.

So Italy stumbled back to the voting booth, to the delight of the many schoolchildren who would have a few days holiday because their schools were to be used as polling centers. The leading questions were: Would the mood of protest in Northern Italy save the Lega? Did Berlusconi, discredited among élites, retain his charisma among the masses? Did AC Milan's return to the top of the first division signal the come-back of its owner? On the Center-Left, Prodi would have the chance to give up the role of leader of the opposition and present himself as a prospective prime minister. D'Alema would have to appeal not merely to the PDS but to the electorate. The clashing small parties would have to show that they could unite and govern. The country had to decide whether it wished to be governed.

11

The 1996 Elections: A Victory for the Left or for the "Establishment"?

The question posed by the April 1996 elections was whether or not the political system had caught up: Could it now reshape itself and guide the changes in Italian society? An optimistic judgment is that the elections marked "the baptism of a new kind of Italian identity."[1] So the tale I have been telling would not, after all, end with three dots. It would end with a full stop to mark the refounding of the Italian state. It has been, however, impossible to make such a leap of faith. The Prodi government has presented a mini-budget, which represents its first significant act. Until more evidence is available, the three dots must remain.

One can examine the election campaign and the vote, as well as the new government's various components, its programs, and its worldview. These topics must be set in the double historical context of the process of change initiated in 1992 and of the underlying problem of the state.

THE 1996 CAMPAIGN:
THE GOOD, THE BAD, AND THE LEGA

The campaign that culminated in the April 21 election emerged from the struggle described in the previous chapter. Having broken with Berlusconi, the

Lega had no allies, which meant it could win few seats in parliament because of the predominantly "British," winner-take-all voting system. The logic of isolation led Bossi to redouble his attacks on the "Roman robbers" and to move ever further down the road of federalism. After the election he had little choice but to begin his battle for secession.

Berlusconi could not escape from the hardline position he had taken towards the Dini government. It was not really a matter of policy, although Berlusconi did adopt diverse but unfailingly right-wing policies—such as enterprise zones in the South, where employers would not be bound by existing labor law or by a constitutional change to permit the direct election of the president.

More important, however, were personalities and language. The leading dove in FI, Vittorio Dotti, was removed from politics by the Ariosto affair. Stefania Ariosto, Dotti's lover, made serious allegations of wrongdoing against Fininvest executives. Why she made them, how much Dotti knew, and why she chose to make his position in FI impossible are questions that remain unanswered. But the affair strengthened the position of hawks like Cesare Previti. When he declared that, if the Center-Right won the elections, it "would take no prisoners,"[2] Previti was imitating Berlusconi's tone of anger, his sense of politics as total war, and his manichaean vision of society. Another FI dove declared that the electorate was disturbed by the "arrogance" and "truculence" of such language.[3]

By contrast the Center-Left adopted the tone of sweet reasonableness that Prodi had introduced in the Spring of 1995. Against Berlusconi's messianic sense that he was chosen to lead by a people that existed only to follow him, the Center-Left stressed consultation and solidarity. Its spokesmen varied their vocabulary: D'Alema avoided all mention of class. He was relentlessly rational and frequently spoke of "serenity."[4] But these were variations on the same theme. Whereas Berlusconi had won the 1994 elections because he inspired people more than Occhetto did, he lost two years later because he frightened people, while his opponents reassured them.

The first round of the campaign was won by Berlusconi, and that may have misled him. In March, Prodi was, as described in Chapter 10, shouted down by the Turin shopkeepers who were exasperated by a complicated tax code that made demands on their time and exposed them to substantial penalties if they failed to observe it. Both Berlusconi and Fini tried to exploit the strong current of anti-statism and, in so doing, they gave the impression that a Center-Right government would spark social conflicts. Moreover Fini's suggestion that income tax not be withheld at source was quite simply preposterous. Although there were votes to be won in Northern Italy by denouncing the state, the general mood in the country was more complex. The historic need for the state had not vanished: Even the small businessmen in the Veneto knew that only the state could provide the infrastructure and organize the research and development that they needed. They wanted a different kind of state rather than no state at all. The Center-Right's program described a limited but not absent state; the Center-Right's rhetoric, which culminated in the slogan of "No rules on the people,"[5] seemed to promise anarchy.

Certainly FI and AN sounded violent. Berlusconi reinforced this impression when he compared the Milan magistrates, who were continuing their investigation of Fininvest, with a group of policemen who had turned to armed robbery and murder.[6] As the magistrates became a campaign issue, the Center-Right suffered from its divisions. AN generally supported the magistrates and, while Berlusconi's pleas that he was being persecuted may have aroused some sympathy, his anathemas conveyed the impression that a government led by him would wage war against the magistrates.

Towards the end of the campaign, as his own polls began to show the Center-Right running behind the Center-Left, Berlusconi grew desperate. He beat the drum of anti-communism, denouncing Prodi as a mere front for D'Alema and repeating that, if the Center-Left won, there would be no more free elections in Italy.[7] Berlusconi returned to his use of religious language and appealed to God to send His light upon the electorate.[8]

This was not the only case when Berlusconi went back to tactics that had worked in 1994. The trouble was that in 1994 he had the advantage of novelty, whereas in 1996 both the electorate and his opponents knew what to expect. This was apparent in his use of TV. I have argued in Chapter 8 that the politics of spectacle was merely one part of "the Berlusconi phenomenon" and that TV was merely one reason for his victory. But even if I were wrong, TV could not exert the same influence the second time around.

Romano Prodi was bad on TV and initially took pride in being bad: It was proof that he was an authentic, ordinary person. However Prodi's performance improved as the campaign went along and he learned how to use TV to project an image of authenticity. His two debates with Berlusconi went better than his advisors had expected.[9] Meanwhile, Berlusconi went on TV too often and wore out his welcome. A key difference between 1994 and 1996 was his smile. In 1994 he had radiated health—via a permanent suntan—wealth, success, and seduction.[10] In 1996 his smile flashed on and off and, in the frequent periods when it was off, Berlusconi looked tired and exasperated.[11] Meanwhile Gianfranco Fini, whose penchant for grand platitudes had helped convince the 1994 voter that AN was no longer a fascist party, found it harder to convince the 1996 voter that the Center-Right would govern more competently than it had done during its eight months of power.

This defeat of the Center-Right refuted the thesis that European elections have been reduced to image and spectacle, unless one argues that the Center-Left deployed a sophisticated brand of anti-image and anti-spectacle. The PDS leaders sought to legitimize their party as a party of government by stressing its moderation. D'Alema's use of terms like "the rules of society," and his claim that social conflicts could take place only within a "common frame of reference," conveyed the admittedly vague vision of a rational party that would govern by consensus.[12] Walter Veltroni reassured the voters by offering the American Democratic Party as the model for the PDS.

Further legitimacy came from the PDS's allies. Since the Center-Left was stressing competence, Lamberto Dini's role was to defend the economic record of his government and to attack the record of Berlusconi's government. He did so with a vigor that provided yet more proof of his skills as a politician. Meanwhile Prodi continued to tour Italy in his bus and to use the language of the Church's social teaching, stressing "solidarity," "community," and each person's "creative ability."[13] Now that the campaign had begun Prodi's position within the Center-Left coalition was stronger. The doubts he inspired in D'Alema and the rivalry between him and Dini remained, but were at least temporarily smoothed over.

The different languages of the Center-Right and the Center-Left indicated different ways of running the state. It is not too great an exaggeration to say that they repeated, although obviously with many new nuances, the argument between Crispi and Giolitti that is mentioned in chapter 1, as well as the "Gaullist" and "Austrian" solutions discussed in chapters 3 and 8. So the thesis that the 1996 elections were fought over differences of policy rather than over the nature of the state is unconvincing. Such a thesis is based on an examination of the problems that seemed important to the electorate: When interviewed, 34.4 percent of people said healthcare was their prime concern, while the next largest group—32.7 percent—declared that taxation was the dominant issue. By contrast a mere 12.7 percent said they were most interested in the institutions of the state.[14] This might seem to indicate that problems such as electoral reform, which had been so widely discussed in the years since 1992, had been pushed into the background by more concrete, everyday concerns.

However the nature of the two dominant issues reveals that this is not so. Healthcare lies at the core of the welfare state, while cuts in taxation were originally the hallmark of the neoliberal state. Social groups assessed the relative weight of the issues very differently: 43.2 percent of entrepreneurs considered taxation reform their first priority, while only 25.1 percent placed healthcare at the top of their list. Housewives reversed this order, 43.7 percent ascribing greater importance to healthcare and 30.3 percent to taxation.

The task of responding to these conflicting demands falls on all European governments, but it is exacerbated in Italy. Both issues are inseparable from the reform of the state bureaucracy, which was cited by 15.3 percent of people interviewed as their prime concern. All reforms are obstructed by the government debt, which remains, obstinately, at approximately 120 percent of GDP. In turn this raises the questions of the Maastricht agreement and Italy's European policy. One returns to the theme that the crisis of the Italian state is, in part, a crisis of modernization. From this viewpoint the meaning of the election campaign was the struggle to demonstrate which of the two contenders could better carry out this process of modernization. The Center-Left won because it promised to combine efficiency with protection of the weaker social groups, to consult rather than to dictate, and to reform the state with as few upheavals as possible.

However distorted it may have been, this was the choice that the two kinds of discourse conveyed. A glance at the varying roles of other actors will reinforce my interpretation. The Church had little choice but to remain on the sidelines. Prodi was too good a Catholic to be chastised for forming an alliance with the ex-communists. But although Cardinal Martini of Milan and the influential magazine, *Famiglia cristiana,* openly supported him, a majority of bishops probably felt happier with the Center-Right. They knew, however, that some of the most committed Catholics—those who led the voluntary organizations, although not necessarily those who worked in them—had chosen the Center-Left. On March 25 Cardinal Ruini reiterated a statement made by Pope John-Paul II in November 1995: The Church would endorse certain values but would not distinguish among parties.

The Mafia also sat out the elections. FI was the strongest party in Sicily but there is no hard evidence that the Mafia campaigned for it. The Corleonesi suffered another blow when the news broke that the young son of Santo Di Matteo had been strangled and his corpse dissolved in acid. Di Matteo was a mafioso who had turned state's evidence and, although it was generally known that the Mafia struck at the families of members who "repented,"[15] this was a particularly brutal case that helped provoke further defections from among the Corleonesi.

The trade unions worked hard for the Center-Left. They wished to continue being consulted as they had been during the PDS-backed Dini government. They also wished to preserve the July 1993 agreement as well as the 1995 pensions reform. Most intriguing was the role of the business élite. Antonio Maccanico, who joined forces with the PPI, had worked for Mediobanca. Cuccia's opinion of Berlusconi had not improved, and neither had Gianni Agnelli's. By contrast, Prodi and Dini were competent economists who understood the need to cut the debt and to combat rising inflation in order to obtain lower interest rates and to participate in the EU's drive towards monetary union. The Marzotto family, leading producers of textiles, provide another example of industrialists who supported Prodi.

Can one see in the PPI-Maccanico alliance the meeting of a reformed DC and the lay business élite? One might go further and consider a third component: the Bank of Italy. Ciampi had also joined the Prodi camp, bringing with him the Bank's record of integrity and economic rigor. One should not exaggerate the homogeneity of these forces, if only because the Bank's governor, Antonio Fazio, had criticized industrialists for unnecessary price increases that fuel inflation. Moreover the term "establishment" implies a longstanding élite endowed with a common culture. Yet it is tempting to see behind the Center-Left coalition the kind of would-be establishment discussed in Chapter 5.

In that context the presence of the PDS in the coalition constitutes not merely the third attempt since 1945 at a catholic–ex-communist meeting, but also an updated version of the producers' pact that hovered on the horizon, like a mirage, during the 1970s. Nor can one omit to mention, when D'Alema has supported Prodi's call for budget cuts, the legacy of rigor bequeathed to the PDS by Enrico Berlinguer. Here again one remains skeptical because of the socioeconomic and cultural rifts in the coalition. But its various worldviews contain elements—such as a rather uncritical Europeanism, the need for social cooperation, and an emphasis on the family[16]—that are shared by most groups in the coalition. Some of these elements are "conservative" or at least are not a part of the tradition of the West European left. But comparative politics is less useful than Italian history in providing insights into the nature of the new government.

THE ELECTION—THE NEED FOR ALLIES

In the closing days of the campaign the polls showed that the Lega's vote, far from collapsing, was increasing. This was another drawback of Berlusconi's choice of language: In the struggle to win the protest vote, he had to compete with "Braveheart" Bossi who spoke of "decapitating Rome."[17] Neither Berlusconi nor Fini could equal the anti-statism of a movement whose goal was to do away with the Italian state. The Lega's 10.1 percent share of the House vote blocked the expected break-through of AN in Northern Italy. Yet Fini's vote increased by 2.2 percent, while FI's vote was virtually the same as in 1994 when the CCD was included in it. The paradox was that the Center-Right group received 44.9 percent of the vote, whereas in 1994 it had, if one discounts the Lega, only 41 percent. Conversely the parties of the Center-Left won 43.7 percent, whereas in 1994 an equivalent group of parties won 47.7 percent.[18] This meant that the Center-Right gained more votes than the Center-Left.

In turn, such a result calls into question our thesis that Berlusconi's violent language damaged his coalition. One answer to this objection is that the Center-Right won only 38 percent of the 1994 PPI-Patto Segni voters, whereas the Center-Left won 59 percent. Berlusconi needed to find many new voters to compensate for the voters he lost when the Lega left his coalition. This is why the campaign was important and why Berlusconi's language damaged him. The main factor in his defeat, however, was that he was outmanoeuvred in the art of coalition-building. In 1994 he had defeated Occhetto by forming an alliance with the Lega, whereas Left and Center were divided. In 1996 the reverse was true.

The "British" voting system penalizes smaller parties and encourages coalitions. It worked against the Lega, which saw its vote increased and its parliamentary representation halved. Although it cannot change deepseated social patterns, the "British" system is a partial cure for the fragmentation that weakened the postwar political system. With a percentage of the popular vote comparable to Margaret Thatcher's, the Center-Left won an outright majority of seats in the senate, while in the House it and RC had an outright majority. Across Northern Italy, Prodi's army won seats that Occhetto's battalions had lost because the Lega split the Center-Right vote. So Prodi could claim, with some exaggeration, that he was able to offer Italy five years of stable government. This is enough time to undertake a serious privatization program and to be in power when the fruits of rigor ripen. Yet Prodi's lack of an autonomous majority in the House is likely to spur further electoral reform.

Another conclusion to be drawn from the assertion that allies not votes were decisive is that the Center-Left's victory does not mark a great swing to the left among Italians. It was inevitable that a myth should be created on the day the results were declared: For the first time since 1947 the (ex-)communists were to come to power. One suspects that the PDS encouraged the myth of a historic triumph for the left in order to make it more difficult for RC to bring down the government in the House.

A glance at the voting patterns reveals no great swings in any direction; instead there is a complex blend of continuity and change. The PDS was the largest party, but its 21.1 percent was lower than it had hoped. FI remained virtually static at 20.6 percent. Prodi brought few new voters to the PPI, which won 6.8 percent. Dini's new party barely succeeded in going above the 4 percent minimum needed to win any seats. The Verdi fell below it: Once more, environmentalism failed to make an impact in Italy. The segments of the DC that had gone over to the right gained 1 percent fewer than the PPI. Protest accounted for most, although not all, of the votes that went to the Lega and to RC, which went up to 8.6 percent. A further indication of protest was the 23 percent who either did not vote or cast an invalid ballot. This percentage has more than doubled in the last twenty years and has continued to rise since 1992. Yet these statistics do not indicate an electoral earthquake.[19] The only striking feature to emerge from a study of the regions was the Lega's success in the North, where it became the largest party with 20.5 percent. If we switch to the Senate, we see that Bossi's legions swelled to 19.1 percent in Piedmont, 24.4 percent in Lombardy, and a triumphant 30.3 percent in the Veneto. There is a link between the recent economic growth in the Veneto and the surge of support for the Lega: The small entrepreneurs and their employees, successful but insecure and still politically underrepresented, were disappointed with the Berlusconi government and turned (back) to Bossi. In Northern Italy as a whole, the Lega's strongholds lie in the "pre-alpine" area that runs from Varese and Como, via Brescia, across to Belluno and Treviso.[20] However the cities, endowed with large industries or financial and service sectors, are contemptuous of the Lega. Although it won the mayoral election in Milan in 1993, its following has ebbed. In the rich center of the city, Bossi ran a bad third behind Berlusconi and the Center-Left candidate in the House race. In Milan as a whole the Lega won only 12 percent, and in Turin it reached a mere 9.7 percent.

Meanwhile the Center of Italy remained red or at least pale pink. In the House elections the PDS won 28.6 percent of the vote, while RC reached 11.2 percent. FI was weak—15.7 percent—and the leading party of the Center-Right was AN with 22.3 percent. In the South, excluding the islands, the Center-Right dominated. FI won 22.3 percent and AN 19.2 percent, although the PDS achieved virtually its national level with 20.9 percent. This region, so long dominated by the DC, gave only 7.3 percent of its votes to the PPI and 8.1 percent to its right-wing rival, the CCD-CDU. FI also swept the islands where it won nearly 30 percent of the vote.

Sociologically the Lega paid for its macho swagger: only 45 percent of its voters were women, whereas both the Center-Right and the Center-Left voters were 50 percent women. No party had a special appeal for the young; 16 percent of Center-Right voters and 15 percent of Center-Left voters came from the 18-24 age-group. Predictably the Center-Left found more of its voters among workers than the Center-Right did: 15 percent to 11 percent. However the Lega found 26 percent of its voters among workers, which demonstrates its ability to overcome class differences in the name of region. The old appeared un-troubled by a neoliberal assault on the social services: They voted in roughly equal numbers for the Center-Right and the Center-Left. Entrepreneurs, free professionals, shopkeepers, and artisans were less tolerant: Twice as many of them voted for the Center-Right as for the Center-Left.

In this brief analysis, sociological and geographical continuity is apparent, although class differences are softening. Signs of change are the Lega's strength and the Church's absence. Fewer than 25 percent of practicing Catholics voted for the parties that emerged from the old DC. Continuing a trend that began in the 1970s, the electorate demonstrated its mobility: One third of voters declared that they could have changed their minds in the course of the campaign.[21] So the best way to interpret the election result is to see it as a political choice: The electorate went shopping for the best basket of leaders, alliances, programs, and discourse, and it bought the Center-Left's basket. There was nothing definitive about the choice and next time the electorate may reverse it. The politicians' task is not to make or unmake revolutions, but to prepare the baskets.

Just as the Berlusconi government was an experiment that Italy, given its liking for populism and charisma, was likely to try, so the Center-Left government, which wove together many different policies and groups, was a logical reaction against it and a logical successor to it. The most revealing statistic may be that, in the constituency-based vote for the House, the candidates running under the Center-Left banner gained some 500,000 votes more than the parties that made up the Center-Left coalition gained in the PR vote. The opposite was true of the Center-Right. This was not a matter of the individual candidates, about whom most voters knew little. It was a vote for a project, the outlines of which we must now describe.

FRAGMENTATION, SHARED RIGOR, AND—PERHAPS—A NEW STATE

On May 18, the Prodi government was sworn in. It contained 20 ministers, a relatively low number of which sent a message that the war for spoils, characteristic of the old regime, was less ferocious. Only three of the twenty were women and even these were restricted to traditionally "female" concerns—health, social solidarity, and equal opportunity. The chance to make another break with the past was thus lost. Yet, even opponents admitted that the quality of the ministers was high, which constituted a second innovation.

The PDS, which had brought the coalition approximately half its votes, received nine ministries—including the deputy-premiership, which went to Walter Veltroni, and the Interior, which was given to Giorgio Napolitano. Since

Luciano Violante became Speaker of the House and the PDS also obtained a good number of undersecretaries, the debate about the excessive weight of the ex-communists grew unnecessarily heated. The Emilia-Romagna PDS was rewarded for its efforts, which had often been made on behalf of candidates from other parties, when Pierluigi Bersani, the president of the region, was named Minister of Industry.

Antonio Di Pietro became Minister of Public Works, a clever appointment since it prevented him from straying off to the right, and since he is an expert at preventing the buying and selling of public contracts. It remains to be seen whether the charismatic Di Pietro can tolerate the trade-offs inherent in working as one of a team of ministers. Prodi had to fight for Giovanni Maria Flick as Minister of Justice. Flick was a lawyer who had defended people brought to trial by the Milan magistrates, and his appointment was a sign that the Center-Left government, while allied with the magistrates, wanted to avoid being identified with them. The example of Biondi is likely to deter Flick from instant amnesties, and Flick serves rather as an example of Prodi's desire to reconcile the various political and social groups. Different versions of this goal led the government to offer to the Center-Right the post of Speaker of the Senate and led D'Alema to renew his bid to involve Berlusconi in discussions about constitutional change.

Such ecumenism has brought to the Center-Left the familiar charges of "change-without-change," which were discussed in Chapter 1. But such charges do not seem justified since the worst examples of buying off challengers and of watering down decisions to suit as many people as possible—the normal practice of the DC-led coalitions—occurred when the opposition—in this case the PCI—sought, or supposedly sought, to overthrow not just the government but the political and social order. D'Alema's view is that consensus on such an order and on the opposition's role in maintaining it allows for sharper clashes over concrete issues. This is plausible, but history has left Italian society with a distaste for sharp clashes so that the sociological and cultural reasons to be suspicious of the Center-Left's ecumenism remain valid.

The goal of cooperation was one reason for Ciampi's appointment as Treasury Minister: He is identified with the agreement of July 1993. Other reasons include the attempt to link this government with Ciampi's government, which is correctly seen as an earlier expression of the reform process begun in 1992. Ciampi's presence is also a signal to the markets that priority will be given to setting the state's finances in order.

Finally the Center-Left's internal ecumenism, its need to include all its components, found expression in the appointment of Dini as Foreign Minister and of Antonio Maccanico, reputedly an associate of Enrico Cuccia, as Minister of the Post, which includes the sensitive issue of TV. The same motive prompted the appointment of 49 undersecretaries, five more than was originally stated. Nine were women, which partially corrected the previous insensitivity. Ten were "technicians": experts in their fields who are supposedly free of any political affiliation. They represent the post-1992 rejection of the excessive role previously played by the parties and the new emphasis on competence. Prodi and Dini were considered "technicians" and Ciampi still is. The establishment looks kindly on technicians and its approval is reciprocated.

As argued in chapter 10, the Center-Left groups are far from united and four potential splits have already appeared. The most obvious is the position of RC, which had an electoral alliance with the Center-Left but which, according to Bertinotti "is not part of the government's majority, although it does not view the government with indifference."[22] Bertinotti added that RC wished to be consulted regularly, but he also stated that his party would view each issue on its merits.

Since RC is reluctant to privatize, supports wage-indexation, criticizes the Maastricht agreement, and is hostile to NATO, Bertinotti's last statement has an ominous ring. There is a widespread view, shared by Prodi, that RC will simply be unable to bring down a leftwing government that can only be replaced by the right. This is true at the moment but, if the policy of economic rigor arouses popular discontent, RC may find it difficult to vote with the government. This would at the very least weaken the government and it might lead to the disintegration of the Center-Left.

The threat from the left reinforces the threat from the right. Although he worked well with the PDS while he was Prime Minister, Dini entered politics on the right and continues to surround himself with Andreottiani. He has stated that he views the existing coalitions as temporary and that he might like to form a center-right party. He cited the American Republicans as a model.[23] In the meantime Dini, who feels his supporters are underrepresented in the government, looks with interest at the CCD-CDU and at the many FI parliamentarians—his supporters in 1994—who are worried by Berlusconi's erratic leadership. Dini's interest is reciprocated and, if the Center-Right coalition were to break up, Dini could pick up the pieces and perhaps form a government without the PDS.

In this scenario, Dini's closest ally might be the Church. After the elections Cardinal Ruini reiterated that the bishops would not choose parties but would indicate values. However he called on Catholic politicians to find ways of working together to promote those values. Implicit in Ruini's statement was that they might choose to unite in one group.[24] *Avvenire* was blunter. Commenting on the election results, it noted that "within the victorious coalition a massive influence is exerted by parties whose physical make up leads them to behave differently from the way christians behave." The title of the article "A new scenario and old dilemmas" could not be more appropriate because *Avvenire* was harking back to a Cold War view of the PDS and RC. Nor did this catholic newspaper refrain from expressing its preference for a coalition of CCD-CDU, Forza Italia (with or without Berlusconi?), the PPI including Maccanico's group, and Dini's movement.[25]

The fourth threat to the coalition comes from the strength and strategy of the PDS. *Avvenire*'s argument, repeated with different nuances by most components of the Center-Left coalition, is that the PPI, the Verdi, and the mini-formations like the Rete are too small to counterbalance the PDS. With regard to the complaint about strength, there are two answers. First, although the PDS is still well organized, it no longer possesses, outside Emilia-Romagna, the mass base that Berlinguer's PCI enjoyed in the 1970s. In short the PDS is less strong than its legend proclaims. Second, the solution is for the other groups to unite because Italian politics needs larger units.

The complaint about strategy is that, while Veltroni favors dissolving the PDS into the Center-Left coalition, which would become an organized, united movement, D'Alema rejects this. He has a vision of the PDS as an Italian version of the German Social Democrats or of Tony Blair's British Labour Party. At first sight this complaint is more plausible because, unlike Blair's party, the PDS cannot hope to win an election on its own. But, although Veltroni's vision of the Center-Left coalition as an Italian version of the U.S. Democratic Party answers the need for fewer and larger parties, it is in my opinion utopian. The risk is that the PDS's relative strength would be eroded, while the coalition would remain an amalgam. In recent days D'Alema has talked about merging the PDS with other left-wing movements, perhaps with the help of Giuliano Amato. This appears a more realistic goal, although one doubts whether Amato would bring many extra votes, and inevitably he would become a rival to Prodi for the post of prime minister.[26]

The threats to the Prodi government come more from within than without. Will it, and the coalition, be strong enough to withstand the discontent that is an integral part of a changing Italy and that the policy of rigor will exacerbate? Will Prodi prove to be a better prime minister than he was a leader of the opposition? The Center-Right is going through the period of self-scrutiny that usually follows electoral defeat. Fini, whose domination of his party was absolute as long as it kept winning, has become an ordinary mortal. The CCD-CDU are wondering aloud whether their future still lies in the Center-Right coalition, as it exists now. FI's plight is even more serious: A virtual party with a charismatic leader, it now doubts that leader. Berlusconi's financial position will be improved if the plan to launch the media components of Fininvest as a public company, under the name of Mediaset, is welcomed on the Milan stockmarket.[27] He would, however, still face serious legal problems. The decisive issue is whether or not Berlusconi has exhausted his political appeal.

While the Center-Right agonizes over its failings, Bossi is leading "Padania" towards independence. Disappointed that he did not hold the balance of power in parliament, Bossi is now advocating the secession of Northern Italy. His crusade is both splendid political theater and deadly serious. The theater is the Mantua parliament, the government of the North headed by the ex-minister, Giancarlo Pagliarini and the liberation committee. Still acting out *Braveheart,* Bossi talks of the forthcoming war of independence. Enthusiastic supporters from the Veneto bear the banner under which their city-state went into battle seven hundred years ago: It depicts a lion with a sword and a closed book.

The serious element is that the Lega is expressing the discontent of a hard-headed, economically dynamic segment of Northern Italy. From Varese to Treviso exasperated voters are proclaiming, via Bossi's virulence and his myths, that they want more control over their own affairs. Prodi must give priority to decentralization. He must not expect gratitude: the alienation and the superiority complexes of many Lega voters run too deep. Like those Sicilians who look on in silence while the Palermo magistrates combat the Mafia, they incarnate the need for reforms.

The Center-Left's economic policy is designed to revive the state by setting its finances in order. Economics is linked with both decentralization and the anti-Mafia struggle. In his first speeches to the House and Senate, Prodi promised the regions and the cities greater financial autonomy and a simplified system of local taxation. In discussing the Mafia he stressed the need to offer Sicilians the chance to develop a legitimate economy.[28] The new government had just received a boost when Giovanni Brusca, a Corleonese chieftain who is thought to have murdered the young Di Matteo, was arrested on May 20. It was a triumph for the Palermo police and magistrates, and it reduced the number of Sicilians who look on in silence.

The state's ability to act is limited by its chronic indebtedness, so rigor is the new government's key policy. Prodi stressed that there could be no reduction of taxation for the next three years and that a mix of public spending cuts and increased public revenue would reduce borrowing by nearly 1 percent of GDP in 1996 and by 1-2 percent in 1997. Meanwhile priority would be given to the struggle against inflation, which would strengthen the lira and bring about lower interest rates. Since the debt is fuelled by interest payments on the extravagances of the pre-1992 regime, lower rates are essential. Following the practice of the old regime, Prodi wrapped his austerity package in Europeanism: These measures would enable Italy to meet three of the Maastricht requirements—lower inflation and interest rates and an annual deficit of no more than 3 percent of GDP. More novel was Prodi's assertion that in Italy the executive branch must be strengthened.

The national strategy in the Center-Left's Europeanism is obvious. A stronger Italian state will be better able to bargain in the EU. In the meantime, Italy wants to rejoin the EMS and seeks membership in the group of EU countries that will found the EMU. The former will be an extra help in bringing down interest rates, while the latter should resolve the problem altogether as the risk penalty factor will supposedly be eliminated.

Two question marks hang over the Center-Left's Europeanism. How realistic is it? Italy cannot possibly meet the criterion that total debt be no more than 60 percent of GDP. The inflation and deficit targets look difficult. One way around such problems lies in the Maastricht's wording that moving towards a target "at a satisfactory pace"[29] could be considered the same as reaching it. The Italian press optimistically reported that Ciampi had won his German colleague, Theo Waigel, over to this view in June.[30] If true, this is a fresh example of Italy's ability to exploit its EU partners, as was discussed in chapter 3. However, the groundswell of opposition to monetary union in Germany makes it hard for Waigel to honor any promises Ciampi may have extracted from him.

This leads to the second question mark, which was already mentioned in chapter 10: How will the EMU unfold in Europe as a whole? A full answer would require another book but one may hazard the suggestion that the EMU is, at the very least, shrouded in uncertainty. Maintaining the effort of austerity at a time when growth forecasts are being revised downwards has provoked unrest in France as well as in Germany. It is far from certain that a reunited Germany can be a model in the year 2000, as West Germany was during the early years of the EMS. Which and how many countries will be in the founding group? Will the euro be a strong or weak currency? How will internal monetary discipline be enforced? What will the relationship be between the member-countries and the other EU countries? These are merely some of the unknowns. Prodi has admitted that "the immediate situation has grown worse,"[31] but he has not wondered—at least not aloud—whether it is wise to tie the Center-Left's economic policy and its political fortunes so closely to "Europe." RC supporters have made their doubts clear: Only 44 percent of them are willing to make sacrifices in order to be part of Europe.[32]

The choice of Europeanism is a gamble. If monetary union works as the Bundesbank hopes it will, then Italy risks being trapped on a treadmill of eternal rigor. If the markets decide it will not work, then they will attack its weaker members, like Italy. A compromise might be to enter a second group of countries that plan to join the EMU later. But it is unlikely that France and Germany would allow such a group the freedom to devalue its currencies whenever its member governments wish. Another solution might be to make the effort of rigor, while postponing decisions about EMU. To ask Italians to make sacrifices in the name of Italy would be a stunning innovation. Is it unthinkable?

However the establishment has long believed in using Europe to bring discipline to Italy, while the PDS sees in Europeanism another way to legitimize itself. The gamble involves domestic dangers too, such as an exacerbation of the splits in the coalition, social unrest, and a government that undermines its credibility by setting unrealistic targets. In the years before 1992 Andreotti's government blithely agreed to EC policies but did nothing to prepare the country to meet them. The Prodi government risks trying to do too much.

The first practical expression of the Center-Left's policy was the mini-budget, which saved approximately $11 billion. Its mixture of cuts and new taxes included an increase in social security payments for employers, which brought a howl of pain from businessmen. The pharmaceutical industry had a special grievance because medicines were recategorized, and some that had formerly been paid for by the healthcare system had now to be paid for by patients, which meant sales were likely to drop. By contrast the unions were generally satisfied because a proposal to make some pensioners contribute to their medical expenses was left out of the final package.

A suggested freeze on hiring in the bureaucracy also vanished: This does not augur well for the vital reform of the civil service. New efforts to reduce tax evasion and fake invalidity pensions depend on the performance of the bureaucracy. Cuts in the Ministry of Foreign Affairs' budget are unlikely to help Italy develop a more independent foreign policy.

Although the mini-budget displayed solidarity and RC was ostentatiously uncritical, there were clashes between the PDS and the government. The reasons become clearer when one considers the three-year plan announced by Prodi on June 27. Although generic, the plan aims at cutting the deficit to 4.5 percent of GDP in 1997 and to 3 percent in 1998. Thus Italy would meet one Maastricht criterion, albeit a year late. Savings, in the form of unspecified spending cuts and revenue increases, would amount to $14 billion in 1997.[33]

A controversial feature was the goal of reducing inflation, which stood at 5.2 percent in 1995, not merely to 3 percent, the figure cited by Fazio, but to 2.5 percent in 1997. One can wonder how realistic these targets are: Nongovernmental forecasts for 1997 are an inflation rate of 3.5 percent and a deficit that is 5.5 percent of GDP. Such discrepancies could mean that the lira will rejoin the EMS only to be forced out again. One can also wonder whether or not such rigor is desirable when the forecasts of real GDP growth are 1.2 percent for 1996 and 1.5 percent for 1997.[34] Moreover unemployment went up from 11.3 percent in 1994 to 12 percent in 1995.

The risks to the Center-Left coalition are not negligible. The PDS dislikes Ciampi's 2.5 percent because it is supposed to act as a benchmark for wage-increases in the upcoming bargaining round. Unions that have completed their bargaining used a benchmark figure of 3 percent inflation. Is it just or wise to split the workforce by changing the rules of the game? The militant metalworkers union thinks not. A bitter dispute would threaten the July 1993 agreement that has been the linchpin of the "Austrian" solution. Meanwhile Bertinotti has announced that RC parliamentarians will vote against Ciampi's figure of 2.5 percent. This is only one of the many possible rifts the government must face as it seeks to emulate Mitterrand's 1983 policy and to impose a lasting deflation. Its chances of success depend on its ability to hold together without, however, shunning the hard choices. Meanwhile the erosion of growth in France and Germany does not help: World time is unkind to the Center-Left.

Prodi is aware that rigor is above all a way to reform the state. He sees his government as the continuation of Unification and of the Liberation as well as the heir to the process of change that began, in his eyes, not with the Clean Hands investigation but with the 1991 referendum on institutional reform.[35] He sees the trap of the "overworked" state, but also the need to liberate/regulate the market and to defend the "underprivileged."[36] Although Prodi sets his thought in a Catholic tradition and claims De Gasperi and Sturzo as his masters, there are few concrete differences between his remedy for Italy's ills and the diagnosis contained in the PDS program for the 1994 elections that was discussed in chapter 8. The worldviews of the catholics and the ex-communists are significantly different, but both depict a state unlike the clientelistic state of the DC-PSI coalitions.

The new state—if it materializes—will enable Italy to bargain better within the EU, the G7, and other international bodies. In a circular process, the government will derive legitimacy from membership in such groups, and the popular support it gains is a bargaining chip in the next round of negotiations. Such a state will be able to demonstrate to the Lega voters that it can obtain, better deals than their mythical Padania could obtain and it will convince Southern Italians that they will not be left out of the bargains that are struck.[37]

Naturally this is a distant, perhaps utopian goal. Meanwhile the example of Britain demonstrates that establishments can make a sorry mess of things, and the Italian business élite has chosen this moment to reveal its failings in the Gemina affair, which has returned to the headlines. Perhaps the would-be establishment is subject to the inherited vice of fragmentation. Or is it just another clan? Will D'Alema be able to continue juggling Amato and Prodi? Will someone, anyone, please privatize Stet? How real is the chance that the political system will be able to take charge of the process of change? When will Italy have a government that can pass not one but two or three budgets before it collapses? Is the fabric of Italian society strong enough to withstand the strains of decentralization? The process of change that started in 1992 is continuing against much resistance. It is time for the three dots . . .

Conclusion:
The Elusive Citizen

Throughout this study I have invoked writers to provide insights into politics and society because, whatever else the postwar period may or may not have been, it was a great period of Italian writing and cinema. Of all these writers, the one most central to our preoccupations is Leonardo Sciascia, who has been much read during the last three years. Totò Riina, supposedly illiterate, quoted from *The Day of the Owl*, while *L'Unità* copublished four small volumes of Sciascia's occasional writings. That he would be cited in the Mafia debate was inevitable, but the real reason why Sciascia is being reread is that the concept of citizenship is at the core of his writing.

He has recounted that when he worked as an elementary schoolteacher in the years after the World War II, he was struck by the absurdity of explaining Italian unification to the hungry, barefooted children who were his pupils.[1] The schoolmaster is the incarnation of the state and Sciascia realized that his was a non-state and his pupils noncitizens.

Several of his novels depict the same discovery and *The Day of the Owl* may serve as an example. The policeman, Bellodi, who comes from Emilia with its civic traditions, learns, as he sets about finding a murderer in Sicily, that bystanders have seen nothing, informers are killed, and the mystery recedes. Bellodi succeeds in interrogating a Mafia chieftain, Don Mariano, but behind the Don stand Roman politicians and Bellodi finds himself transferred out of Sicily. Sciascia reverses the traditional detective story to recount a parable of the absent state. The policeman is its representative, the bystanders are its noncitizens, the Mafioso strips it of its power and substitutes for its laws a counterstate based on violence while his accomplices, the politicians, divert the instruments of government to private ends.

That they are in the capital, Rome, demonstrates that Sciascia considers Sicily and its Mafia as emblematic of Italy. To Roman unreason he opposes a mythical Paris, citadel of the Enlightenment and inhabited by writers like the inevitable Stendhal, Diderot (whom Sciascia seeks to emulate), Pascal, and La Rochefoucauld. The last of these may guide us in our discussion of the second phase of Sciascia's discourse on citizenship.

So far we have seen how the self, as it moves outward to make contact with a social order that is ideally inspired by justice and reason, discovers only chaos. Self-identification takes place in solitude: I do not trust, therefore I am. Sciascia himself explains that his family defended him against the Fascist state. But in his novels the family does not even possess the crude unity of "amoral familism"; it is conflict-ridden and irrational. So the violence of the counterstate penetrates the self and Sciascia admits that when he attacks the Mafia he feels a "split, a laceration" within himself. As La Rochefoucauld tells us, there is no united, much less reasonable, self. Bellodi finds himself admiring Don Mariano, while in *Todo modo* the narrator feels an affinity with Don Gaetano, but he also accuses himself of killing him, thus admitting his complicity in DC misgovernment.

The quest turns into a circle in which there are no citizens, no families, no regional or professional groups, no genuine institutions, and hence no state. Instead there is "the system," a Foucaultian monstrosity that draws its critics into its self-alienation.[2] Sciascia denounced the historic compromise, because, in his eyes, the PCI ceased to criticize the Christian Democrats and joined in their misgovernment. Similarly he turned against Leoluca Orlando, whom he accused of using the anti-Mafia struggle as a means of gaining power.

The absence of legitimate power explains why Sciascia offers as a model the kidnapped Aldo Moro, a dominant figure in the system who is expelled from it by an unholy alliance of the Red Brigades, the Communists, and the Catholics. Suddenly powerless, Moro can tell the truth in his prison letters. Similarly Sciascia intimates that he, the narrator, can transcend the laceration of the self by using the language of literature. However it is hard to see why literature should, by some special grace, escape the general alienation. The powerless Moro and the omniscient artist are subterfuges behind whom lies the absent state. Sciascia's vision of Italian history, in which the governing group draws in a segment of the governed and resumes oppression under a different name, is akin to the pessimism of the Lampedusa whom he came to admire.[3] But unlike Tancredi, Sciascia's characters try desperately to become citizens:

the hero of his last novel, *Una storia semplice,* accomplishes his duty but is rewarded by being forced into an act of violence.

The quest for citizenship is a parable of the last three years of Italian history. To probe it using very different methodological tools we might consider Robert Putnam's suggestive thesis that the key to good government is the presence of the "civic community."[4] Since Putnam deals with Italy's regional governments and poses the question of why Emilia-Romagna is a success and Calabria a failure, we must twist his argument. However we may begin with his assertion that the determining factor is the civic community, which is rich in associational life, encourages horizontal interaction, and engenders trust among its participants. The historical model is the medieval commune and the memory of its democratic procedures has survived into the twentieth century.

Certainly Putnam's remarks on clientelism are apt. A vertical relationship, clientelism breeds narrow self-interest and distrust of one's equals who are also competitors. Putnam's view of the Catholic Church as providing an alternative to the civic community is akin to my interpretation of Pius XII. I would add, however, that along with its vertical bonds, the Church can also create—via parish life—horizontal links, one example of which would be the white cooperatives of the Veneto.

However it is the nature of the participation in associations that appears to me more problematic than Putnam maintains. Admittedly I have the unfair advantage of writing after the revelations of systemic clientelism in northern Italy—revelations that would appear to contradict the notion of a successful civic community. Participation in associations is obviously not the same in all countries: parent-teacher organizations offer a very different kind of experience in Bologna than in Washington. But there may also be differences of quality. Sociologists of the Third Republic have argued that French associations were often merely delinquent peer groups. In Italian associations, as in political parties, the tendency toward fragmentation is masked by a facade of unity. As in the student assemblies of the 1970s, belonging is its own goal—once more the importance of *stare insieme*—and decisions are infrequent, which means that the associations do not lead outward to wider groups.

Such traits are easily explicable if we reverse Putnam's historical schema and argue in a more banal fashion that the formative experience was not the early medieval commune but the centuries of foreign occupation. From this experience stem the suspicion of others, the fear of conspiracies—to which Berlusconi is as prone as Craxi was—and the disenchanted pessimism. Just as Salvadori and Cammelli depict the besieged state, so one might talk of the besieged individual, who trusts only organizations that are close, tight, and equipped for war, such as the clan or the family.

Of the clan we have said enough. Of the family Paul Ginsborg notes that it has maintained its strength by adapting: adolescents remain at home for longer because jobs and housing have grown more scarce. The problem lies in turning the family outward toward the broader society.[5] The inward-directed family is brilliantly depicted in Ettore Scola's *La Famiglia* (1987). In each generation political society fails the family: The grandfather laments the decline of his friend Carducci, who has degenerated into the poet laureate of the new and artificial Italy; the son places his hopes in the Partito d'Azione, while his grandson, a child of the late 1960s, roams the world but returns to the family flat, where the entire film takes place. The final shot is of the family assembled: biological continuity, a society unto itself.

That Scola, a director with close ties to the PDS, should make such a film is intriguing. Of course I am not using it to argue that Robert Putnam's civic community does not exist. That would be foolish, faced as I am with the red cooperatives of Emilia-Romagna. However I am suggesting that in Italy the civic community is very much a *Gemeinschaft*, dependent on close relations and emotional bonds. The PCI and the Church, as well as the Lega and FI, have fostered this kind of community. Moreover some of the great demonstrations of citizenship in the last three years have been passionate, spontaneous, and defensive. The fax people are an example, despite their advanced technology.

Putnam maintains correctly that a modern system of government requires a broader, social trust. In our terms this would be more of a *Gesellschaft*, a cool, rational calculation that enlightened self-interest is best served by collaboration with people one does not know but whose self-interest points them in the same direction. This kind of community deals in contracts and above all in institutions. One returns to Violante's comment that the anti-Mafia struggle cannot be left to the police and the magistrates. Pressure from public opinion is necessary in any country, but if perpetual demonstrations are required to enable or to convince public representatives to do their job, then something is amiss.

Many issues do not lend themselves to the "everybody-in-the-piazza" approach. Prominent among them are institutions and laws regulating the market: it is difficult to organize demonstrations in support of a stronger Consob (the equivalent of the Securities and Exchange Commission). Yet the need to regulate the stock market and to encourage companies and brokers to provide more information is great. Similarly the bizarre situation of a Prime Minister who exercised power over state TV, with which his own networks competed, would not have arisen if codes of conduct for public officials had been in place.

The example of electoral reform, long considered a matter to which most people were indifferent, demonstrates how an alliance of political leaders and experts can create an interest in supposedly remote issues. While it is possible that this is no longer the key issue, Pasquino has pointed out that the struggle to change institutions is a learning process that does not end with the first changes. To take another example, Berlusconi may have educated the electorate on the importance of the public-private divide by his July 24 meeting at Arcore. The privatizations have widened interest in the workings of the stock market. Credito Italiano's present bid to take over Credito Romagnolo, unthinkable five years ago, is providing small shareholders and even the general public with precious insights into contemporary capitalism.

The history of the last three years in Italy has instilled a hope that the actions of the Berlusconi government have not extinguished. Institutional change does not mean much unless the public servants believe in it and in themselves. But here again an evolution has taken place. The magistrates have had to fight so hard to defend an independence that they had previously surrendered that they will surely not relinquish it again. The memory of Di Pietro's impassioned TV performance should remove the need for future such performances.

A nation should build on its strengths. Since local ties are strong in Italy, a fruitful approach would be to expand them so that they embrace more people and a wider range of tasks. Decentralization could strengthen rather than undermine the state, provided that it is undertaken without rhetoric and that responsibility and power move together from center to periphery. The tendency toward what has been called "neo-feudal anarchy,"[6] which results from the inadequacy of the overworked state, should be corrected by widening the sense of community.

The changing Italy will of course remain Italy. The family is not going to wither away and even if governments perform better, admiration for Franco Baresi will not decline. This is entirely as it should be. Throughout this book I have drawn parallels with France and Britain, but these elucidate arguments and do not create models. Indeed the excessive admiration for foreign models is a damaging trait of Italian political culture. The state may cease to be overworked but it will and must remain interventionist. Italy cannot adopt the "Erhard" solution, but it can produce its own *Italian* version of the Austrian solution.

Above all Italy can produce citizens. The gamble of the last three years has been that the protesting social groups—the urban middle classes of northern Italy, the small- and medium-sized entrepreneurs of Lombardy, the anti-Mafia movement in Sicily, and so on—will not be able to realize their goals merely by gaining a greater share of power in a clientelistic state. Nor will they be bought off by the new version of clan government offered by Berlusconi. Rather they will have to create a state, which is neither overbearing nor absent because it is no longer overworked, in which the market functions and public goods are not sold to the highest bidder but are distributed in a manner that is recognizably fairer and more efficient. In short these and other groups will break out of the trap depicted by Sciascia and citizenship will cease to be elusive.

NOTES

Chapter 1

1. The newspaper *Il Manifesto* marked the celebration with a book, *Il crac della Banca Romana* (Rome: Il Manifesto, 1993).
2. Ralph Dahrendorf, *Espresso,* June 27, 1993, p. 51.
3. Gianfranco Pasquino, "A Case of Regime Crisis" in G. Pasquino and P. McCarthy, eds., *The End of Postwar Politics in Italy: The Landmark Elections of 1992* (Boulder: Westview, 1993), p. 1.
4. Franco Cazzola, *L'Italia del Pizzo* (Turin: Einaudi, 1992), pp. 10-59.
5. For Giuseppe Garofano's judgment of Gardini, see *La Repubblica,* November 23, 1993. For Romiti's mishaps, see *La Repubblica,* February 16, 1994, and March 1, 1994. For Agnelli and Valletta, see Piero Bairati, *Valletta* (Turin: Unione Tipografico-Editrice Torrinese, 1983), pp. 62 and 310.
6. Sergio Romano, *L'Italia scappata di mano* (Milan: Longanesi, 1993), pp. 10-16.
7. Giorgio Bocca, *Espresso,* July 15, 1994, p. 5.
8. The Italian name for it is *gattopardismo* and the historical process of change without change is called *trasformismo.*
9. Massimo L. Salvadori, *Storia d'Italia e crisi di regime* (Bologna: Il Mulino, 1994), p. 36. See also Marco Cammelli, "Sistema politico bloccato, stato accentrato" (manuscript version).
10. Vera Zamagni, *Dalla periferia al centro* (Bologna: Il Mulino, 1990), p. 143. I have drawn much on this book for the economic data in this chapter and on Denis Mack Smith, *Italy, a Modern History* (Ann Arbor: University of Michigan Press, 1969), for the political data.
11. Giulio Sapelli, *Sul capitalismo italiano* (Milan: Feltrinelli, 1993), p. 156.
12. Salvatore Lupo, *Storia della Mafia* (Rome: Donzelli, 1993), p. 158. See also pp. 19-66 for a discussion of the Mafia during this period. Also Raimondo Catanzaro, *Il delitto come impresa: storia sociale della Mafia* (Padua: Liviana, 1988), pp. 84-141.

13. Giorgio Galli, *Storia della Democrazia cristiana* (Bari: Laterza, 1978), pp. 7-19. Galli goes as far as to say that the Church hierarchy "liquidated" the PPI (p. 5).

14. Giovanni Gentile, quoted in Alberto Asor Rosa, *Storia d'Italia,* vol. 4, t. 2 (Turin: Einaudi, 1975), p. 1411.

Chapter 2

1. Statistics on the 1992 and 1994 elections are taken from *La Repubblica,* March 30, 1994.

2. Gianni Baget-Bozzo, *Il Partito cristiano al potere* (Florence: Vallechi, 1974), vol. 1, p. 220.

3. *Avvenire,* September 21, 1993.

4. *La Repubblica,* October 26, 1993, and *L'Unità,* October 27, 1993.

5. *La Repubblica,* January 11, 1994.

6. *Il Manifesto,* March 15, 1994.

7. The figures on mass attendance are taken from F. Spotts and T. Wieser, *Italy, A Difficult Democracy* (Cambridge: Cambridge University Press, 1986), p. 247.

8. *La Repubblica,* March 30, 1994.

9. *L'Unità,* April 15, 1994.

10. *La Repubblica,* April 14, 1994.

11. *La Stampa,* October 4, 1993.

12. *La Repubblica,* March 29, 1994.

13. The main historical works, on which I have drawn heavily in this chapter, are: Pietro Scoppola, *La repubblica dei partiti* (Bologna: Il Mulino, 1991), and *La proposta politica di De Gasperi* (Bologna: Il Mulino, 1977); Silvio Lanaro, *Storia dell'Italia repubblicana* (Venezia: Marsilio, 1992); Aurelio Lepre, *Storia della prima Repubblica* (Bologna: Il Mulino, 1993); Paul Ginsborg, *Storia d'Italia dal dopoguerra a oggi* (Turin: Einaudi, 1989). On the Resistance I have used Claudio Pavone, *Una guerra civile: un saggio storico sulla moralità della Resistenza* (Turin: Bollati Boringhieri, 1991). See also "L'Italia repubblicana: tre autori a confronto," *Passato e presente,* a. XI, n. 29 (1993), pp. 11-32.

14. For a debate on this issue see "L'Italia repubblicana: tre autori a confronto," op. cit., p. 18.

15. Silvio Lanaro, op. cit., p. 44. On the general issue see John L. Harper, *America and the Reconstruction of Italy* (Cambridge: Cambridge University Press, 1986), p. 87. Harper argues that Italian groups had more freedom than is commonly thought with respect to the United States and that they exploited it skillfully. On the 1948 elections, see David Ellwood, "The 1948 elections

in Italy: A Cold War Propaganda Battle" in *Historical Journal of Film, Radio and TV*, vol. 13, n. 1 (1993): 19-33. See also James E. Miller, *The United States and Italy, 1940-1950* (Chapel Hill: University of North Carolina Press, 1986), pp. 213-74.

16. A. Lepre, op. cit., p. 9.

17. Paul Ginsborg, op. cit., pp. 42-44.

18. Vera Zamagni, *Dalla periferia al centro* (Bologna: Il Mulino, 1990), p. 403.

19. P. Scoppola, *La repubblica dei partiti*, pp. 74-81.

20. The Italian term is *poliedricità*—see Marina Addis Sabe, *Gioventù italiana del Littorio*, Prefazione di U. A. Grimaldi (Milan: Feltrinelli, 1973), p. 33.

21. P. P. Pasolini to Luciano Serra undated (August 1943) in P. P. Pasolini, *Lettere 1940-1954* (Turin: Einaudi, 1986), p. 184. For his early writings, see Mario Ricci, ed., *Pasolini e "Il Setaccio"* (Bologna: Cappelli, 1977).

22. Salvatore Satta, *De Profundis* (Milan: Adelphi, 1980), pp. 79, 175, and 16. Satta's book was written between June 1944 and April 1945. It was first published in 1948.

23. Ennio Di Nolfo, *Vaticano e Stati Uniti 1939-1952* (Milan: Franco Angeli, 1978), p. 427.

24. A. Lepre, op. cit., p. 18. On Pius XII, see also S. Lanaro, op. cit., pp. 96-103. On the Church under Fascism, see Guido Verucci, *La Chiesa nella società contemporanea* (Bari: Laterza, 1988), pp. 33-57. For Fellini's comment, see *L'Unità*, October 20, 1993.

25. Cardinal Domenico Tardini, Ennio di Nolfo, *Vaticano e Stati Uniti 1939-1952*, op. cit., pp. 279-81. I have used these documents as a major source for the Vatican's role, although they must be treated with care as they constitute the Vatican's campaign to win the U.S. government over to its views.

26. Lanaro thinks the Vatican's flirtation with a Salazar-like solution was blocked by the rise of anti-Fascism—op. cit., pp. 90-95. Scoppola agrees—*La proposta politica di De Gasperi*, p. 46—but argues that the Vatican continued to be tempted by authoritarianism.

27. Ennio Di Nolfo, op. cit., p. 450. Tardini gives Italy away on p. 293.

28. For good discussions of this issue, see Paul Ginsborg, op. cit., p. 106 and Antonio Gambino, *Storia del dopoguerra* (Bari: Laterza, 1975), p. 103.

29. P. Scoppola, *La proposta politica di De Gasperi*, p. 73.

30. On Pius XII and the state, see G. Baget Bozzo, op. cit., vol. 1, p. 261.

31. P. Scoppola, ed., *Chiesa e Stato nella storia d'Italia* (Bari: Laterza, 1967), pp. 783, 786, and 794.

32. At the same moment the Vatican was wondering whether the Axis powers would not be better than the Allies at maintaining order once the war ended. See Ennio Di Nolfo, op. cit., pp. 190-200. For De Gasperi's statement, see p. 54.

33. G. Verucci, op. cit., p. 218. See also Enzo Collotti, "Collocazione inter-
    nazionale dell'Italia dall'armistizio alle premesse dell'alleanza atlantica," in
    L'Italia dalla Liberazione alla repubblica (Milan: Feltrinelli, 1976), pp. 79-107.
    Collotti argues that domestic actors used the international situation to advance
    their cause and that De Gasperi saw the coalitions with the Left as a temporary
    phase.
34. The thesis of the three overlapping struggles is found in Claudio Pavone, op.
    cit.
35. Renata Viganò, *L'Agnese va a morire* (Turin: Einaudi, 1949), p. 142.
36. Carlo Levi, *L'Orologio* (Turin: Einaudi, first published 1949, re-edited 1989),
    p. 308. Unsurprisingly Levi's novel has been much discussed in the last two
    years.
37. For an assessment of De Gasperi's government as conservative, see F. Catalano,
    "The Rebirth of the Party System 1944-1948," in S. J. Woolf, ed., *The Rebirth
    of Italy 1943-1950* (New York: Humanities Press, 1971), pp. 57-94. The
    majority of Italian historians take this view. See Giorgio Galli, op. cit., p. 74.
    Pietro Scoppola, who argues passionately that De Gasperi was not a conserva-
    tive, states his case in both of his books and also in "L'avvento di De Gasperi,"
    in *L'Italia dalla Liberazione alla repubblica*, op. cit., pp. 315-49.
38. Guido Carli, *Intervista sul capitalismo* (Bari: Laterza, 1977), p. 71.
39. These figures are taken from A. Lepre, op. cit., p. 128. David Ellwood notes
    that 36 labor leaders were killed in Sicily alone at the time of the 1948
    elections—op. cit., p. 23.
40. Silvio Lanaro uses the term *real cultural repression* to describe the atmosphere
    in the schools in the 1950s—"L'Italia repubblicana: tre autori a confronto,"
    op. cit., p. 27.
41. Nicola Tranfaglia, ed., *Mafia, Politica e Affari 1943-1991* (Bari: Laterza,
    1992), pp. 20-42.
42. Carlo Guarnieri, "Burocrazie pubbliche e consolidamento democratico: il
    caso italiano," *Rivista italiana di scienza politica,* a. XVIII, n. 1 (April 1988):
    73-103. See also Marco Cammelli, op. cit.
43. The two outstanding historians of the DC, Scoppola and Baget Bozzo, take
    radically different positions on De Gasperi. Scoppola has dedicated great
    learning and passion to defending the thesis that De Gasperi fought to create
    a DC that was autonomous of the Vatican, that De Gasperi should not be
    considered a conservative, and that even after 1947 he maintained a link with
    the PCI, which he considered an authentic part of the new republic. Baget
    Bozzo, whose *Il Partito cristiano al Potere* is written with equal erudition and
    passion, denies that De Gasperi saved Italy from Pius XII (p. 359), declares
    that at least from 1946 on De Gasperi should be considered a conservative

(p. 508), and concludes that De Gasperi left the DC without a worldview (p. 510). For a non-Italian historian's view of De Gasperi see S. J. Woolf, *The Rebirth of Italy,* op. cit., pp. 224-43.

44. Giorgio La Pira, "L'attesa della povera gente," *Cronache sociali* (January 1950): 2-6. For this discussion of Dossetti I have relied much on Baget Bozzo who was himself a Dossettiano. He is not uncritical of Dossetti (op. cit., p. 347) whom he accuses of not standing up to De Gasperi. However the judgment in the paragraph that follows is my own.

45. G. Baget Bozzo, op. cit., p. 67.

46. Ibid., p. 510.

47. L. Domenici, "Unificazione e pluralità in Gramsci," *Critica Marxista* (1989/5): 76.

48. On Togliatti's use and abuse of Gramsci see Paul Ginsborg, op. cit., p. 57. On hegemony see Aldo Schiavone, *Per il nuovo Pci* (Bari: Laterza, 1985), p. 85. For an analysis of Togliatti's strategy and the interpretations of it, see Donald Sassoon, *Togliatti e la via italiana al socialismo* (Turin: Einaudi, 1980), pp. 1-62. The most complete history of the PCI at the end of the war remains Paolo Spriano, *Storia del Partito comunista italiano,* vol. 5 (Turin: Einaudi, 1975).

49. Giorgio Bocca, *Palmiro Togliatti* (Rome: L'Unità, 1992 edition), pp. 341-58. Bocca is sharply critical of Togliatti's attitude.

50. Antonio Gambino, op. cit., p. 492.

51. Giorgio Bocca, op. cit., p. 411. Sergio Bertelli, whose *Il Gruppo* contains brilliant if unflattering insights into the PCI leadership, argues that Togliatti relied on his secret diplomacy with the Vatican, see *Il Gruppo* (Milan: Rizzoli, 1980), pp. 340-51.

52. Franco Rodano, quoted in G. Bocca, op. cit., p. 405.

53. Claudio Napoleoni, "Due opposti giudizi sull'economia italiana," *Rinascita,* (May 1949): 234. For a longer discussion of the postwar PCI and the reformist state, see my "I comunisti italiani, il New Deal e il difficile problema del riformismo," *Studi storici,* n. 2/3 (1992): 457-78.

54. Pietro Di Loreto, *Togliatti e la "Doppiezza"* (Bologna: Il Mulino, 1991), p. 169. My discussion of duplicity is based partly on Di Loreto's book but my conclusion, namely, that the PCI was pretending to be revolutionary when it was not, is different from his. Nor do I agree with Pietro Scoppola that the PCI presented "the gravest of threats" to Italian democracy, see *La repubblica dei partiti,* op. cit., p. 108. Scoppola feels that new material from Cominform files indicates that Togliatti considered resorting to force after the PCI was expelled from the government. But my interpretation of the evidence—presented by Aldo Agosti, "Il PCI e la svolta del 1947," in *Studi storici,* n. 1 (1990):

53-88—is that Togliatti was feigning toughness to conform with Soviet criticism of him and to disarm his opponents within the PCI.

55. For the assassination attempt, see G. Bocca, op. cit., pp. 465-75. Secchia's comment is given on p. 509.

56. The success story of Emilia-Romagna is recounted by Fausto Anderlini, *Terra rossa, comunismo ideale, socialdemocrazia reale* (Bologna: Istituto Gramsci, 1991). For the parallels with the DC in the Veneto, see Carlo Trigilia, *Grandi partiti e piccole imprese,* (Bologna: Il Mulino, 1986).

Chapter 3

1. Sergio Romano, *L'Italia scappata di mano* (Milan: Longanesi, 1993), p. 123.

2. *L'Unità,* January 28, 1994.

3. Sergio Romano, "Italy and the New Europe," in D. Calleo and P. Gordon, eds., *From the Atlantic to the Urals* (Washington: Foundation of European Studies, 1992), p. 169.

4. For this account of the 1948 elections I have drawn heavily on James Miller, *The United States and Italy 1940-1950* (Chapel Hill: University of North Carolina Press, 1986), pp. 213-74.

5. Pietro Pastorelli, *La Politica estera italiana del dopoguerra* (Bologna: Il Mulino, 1987), p. 118.

6. Claudio Gatti, *Rimanga tra noi* (Milan: Longanesi, 1990), p. 40.

7. Piero Bairati, *Valletta* (Turin: Unione Tipografico-Editrice Torrinese, 1983), pp. 254-69.

8. Claudio Gatti, op. cit., p. 120.

9. Sergio Zavoli, *La notte della Repubblica* (Rome: l'Unità, 1994), p. 23.

10. Claudio Gatti, op. cit., p. 133. In general Gatti exonerates the CIA, but he is not altogether convincing; see my review of his book *Polis* (1992/3): 597-99.

11. Giorgio Bocca, *Il terrorismo italiano* (Milan: Rizzoli, 1978), p. 14.

12. Giorgio Galli, *Storia del partito armato* (Milan: Rizzoli, 1986), pp. 326-30.

13. Claudio Gatti, op. cit., pp. 29-44. Gatti's American sources deny that Gladio was to be used against the PCI, but see Franco Ferraresi, "Una struttura segreta denominato Gladio," *Politica in Italia Edizione 92,* a cura di S. Hellman e G. Pasquino, (Bologna: Il Mulino, 1992), p. 94.

14. P. Pastorelli, op. cit., p. 176.

15. Ibid., pp. 129-44. The offer to join was made in guarded language in Bevin's Commons speech of January 22 and was repeated explicitly by the United States in March 1948.

16. G. Baget-Bozzo, *Il partito cristiano al potere,* op. cit., pp. 272 and 409.

17. Nico Perrone, *Mattei, il nemico italiano* (Milan: Leonardo, 1989), pp. 97-105. Perrone notes that De Gasperi resisted strong U.S. pressure in 1951 when he granted Mattei exclusive rights in the Po Valley (p. 54). On Mattei, see also Dow Votaw, *The Six-legged Dog* (Berkeley: University of California Press, 1964).

18. John Harper, "Il vertice di Venezia," *Politica in Italia Edizione 88,* a cura di P. Corbetta e R. Leonardi (Bologna: Il Mulino, 1988), pp. 69-92. Also Istituto Affari Internazionali, *L'Italia nella politica internazionale 1985-1986* (Milan: Angeli, 1988), pp. 25-72.

19. "Il cerchioquadrato," supplement to *Il Manifesto,* February 13, 1994. For Craxi and Siad Barre, see Sergio Turone, *Corrotti e corruttori* (Bari: Laterza, 1984), p. 283. Craxi was not of course unique in Italy. For the diversion of Italian foreign aid to Senegal into the pockets of Senegalese and Italian government officials, see *Sud* (Dakar) November 11, 1993.

20. Beniamino Andreatta, "Una politica estera per l'Italia," *Il Mulino,* (1993/5): 881-91.

21. "Il cerchioquadrato," op. cit.

22. *La Stampa,* February 21, 1994.

23. *La Repubblica,* October 1, 1993.

24. Luigi Spaventa, *La Repubblica,* August 2, 1978.

25. Sergio Romano, *L'Italia scappata di mano,* op. cit., p. 114.

26. F. R. Willis, *Italy Chooses Europe* (Oxford: Oxford University Press, 1971), pp. 30-41.

27. Ibid., pp. 23 and 72.

28. Peter Ludlow, *The Making of the EMS* (London: Butterworth, 1982), pp. 205-17.

29. Beniamino Andreatta, op. cit., p. 888.

30. *Alla ricerca del buon governo,* campaign material of Forza Italia, p. 31.

31. See Vera Zamagni, *Dalla periferia al centro,* op. cit., pp. 403-20. See also "Una scommessa sul futuro: l'industria italiana nella ricostruzione," in *L'Italia e la politica di potenza in Europa* (Milan: Marzorati, 1988). For the view that more government intervention was possible, see Marcello De Cecco, "Economic Policy in the Reconstruction Period," in S. J. Woolf, ed., *The Rebirth of Italy* (New York: The Humanities Press, 1972), pp. 135-55.

32. Pasquale Saraceno, *Intervista sulla Ricostruzione,* a cura di Lucio Villari (Bari: Laterza, 1977), p. 104.

33. Michele Salvati, *Economia e Politica in Italia dal dopoguerra a oggi* (Milan: Garzanti, 1984), p. 68.

34. Vera Zamagni, "Una scommessa sui futuro," op. cit., p. 480. See also P. Saraceno, op. cit., p. 127.

35. P. Saraceno, op. cit., p. 163.
36. David Ellwood, *Rebuilding Europe* (London: Longmans, 1992), p. 196. This is also Michele Salvati's main theme.
37. Commissione Antimafia, *Relazione sulla Camorra,* December 21, 1993, pp. 7-22.
38. Michele Salvati, op. cit., p. 60.
39. Vera Zamagni, "The Italian Economic Miracle revisited," Ennio di Nolfo, ed., *Power in Europe 11* (New York: Walter de Gruyter, 1992), p. 207.
40. *The Economist,* January 29, 1994, p. 63.
41. Patrick McCarthy, "Italy: The Absent State," *International Economic Ideas,* (November-December 1993): 6-9.
42. See Carlo Trigilia, *Grandi partiti e piccole imprese,* op. cit.
43. Michele Salvati, op. cit., p. 134.
44. Pier Paolo D'Attorre, "Sogno americano e mito sovietico nell'Italia contemporanea," in his edited *Nemici per la pelle* (Milan: Franco Angeli, 1991), p. 31.

Chapter 4

1. *Espresso,* July 18, 1993, pp. 40-46 and August 1, 1993, pp. 24-34.
2. *Espresso,* July 18, 1993, pp. 67-69.
3. P. A. Allum, *Politics and Society in Post-war Naples* (Cambridge: Cambridge University Press, 1973), pp. 72-77.
4. Edward C. Banfield, *The Moral Basis of a Backward Society* (New York: The Free Press, 1958), p. 83.
5. Giorgio Galli, *Storia della Democrazia cristiana* (Bari: Laterza, 1978), p. 299.
6. Paul Ginsborg, *Storia d'Italia dal dopoguerra a oggi* (Turin: Einaudi, 1989), p. 193.
7. G. Baget Bozzo, *Il Partito cristiano e l'apertura a sinistra* (Florence: Valleschi, 1977), p. 119. For this section I have drawn heavily on Baget Bozzo as well as on Giorgio Galli, *Fanfani* (Milan: Feltrinelli, 1975), pp. 1-82.
8. For the DC factions, see G. Pasquino, "Italian DC: A Party for All Seasons," in *Italy in Transition,* P. Lange and S. Tarrow, eds., (London: Cass, 1980), pp. 88-109. See also Mario Caciagli, "Il resistibile declino della DC," in *Il Sistema politico italiano,* G. Pasquino, ed., (Bari: Laterza, 1985), pp. 101-27.
9. For a full analysis of the political system, see Giovanni Sartori, *Teoria dei partiti e caso italiano* (Milan: SugarCo, 1982). See also Sidney Tarrow, "The Italian Party System Between Crisis and Transition," *American Journal of Political Science,* vol. 21, n. 2 (May 1977): 193-221.
10. Sergio Romano, *L'Italia scappata di mano* (Milan: Longanesi, 1993), p. 15.
11. The Italian word for this is *dietrologia.*

12. Joseph La Palombara, *Democracy Italian Style* (New Haven: Yale University Press, 1987).

13. Sidney Tarrow, *Between Centre and Periphery* (New Haven: Yale University Press, 1977). See also Gianfranco Pasquino, *La Repubblica dei cittadini ombra* (Milan: Garzanti, 1991), p. 17.

14. For a discussion of fragmentation, see Joseph La Palombara, *Interest Groups in Italian Politics* (Princeton: Princeton University Press, 1964), pp. 137-42.

15. This account is taken from Giampaolo Pansa, *Bisaglia, una carriera democristiana* (Milan: SugarCo, 1975).

16. Joseph La Palombara, *Interest Groups in Italian Politics*, op. cit., pp. 235-46.

17. Giorgio Galli, *Storia della Democrazia Cristiana*, op. cit., pp. 255-59.

18. Paul Ginsborg, op. cit., pp. 201-08.

19. Gianfranco Pasquino, "Italian DC," op. cit., p. 108.

20. Giorgio Galli, *Storia della Democrazia Cristiana*, op. cit., p. 285.

21. For Lauro and for Gava's career until the 1970s I have drawn heavily on Percy Allum, op. cit., pp. 274-324. This superb study caused Gava a certain amount of trouble.

22. *Il Manifesto*, December 12, 1992.

23. Giorgio Bocca, *L'Inferno* (Milan: Mondadori, 1992), p. 210.

24. Commissione Antimafia, *Relazione sulla Camorra*, December 21, 1993, p. 159. See also Commissione Antimafia, relatore Luciano Violante, *Relazione sui rapporti tra Mafia e politica*, May 28, 1993, p. 97.

25. *L'Unità*, March 13, 1992.

26. Raimondo Catanzaro, op. cit., p. 190.

27. Salvatore Lupo, op. cit., p. 165. There are major differences of interpretation between Lupo and Pino Arlacchi, *La Mafia imprenditrice* (Bologna: Il Mulino, 1993). Where Arlacchi distinguishes between an old and a new Mafia, Lupo stresses continuity. Whereas Arlacchi considers the emergence of the criminal as businessman to be the major development in recent Mafia history, Lupo depicts it as a normal phase in the Mafia's evolution. In general Catanzaro is closer to Lupo.

28. *La Repubblica*, February 26, 1994.

29. A fresh controversy over Sciascia's interpretation of the Mafia broke out in 1993. For a balanced judgment, see Nicola Tranfaglia in *La Repubblica*, December 21, 1993. For Lupo's view, see op. cit., p. 219.

30. Commissione Antimafia, *Insediamenti e infiltrazioni di soggetti ed organizzazioni di tipo mafioso in aree non tradizionali*, December 17, 1993, p. 21.

31. S. Lupo, op. cit., p. 195. For the history of the drug trade see R. Catanzaro, op. cit., p. 238.

32. *Il Manifesto*, October 21, 1993.

33. Tiziana Parenti, Forza Italia Convention, Rome, February 6, 1994, text provided by Press Office of Forza Italia. Silvio Berlusconi, *La Stampa*, March 21, 1994.

34. *La Stampa*, November 15, 1993; *La Repubblica*, November 17, 1993; and *Avvenire*, December 9, 1993.

35. *L'Espresso*, July 22, 1994, p. 49.

36. For the historical account I have drawn heavily on Carlo Guarnieri, *Magistratura e Politica in Italia* (Bologna: Il Mulino, 1992). However Guarnieri's account of the 1980s differs slightly from mine.

37. Giampaolo Pansa, *Lo Sfascio* (Rome: L'Unità-Sperling e Kupfer, 1993), pp. 91-98.

38. Giorgio Bocca, op. cit., p. 34.

39. Claudio Fracassi e Michele Gambino, *Berlusconi, una biografia non autorizzata* (Rome: Avvenimenti, 1994), p. 61.

40. *L'Espresso*, July 22, 1994, p. 48.

41. Giampaolo Pansa, *I Bugiardi* (Rome: L'Unità-Sperling e Kupfer, 1993), p. 189.

Chapter 5

1. The quotations from Berlusconi are taken from "Il Messaggio di Berlusconi in TV," reproduced in Claudio Fracassi e Michele Gambino, *Berlusconi, una biografia non autorizzata* (Rome: Avvenimenti, 1994), pp. 56-58, and from Berlusconi's February 6 speech to the Forza Italia Convention (text supplied by Press Office of Forza Italia).

2. For Fininvest's troubles with the Milan magistrates, see *L'Espresso*, July 29, 1994, pp. 57-59.

3. C. Fracassi e M. Gambino, op. cit., p. 44.

4. Giampaolo Pansa, *I Bugiardi* (Rome: L'Unità-Sperling e Kupfer, 1994), p. 19.

5. The term *state bourgeoisie* was popularized in the 1970s by Eugenio Scalfari and Giuseppe Turani as well as by Guido Carli—see note 7. They used it to indicate groups that worked in the public sector and were part of the DC-PSI power system. Such groups were contrasted with the private sector. Since the state bourgeoisie has expanded since the 1970s, I have expanded the term to include private sector groups that rely heavily on political power. Because the entire Italian private sector is linked with the state—see chapters 1 and 3—this involves a difficult but necessary distinction. Moreover because politicians in the 1990s intervened more massively in business than they did during the 1970s, they too may, when they play this role, be included in the state bourgeoisie.

6. Aurelio Lepre, *Storia della prima Repubblica* (Bologna: Il Mulino, 1993), p. 215.

7. On the nationalization, see Giorgio Mori, "La nazionalizzazione in Italia: il dibattito politico-economico," in *La nazionalizzazione dell'energia elettrica: Atti del Convegno per il XXV anniversario dell'istituzione dell'Enel* (Bari: Laterza, 1989), pp. 91-116. My account of Edison's misadventures owes much to Eugenio Scalfari e Giuseppe Turani, *Razza padrona* (Milan: Feltrinelli, 1974). See also Guido Carli, *Intervista sul capitalismo italiano,* a cura di Eugenio Scalfari (Bari: Laterza, 1976), pp. 76-112. Carlo Scognamiglio, the new Speaker of the Senate, saw in the nationalization of the electrical industry the first sign of the shift of economic power from Milan to Rome, see *Espresso,* April 29, 1994, p. 62.

8. *Espresso,* July 4, 1993, p. 89.

9. For Cuccia I have drawn on Fabio Tamburini, *Un Siciliano a Milano* (Milan: Longanesi, 1992). See also Steven Solomon, "The Last Emperor," *Euromoney* (October 1988): 42-60 and Geoffrey Dyer, "Cuccia's Last Stand," *Euromoney* (December 1993): 26-32. Another good portrait of Cuccia is, Alan Friedman, *Agnelli and the Network of Italian Power* (London: Harrap, 1988), pp. 87-109.

10. *Espresso,* July 11, 1993, p. 43.

11. F. Tamburini, op. cit., p. 299.

12. *L'Unità,* February 25, 1994.

13. For the Cuccia-Sindona struggle I have used E. Scalfari and G. Turani, op. cit., pp. 280-95; F. Tamburini, op. cit., pp. 237-304; and Giorgio Galli, *L'Italia sotteranea* (Bari: Laterza, 1983), pp. 169-77.

14. E. Scalfari e G. Turani, op. cit., p. 281.

15. Ibid., p. 288.

16. *Espresso,* July 11, 1994, p. 46. Fininvest's estimate is around $2 billion and Cuccia's around $4 billion. For recent data we have used an exchange rate of LIT 1,500 to the dollar, which is a rough average for the years 1990-94.

17. E. Scalfari e G. Turani, op. cit., p. 356.

18. Giorgio Galli, op. cit., p. 180.

19. Giampaolo Pansa, *Bisaglia,* op. cit., pp. 320-36. For the PCI view, see *Rinascita,* February 21, 1975, and June 20, 1975.

20. G. Carli, op. cit., p. 69.

21. G. Galli, op. cit., p. 180.

22. *La Repubblica,* February 22, 1994.

23. *Economist,* February 12, 1994.

24. This is my interpretation of Alan Friedman's exhaustive account of the arms-for-Iraq affair—*Spider's Web* (New York: Bantam Books, 1993).

25. *Espresso,* June 27, 1993, pp. 22-30.

26. Cesare Romiti, *Questi anni alla Fiat* (Milan: Rizzoli, 1988), p. 82.

27. See, for example, Napoleone Colajanni, "Dietro Cefis chi governa?" *Rinascita,* March 21, 1975.

28. Cesare Romiti, op. cit., p. 17.

29. E. Scalfari e G. Turani, op. cit., p. 460.

30. Steven Solomon, op. cit., p. 57; F. Tamburini, op. cit., pp. 386-404. For a view favorable to Schimberni, see Alan Friedman, *Agnelli,* op. cit., pp. 242-57. For the establishment's view, see Cesare Romiti, op. cit., pp. 240-64.

31. *Espresso,* August 8, 1993, pp. 64-70 and August 15, 1993, pp. 46-54.

32. *Espresso,* August 1, 1993, p. 59.

33. The Sergio Cusani trial did not provide precise information on the amount of money or how much went to Craxi.

34. *La Repubblica,* March 9, 1994.

35. E. Scalfari e G. Turani, op. cit., pp. 29 and 460.

36. *La Repubblica,* February 3, 1994.

Chapter 6

1. Communist spokesmen have tried to distinguish between the project of the historic compromise and the reality of the governments of National Solidarity during 1976 to 1979, see Alessandro Natta, *Critica marxista 2,* (1985), p. 29. But this is specious.

2. Antonio Bisaglia in Giampaolo Pansa, *Bisaglia: una carriera democristiana* (Milan: SugarCo, 1975), p. 355.

3. Cesare Romiti, *Questi anni alla Fiat* (Milan: Rizzoli, 1988), p. 17.

4. Enrico Berlinguer, "Imperialismo e coesistenza alla luce dei fatti cileni," *Rinascita,* September 28, 1973, p. 3. Reprinted in *La questione comunista,* Antonio Tatò, ed., (Rome: Riuniti, 1975), p. 609.

5. *Time* (European edition), June 30, 1975, cover page.

6. Enrico Berlinguer, "Intesa e lotta di tutte le forze democratiche e popolari per la salvezza e la rinascita dell'Italia," *XIV Congresso del PCI, Atti e risoluzioni* (Rome: Riuniti, 1975).

7. Ibid., p. 25.

8. Ibid., pp. 45 and 51.

9. "Intervento di Bruno Trentin," *XIV Congresso del PCI, Atti e risoluzioni* (Rome: Riunite, 1975), p. 446.

10. Aldo Schiavone, *Per il nuovo PCI* (Bari: Laterza, 1985), p. 85.

11. Ibid., p. 76.

12. Giuseppe Are, *Radiografia di un partito: il PCI negli anni 70* (Milan: Rizzoli, 1980), p. 51.

13. E. Berlinguer, "Conclusioni," *XIV Congresso del PCI*, p. 634.

14. Alberto Asor Rosa argues that Moro wanted the DC to retain its central role but to become a more popular party, see A. Asor Rosa, "La cultura politica del compromesso storico," *Laboratorio politico*, nos. 2-3, (1982): 12. But it is hard to see how Moro pursued the second goal between 1976 and 1978.

15. *Intervista*, February 3, 1976, reprinted in *Conversazioni con Berlinguer*, Antonio Tatò, ed., (Rome: Riuniti, 1984), p. 60. This surprising omission is noted by Gianni Baget Bozzo—"Communist culture has never attempted . . . a political analysis of the Catholic Church and especially of the Italian Church." Gianni Baget Bozzo, "La DC, la Chiesa e Il compromesso storico," *Laboratorio politico*, nos. 2-3, (1982): 339.

16. Leonardo Sciascia, *Il Contesto* (Turin: Einaudi, 1971), p. 74.

17. P. P. Pasolini, *Lettere luterane* (Turin: Einaudi, 1976), p. 51.

18. Giorgio Amendola, "Coerenza e severità," *Politica ed economia*, July-August 1976, p. 7.

19. For Berlinguer's language, see *Austerità, occasione per trasformare l'Italia* (Rome: Riuniti, 1977).

20. Marzio Barbagli e Piergiorgio Corbetta, "Partiti e movimenti: aspetti e rinnovamento del PCI," *Inchiesta*, January-February 1978, p. 11. For the FGCI figures see Marcello Fedele, *Classi e partiti negli anni 70* (Rome: Riuniti, 1979), p. 184.

21. Barbagli e Corbetta, op. cit., p. 8.

22. Paul Ginsborg, *Storia d'Italia dal dopoguerra a oggi*, vol. 2, (Turin: Einaudi, 1989), p. 462.

23. The judgment that the Historic Compromise was primarily defensive is put most clearly by Gianfranco Pasquino, "Il PCI nel sistema politico italiano degli anni settante," *La Giraffa e il Liocorno*, a cura di S. Bellgini (Milan: Franco Angeli, 1983), p. 45. His interpretation was attacked by Aldo Schiavone—op. cit., p. 16—who argues that Berlinguer aimed at a Socialist transformation of Italy. My interpretation is closer to Pasquino's, but the fact that PCI strategy could be interpreted so differently is yet another sign of its ambiguity.

24. P. P. Pasolini, "10 giugno 1974. Studio sulla rivoluzione antropologica in Italia," *Scritti corsari* (Milan: Garzanti, 1977), pp. 46-52.

25. Italo Calvino, *La giornata di uno scrutatore* (Turin: Einaudi, 1963), p. 37.

26. Arturo Parisi e Gianfranco Pasquino, eds., *Continuità e mutamento elettorale in Italia* (Bologna: Il Mulino, 1977), p. 30.

27. Giuseppe Are, op. cit., p. 132.

28. Patrick McCarthy, "The Parliamentary and Non-Parliamentary Parties of the Far-Left," in *Italy at the Polls 1979*, Howard R. Penniman, ed., (Washington: American Enterprise Institute, 1981), pp. 193-211.

29. G. Pasquino and A. Parisi, op. cit., p. 28.

30. Robert Flanagan, David Soskice, and Lloyd Ulman, *Unionism, Economic Stabilization and Incomes Policy* (Washington: Brookings Institute, 1983), pp. 529-61. I have relied much on this analysis of what the authors call Eurocommunism as incomes policy.

31. Michele Salvati, "Col senno di poi," *Quaderni piacentini* 6. (1982): 7.

32. Ibid., p. 10.

33. Fernando di Giulio e Emmanuele Rocco, *Un ministro ombra si confessa* (Milan: Rizzoli, 1979), p. 39.

34. Ibid., pp. 152-53.

35. For more detailed analysis of these laws see Gerardo Chiaromonte, *Le scelte della solidarietà nazionale* (Rome: Riuniti, 1986), pp. 48-49, and Giuseppe Vacca, *Tra compromesso e solidarietà* (Rome: Riuniti, 1987), p. 107 ff. For a negative judgment on them, see Leonardo Paggi e Massimo D'Angelillo, *I Comunisti italiani e il riformismo*, (Turin: Einaudi, 1986), p. 149.

36. Alberto Franceschini, *Mara, Renato e io* (Milan: Mondadori, 1988), pp. 3-6.

37. Stephen Hellman, *Italian Communism in Transition: The Rise and Fall of the Historic Compromise in Turin* (Oxford: Oxford University Press, 1989), pp. 87-90.

38. Leonardo Sciascia, *L'Affaire Moro* (Palermo: Sellerio, 1978), p. 32.

39. Both Hellman—op. cit., p. 91—and Ginsborg—op. cit., p. 512—suggest that the PCI's Third International heritage re-emerged in its lack of sensitivity towards civil liberties.

40. Paul Ginsborg, op. cit., p. 539.

41. Enrico Berlinguer, *Per uscire dalla crisi. Rapporto al Comitato centrale*, December 10, 1974, op. cit., p. 22.

42. Joan Barth Urban, *Moscow and the Italian Communist Party* (London: Tauris, 1986), p. 304.

43. Enrico Berlinguer, "Intesa e lotta," op. cit., p. 20.

44. Ibid., p. 34.

45. Adriano Guerra, "Condizioni per un nuovo internazionalismo," *Rinascita*, March 7, 1975, p. 19.

46. *Intervista*, June 15, 1976. Reprinted in *Conversazioni con Berlinguer*, p. 70.

47. For an analysis of the speech, see Giuseppe Fiori, *Vita di Enrico Berlinguer* (Bari: Laterza, 1984), p. 333. See Aldo Schiavone, op. cit., p. 87, who stresses that Berlinguer's remarks shocked many Italian Marxists.

48. Giampaolo Pansa, *Ottobre addio* (Milan: Mondadori, 1982), p. 111.

49. "Il discorso di Berlinguer a conclusione del Festival di Genova," *L'Unità,* September 18, 1978.

50. *Intervista,* July 15, 1976. Reprinted in *Conversazioni con Berlinguer,* p. 65.

51. *La Repubblica,* July 4, 1990.

52. For this interpretation of U.S. foreign policy I have drawn heavily on Dana Allin's Ph.D. thesis, "Understanding the Soviet Threat to Western Europe: American Views 1973-1985," Paul H. Nitze SAIS, European Studies. However the judgments are my own.

53. Henry Kissinger, "Communist Parties in Western Europe," *Eurocommunism: The Italian Case,* Austin Ranney and Giovanni Sartori, eds., (Washington: AEI, 1978), pp. 185-88.

54. Giuseppe Fiori, op. cit., pp. 288-89. He takes the tone of nationalist outrage, which was a frequent and unsuccessful PCI tactic. Schmidt's hostility did not prevent him two years later from appealing personally to Berlinguer not to block Italian entry into the EMS, see Chiaromonte, op. cit., pp. 138-39. The Tribune wing of the Labor Party showed some sympathy for the PCI.

55. Mario Margiocco, *Stati Uniti e PCI* (Bari: Laterza, 1981), pp. 233-37 and 278.

56. Ibid., p. 270.

57. Richard N. Gardner, *Il Corriere della Sera,* November 15, 1977, p. 6. Roberto Leonardi, "Gli Stati Uniti e il compromesso storico," *Il Mulino,* May-June 1978, p. 387, notes that there was no pressure on the United States from the DC groups supposedly favorable to the PCI.

58. Zbigniew Brzezinski, *Power and Principle: Memoirs of the National Security Advisor* (London: Weidenfeld, 1983), pp. 311-13.

59. Stephen Hellman, op. cit., p. 147.

60. Paolo Franchi e Luciano Canfora, "Due ipotesi su Enrico Berlinguer," in *Micromégas,* 1 (1988): 79-88.

61. One Emilia leader, who asked to remain anonymous, told me that Berlinguer was the last great Communist leader and that he had brought this distinction on himself! For a more favorable judgment on Berlinguer's last years by the new secretary of the PDS see Massimo D'Alema, "Berlinguer non era triste," *L'Espresso,* June 17, 1994, pp. 48-50.

62. Marc Lazar, *Maisons rouges* (Paris: Aubier, 1992), p. 325. Lazar's thesis is that historians, both Italian and Anglo-Saxon, have overstressed the heretical aspect of the PCI, which was very much a Communist party. The same conclusion could also be drawn from Piero Ignazi's *Dal Pci al Pds* (Bologna: Il Mulino, 1992).

63. "Documento approvato dalla Direzione del PCI, November 27, 1980," reprinted in *Conversazioni con Berlinguer,* op. cit., p. 213.

64. Guido Carli, op. cit., p. 23.
65. *Intervista*, July 28, 1981. Reprinted in *Conversazioni con Berlinguer*, op. cit., p. 251.

Chapter 7

1. Ilvo Diamanti, "Così compatti gli squadroni del Nord?" *Reset*, December 1993, p. 13.
2. See John L. Harper, *Bettino Craxi and the Second Center-Left Experiment*, Johns Hopkins University Bologna Center Occasional Papers, Bologna, Italy, 1986.
3. Gerardo Chiaromonte, *Le scelte della solidarietà democratica* (Rome: Riuniti, 1986), p. 30.
4. Gianni Riccamboni, *L'identità esclusa* (Turin: Liviana, 1992), pp. 169 and 188.
5. Carlo Carboni, "Introduzione," in C. Carboni, ed., *Classi e Movimenti in Italia 1970-1985* (Bari: Laterza, 1986), p. xiii.
6. Alessandra Venturini, "Il mercato del lavoro negli anni Ottanta," in Giangiacomo Nardozzi, ed., *Il ruolo della Banca Centrale nella recente evoluzione dell'economia italiana* (Milan: Franco Angeli, 1993), p. 108.
7. Paolo Sylos Labini, "Struttura sociale, sviluppo e classi sociali," in C. Carboni, op. cit., p. 218.
8. Marco Revelli, *Lavorare in Fiat* (Milan: Garzanti, 1989), p. 122.
9. Arnaldo Bagnasco, "La struttura di classe nelle tre Italie," in C. Carboni, op. cit., p. 75.
10. Bettino Craxi, "Il Vangelo socialista," *L'Espresso*, August 27, 1978, pp. 24-29. For a contemporary reaction see my "The Italian Socialist Party Launches an anti-Communist Crusade," *Tribune*, September 28, 1978.
11. On the 1976 to 1979 period, see Gianfranco Pasquino, "The Italian Socialist Party: Electoral Stagnation and Political Indispensability," in Howard R. Penniman, ed., *Italy at the Polls 1979* (Washington: American Enterprise Institute, 1981), pp. 141-71. See also David Hine, "The Italian Socialist Party under Craxi: Surviving But Not Reviving," in *Italy in Transition*, P. Lange and S. Tarrow, eds., (London: F. Cass, 1980), pp. 133-48.
12. On this period, see G. Pasquino, "Modernity and Reforms: The PSI Between Gamblers and Entrepreneurs," *West European Politics* (January 1986): 112-35.
13. John L. Harper, op. cit., p. 14. On Craxi's premiership, see also David Hine, "The Craxi Premiership," in Robert Leonardi and Raffaelle Nanetti, eds., *Italian Politics*, vol. 1 (London: Frances Pinter, 1986), pp. 105-16.

14. See Jan Kregel, "La politica del cambio della Banca d'Italia e la ristrutturazione della industria italiana 1980-1985," in Giangiacomo Nardozzi, op. cit., pp. 59-98.

15. Aurelio Lepre, op. cit., pp. 299-301.

16. Censis, *L'Italia in Politica 3* (Rome: Censis, 1994), p. 16.

17. Umberto Bossi con Daniele Vimercati, *Il Vento dal Nord* (Milan: Sperling and Knupfer, 1992), p. 47.

18. For the Lega's language, see Roberto Iacopino e Stefania Bianchi, *La Lega ce l'ha cruda* (Milan: Mursia, 1994).

19. *La Voce,* April 12, 1994.

20. *La Voce,* May 10, 1994. In April 1994, when the prime rate was 8.35 percent, the average small company in Lazio paid 15 percent, see *La Voce,* May 12, 1994.

21. Antonio Bisaglia, quoted by Ilvo Diamanti, op. cit.

22. Renato Mannheimer, "La crisi del consenso per i partiti tradizionali," in R. Mannheimer, ed., *La Lega Lombarda* (Milan: Feltrinelli, 1992), pp. 13-33. See also Gianfranco Pasquino, *La Nuova Politica* (Bari: Laterza, 1992), pp. 3-15.

23. Roberto Biorcio, "La Lega come attore politico," in *La Lega Lombarda,* op. cit., p. 43. For the phases of Lega history I have relied on this article, on Biorcio's "Nel ventre della Lega," *Il Manifesto,* July 16, 1993, and on G. Pasquino, *La Nuova Politica,* op. cit., pp. 15-36.

24. Ilvo Diamanti, "Intervista," *L'Unità,* December 10, 1993.

25. Renato Mannheimer, "The electors of the Lega Nord," in G. Pasquino and P. McCarthy, eds., *The End of Postwar Politics in Italy* (Boulder: Westview, 1993), pp. 85-107.

26. R. Iacopino e S. Bianchi, op. cit., p. 96.

27. Gustavo Zagrabelsky, "Pathos e realtà del Federalismo," *Reset,* op. cit., p. 18. For the Lega's federalism, see *Il Manifesto,* December 12, 1993.

28. Gianfranco Pasquino, *La Repubblica dei cittadini ombra,* op. cit., p. 74.

29. Enzo Balboni, "I nodi costituzionali di una difficile crisi di governo," *Politica in Italia, Edizione 1988,* Piergiorgio Corbetta e Robert Leonardi, eds., (Bologna: Il Mulino, 1988), pp. 47-68.

30. Gianfranco Pasquino, "La crisi del governo Di Mita," *Politica in Italia, Edizione 1990,* Raimondo Catanzaro e Filippo Sabetto, eds., (Bologna: Il Mulino, 1991), pp. 51-68. On the PSI between 1987 and 1992, see David Hine, "The Italian Socialist Party and the 1992 Election," in *The End of Postwar Politics in Italy,* op. cit., pp. 50-62.

31. An ex-DC parliamentarian, Angelo Rojch was arrested for allegedly pocketing vocational training funds, see *La Voce,* May 13, 1994. For Kohl's comment, see Giorgio Bocca, *L'Inferno* (Milan: Mondadori, 1992), p. 10.

32. Sabino Cassese e Giulio Vesperini, "Come sono cambiati i rapporti tra sistema politico e burocrazia," *Stato dell'Italia*, a cura di Paul Ginsborg (Milan: Il Saggiatore-Bruno Mondadori, 1994), pp. 488-93. See also Marco Cammelli, op. cit.

33. Censis, *Italy Today 1990* (Rome: Fondazione Censis, 1991), p. 9.

34. Gianfranco Pasquino, *La Repubblica dei cittadini ombra*, op. cit., p. 77.

Chapter 8

1. Giampaolo Pansa, *I Bugiardi* (Rome: L'Unità-Sperling e Kupfer, 1994), p. 190.

2. Giampaolo Pansa, *Lo Sfascio* (Rome: L'Unità-Sperling e Kupfer, 1993), pp. 107-14. First published in *La Repubblica*, December 14, 1983.

3. See our "The Communists Divide and Do Not Conquer," in *The End of Postwar Politics in Italy* (Boulder: Westview, 1993), Gianfranco Pasquino and Patrick McCarthy, eds., pp. 31-49.

4. OECD, *Economic Survey 1992-1993, Italy* (Paris: Organization of Economic Cooperation and Development, 1993), pp. 13-29.

5. Commissione Parlamentare d'Inchiesta sul fenomeno della Mafia, *Relazione sui rapporti tra Mafia e Politica*, Relatore: Luciano Violante, p. 57.

6. *La Voce*, May 26, 1994.

7. OECD, op. cit., pp. 45-49, 60, and 68-76.

8. OECD, *Economic Survey 1994, Italy* (Paris: Organization of Economic Cooperation and Development, 1994), p. 13.

9. See our "Inching Towards a New Regime," in G. Pasquino and P. McCarthy, eds., op. cit., pp. 168-70.

10. Censis, *Rapporto sulla situazione del Paese 1992* (Rome: Censis Foundation, 1993), p. xxii.

11. Gianfranco Brunelli, "Nel tramonto della DC," *Chiesa in Italia 1993, Annale di "Il Regno"* (Bologna: Edizioni Dehoniane, 1993), p. 100.

12. Commissione Parlamentare d'Inchiesta, op. cit., p. 34.

13. Ibid., p. 55.

14. *L'Unità*, May 28, 1994.

15. Commissione Parlamentare d'Inchiesta, op. cit., p. 105. This section of the report was written by Alfredo Galasso.

16. See Giorgio Bocca, *L'Espresso*, June 10, 1994, p. 5.

17. *Espresso*, May 27, 1994, pp. 66-68.

18. *La Repubblica*, April 13, 1994.

19. For Ciampi's economic policy see OECD, *Economic Survey 1994, Italy* op. cit., pp. 11-53.
20. *European Industrial Relations Review* 236 (September 1993): 15-19.
21. *La Repubblica,* September 29, 1993, and October 1, 1993.
22. *Economist,* January 29, 1994, p. 63; *L'Unità,* February 11, 1994, and February 23, 1994.
23. *Espresso,* July 1, 1994, pp. 152-57.
24. *Economist,* May 14, 1994, p. 81.
25. *La Voce,* April 26-28, 1994.
26. Banca Commerciale Italiana, *Monetary Trends* n. 49 (August 1993): p. 13.
27. *La Repubblica,* February 18, 1994.
28. Luciano Benetton speaks of "a new period of the Italian economy with new entrepreneurs," see *La Repubblica,* March 5, 1994.
29. *La Voce,* May 12, 1994.
30. *Espresso,* April 15, 1994, p. 140, and June 10, 1994, p. 45.
31. The election figures are taken from *La Repubblica,* March 30, 1994. The figures on switching votes come from Censis, *L'Italia in Politica 3* (Rome: Censis, 1994), pp. 14-16.
32. *Panorama,* February 4, 1994, p. 11.
33. *Programma di governo del PDS,* p. 11.
34. This summary of MSI history draws heavily on Piero Ignazi, *Il Polo escluso* (Bologna: Il Mulino, 1989). I also wish to thank the author for allowing me to consult the manuscript version of his article "Il MSI da Almirante a Fini."
35. *Il Polo escluso,* op. cit., p. 246.
36. *L'Unità,* January 20, 1994.
37. *La Repubblica,* December 7, 1993.
38. Ibid.
39. Domenico Fisichella, *La Voce,* May 20, 1994.
40. *Il Manifesto,* December 12, 1993.
41. *Espresso,* April 8, 1994, p. 62.
42. *La Repubblica,* January 29, 1994.
43. *L'Unità,* March 11, 1994.
44. Stefano E. D'Anna e Gigi Montecalvo, *Berlusconi in Concert* (London: Otzium, 1994), p. 191.
45. Ibid., p. 59.
46. *Il Programma di Forza Italia,* p. 6.
47. For a longer but still incomplete study of Berlusconi's language see my "Il linguaggio di Silvio Berlusconi," *Il Regno,* May 15, 1994, pp. 276-78.
48. Diakron was not legally a part of Fininvest but its independence was a fiction. On FI, see Alessandro Gilioli, *Forza Italia* (Bergamo: Ferruccio Arnoldi

Editori, 1994). For a longer account of the campaign see my "Forza Italia: The New Politics and Old Values of a Changing Italy," to be published in Stephen Gundle and Simon Parker, eds., *The New Italian Republic: From the Fall of Communism to the Rise of Berlusconi* (London: Routledge, in press).

Chapter 9

1. The figures on seats are taken from Gianfranco Pasquino, *The Unexpected Alternation: the Italian Elections of 1994* (Bologna Center Occasional Papers, Bologna, 1994), p. 11. The author warns that the figures are imprecise because members change their party affiliation. Thirteen parliamentarians left the Lega between May and December.
2. *L'Espresso,* May 27, 1994, p. 42.
3. For the changes in Berlusconi's language see my "Silvio Berlusconi: La parola crea l'uomo politico," *Europa/Europe,* 3 (1994): 243-58.
4. Romano Prodi, *La Voce,* November 17, 1994.
5. *La Voce,* September 10, 1994.
6. *L'Espresso,* June 10, 1994, p. 25.
7. *L'Espresso,* August 12, 1994, p. 36.
8. *Economist,* July 30, 1994, p. 23.
9. *La Repubblica,* September 20, 1994.
10. The names of these men were Carlo Rossella and Clemente Mimun. As the head of Channel 1 Moratti appointed Brando Giordano, an ex-DC member; this revived the change-without-change dispute. The new head of Channel 3 was Daniele Brancati. The regional TV network was placed in the hands of Piero Vigorelli, another ex-Craxi supporter who had gone over to Berlusconi, see *Il Manifesto,* September 18, 1994.
11. *La Voce,* May 13, 1994.
12. *La Voce,* July 16, 1994.
13. Ibid.
14. *La Repubblica,* October 6, 1994.
15. Among the many who made such statements were Domenico Contestabile and Tiziana Maiolo, the chairperson of the House Justice Commission, see *La Voce,* September 11, 1994. Both had been New Left militants who had fought for the rights of imprisoned comrades. They had changed their minds about politics but not about prisoners.
16. *L'Unità,* December 9, 1994.

17. Pino Mandalari's phone had been tapped and his conversations with and about FI and AN candidates were recorded, see *Panorama,* January 12, 1995, pp. 28-30.

18. *La Voce,* December 14, 1994.

19. *La Repubblica,* November 26, 1994.

20. At least one sports journalist attributed this slide to Berlusconi's absence, see *La Stampa,* October 30, 1994.

21. Giorgio Bocca, *La Repubblica,* December 7, 1994.

22. The translation loses the alliteration of the Italian: "Le chiachiere se le porta il vento ma carta canta." The expression "carta canta," literally "paper sings," is also much used by Bossi.

23. *La Voce,* December 14, 1994.

24. *La Voce,* December 14, 1994, and *La Repubblica,* November 23, 1994.

25. Romano Prodi, *La Voce,* November 17, 1994.

26. *Economist,* December 3, 1994, p. 78.

27. *Economist,* June 30, 1994, p. 23. The Anglo-Saxon financial press became willy-nilly a protagonist in the Italian political struggle. Its criticism of Berlusconi's financial laxity damaged him in the eyes of the Italian elites.

28. Ibid.

29. *La Voce,* September 29, 1994.

30. Gianfranco Pasquino, op. cit., p. 14.

31. *Financial Times,* December 16, 1994.

32. *La Repubblica,* January 8, 1995.

33. *La Repubblica,* January 10, 1995.

34. Mauro Calise, *Dopo la Partitocrazia* (Turin: Einaudi, 1994), p. 102.

35. *La Stampa,* January 9, 1995.

36. *Forza Italia informa,* October 31, 1994. (Text obtained from the FI Press Office in Rome).

37. *La Repubblica,* November 3, 1994.

38. *La Voce,* December 20, 1994.

39. For a longer analysis of the groups in FI see my "Forza Italia, le vittorie e vicissitudini di un partito virtuale," in Piero Ignazi and Richard Katz, eds., *L'anno politico in Italia 1994* (Bologna: Il Mulino, in press).

40. *L'Espresso,* December 23, 1994, p. 17.

41. *La Repubblica,* November 8, 1994.

42. Piero Ignazi, *Postfascisti? Dal MSI ad AN* (Bologna: Il Mulino, 1994), pp. 113-21.

43. *La Repubblica,* November 23, 1994.

44. *Secolo d'Italia,* November 25, 1994.

45. *La Repubblica,* March 29, 1994.

46. *La Repubblica,* December 23, 1994.

47. *La Repubblica,* December 11, 1994.

48. *Avvenire,* November 25, 1994.

49. *La Repubblica,* December 11, 1994.

50. *Panorama,* January 13, 1985, p. 16.

51. *L'Espresso,* January 5, 1995, pp. 44-46.

52. Gianni Vattimo, *La Stampa,* January 9, 1995.

53. *L'Espresso,* January 5, 1995, p. 29.

54. *La Repubblica,* December 24, 1995.

55. This group was animated by Alberto Michelini, who had gone over from Segni to Berlusconi and who is widely regarded as a spokesman for Opus Dei.

56. *La Voce,* January 6, 1995.

57. *Il Giornale,* January 13, 1995.

<hr />

Chapter 10

1. Censis, *Rapporto sulla situazione sociale del paese 1994* (Rome: Censis Foundation, 1994), pp. 11 and 23.

2. Censis, *Rapporto 1995,* op. cit., p. 12.

3. Ibid, p. 57.

4. Giovanni Pitruzzella, "I poteri locali" in *Stato dell'Italia,* a cura di Paul Ginsborg (Milan: Il Saggiatore-Bruno Mondadori, 1994), p. 474.

5. Censis, *Rapporto 1995,* op. cit., p. 49.

6. Ibid, p. 57.

7. Massimo Cacciari "L'invenzione dell'individuo," *Micromega,* supplement, 1995/5, pp. 121-27.

8. Information provided by the Ufficio Stampa of CGIL-CISL-UIL, Emilia-Romagna.

9. Michele La Rosa, "Il Lavoro tra senso, tempo, qualità e quantità," manuscript version.

10. *Il Corriere della Sera,* January 22, 1996.

11. *La Stampa,* March 4, 1996.

12. *Economist,* January 13, 1996.

13. Censis, *Rapporto 1995,* p. 407. See also Censis, *Accompagnare la crescita del nuovo spazio economico* (Rome: Censis Foundation, 1995).

14. Svimez, *Rapporto 1995 sull' economia del Mezzogiorno* (Bologna: Il Mulino, 1995), pp. 526-33.

15. Filippo Cavazzuti, *Privatizzazioni, imprenditori e mercati* (Bologna: Il Mulino, 1996), manuscript version.

16. David Lane, "Losers not choosers," *The Banker,* February 1996, pp. 26-27.

17. *La Repubblica,* March 9, 1996.

18. See in particular *La Repubblica,* September 13, October 31, and November 11. See also Robert Graham's coverage in *Financial Times.* The latest battle of Montedison went on throughout autumn 1995. For information on the stockmarket see Consiglio di borsa, *An Overview of the Italian stock market* and *1996: Facts and figures on the Italian stock exchange* (Milan: Consiglio di borsa, 1995 and 1996).

19. *Corriere della Sera,* December 12, 1995.

20. *La Repubblica,* September 16, 1995.

21. *La Repubblica,* January 20, 1996.

22. *La Repubblica,* April 18, 1995.

23. Claudio Rinaldi, "Compagno Rospo," *L'Espresso,* August 25, 1985, pp. 32-37.

24. *La Stampa,* March 17, 1995.

25. G. Pasquino, "Il governo di Lamberto Dini," to appear in *Politica in Italia 1995,* a cura di Mario Caciaghi e David Kertzer (Bologna: Il Mulino, 1996), manuscript version.

26. *Ibid.*

27. *La Repubblica,* April 29, 1996.

28. *La Repubblica,* March 5,1995.

29. *La Voce,* March 17, 1995.

30. For a description of the pension plan and the debates surrounding it see *European Industrial Relations Review,* n. 253, February 1995 to n. 264, January 1996. For a critical analysis see Giuliano Cazzola, "Le pensioni sotto il segno del Gattopardo" in *Diritto delle Relazioni industriali,* 1995/2, pp. 125-133.

31. *La Repubblica,* March 21,1995.

32. *L'Unità,* March 22, 1995.

33. Gianfranco Pasquino, *op. cit.*

34. *La Repubblica,* April 26, 1995.

35. "Parla Dini" *L'Espresso,* August 11, 1995 pp. 32-34.

36. *La Repubblica,* September 17, 1995.

37. Filippo Cavazzuti, *op. cit.*

38. *La Repubblica,* October 24, 1995.

39. *Il Manifesto,* October 20, 1995.

40. *La Repubblica,* October 27, 1995.

41. *La Repubblica,* September 28, 1995.

42. *La Repubblica,* December 15, 1995.

43. *Economist,* January 13, 1996.

44. *Il Corriere della Sera,* January 22, 1996.

45. See Susanna Agnelli, "The Mediterranean and the Future of Europe," JHU Bologna Center Occasional Papers 1996, manuscript version.

46. *La Stampa,* November 3, 1995.

47. *L'Unità,* September 14, 1995.

48. See John L. Harper, "Italy's American Connection: Past, Present, Future," manuscript version.

49. Gaspare Nevola e Gian Enrico Rusconi, "Politica: democrazia doc o pop" *L'Informazione bibliografica* A XXl, N. 2, Aprile-Giugno, 1995, pp. 199-210.

50. *Il Manifesto,* January 22, 1995.

51. *Secolo d'Italia,* January 25, 1995.

52. On the confusion of Scotland and Ireland see *La Repubblica,* December 5, 1995. For the warning to D'Alema see *L'Unità,* January 12, 1996. For the English pigs see *La Repubblica,* February 29,1996.

53. See our "Prodi sfida Berlusconi: una guerra filologica" *Il Regno,* December 1995, pp. 338-40. Bartali and Coppi were Italy's greatest cyclists in the post-war period. Since Bartali was a devout Catholic, it was thought that his rival Coppi *had* to be a Communist, although in fact he was not.

54. On the divisions in Prodi's coalition, see Gianfranco Brunelli, "Scheglie il centro" and "Il ritorno dei partiti," *Il Regno,* October 1995, p. 272 and February 1996, pp. 17-18. On the PDS's lust for interlocutors, see G. Pasquino, "Il paradosso di Segni," *L'Unità,* February 26, 1996.

Chapter 11

1. *La Repubblica,* April 22, 1996.

2. *La Repubblica,* April 16, 1996.

3. *La Repubblica,* April 27, 1996. The judgment was made by Raffaele Della Valle, former deputy speaker of the House.

4. The word recurred in his April 17 speech in Bologna. Author's notes.

5. Vittorio Sgarbi, *La Repubblica,* March 10, 1996. Admittedly Sgarbi, who is also an excellent art critic, is particularly outspoken.

6. *Corriere della Sera,* March 15, 1996. The comparison was with the Uno bianca criminals.

7. *La Repubblica,* April 14, 1996. This view was spelled out in *Il Giornale,* April 26, 1996. This clever, right-wing paper is officially owned not by Silvio but by Paolo Berlusconi.

8. *La Repubblica,* April 18, 1996.

9. For information on the TV debates I am indebted to Roberto Grandi.

10. Stephen Gundle, "Il sorriso di Berlusconi," manuscript version.

11. Interviewed off the record FI and Fininvest officials complain that their advice was never sought and that Berlusconi ran the campaign on his own. For a longer but still incomplete analysis of the language of the campaign see my "The Discourse of Serenity: A Linguistic Victory In the 1996 Italian Elections" to be published in Luciano Cheles and Lucio Sponza, editors, *The Art of Persuasion: Political Language In Italy From 1945 to the Present* (Manchester: Manchester University Press, 1997).

12. *L'Unità*, March 24, 1996.

13. For a sample of Prodi's language see his *Governare l'Italia*, (Rome: Donzelli, 1995).

14. Censis, *Dal voto al governo: le aspettative degli italiani* (Rome: Censis Foundation, 1996), p. 12.

15. There is a revealing difference between the English expressions "to turn state's evidence" or in Britain "to turn queen's evidence," which set the action in the context of citizen and state, and the Italian word *pentito* or "one who has repented," which emphasizes the moral rather than legal decision of an individual whose interlocutor is the Church.

16. Censis, *Dal voto al governo*, p. 21. However the judgment that the Europeanism is "uncritical" is my own.

17. *La Repubblica*, April 21, 1996.

18. Istituto Carlo Cattaneo, "Comunicato stampa," April 1996. These are the figures of the PR vote.

19. Election statistics, unless otherwise stated, are taken from *Il Corriere della Sera*, April 24, 1996 and from *La Repubblica*, April 23, 1996.

20. Ilya Diamante, *La Repubblica*, May 7, 1996.

21. Censis, *Dal voto al governo*, p. 59.

22. *La Repubblica*, May 1, 1996.

23. *La Repubblica*, May 18, 1996.

24. *Avvenire*, May 7, 1996.

25. *Avvenire*, April 23, 1996. For a good analysis of the Church's positions see Gianfranco Brunelli, "La Svolta," *Il Regno*, May 15, 1996, pp. 257-60.

26. For D'Alema's views see "L'Intervista" *L'Unità*, May 19, 1996. For the approach to Amato see *L'Unità*, June 5, 1996.

27. *Economist*, June 22, 1996.

28. *La Stampa*, May 23-25, 1996.

29. Council for the European Communities, *Treaty of European Unity*, (Brussels: European Union, 1992), p. 27.

30. *La Repubblica*, May 6, 1996.

31. *La Repubblica,* May 29, 1996.
32. Censis, *Dal voto al governo,* p. 37. The figure for the PDS is 60 percent and for FI 67.5 percent.
33. *Financial Times,* June 28, 1996. For the government's explanation of its three-year plan see its "Documento di Programmazione Economico-Finanziaria," June 1996.
34. Morgan Stanley, *Inside the Italian Economy* (London: Morgan Stanley, June 1996), p. 15.
35. "Intervista a Romano Prodi," *Il Regno,* June 30, 1996.
36. Romano Prodi, *Governare l'Italia* (Rome: Donzelli, 1995), pp. 19 and 15.
37. For the "bargaining state" see Patrick McCarthy and Erik Jones, "The Crisis of the State in Advanced Industrial Societies" in their edited *Disintegration or Transformation* (New York: St. Martin's Press, 1995), p. 7.

Conclusion

1. Leonardo Sciascia, *La Sicilia come metafora,* intervista di Marcelle Padovani (Rome: Mondadori, 1979), p. 23. This is the most complete statement of his political views that Sciascia was ever persuaded to make. For the "laceration," see p. 74.
2. The Italian word is *contesto,* which is the title of one of Sciascia's novels.
3. Leonardo Sciascia, *Fatti diversi di storia letteraria e civile,* vol. 2 (Rome: L'Unità-Sellerio, 1993), p. 15.
4. Robert D. Putnam, with Robert Leonardi and Raffaella Y Nanetti, *Making Democracy Work: Civic Traditions in Modern Italy* (Princeton: Princeton University Press, 1993), p. 86.
5. Paul Ginsborg, "La famiglia italiana oltre il privato per superare l'isolamento," in his edited *Stato dell'Italia* (Milan: Il Saggiatore-Bruno Mondadori, 1994), pp. 284-90. The family has of course undergone changes, see Censis, *Rapporto sulla situazione sociale del Paese 1994* (Rome: Censis Foundation, 1994), pp. 308-16.
6. Ibid., p. 16.

INDEX